MEDIEVAL WOMEN MONASTICS

Wisdom's Wellsprings

edited by

Miriam Schmitt, O.S.B.
and
Linda Kulzer, O.S.B.

illustrated by

Mary Michael Kaliher, O.S.B.

Bernadette
May you enjoy reading about the lives of these gifted women and may it inspire you as you use your own gifts creatively in your ~~letter~~ ministry. *S. Miriam Schmitt OSB*

A Liturgical Press Book

THE LITURGICAL PRESS
Collegeville, Minnesota

Illustrated by Mary Michael Kaliher, O.S.B.

Cover design by Greg Becker

1   2   3   4   5   6   7   8

Library of Congress Cataloging-in-Publication Data

Medieval women monastics : wisdom's wellsprings / edited by Miriam
  Schmitt, O.S.B. and Linda Kulzer, O.S.B. ; illustrated by Mary Michael
  Kaliher, O.S.B.
      p.   cm.
    "A Liturgical Press book."
    Includes bibliographical references.
    ISBN 0-8146-2292-5
    1. Monasticism and religious orders for women—Europe—History—
  Middle Ages, 600–1500. 2. Monastic and religious life of women—
  Europe—History—Middle Ages, 600–1500. 3. Europe—Church his-
  tory—600–1500. I. Schmitt, Miriam. II. Kulzer, Linda.
  BX4200.M43   1996
  271'.90022—dc20
  [B]   95-52012
                                                            CIP

Contents

Acknowledgements

It is impossible to mention everyone who helped to compile these spiritual biographies of seventeen early monastic, primarily Benedictine, holy women. But we are particularly indebted to those women who were the abbesses and prioresses of the communities to which the authors and illustrator belonged when they were involved with their labors. As co-editors, Sister Linda Kulzer and I also want to express our gratitude in a special way to others who have helped us: our prioresses, Susan Lardy, O.S.B., and Mary Reuter, O.S.B., for giving us the time and resources to investigate our heritage; the Board of Directors of the American Benedictine Academy and its president, Jeanne Ranek, O.S.B., for their support; Bonnie Staiger, a Benedictine Oblate, for her generous assistance in reading and editing articles; Knute Anderson, O.S.B., for his ready response in locating resources at the Hill Monastic Manuscript Library, St. John's Abbey; Rosemary Rader, O.S.B., who aroused enthusiasm for this venture in England while studying at Oxford University.

We would also like to thank the following abbesses and nuns of these European abbeys: Abbess Domitilla Veith, O.S.B., (Frauenchiemsee) for sending resources on Irmengard of Chiemsee; Franziska Kloos, O.S.B., and Mechtildis Denz, O.S.B. (Eichstätt); Ancilla Ferlings, O.S.B., and Adelgundis Führkötter, O.S.B., now deceased (Eibingen); Abbess Gabriella Sinabel, O.S.B. (Nonnberg); and Abbess Gertrude Schaller, O.C.S.O., (Fribourg, Switzerland) who, when they visited with me at their abbeys in 1990–1991, planted the seed which later developed into this book about the spiritual journeys of seventeen monastic women who went before us, leading the way.

Miriam Schmitt, O.S.B.

List Of Illustrations

Introduction

Miriam Schmitt, O.S.B.

Hildegard of Bingen, in a letter to Guibert of Gembloux, describes herself as reaching out her hands to God and being "carried along as a feather is borne weightlessly by the Wind *(Ruah)."* This image captures the inspiration and encouragement that Sr. Linda Kulzer and I experienced co-editing these spiritual biographies of seventeen early Benedictine women.

Within the last decade both women and men have shown unusual interest in the spiritual legacy bequeathed to us by medieval women monastics. This has been particularly evident in the discussions flowing from papers pertaining to them that have been presented at the annual International Congress on Medieval Studies each May at Kalamazoo, Michigan. Since 1987 both Benedictines and Cistercians have made research presentations on all but four of the monastic women featured in this volume. Increasingly evident among English-speaking Benedictine communities of women is a pervasive interest in studying the lives, spirituality, and contributions made by these gifted, European, medieval women monastics. Because of the lack of English resources presently available, much of our heritage rooted in an Anglo-Saxon and Germanic tradition— is unknown to us. Consequently, we have neglected this legacy. In teaching monastic and Benedictine history, even to our incoming members, we have not been aware of nor claimed a significant part of our heritage.

In the summer of 1992, Sr. Linda Kulzer, O.S.B., and I felt impelled to make available in English a strand of our rich monastic and Benedictine legacy by gathering the life stories of outstanding medieval women monastics. Through announcements at the Conference of American Benedictine Prioresses, letters to prioresses and monastic researchers, and our own contacts with writers who were potential contributors, we selected eighteen contemporary, Benedictine women to write these stories.

They represent three countries—the United States, England, and Australia—and thirteen religious communities steeped in varied monastic traditions. Sister Mary Michael Kaliher, O.S.B., graciously agreed to be the illustrator of our book.

Because our original purpose was primarily to acquaint English-speaking monastics with their roots in the Anglo-Saxon and Germanic expressions of Benedictinism, we solicited contributions from Benedictine women who were willing to do research and share their findings in a manuscript approximately twenty-five pages long. Naturally, this limitation on length influenced the amount of historical background that could be shared in an essay. Our aim was to involve members from a variety of Benedictine communities in English-speaking countries. This approach necessarily resulted in differing emphases and styles of writing; however, it also lent the project the expertise, enthusiasm, and creativity of writers of varying Benedictine traditions.

This book is an initial attempt to make available brief accounts of selected medieval women monastics beginning with St. Scholastica of Norcia (sixth century) and culminating with Dame Gertrude More of Cambrai (seventeenth century). Its focus is primarily on Anglo-Saxon, Austrian, and Germanic monastic women since many of our American monasteries have their roots in the Abbeys of Wimborne, Nonnberg, and Eichstätt. The book portrays seventeen multitalented nuns and canonesses who helped Christianize Europe across eleven centuries. The arrangement of the essays attempts to reflect the development of the women's monastic movement chronologically.

From its beginnings in Norcia and Monte Cassino, Italy, women's monasticism flourished in the seventh century, often in the form of double monasteries among the Anglo-Saxons in England. It spread to Germany during the Merovingian and Carolingian eras of the Franconian Empire via the Anglo-Saxon missionaries from Wimborne Abbey who responded to the call of Boniface, the Apostle of Germany. During the twelfth and thirteenth centuries, monasticism took on a literary, prophetic, and mystical emphasis among the Germanic women's communities. Finally, in the seventeenth century, we conclude with the return of women monastics from Cambrai to England and the eventual founding of Stanbrook Abbey.

Each chapter provides a brief biography of a particular woman monastic, a synopsis of her spirituality, and a summary of her significance for our contemporary Church, for monasticism, and for the whole world. Our original purpose was to delve into the richness of our own tradition and thereby to empower our own members with their heritage, primarily monastic and Benedictine. As their stories unfolded and the varied contributions of these early women were revealed with greater clarity, we began to view this project in relation to a much wider audience that would include women of all beliefs and all traditions.

Chapter 1 begins with St. Scholastica, the sister of Benedict, whom Gregory the Great praises for her remarkable capacity to love. The author presents her as "a strong, resourceful woman who would not let herself be limited unfairly." We are given "an inspiring portrait of a surprisingly modern, resolute woman, who saw life as a series of decisions and doubted not at all her own ability to make them."

Our focus in chapters 2 and 3 centers on the unusual contributions made by two seventh and eighth-century Anglo-Saxon monastics, Hilda of Whitby and Frideswide of Oxford. Hilda, the abbess of a double monastery and an erudite church leader, was instrumental in ending the controversy over the date of Easter between the Roman Church and the Celtic Christians at the celebrated synod held at her abbey in Whitby. Frideswide is the monastic founder and patron saint of the city and university of Oxford. In the words of our author, she was "the abbess whose leadership was the initial heartbeat of ecclesial, academic, and civic life in Oxford."

At the turn of the seventh century, Erentrude, the niece of St. Rupert, founded Nonnberg Abbey in Salzburg (see chapter 4). Rupert not only invited Erentrude to become the first abbess of the new women's foundation but also established St. Peter's Abbey for monks in the same city. Nonnberg, the oldest Benedictine women's abbey in Germany and Austria, has had an unbroken monastic tradition since its beginning around 700 A.D. It is from this abbey in 1035 that the Abbey of St. Walburg, Eichstätt, originated.

At the urging of Boniface in the eighth century, Abbess Tetta of Wimborne Abbey sent thirty exemplary Anglo-Saxon women missionaries to Germany. Our attention in chapters 5 through 7 is on Walburga, Leoba, and Thecla who helped transplant their Benedictine heritage primarily into the areas of Saxony, the Rhineland, and Bavaria. Walburga succeeded her brother Wunibald in governing the double monastery of Heidenheim. Today, her name is associated with miracles of healing attributed to faith in her intercessory power. Leoba, the wise confidant not only of Boniface but also of Queen Hildegard, the wife of Charlemagne, was greatly admired for her wisdom, learning, and holiness. The third woman of this Anglo-Saxon trio, Thecla, "shining like a light in a dark place," served as the abbess of Ochsenfurt and later founded the Abbey of Kitzingen. Indications are that during this missionary period these Anglo-Saxon abbesses who governed double monasteries also administered the surrounding parishes, working in collaboration with the monks as their counterparts.

From the ninth to the twelfth centuries, Germany gave the Church and monasticism many gifted nuns and canonesses. Among them were foundresses and abbesses, poets, dramatists, illuminators, historians, herbalists, mystics, seers, and prophets. In chapters 8 through 12, we consider Irmengard of Chiemsee, Hrotsvit of Gandersheim, Hildegard of Bingen and her *magistra* Blessed Jutta of Spanheim, Elisabeth of Schönau, and Herrad of Hohenbourg.

In the mid-ninth century, Irmengard (chapter 8) refounded Frauenwörth, the oldest Benedictine abbey for nuns in Germany proper. It was originally founded in 766 by Duke Tassilo III, shortly after Nonnberg. This Carolingian princess continues to be revered today for her contemplative spirit and her great love for the poor. She has the distinction of being canonized a Benedictine woman-saint in the twentieth century, more than a millennium after her death. Hrotsvit of Gandersheim, a tenth-century Saxon canoness, holds three unique honors. She is the first known dramatist of Christianity, the first Saxon poet, and the first woman historian of Germany. In her six literary plays modeled on those of the Roman writer, Terence, she consciously attempted to remold and counteract his view of women as evil and depraved. Her plays provided literary models of exemplary behavior for Christian readers to emulate.

The twelfth-century Benedictines—Hildegard of Bingen; her teacher, Jutta of Spanheim; and Elisabeth of Schönau—are presented in chapters 10 and 11 as our foremothers in Wisdom. They witnessed to the gospel through their visionary insights, their gift of healing, and their prophetic witness flowing from their contemplative vision. The chapter on Hildegard and Jutta places special emphasis on the Rule of Benedict as a Wisdom document through which they were guided and transformed by *Sapientia* in their spiritual return journey to God. Elisabeth, in the words of the author, is noted for her "intensely felt accounts of her visionary experiences" and "more closely resembles the mystics of the twelfth and thirteenth centuries who came after her than she does her contemporary, Hildegard." Herrad of Hohenbourg created a pictorial encyclopedia of her twelfth-century world in the *Garden of Delights,* depicting her extensive knowledge of the biblical and the secular in more than six hundred miniature illuminations.

From the prophetic expression of the Benedictine charism, we turn in chapters 13 through 16 to the mystical tradition represented by four thirteenth-century mystics: Lutgard of Aywières (emphasis in this essay is on her years as a Benedictine); and Mechtild of Magdeburg, Mechtild of Hackeborn, and Gertrud of Helfta, the three Saxons who belonged to the abbey of Helfta, "the crown of German cloisters." Characteristic of their Trinitarian, Christocentric, and bridal mysticism is a focus on Scripture, particularly on the Song of Songs, and an emphasis on the humanity of Christ in which the heart becomes the symbol of this love. The mysticism of Gertrud the Great and Mechtild of Hackeborn was a fusion of the biblical, liturgical, and mystical integrated with the cenobitic thrust of the Rule of Benedict.

The book concludes with chapter 17 describing the spirituality of Dame Gertrude More who lived in the early part of the seventeenth century. She was among the original group who left England, settled at Cambrai, France, and was guided by Dom Augustine Baker in her brief but intense spiritual journey to God. The small Cambrai community suffered untold hardships in their expulsion from Cambrai and their consequent imprisonment during the French Reign of Terror. Their community, numbering seventeen members, returned to England in 1795 and eventually founded Stanbrook Abbey at Worcester. Thus the circular monastic movement begun by the Anglo-Saxon missionaries who went from England to Germany came full circle in the return of the Cambrai nuns to England from the continent of Europe.

We invite our readers to investigate further the stories of these and other medieval monastic forerunners and the precious and varied spiritual legacy they bequeathed to us. It is our hope that their contemplative and prophetic witness will spur us on to be as courageous, daring, and passionate in our quest for God in our era as they were in theirs.

Emerging from the Shadows: St. Scholastica

Mary Richard Boo, O.S.B., and Joan M. Braun, O.S.B.

We have all but lost the person. Scholars have largely neglected her. Library holdings are negligible. Even St. Gregory, whose sixth-century *Dialogues* offer the only known primary account of her, presents her chiefly as a character in the life of her illustrious brother. Although a plethora of buildings bear her name—wherever there are Benedictine sisters, there is a "St. Scholastica" this or a "St. Scholastica" that—St. Scholastica herself has been hidden in Benedict's shadow and relegated to an existence somewhere between myth and reality.

Let us admit at the outset that little is known of Scholastica. Gregory's *Dialogues* alone recount the story of a final meeting between brother and sister and, subsequently, the fact of her death.

> His [Benedict's] sister Scholastica, who had been consecrated to God in early childhood, used to visit with him once a year. On these occasions he would go down to meet her in a house belonging to the monastery a short distance from the entrance. [No women were allowed to enter the monastery itself.]
>
> For this particular visit he joined her there with a few of his disciples and they spent the whole day singing God's praises and conversing about the spiritual life. When darkness was setting in, they took their meal together and continued their conversation at table until it was quite late. Then the holy nun said to him, "Please do not leave me tonight, brother. Let us keep on talking about the joys of heaven till morning."
>
> "What are you saying, sister?" he replied. "You know I cannot stay away from the monastery."

The sky was so clear at the time, there was not a cloud in sight. At her brother's refusal Scholastica folded her hands on the table and rested her head upon them in earnest prayer. When she looked up again, there was a sudden burst of lightning and thunder accompanied by such a downpour that Benedict and his companions were unable to set foot outside the door.

By shedding a flood of tears while she prayed, this holy nun had darkened the cloudless sky with a heavy rain. The storm began as soon as her prayer was over. In fact, the two coincided so closely that the thunder was already resounding as she raised her head from the table. The very instant she ended her prayer the rain poured down.

Realizing that he could not return to the abbey in this terrible storm, Benedict complained bitterly. "God forgive you, sister!" he said. "What have you done?"

Scholastica simply answered, "When I appealed to you, you would not listen to me. So I turned to my God and He heard my prayer. Leave me now if you can. Leave me here and go back to your monastery."

This, of course, he could not do. He had no choice now but to stay, in spite of his unwillingness. . . . We need not be surprised that in this instance she proved mightier than her brother; she had been looking forward so long to this visit. Do we not read in St. John that God is love? Surely it is no more than right that her influence was greater than his, since hers was the greater love. . . . The next morning Scholastica returned to her convent and Benedict to his monastery. Three days later as he stood in his room looking up toward the sky, he beheld his sister's soul leaving her body and entering the heavenly court in the form of a dove. . . . The bodies of these two were now to share a common resting place, just as in life their souls had always been one in God.[1]

And that is it. All the rest is surmise, secondary sources, and interpretation.

Scholarly monks and nuns will no doubt continue for years to come to pore over what is known about Scholastica, while those who are intrigued less by research than by the woman herself will go on trying to discover what she was really like and what she has to offer the contemporary Christian.

Much of the attention given Scholastica has centered understandably on the famous "Thunderstorm Episode."[2] Here she demonstrated in the span of a few brief hours that she possessed "the greater love." Having dared more, she received more. In this instance, love took precedence over law (although, as Adalbert de Vogüé reminds us, Gregory only a few chapters later again lauds Benedict's great Rule).[3] All this is impressive enough. It behooves us, however, to glance back over the preceding sixty years of Scholastica's life to consider what is not literally stated but is unquestionably clear: saints are not made overnight nor during the course of a single downpour, however precipitous their conversions may sometimes seem. Gregory's thunderstorm chapter is a vignette drawn from a much longer, more serious drama in which Scholastica figures as a woman aware of her freedom in God.

Scholastica must have understood that in making any major decision in her life, she had options as we all do; she was not locked into one course of action but could look about her at a range of choices. One choice was, of course, deferential obedience to her brother and his interpretation of the Rule he himself had written. This option might well have been coupled with silent, passive, and potentially depressing disappointment.

Or she might have chosen to display frustration, even anger, perhaps in the hope of moving Benedict to change his mind. Or a third option—and the one she selected—she could turn in prayer to God to ask of Him what her brother refused.

Her action suggests a strong, resourceful woman who would not let herself be limited unfairly. But, we ask, how could she be confident that she was not simply asserting her own will, defying God as well as her brother? The answer is plain: long years of discerning the will of God had empowered her with penetrating vision and deep desire.

Theologians define discernment in a spiritual context as habitually turning toward God in a constantly receptive effort to determine what He wills for us. It is, as Johnette Putnam puts it, "not a process, but . . . a way of life which is always attentive to the will of God."[4] Without the habit of discernment, Scholastica would not have dared to presume that God's will for her was expressed in his sudden intervention and the granting of her request.

One can only speculate about Scholastica's possible influence on the spirit of the Rule itself. Abbot Butler and other scholars have made it clear that the Rule is derived from dozens of sources—some religious, some not—but we must agree with Gregory, who explains with disarming simplicity that the discretion and charity for which the Rule is famous must flow from Benedict himself. But what did Scholastica contribute to the formation of Benedict? Is it conceivable that she was so docile and submissive that she had no impact on her forceful brother? Hardly, if we read Gregory with care. Surely they must have talked of Benedict's work during their lengthy, if infrequent, conversations. Would he not have asked her to read what he was compiling and writing? Perhaps it was partially because of her that the Rule mandates profound respect for every individual, in and out of the monastery. Perhaps she reminded Benedict to be a little easier on the young boys in the monastery and on the old and sick who could no longer fulfill a demanding life style. Did she ask him to increase a bit the daily allotment of wine and did he grumble as he did it? Did she suggest that the monks be given better clothing for journeys outside the monastery walls, and did her brother mumble something about those monks returning the clothing when they came home? Was it her insight that saw all religious, including Benedict and herself, as mere beginners in a lifelong race toward love? We cannot know, of course, the relationship between brother and sister and can only assume that Scholastica may have influenced Benedict's thinking. Such influence would seem to be entirely probable: as he gave to her, so she returned her gifts to him.

What, then, do we see in this woman distanced from us by centuries of silence and obscurity? Certainly a woman for our time: a completely human person dedicated to the search for the Divine, steadily growing in her realization that the search must culminate, not in constraint, but in freedom; not in weakness, but in strength. By the time of her death, her soul was ready to fly into the sun like the dove by which she is tradition-ally symbolized.

Tradition has woven a fuller story of Scholastica. It depicts her as a twin sister to Benedict, born about 480 at Norcia, Italy, the daughter of Abundantia, who died in childbirth, and Euproprius, who was both illus-trious and wealthy. As a young child, she was consecrated to the Lord; this was already a common practice in the Church, but she was said to be younger than the law allowed when she participated in the ceremony. When Benedict established his monastery at Monte Cassino, she settled nearby, putting herself under her brother's spiritual direction. The precise location of her place of residence has never been conclusively estab-lished.[5] A pious tradition, recaptured by Salvatore Petrini, holds that the maternal home of the saint was where she would have lived for some time before going to the Cassino area. The site of the ancient maternal home was supposedly later the location of the current Church of St. Scholastica "at the Cemetery" near Norcia. When she was aged, according to Aldo Cicinelli, Scholastica lived with other pious women in Plumbariola, next to Cassino.[6] Gregory tells us that Scholastica died shortly after her final visit with Benedict: Ildephonse Cardinal Schuster sets that meeting on February 7, 547, the Thursday preceding the first Sunday of Lent in that year. This differs slightly from other researchers, who put the year of her death about four years earlier, in 543.

Scholastica's existence is not in doubt. Gregory wrote only fifty years or so after the events he recounts, and he himself names as his major sources of information four of Benedict's companions or contemporaries: Constantine, who followed Benedict as abbot of Monte Cassino; Simplicius, third abbot of Monte Cassino; Honoratus, abbot of Subiaco when Gregory was writing the *Dialogues*; and Valentinian, superior of the monastery at the Lateran Basilica.[7] Gregory mentions, too, three eyewit-nesses of many of Benedict's miracles: Exhilaratus; the "distinguished Anthony"; and Benedict's own follower, Peregrinus. These men would certainly have known of Scholastica or even known her personally. As for

Gregory himself, Schuster speaks confidently of his "historical exactitude and his literary probity."[8]

Gregory does not stand alone, however. The liturgy solidly supports him. In the eighth century, only two hundred years after her death, Scholastica was included in the calendar of the liturgical year. The earliest documentation of her existence following publication of the *Dialogues of St. Gregory* (II) is in two Cassinese calendars from the eighth and ninth centuries. The presence of her name on February 10 in the Parisinus 7530, 778–797 A.D., and in the Casanatensis 641, 811–812 A.D., on the same date establishes that she was venerated as a saint at Monte Cassino from the eighth century onward. The Parisinus 7530 also records the observance of the dedication of a church to St. Scholastica on June 19.[9] This church is believed to have been built, appropriately, on the site traditionally identified as the final meeting place of Benedict and Scholastica.[10]

In about 1058, the *Codex Benedictus,* Vat. Lat. 1202, was produced at Monte Cassino at the request of Abbot Desiderius.[11] A lectionary for the feasts of Saints Benedict, Maurus, and Scholastica, it functioned as the book from which lessons were read in choir for the liturgy of the Night Office.[12] (It is interesting to note that for the four lessons of the Night Office of the feast of St. Scholastica, a choice was available between the works of Abbot Bertharius and those of Alberic of Monte Cassino, but that both sets of lessons about Scholastica were shorter than those for either Benedict or Maurus.[13])

Although Alberic, monk of Monte Cassino and author of "The Homily of Alberic the Deacon on Saint Scholastica,"[14] did not write about Scholastica until sometime after the middle of the eleventh century, knowledge of her had obviously persisted over the four hundred years that separated Alberic from Gregory. In addition to his famous homily, Alberic also wrote two little-known poems that cite Scholastica; one, an eighty-line elegy, is in the *Codex Benedictus*; the other was printed in Mabillon's *Acta Sanctorum, O.S.B.,* 11. 44–45. The latter seems to be a refined version of a similar poem in honor of St. Benedict by Abbot Bertharius.[15]

A relatively recent and rich source of information, particularly traditional material, regarding Scholastica is the 1981 report of the restoration of the frescoes of the Church of St. Scholastica in Norcia.[16] (This church has a significant place in the histories of both Benedict and Scholastica who are considered patrons of the city; moreover, it is the church believed to have been built on the site of their maternal ancestral home.) On the morning of February 10, 1978, the feast of St. Scholastica, during the restoration of the frescoed walls of the Norcian church, a hitherto unknown painting of Scholastica was revealed beneath the falling plaster. This fourteenth-century work had been covered by a cycle of fifteenth-century frescoes depicting the life of Benedict and had been forgotten over the years.[17] Its existence adds still further credibility to the legend of Scholastica.

The unanswered questions about Scholastica, then, are not centered on her existence, but on whether she was simply a holy woman who lived near Monte Cassino under the spiritual direction of Benedict or was authentically his sister—perhaps even his twin.

In a brief essay published in 1965, J. H. Wansbrough deals with the identity issue by skirting it, concerning himself instead with what he considers Gregory's deliberate use of allegory:

> Gregory gives the characters in his *Dialogues* names which indicate their character, or the function he wishes them to perform, the moral which he will use them to illustrate. . . . So when we claim that the name Scholastica indicates leisure for contemplation this leaves the question of her historicity untouched. . . . She stands for contemplation.[18]

Creative as Wansbrough's exegesis is, it was refuted some fifteen years later by the noted Benedictine scholar, Adalbert de Vogüé, of the monastery of La Pierre-qui-Vire.[19]

Pearse Cusack also devotes some pages of rather dashing scholarship to Scholastica's identity. His hypothesis, like Wansbrough's, rests on Gregory's intention in writing the *Dialogues,* especially chapter 33. If, as Cusack maintains, Gregory wrote to inspire his readers and to carry to its conclusion in both content and structure a thesis that love has precedence over law, he may well have deliberately used literary conventions and been influenced by medieval biographies which frequently linked a "sister figure" with a stronger, more independent brother. (In chapter 33, these roles are, of course, reversed.)[20] There is, nevertheless, the distinct possibility that Gregory did not write primarily to inspire, as Cusack would have it, but to chronicle the factual matter of Benedict's (and thus, partially at least, Scholastica's) life. Although it is not possible to write fact and fiction simultaneously, facts can be written with a clearly secondary intention of motivating the reader. It seems probable that Gregory adhered strictly to the truth but hoped at the same time that the facts would speak inspirationally to those who read them. As even Cusack concedes: "It is psychologically predictable that a sister, especially a younger one, will identify with a brother and, indeed, follow him to holiness—and brothers do have sisters!"[21]

Were Benedict and Scholastica twins? To paraphrase Pearse Cusack: twins *do* exist. Gregory describes Scholastica as simply Benedict's sister. Later sources describe the two as twins. Whether this designation alludes to actual birth or to the unity of spirit that traditionally binds twins, or to both, is hardly significant. Gregory states only that "their souls had always been one in God."[22]

Their unity was demonstrated when Scholastica died: Benedict chose to share his grave with her.[23] He had previously selected for his own burial site a small chapel dedicated to John the Baptist in the community cemetery at Monte Cassino.[24] Here he had the body of Scholastica placed in the lower part of the grave and covered with a horizontal slab, so that the grave could again be opened for the body of Benedict himself only a few months later. Their remains lay here together for more than a century, while overhead, in the closing years of the sixth century,[25] marauding Lombards under the command of Zoto of Beneventum invaded the monastery and evicted, but did not kill, the monks—nor did they disturb the common grave of Benedict and Scholastica.

Brother and sister slept on while the monks of Monte Cassino regrouped to form a community beside the Lateran Basilica in Rome, thus bringing the Rule of Benedict out of provincial obscurity and laying the foundations for its eventual worldwide observance. Monte Cassino itself was all but deserted for some 130 years, although its silence was broken during those dormant years when monks from the monastery of Fleury in France arrived to find and claim the remains of Benedict and Scholastica.[26] Although the two skeletons taken to Fleury have never been conclusively proved to be those of Scholastica and Benedict, tradition strongly affirms that they are. Until modern technology renders a final judgment on their identity, we can concur with Philip Le Maitre that the French without doubt believed in good faith that they brought back the prestigious remains of the Patriarch and his sister.[27]

Schuster is blunt in his description of the expedition from Fleury: "After the dispersion of the monks of Monte Cassino as a result of Zoto's occupation of the monastery, since the place remained unguarded and deserted, about the year 703, while Gisulph was duke of Beneventum, some Flemish monks arrived to steal the relics, which were then carried off to Fleury."[28] Schuster adds, a few lines later: "At the time of the restoration of Monte Cassino [in 718] through the efforts of Popes Gregory II and Zachary, the monks, as legal heirs of the former monastery, demanded, but in vain, that the bones of the Patriarch be returned to them. [Schuster makes no reference to those of Scholastica.] The monks of Fleury as well as the Frankish bishops turned a deaf ear to the letters of Pope Zachary."[29] A few scattered bones and ashy remains had been left at Monte Cassino, but by far the greater part of the remains of both saints are very likely still in France, having never been returned. (Following the World War II bombing of Monte Cassino by Allied forces in an effort to destroy German fortifications there, two skeletons—one male, one female—were discovered beneath the rubble of an ancient altar. These remains are also alleged to be those of Benedict and Scholastica.)

If Scholastica's bones were indeed taken to Fleury, they were not to find rest even there. A widely accepted tradition holds that during the epis-copate of St. Berecharius (655–70) the body of St. Scholastica was brought from the monastery of Fleury to Le Mans.[30] According to this ac-count, when Le Mans was invaded by Northmen in the latter half of the ninth century, some of the relics were brought to the monastery of Juvigny les Dames under the sponsorship of the Empress Richilda. Almost all of the remaining bones were destroyed by fire in September 1134. This tra-dition, completely accepted in the eighth and ninth centuries, is not with-out its modern challengers. W. Goffart of the University of Toronto proposes a number of hypotheses addressing the question of what hap-pened to Scholastica's relics in the light of ancient commentaries.[31] He states:

> The controversy among modern scholars over the translation of St. Benedict and St. Scholastica has centered on the question whether or not the remains of the saints ever left Monte Cassino and were taken to the monastery of Fleury, near Orleans. In the eighth and ninth centuries, this question was not in doubt; everyone accepted that the translation had taken place. The early evidence does disclose a discrepancy, however, over what happened to the relics when they reached northern France. Some of the texts speak of a translation to Fleury only, others of a division between Fleury, which retained the relics of St. Benedict, and Le Mans, which acquired those of St. Scholastica. This discrepancy affects the indirect evidence for the translation as well as the intentional narrative accounts.

Goffart casts a dubious eye on those sources—perhaps forged—that place the remains of Scholastica at Le Mans at any time; he is not im-pressed by the apparent success of Queen Richilda in locating there what she believed to be Scholastica's bones. Still, he concedes, the study of rel-evant manuscripts must continue before the total truth can be known.

That the truth will gradually emerge is almost certain. In the meantime, we have an inspiring portrait of a surprisingly modern, resolute woman who saw life as a series of decisions and doubted not at all her own abil-ity to make them. Let her bones lie where they will; her spirit transcends the centuries.

NOTES

1. St. Gregory the Great, *Life and Miracles of St. Benedict,* trans. Odo J. Zimmermann, O.S.B., and Benedict R. Avery, O.S.B. (Collegeville: The Liturgical Press, n.d.) 67–70.

2. Ibid., 67–9.

3. Adalbert de Vogüé, "The Meeting of Benedict and Scholastica: an Interpretation," *Cistercian Studies* 18 (1983) 182.

4. Johnette Putnam, *Discerning Community Leadership: The Benedictine Tradition* (Conference of American Benedictine Prioresses, 1988) 2.

5. Numerous scholars (e.g., Don Angelo Pantoni, "Sulla Localita Del Convegno Annuale Di S. Benedetto E S. Scolastica, E Sul Monastero Di Piumarola," *Benedictina* 15 (1968) 206–228; D. H. Farmer, "Scholastica," *The Oxford Dictionary of Saints,* Oxford, (1978) place her in the convent of Piumarola, some three miles from Monte Cassino, and some depict her as an abbess there. On this matter of her dwelling place, Pantoni—himself a monk of Monte Cassino—disagrees with Ildephonse, Cardinal Schuster, who holds that Scholastica resided at the base of Monte Cassino where an oratory was later dedicated to her. She did not, according to Schuster, "live with a community of nuns. It must have been a kind of hermitage with a few religious; there were others like it on the mountain of Casinum." (Ildephonse Schuster, *Saint Benedict and his Times,* trans. Gregory J. Roettger [St. Louis: B. Herder Book Co., 1951.] 338).

6. Aldo Cicinelli, *Una Mostra, Un Restauro* (included in *Gli Affreschi Della Chiesa di S. Scolastica a Norcia*, Norcia, 1981) Norcia, 1979, 27.

7. Gregory, *Life and Miracles,* 2.

8. Schuster, *St. Benedict,* 6.

9. Germain Morin, "Les Quatre Anciens Calendriers du Mont-Cassin (VIIIe et IXe Siecles)," *Revue Benedictine* 25 (1908) 486, 489.

10. Morin, 492, n.3.

11. The *Codex Benedictus* has recently (copyright 1982, 1981) been reproduced in facsimile form by Johnson Reprint Corporation (New York and Belser Verlag, Zurich) and Harcourt Brace Jovanovich. Writing in that facsimile volume, both Paul Meyvaert ("The Script and the Scribe of the *Codex Benedictus,*" 30-31) and Penelope Mayo ("Art Historical Introduction to the *Codex Benedictus,*" 44) place the original production of the Codex somewhere between 1058 and 1072.

12. Louis Duval-Arnold and Agostino Bagliani, "Codicological Introduction to the Manuscript Vaticanus Latinus, 1202," *Codex Benedictus, Vat. Lat. 1202* (New York and Zurich: Johnson Reprint Corporation, 1981, 1982) 18.

13. Paul Mcyvaert, "The Historical Setting and Significance of the *Codex Benedictus,*" *Codex Benedictus* Vat. Lat. 1202 (New York and Zurich: Johnson Reprint Corporation, 1981, 1982) 24.

According to Meyvaert, until the time of Desiderius, Bertharius's two works were undoubtedly the only lessons used for the Night Office on the feast of St. Scholastica. We can rightly say, then, that from at least the last quarter of the ninth century, St. Scholastica was commemorated with lessons.

Bertharius assured a text of appropriate length for the lessons of the Night Office by writing a sermon in Scholastica's honor; in the sermon, he takes, in order, all the phrases referring to her in Gregory's *Dialogues* (II) and offers a spiritual commentary on each of them. Bertharius also composed a homily on the Gospel text of the ten virgins recited on her feast. Both the sermon and homily are included in the *Codex Benedictus.*

14. The second set of lessons for the feast of St. Scholastica consists of this life and homily. Herbert Bloch thinks, with substantial reason, that Alberic wrote the pieces on Scholastica specifically for the *Codex Benedictus.* Alberic retells, with many literary embellishments, the material in the *Dialogues*; he adds, too, a number

of miracles attributed to St. Scholastica—all of which result in a text long enough to provide lessons for the Night Office (Meyvaert, 18).

Alberic tells us that Scholastica worried about Benedict's coming down the mountain and reascending the same day, but that she appreciated the solitude afforded by their meeting place. He goes on to describe Scholastica in terms of virtues prized by eleventh-century cenobitics. She was, he states, a woman of continual prayer who kept vigils indefatigably and was so filled with a spirit of compunction that tears of gratitude never ceased flowing from her deep sense of contrition. Don Anselmo Lentini, "L'omilia e la vita di S. Scolastica di Alberico Cassinese," *Benedictina* 3 (1949) 231.

15. Owen J. Blum, "Alberic of Monte Cassino and the Hymns and Rhythms Attributed to Saint Peter Damian," *Traditio* 12: 92, 93.

16. *Gli Affreschi Della Chiesa di S. Scolastica a Norcia,* "Una Mostra, Un Restauro," Norcia, 1981.

17. The earliest epochs of the Church of St. Scholastica did not provide reliable information about it. The first definite reference to the church is from 1294 when Pope Celestine V granted indulgences to visitors there. In 1389 Pope Boniface IX published a similar document. Ibid., 14.

In the rediscovered fourteenth-century frescoes, Scholastica, painted by the Master of the Straus Madonna, is represented in the International Gothic style with an elegant, somewhat courtly demeanor. She is young, slender, and in her graceful left hand holds a book. The two figures are standing; Scholastica's body is slightly turned toward her twin brother, who seems to be looking at her while she gazes off into space away from him. (Benedict, thought to have been done by a follower of Bartolomeo di Tommaso [fifteenth century], is an elderly, portly figure somewhat Giottoesque in form.) The lines of demarcation of the two layers of plaster and the figures typifying two different art styles are evident. Both the fourteenth and fifteenth-century frescoes were covered over in the seventeenth century by elaborate Baroque plaster decorations. Ibid., 24, 29, 41.

One may wonder why the frescoes depicting the life cycle of Benedict were superimposed upon the painting of his sister only a few decades later. Certainly the intent of the monks then resident was not to obscure Scholastica, but rather to find space in which to record the life of Benedict as recounted in the *Dialogues* of Gregory. Their goal was more didactic than artistic. (In fact, Scholastica is included twice in this series of scenes, but in a manner which suggests her dependency upon Benedict). Ibid., 21, 24, 41.

18. J. H. Wansbrough, "St. Gregory's Intention in the Stories of St. Scholastica and St. Benedict, *Revue Benedictine* 75 (1965) 146.

19. Adalbert de Vogüé, "The Meeting of Benedict and Scholastica: an Interpretation," 167–183. De Vogüé dismisses Wansbrough's interpretation of the names *Benedict* and *Scholastica,* pointing out that both were fairly common given names and that, moreover, the correct definition of *scholasticus* is that of an administrator in a high position, a jurist, or simply a very learned man. *Scholastica,* of course, is the feminine form and, like *scholasticus,* carries no connotation of contemplation. De Vogüé does not hesitate to accept literally the identity of any of the figures depicted by Gregory.

20. Pearse Aiden Cusack, "St. Scholastica: Myth or Real Person," *Downside*

Review 92 (April 1974) 145–159. According to Cusack, "It was almost as important for these mythological heroes of medieval hagiography to have a sister as it is for the President of the United States to have a wife. . . . The introduction of a sister adds to the interest of a story; it gives edification to both sexes and avoids the embarrassment of pairing the saint with a female who is otherwise unrelated to him" (148). This sister figure would not have necessarily, or even probably, been Benedict's actual blood sister, but rather some holy person living nearby who, like a number of other individuals, had chosen Benedict as her spiritual director. Beyond that, Cusack states, all is simply "unwarranted inference. . . . It seems . . . that although Scholastica was a real person, her personality is so shrouded in the mists of time and the obscurity of myth that we cannot really be sure that she was sister german to the Patriarch of Western Monasticism." Although Cusack's article received no literary response (letter, Pearse Aidan Cusack, July 18, 1993), it again raises an area of research—one which he continues to pursue in his new work, *An Interpretation of the Second Dialogue of Gregory the Great* (The Edwin Mellen Press, Lewiston, N.Y., 1993).

Father Cusack must be granted his point—or perhaps, more fairly, a portion of it. There is no single source that states with greater authority than does Gregory that Scholastica was, indeed, the actual sister of Benedict, but Cusack questions Gregory's intentions and therefore his validity.

21. Ibid., 148.

22. Gregory, *Life and Miracles*, 70.

23. Ibid., 70.

24. Ibid., 75–6.

25. Specifically in the year 580, according to G. R. Huddleston, *Catholic Encyclopedia* 10 (1911) 527a.

26. Schuster holds out for their coming in 703, but Antoine Beau and others (*The Veneration and the Relics of St. Benedict and of St. Scholastica* [A. & J. Picard, 1980] 395-398; reviewer, Philippe LeMaitre, *Monastic Studies* 21 (1979) agree on the latter half of the seventh century, most likely c. 660, and consider even early eighth-century dates based on unreliable sources.

27. LeMaitre, Philippe, reviewer, *The Veneration and the Relics of St. Benedict and of St. Scholastica*, Antoine Beau and others; *Monastic Studies* 21 (1979) 398.

28. Schuster, 364.

29. Ibid., 365.

30. Georges Goyau, "Le Mans," *Catholic Encyclopedia* (New York: Robert Appleton Co., 1910) IX:144.

31. W. Goffart, "Le Mans, St. Scholastica, and the Literary Tradition of the Translation of St. Benedict," *Revue Benedictine* 27 (1967) 107–141.

2

Abbess Hilda of Whitby:
All Britain Was Lit by Her Splendor

Nancy Bauer, O.S.B.

Intertwined with the vast troupe of kings, bishops, and monks that makes its way across the stage of Bede's *History of the English Church and People* is a smaller, but no less revered, parade of monastic women. Bede names twenty women of the Anglo-Saxon period, most of them from the seventh century and most of them members of royal families, who became nuns either in their homeland or abroad. Of these twenty, some are mentioned merely in passing, playing only a small part in a greater story. Heriburg, the abbess of Watton, and her daughter Coenburg, for example, appear only as recipients of the miraculous cures effected by St. John of Beverly.[1] A few more, such as Earcongota, Saethryd, and Ethelberga, are presented as examples of those who traveled to the Frankish realm to join the double monastery of Brie because, we are told, there were as yet few monasteries in English territory to accommodate them.[2] A few more are mentioned in the context of particular events at their monasteries. Abbess Ebba, for example, finds her way into Bede's history for two reasons. It is to her monastery of Coldingham that the long-suffering Etheldreda fled when her husband, the equally long-suffering King Egfrid, finally released her from her marriage vows to pursue monastic vows.[3] It is also Ebba's Coldingham that is the locale of the only scandal reported by Bede in the growing number of double monasteries dotting the English landscape. Though Ebba herself is not accused of impropriety, her monks and nuns seemed to have been so lax that the destruction of the monastery by fire after her death is seen as a fitting punishment.[4] Still another of the Anglo-Saxon nuns merits considerable space for a variety of reasons. The Abbess Ethelburga ran the monastery of Barking in such admirable fashion that it was the scene of several miracles, and Bede, who always enjoyed a good miracle, felt compelled to interrupt his progression of kings and clerics to park his readers at Barking's gates long enough for them to be duly edified by the goings on there.[5] But Ethelburga herself is introduced not so much as a monastic foundress and capable administrator in her own right, but as someone who "bore herself in a manner worthy of her brother the bishop," that is, Bishop Earconwald who built monasteries for himself and his sister. It is he who is credited with establishing "an excellent regular discipline in both houses."[6]

Of course there were numerous Anglo-Saxon nuns who never came to Bede's attention. Bede's history is, after all, uneven. Considerable space is sometimes given to relatively minor characters, while scant attention is sometimes paid to major players in the political, ecclesiastical and monastic events of Anglo-Saxon England. As much depended on Bede's access to information as on his own preferences of heroes and heroines. Ethelberga, though surely deserving of attention, got plenty of it for the simple reason that there was a book of her holy deeds from which to draw information. Bede tells us so.[7] Other nuns, whom Bede barely mentions, were actually the subjects of considerable devotion and in some cases their accomplishments were recorded elsewhere.

But of the twenty nuns in Bede's repertoire, two stand out: Etheldreda of Ely (c. 630–679) and Hilda of Whitby (614–680). These two alone earn something akin to biographies based primarily on their own initiatives and achievements. And what he wrote of these two women assured them a permanent place among the company of great monastic founders and, and even more importantly, propelled them into the hearts and imaginations of succeeding generations of monastics and non-monastics alike. Interestingly, however, only one of these commands sufficient interest among contemporary monastic women to have a chapter in this book. Yet if previous generations, indeed if Bede himself had to choose between the two, the other would most likely have emerged the winner. That Hilda is more popular now than in previous centuries says as much about us as it does about Hilda. That Etheldreda was more popular in previous centuries says as much about our predecessors as it does about Etheldreda. That Etheldreda and Hilda have not sustained equal popularity through all the centuries also says something about the kind of information available about both of them. The problem seems to be that there has not been enough information on Hilda while there has been too much of the wrong kind of information on Etheldreda.

Bede gives us just enough facts about Hilda to whet our appetites, but too little to assuage our thirst. Unlike many of the other female mystics and monastics of the Middle Ages who have become popular in recent years, Hilda has left us no letters, poems, prayers, hymns, or journals. And with the exception of a chapter in Bede, there is scant primary material from which to draw. There is, for example, no extant Life of Hilda by those who knew her, and scholars disagree on whether there ever was a Life. But while what we have of Hilda is brief, it is believable. And even more importantly, it presents a Hilda who stands as a model for what women, particularly monastic women, hope to achieve today. The same cannot be said for her contemporary—and most likely her acquaintance and perhaps even friend—Etheldreda. What Bede gave us about Etheldreda is no longer fully believable and barely even admirable. Furthermore, what Bede gave us has been embellished by later and less scrupulous "historians" who, in an effort to magnify her sanctity, managed to diminish her humanity. Hilda has been blessedly spared the hyperbole of hagiography. But alas, short of the few biographical notes provided by Bede, what else we know of her must be pried and prodded from the pages of history. Like spies, Hilda's fans search for clues and connections among the events and people that formed the context of her life. And even then, along with Lina Eckenstein, we sigh, "Would that there were more data whereby to estimate her personality."[8] What we have of Etheldreda, on the other hand, must be carefully sifted to separate truth from propaganda and reality from what made a good story.[9]

Let us turn to Bede, then, to discover why, when Hilda and Etheldreda are examined in the context of seventh-century, Anglo-Saxon England, Etheldreda is called forever after the most popular of the many Anglo-Saxon women saints, but Hilda, the most useful and influential.

From Bede we learn that Hilda died in 680 at the age of sixty-six.[10] Her life, therefore, spanned some of the most pulsating years of English Church history and Hilda managed to at least be on the scene, if not trying to direct the outcome, of some of the major events of that history. It was the great age of conversion of the English people from "heathenism" to Christianity, a period that provided opportunities for women of Hilda's talents and circumstances that has seldom, perhaps never, been equaled in the Church. But the spread of Christianity did not progress evenly and without interruption. If a bishop managed to convert one king, and therefore his kingdom, his efforts were easily abolished when that king was defeated in battle and his successor reverted to heathenism. Or perhaps the converted king, such as Redwald, kept an altar to Christ and an altar to his other gods in the same shrine at the same time.[11]

When Christianity finally took hold, there were arguments about how to organize the growing number of believers. There were conflicts of great personalities, all of them saintly in their own way, but who were not always compatible with each other. And there were miracles. Dreams, signs, and coincidences that seemed divinely orchestrated inspired, and sometimes frightened, the great and simple alike. It was a time, for example, when one of the apostles might appear in the night and literally beat common sense into a cleric who cowed in the face of adversity.[12] It was a time when monasticism thrived and throbbed, but those who went to the monastery thinking they were leaving the world behind them had only to look over their shoulder to discover that the world had followed them there seeking advice, seeking inspiration, seeking favors. It was a time, finally, when no one, least of all Bede, liked anything better than the story of a good holy death complete with the struggle to utter final words of spiritual wisdom, followed by visions of the soul advancing to heaven accompanied by light and angels. It was a time that produced great saints—some of them kings, some of them bishops, some of them monks, some of them enemies of each other. And many of them were women.

It was also a time of political turmoil. The Angles, Saxons, and Jutes, invaders of the fifth and sixth centuries, had become settlers by the seventh century. But what we now know as England was at that time divided into several provinces, each with its own king. Hilda's native province of Northumbria, while one of the most powerful during her lifetime, was sometimes ruled by a single king and sometimes divided into the rival kingdoms of Mercia and Deira. There were perpetual wars with neighboring tribes and provinces, either in an effort to acquire more territory or to protect existing borders. Hilda's own father, Hereric, nephew of the future King Edwin, was in exile when she was born or perhaps had already been poisoned before her birth.[13] As an extended member of a royal family, Hilda's fate and fortune were undoubtedly affected by the rise and fall of Edwin and subsequent rulers. But it was also because she was a member of a royal family that Hilda became one of those abbesses who was uniquely positioned to hold sway with both kings and bishops at a time when each was testing the limits of authority over the other, while at the same time each needed the tolerance of the other for furtherance of Church and state.

As abbess and royal grandniece, Hilda shared her stage with some of the most illustrious actors of the day—Bishop Paulinus who brought Christianity to her homeland, the great King Edwin who allowed Christianity to stay, the charismatic monk-bishop Aidan who brought it back, Kings Oswald and Oswy who allowed it to flourish, and the fiery bishop Wilfrid who tried to Romanize it.

Chronologically, Bede himself was not long distant from these events, and, geographically, he was not very far from Whitby. While he completed his history in 731, a bit more than fifty years after Hilda's death, he was entrusted to the monastery of Wearmouth as a boy of seven just about the time she died in nearby Whitby.

He obviously knew, or at least knew of, Hilda's successor, Aelffled, as he speaks of her with admiration in his *Life of Cuthbert*. He derived some of his information from Wilfrid, who knew both Hilda and Etheldreda, but who found favor more with the latter than with the former. Also, Bede was ordained a deacon and priest by John of Beverly, who had been a monk of Whitby almost certainly while Hilda was still alive. Finally, Bede most likely heard of Hilda through informal conversation, the "grapevine" that seems to run from monastery to monastery in every age. For all his opportunities to gather information on Hilda, it seems he could have provided more to satisfy our curiosity. But Hilda was only one of the many players in his great drama which spans more than seven hundred years, and Bede had purposes other than biography. While we would love to know more of the details of her life, what he most wanted his readers to know was that her love for God inspired her life.

Bede tells us only two things about the first half of Hilda's sixty-six years. The first, one of the few hagiographical details attached to her, is that when her mother was still pregnant she dreamt that she found a valuable jewel under her garments and when she looked closely at the jewel, "it emitted such a brilliant light that all Britain was lit by its splendor." That jewel, of course, would prove to be her as-yet-unborn daughter Hilda.[14]

The other detail locates Hilda at one of the most celebrated events in Northumbrian Church history and, no doubt, one of the most important events of her own life—the baptism of her great-uncle King Edwin and his royal household on Easter day in the year 627. Bede tells us that Hilda, who would have been fourteen at the time, was among those instructed by Paulinus and baptized during this mass conversion.[15]

The great mission of Augustine, launched thirty years earlier in the province of Kent, though sometimes credited with the conversion of all England, would actually have had little chance to affect faraway Northumbria prior to this.[16] Christianity came north when Ethelberga, daughter of the Christian king Ethelbert of Kent, married Edwin. In order to win Ethelberga's hand, Edwin had to promise that she could continue to practice her faith. For that reason, the queen brought with her to the Northumbrian court Bishop Paulinus, who had been sent from Rome in 601 to aid Augustine in his mission. Among the first to be baptized in Northumbria by Paulinus was Eanfled, the infant daughter of Edwin and Ethelberga.[17] This Eanfled and her own daughter Aelffled would eventually succeed Hilda as joint abbesses of Whitby.

Paulinus, of course, immediately set about to convert Edwin because in those days, as went the king, so went the province. Edwin was a thoughtful, deliberating man, however. He was tolerant of this new religion and even interested in it, but Bede tells us, "[he] often sat alone in silent converse with himself for long periods, turning over in his inmost heart what he should do and which religion he should follow."[18] Perhaps surprising to Paulinus, Edwin was one "heathen" who took his own religion seriously. Bede tells us that the king decided to discuss the matter with his advisers and if, on examination, they decided this Christianity appeared more holy and acceptable than their own religion, he would adopt it. Their own religion, it turns out, generated little sentiment. The first to abandon it was the high priest himself who reasoned that the gods had never done much to secure success and power for Edwin anyway.[19]

When Edwin was finally convinced of the merits of Christianity, he arranged to be baptized along with his court. And apparently Christianity flourished as long as Edwin ruled. He planned to set up Paulinus in his own see at York; alas, Edwin was defeated and killed in battle in 633 before the plan could be accomplished.[20] There followed a year of violence in which Northumbria was again divided and the Christian faith was officially abandoned in both Bernicia and Deira. Paulinus, Ethelberga, and Eanfled retreated to Kent.[21]

In 634 Oswald secured the throne, and it was he who made sure that Christianity got more than a toehold in Northumbria. Rather than continue the flow of the Christian stream from Rome via Augustine's extended mission, Oswald turned to another source. The new king had spent Edwin's reign in exile among the Scots of the north, and there he learned Christianity from the ascetical monks of Iona.[22] Rather than recall the Roman Paulinus, he petitioned Iona for a monk-bishop to instruct his people in the faith. At first, a monk of austere disposition was sent. He soon returned to Iona complaining that the English were ungovernable, barbarous, and obstinate. The monk Aidan spoke up, however, and suggested that perhaps what was called for in mission territory was a little less perfectionism and a lot more patience: "You should have followed the practice of the Apostles and begun by giving them the milk of simpler teaching, and gradually nourished them with the word of God until they were capable of greater perfection and able to follow the loftier precepts of Christ."[23] As a reward for sharing his wisdom, Aidan got the job. And a providential thing it was for Hilda. As bishop of Northumbria, he saw the advantage of having a woman of Hilda's capabilities on his team and, intercepting her plans at a crucial moment, launched her entire monastic career in her homeland when she was planning to do what so many other monastically inclined Anglo-Saxon women were doing—exporting their talents to Gaul. Indeed, when one reads Bede's characterization of Hilda and that of Aidan, it seems that Aidan perhaps saw in her a feminine incarnation of himself.

Aidan, as described by Bede, was "a man of outstanding gentleness, holiness and moderation," that last being no small feat given the reputation of the monks of Iona and their ascetical founder, Columba. Aidan, who was given the island of Lindisfarne from which to conduct his mission, was successful with the people of Northumbria for that noblest of reasons—he and his clergy practiced what they preached. He showed no interest in worldly possessions except when they could be used to relieve the burden of the poor; he spoke to all he encountered, whether high or low; those who walked with him, whether monks or lay people, were required to meditate, to read the Scriptures, or learn the psalms; if given money, he used it to ransom those unjustly sold as slaves, and many of the ransomed became his own disciples and eventually priests. Bede tells us, "If wealthy people did wrong, he never kept silent out of respect or fear, but corrected them outspokenly."[24] He even challenged the king. When Oswin, who ruled Deira for seven years after Oswald's death, gave a horse to Aidan to make his travels easier, Aidan in turn gave the horse to a poor man. When the king chided him for giving away such a splendid animal, Aidan in turn rebuked the king: "Is this child of a mare more valuable to you than this child of God?"[25] It is a sign of the respect accorded Aidan that the king repented rather than ranted.

Unfortunately, we do not know what Hilda was doing or where she was doing it during this flourish of political and ecclesial activity in her homeland. We do not know if she stayed in Northumbria following the death of Edwin. We do not know what we would perhaps most of all like to know: Did she marry, have children, grandchildren? Why did her life take a sudden turn at the age of thirty-three? Some historians suggest she had to have been married for the simple reason that women of that period did not remain single, and that the change in her life at age thirty-three was prompted by widowhood. As further evidence that she was a widow, Christine Fell points to the fact that Bede never refers to Hilda as a virgin, as he does Etheldreda and Aelffled.[26] However neither does Bede mention any progeny following or leading Hilda to Whitby or to the other monasteries she ruled as he does with other royal women whose daughters and even granddaughters followed or preceded them into monastic life. Nor does a son of Hilda appear in the tangled web of royal men described by Bede. Of course, she could have been widowed and childless. On the question of whether or not she had ever been married, the muddled answer is that we do not know, but it seems likely that she would have been.

We can surmise with more certainty, that whether or not Hilda left Northumbria for a time, she must have lived there long enough for Aidan to become acquainted with her. For the thing she did at age thirty-three was to renounce her home and all that she possessed and travel to the kingdom of East Anglia from whence she planned to travel to Gaul to enter the double monastery of Chelles. Her sister, Hereswith, who had married into the East Anglian royal family had already entered Chelles. Hilda remained in East Anglia for one year, but before she could embark on her trip to the continent, she was recalled to Northumbria by Aidan who had plans of his own for Hilda.[27] Incidentally, Hilda most likely met

Etheldreda while in East Anglia. Etheldreda would have been, at that time, about fifteen years old and living in the court of her father, King Anna. Speculation can be a dangerous thing, but it is not far-fetched to suggest that the two discussed their mutual attraction to monastic life. Etheldreda would have been familiar with this fairly new option opening up for royal women, not only because of Hereswith's departure for Gaul but because her own sister, Ethelberga, and step-sister, Saethryd, and niece, Earcongota, were among those who, according to Bede, went to Brie to pursue their vocations.

Aidan, perhaps recognizing Hilda's skills in organization and administration, arranged for her and a few companions to begin their monastic training at a location along the River Wear in her native Northumbria. A year later he appointed her abbess of a monastery at Hartlepool which had been founded by Heiu who, according to Bede, was the first woman of the province to be clothed as a nun. Heiu, a "devout servant of Christ," reestablished herself elsewhere. We hear no more about her, but it is at this point that we begin to hear of the considerable talent and energy of Hilda. Susan Ridyard points out that the significance of Hilda may be that while others such as Heiu set out with inspiration, Hilda brought skill to the task and was therefore instrumental in getting monasticism firmly grounded.[28] Bede tells us that following the guidance of learned men such as Aidan, Hilda quickly set about establishing regular observance at Hartlepool. These learned men, in turn, quickly came to admire her "innate wisdom and love of God's service." But Aidan, who died in 651, would not have the pleasure of seeing Hilda in her most productive and successful years.

By 655 Hilda had obviously earned a reputation for herself. In that year King Oswy, who succeeded Oswald, vowed that if he were successful in a particular battle against a particularly meddlesome king, he would donate twelve grants of land for monasteries and dedicate his infant daughter, Aelffled, to God "in perpetual virginity." Oswy was successful on the battlefield, and true to his word, he entrusted Aelffled to Hilda.[29] Two years later Hilda set out to found a monastery at a place identified by Bede as Streanaeshalch, reckoned by modern scholars as the place known to later generations as Whitby. It was from Whitby that Hilda let her splendor light all of Britain.

As she had done at Hartlepool, she immediately set out to establish the regular life, a task she conducted, Bede tells us, "with great energy." The regular life as interpreted by Hilda included the observance of righteousness, mercy, purity, and other virtues. No doubt inspired by Aidan and the Celtic monastic tradition, Hilda drew on the Scriptures: "After the example of the primitive Church, no one there was rich, no one was needy, for everything was held in common, and nothing was considered to be anyone's personal property."

Details of day-to-day life at Whitby elude us, however. Whitby, and Hartlepool as well, were double monasteries. We know from Bede and other sources that there were variations in the degree of separation between men and women at such monasteries. In some, the monks and nuns worshiped together; in others there were separate chapels. The idea of the double monastery was imported from Gaul, but surely Whitby's rituals and rules were derived from Irish monasticism. While monasteries were multiplying in England during Hilda's lifetime, there don't seem to have been any established exclusively for women, though there were for men. The double monasteries were always ruled by abbesses, usually women of royal birth. The arrangement was clearly beneficial for women, the men providing sacraments and heavy manual labor. But it was beneficial for men, too, giving them an opportunity to pursue monastic vocations in their homeland, and in the case of Whitby, providing an opportunity for those with priestly vocations to prepare for their ministry.[30]

From several stories in Bede, including the story of Aelffled, it is obvious that there were children at some of the double monasteries. Shortly before she died, Hilda established a dependent monastery at Hackness, and we learn from the story of her death that there was a sisters' dormitory there. One of the nuns, Begu, was reading in the dormitory when she had a vision of Hilda's soul carried to heaven guided by angels.

While the liturgical and architectural splendor of Rome was making its way to England in Hilda's later years, at the time Whitby was established, the Anglo Saxons built to simpler specifications. The buildings were most likely of timber and wattle.

The one thing we know of Whitby is that for which it was most famous—education. To live by Scripture, Hilda's monks and nuns had to know Scripture; thus she required that they make a thorough study of it. They were also required to occupy themselves in good works, though what kind of good works is not mentioned. It was to this combination of learning and good works, however, that Bede attributes the fact that many of the men were found fit for holy orders, and five of them later became bishops. A sixth monk of Whitby was chosen to be a bishop but died before his consecration. The fact that so many of the men of Whitby became bishops is often cited as a mark of respect for Hilda's abilities. But it should be noted that only one of them, Bosa, is known for sure to have been appointed and consecrated during her lifetime, and a second might have been. Some of the others may never have known Hilda, though one of them, Oftfor, was with her at both Hartlepool and Whitby. It may, in fact, have been Aidan's intention that Hilda set up a monastery not only for native Northumbrians to pursue their monastic vocations, but also a monastery that would serve as a training ground for developing a native clergy.[31] On the other hand, since Aidan was dead for six years before

Hilda founded Whitby, it may have been her own inspiration to begin the training of priests.

Whitby most likely served another purpose, that is, as a center that provided instruction and sacraments for the local community, the seventh-century equivalent of a modern-day parish. While much has been made of the cowherd-turned-monk Caedmon as the first English poet, the ever-enterprising Hilda may have been more interested in his gift as something that could be put to practical use in the developing Church. What better way to instruct an illiterate population in the doctrine of Christianity than by delivering the lessons in pleasant, catchy, easily memorized poetic songs?[32]

Hilda herself was as much a teacher as an administrator. She instructed her flock, both privately and publicly. She was still instructing from her deathbed where, Bede says, the handmaids of the monastery had gathered and Hilda was urging them to maintain Gospel peace. Never one to waste an opportunity, Hilda was still speaking the moment she died.

The education Hilda provided, like that of Aidan, was by word and example, and was not limited to a Whitby audience. So great was her prudence, Bede says, that ordinary folk, kings, and princes sought her advice in their difficulties and took it. Thus, "she also brought about the amendment and salvation of many living at a distance, who heard the inspiring story of her industry and goodness." Perhaps the highest compliment paid to Hilda, says Bede, was that all who knew her called her "Mother" because of her wonderful devotion and grace.

But this woman of devotion, grace, prudence, and holiness was far from fainthearted in the face of controversy. Not only did she entertain debate, she took sides. And even when she took the losing side, she emerged with her reputation for devotion, grace, prudence, and holiness intact. That takes a special kind of talent indeed.

From Bede, we learn of one of the two great controversies in which she was involved. In the year 664, a synod was held at Whitby to settle the most contentious issue of the day—the proper way to calculate the date for Easter.[33] What seems unimportant after 1,300 years was no small matter in seventh-century Northumbria. In fact, it was a many-layered controversy that had accumulated various related issues as it arose from time to time over a period of three hundred years in England and Ireland. At issue was the fact that Christians who were instructed by clerics from Rome had one way of calculating the date for Easter and those with Celtic training had another. On a deeper level, at issue was whether England and Ireland would turn to Rome as the authority on ecclesiastical questions or whether they would continue to draw from their Celtic traditions and thereby isolate themselves from the growing, universal Church. It was also the turning point at which the quaint, monk-bishop style of ecclesial administration directed from remote monasteries needed to be replaced by the more efficient Roman, diocesan style. But getting in the way of reason, as so often happens, was a conflict of personalities. And—how could it be otherwise—politics were also involved.[34]

The issue as it emerged in Northumbria in 664 had the following twists and turns. King Oswy, Celtic trained in his religion, observed Celtic customs. His wife, Queen Eanfled, baptized and instructed by Paulinus, observed Roman customs. Most of the time, the method of calculating Easter didn't matter because in most years both methods resulted in Easter occurring on the same Sunday. But it could happen, and Bede says it sometimes did, that the king was celebrating the Resurrection while the Queen was still observing the Lenten fast.

A conflict of personalities entered the picture when Wilfrid emerged as the defender of the Roman system and Colman, a successor to Aidan, the defender of the Celtic. Wilfrid was an up-and-coming star of the Northumbrian Church. With Queen Eanfled as his benefactress, he had entered the monastery of Lindisfarne and had observed there the Celtic monastic style. He wasn't particularly impressed by what he observed and longed to visit Rome. Under Eanfled's patronage he did, and one of the things he learned there was the Roman method of calculating Easter. On his return to England he bent the ear of Oswy's son, Alchfrid, who was sub-king of Deira. Anxious to test his mettle against his father, Alchfrid convinced Oswy to call a synod to settle the Easter question. Alchfrid apparently realized that Northumbria would soon have to do as the Romans do anyway and that perhaps a public defeat for his father on this issue would enhance his own image.[35] Hilda, though trained early in life by Paulinus, by this time sympathized with the Celtic tradition handed on to her so lovingly by Aidan. The fact that her monastery was chosen as the site for this great gathering attended by kings, bishops, and presumably the queen, is testimony to her stature in the kingdom. The fact that Bede records her opinion on the issue, though he does not say whether she spoke during the debate, is testimony that the opinions of women, at least women who were royal abbesses, counted for something in seventh-century England.

The synod turned out to be the ecclesiastical debut for young Wilfrid who was appointed spokesman for the Roman side. He won the battle, but if he made friends in high places that day, he may also have made enemies, Hilda among them. In Bede's version of the synod, Wilfred haughtily demeaned the Celts, calling them people from remote islands who "stupidly contend against the whole world." In a debate symbolic of the decline of the Celtic Church and the rise of the Roman, he pitted the authority of the great Irish monastic, Saint Columba, against the authority of the even greater saint, Peter, who received the keys of heaven from Christ himself.

Wilfrid, of course, was right about Easter and Peter. And King Oswy, perhaps to Alchfrid's disappointment, readily and amiably agreed, thereby avoiding a showdown with his ambitious son. Most of those in attendance accepted the decision, but Colman and his companions left Lindisfarne and a new bishop was appointed. That bishop died soon after, and Wilfrid was appointed.

How eagerly Hilda adopted the Roman system we are not told. But from another source we learn that fifteen years after the synod and just one year before she died, Hilda was partner to an effort to depose Wilfrid. The source of that story is the *Life of Wilfrid* written by the bishop's disciple, Eddius Stephanus. While Bede is the principal source on Hilda, the *Life of Wilfrid* predates the *History of the English Church and People* by ten to twenty years.

There are two mentions of Hilda in the *Life of Wilfrid*. Like Bede, Eddius records the events of the Synod of Whitby which was, he says, held "in the presence of the holy mother and pious nun Hild."[36] Eddius does not record Hilda's position on the Easter question; however, the fact that he refers to her as "holy" and "pious" is magnanimous, indeed, for she was an opponent of his own hero, Wilfrid. Eddius reports that in the year 679 she and Archbishop Theodore of Canterbury, the leading prelate of England, sent representatives to Rome to testify against Wilfrid in the first of his many battles to regain his episcopal see which had been divided and given to three new bishops.[37] We don't know why Hilda opposed Wilfrid, but several reasons can be proposed. Of immediate concern was the fact that one of the three new bishops, Bosa, was selected from among her own monks to preside over Deira, the territory in which Whitby was located. Perhaps she wanted to retain this honor for her monastery and have a more congenial prelate than Wilfrid at her disposal. It's likely that she had had unpleasant encounters with Wilfrid during his episcopacy, as abbesses and bishops are wont to have, and perhaps the unpleasantness of those encounters was magnified by Hilda's memories of Wilfrid's victory at the synod of 664. Also, the sophisticated pomp and ceremony that Wilfrid attached to the episcopacy was a style that contrasted sharply with the humility and simplicity of the Celtic monk-bishops so loved by Hilda and others. We would like to think that a woman of Hilda's stature and holiness was above personal vendettas, but perhaps Hilda with her "innate wisdom" saw where her beloved Church was headed if headed by men too dependent on worldly possessions and power. What a fascinating diary Hilda would have left, if only she had left one. Even maintaining harmony at Whitby must have been a chore. There was Hilda who favored the Celtic customs and opposed Wilfrid; there was Eanfled who favored Wilfrid and the Roman customs but who had entered Whitby after Oswy died in 670; and in the middle of these two powerful women was Aelffled, the daughter of Eanfled and the spiritual daughter of Hilda. The fact that Hilda maintained the respect of even those who disagreed with her—Bede, after all, strongly and repeatedly rejected the Celtic Easter but obviously admired Hilda—and the fact that we do not hear of quarrels erupting from Whitby indicates that she was prudent indeed.

Perhaps even greater testimony to her grace and wisdom is the fact that her successor, Aelffled, the one she raised in the monastery from childhood, was equally respected and admired. It was Aelffled who finally drew together the parties warring over Wilfrid, whose woes continued long after Hilda died. Aelffled, according to Eddius, was "always the comforter and best counselor of the whole province."[38] It is fitting that, since Hilda presided over Whitby when the synod of 664 brought Wilfrid to the fore, her spiritual daughter, "the prudent virgin Aelffled," should reconcile him and his opponents at the Synod of Nidd in 706, near the end of his life. So esteemed was Aelffled that the anonymous monk of Whitby who wrote a Life of Pope Gregory the Great referred to Streanaeshalch as "the well-known monastery of Aelffled, a most religious woman and the daughter of Queen Eanfled."[39] Curiously, he did not mention Hilda, despite the fact that he described in detail the translation of the remains of her great-uncle Edwin to Whitby.

Aelffled died in about 713, and we hear little more about events at the Whitby founded by Hilda. The monastery was destroyed by invading Danes in about 867. According to Symeon of Durham, it was refounded in about 1074 by a knight-turned-monk whose name was Reinfrid. It prospered for a time, becoming an abbey in the early twelfth century but meeting its end in 1540 with the Dissolution.

But what of Etheldreda? While Hilda spent the last thirty-three years of her life making a name for herself as a monastic leader, Etheldreda seems to have spent the first forty years of her life trying to shed her royal responsibilities in order to pursue her monastic inclinations. Etheldreda was born sometime between 630 and 633, one of the daughters of the East Anglian King Anna, all of whom eventually made their way into monasteries and sainthood. But what we learn of Etheldreda from Bede, a careful historian, should be separated from what we learn of Etheldreda from subsequent hagiographers.[40]

Etheldreda, Bede tells us, was first married to a man named Tondbert, a prince of South Gyrwas, a state adjacent to East Anglia. A few years after Tondbert's death, Etheldreda was given in marriage to Egfrid, prince and eventually king of Northumbria. It is this marriage for which Etheldreda became famous. Because she preferred to become a nun, she refused to consummate the marriage for twelve years. Bede must have realized that his readers would have a difficult time believing this, so he noted that Bishop Wilfrid himself "absolutely vouched" for the fact.

Egfrid finally granted Etheldreda her freedom. She spent a year in Ebba's monastery at Coldingham, then returned to her native land to found a monastery in the district of Ely. As abbess she was noted for her ascetical life, wearing woolen rather than linen garments, seldom using hot water for her bath except on great feast days, seldom eating more than one meal a day, and remaining at prayer in church from Matins until dawn. She died only seven years after establishing Ely. She was succeeded by her sister Sexburg, who had also been married to a king. Sixteen years after Etheldreda's burial, Sexburg decided to have her sister's body exhumed and transferred to the church. When the tomb was opened and her body removed, it was free from decay "as if she had died and been buried that very day." Even more amazing was the fact that a tumor on her neck that was lanced shortly before she died had healed after death leaving "only the faint mark of a scar." According to Bede, "The miraculous preservation of her body from corruption in the tomb is evidence that she had remained untainted by bodily intercourse." Bede was so taken with her resolve that in his history he included a hymn in praise of virginity in her honor.[41]

Though Bede does not dwell on Etheldreda's organizational and administrative abilities as he does on Hilda's, there is no reason to believe she was not an equally capable abbess. Nor, according to Susan Ridyard, is there reason to believe Ely did not become as valuable an asset to the developing Church of East Anglia and the surrounding territories as was Whitby to Northumbria. Etheldreda, according to Ridyard, was among the pioneers who established religious life in England having founded one of the first, if not the first, monasteries for women in the eastern territory.[42] Either Bede didn't know any more details on Etheldreda's accomplishments or he chose to ignore them. Obviously, the thing that caught his attention was the phenomenal story of how she tried to preserve her virginity, and virginity was a highly valued virtue at the time Bede was writing. Succeeding authors embellished Etheldreda's piety so that by the time she passed through the Enlightenment and arrived in the late-twentieth century, a period in which marital sex would no longer be seen as such a dreadful threat to sanctity, she was a mere caricature of the monastic foundress she really was. Our generation is perhaps the first generation wanting to know more about Etheldreda's mind and less about the state of her body sixteen years after burial. We must also remember that the circumstances of Etheldreda's life did not afford her the opportunities that presented themselves to Hilda. As the daughter of a king rather than the grandniece of a king, she would have been under greater pressure to contract marriages that would benefit her family's kingdom and maintain peace between provinces. Thus, she had not only her own wishes to consider, but also the welfare of many people. Despite the high regard apparently accorded women in the Anglo-Saxon period, daughters of kings were pawns in their fathers' political maneuverings. Even Aelffled led the life chosen for her by her father.

But if Etheldreda was a victim of circumstances beyond her control, Hilda was a genius at grabbing the opportunities her circumstances presented. Still, through most centuries, Etheldreda enjoyed the esteem and affection of the English people to a greater extent than Hilda. Reginald of Durham names the three most popular Anglo-Saxon saints as Cuthbert of Durham, Edmund of Bury, and Etheldreda of Ely.[43] Aelfric (955–1020), in his Passion of St. Edmund, names this same trio as evidence that the English people were not lacking in the Lord's saints.[44] Again in the nineteenth century, Gueranger calls Etheldreda "one of the most popular saints among our English forefathers," and notes that her shrine at Ely became one of the most famous places of pilgrimage in England.[45] St. Etheldreda appeared on almost every liturgical calendar throughout the Middle Ages while St. Hilda appeared sporadically.

This is not to suggest that Hilda did not have her followers; several churches in England were dedicated to her, commemorating her feast on November 17. Even a few legends were attached to her memory as time went on. Sir Walter Scott, in his poem, "Marmion," preserves some of those legends. Here is what his fictionalized nuns of Whitby say of their earliest mother-abbesses Hilda and Aelffled:

> They told how in their convent cell
> a Saxon princess once did dwell,
>   The lovely Aelffled;
> And how, of thousand snakes, each one
> Was changed into a coil of stone
>   When holy Hilda prayed;
> Themselves, within their holy bound,
> Their stony folds had often found,
> They told how sea-fowls' pinions fail,
> As over Whitby's tower they sail,
> And sinking down, with flutterings faint,
> They do their homage to the saint.[46]

Occasionally Hilda found fans in unlikely places. In the 1890s an American Baptist, William Cathcart, writing a decidedly anti-papal history of the English and Irish Churches, came up with three new names for the most popular of Anglo-Saxon saints: "No more saintly hero appears in the Ecclesiastical History of Bede than King Oswald; no more heavenly minded ecclesiastic than Bishop Aidan, and no more talented, holy and useful woman than St. Hilda."[47]

To what do Oswald, Aidan, and Hilda owe this adulation? These three, according to Cathcart, "belonged to the church of the Scots, who held no communion with the Roman Catholic Church."[48] Furthermore, what Hilda was running, in Cathcart's estimation, was not what we would recognize as a monastery, but rather a Bible school, or, as he says, a Sunday school that operated every day of the week. The members of Whitby, he claims, "could leave at any time, marry, exercise the rights of ownership over such property as they had not surrendered or might acquire, and withdraw the temporary obedience necessary in the monastery, but regarded as un-pledged and unjust, in the case of withdrawal."[49] This, of course, is an as-sessment of Hilda and Whitby that results more from wishful thinking than from reality.

Hilda found more recent fans among a group of dissenters in the Church of England. The controversy stems from yet another synod. In the 1986 synod in York, a measure to allow women priests from other coun-tries to celebrate Holy Communion in England was defeated. Some Anglicans, disappointed with the decision, started meeting "to design a radical new way of 'being church.'"[50] Their goal was to organize them-selves into a "non-sexist" worshiping community that would provide "non-sexist" liturgies. Meeting for the first time in February, 1987, the group decided to call itself the "St. Hilda Community." Hilda "was chosen partly because she was a strong, intelligent woman—according to legend the chairperson of the Synod of Whitby—as someone remarked, a nice change from all those neurotic women saints."[51]

The St. Hilda Community began designing and writing liturgies with the presiders being women lawfully ordained abroad. The community also began generating headlines and finally a letter of protest from the vicar, rural dean, and bishop of Whitby, and the prioress of the Order of the Holy Paraclete, complaining that they were "disgracing St. Hilda's name, and that the saint would surely disapprove." The community replied "that there was no patent in saints, and that we believe Hilda might have a stomach for what we were doing."[52]

We don't really know what Hilda would stomach today, but clearly she has become the choice of feminists, and Etheldreda (one of those "neu-rotic women saints"?) has not, though there's something to be said, too, for the abbess of Ely's struggle to choose her own path in life. The biggest Church controversy of Hilda's time was that of the Easter question and all it entailed. We know where she stood on that issue. One could interpret her position as fear of change and a clinging to traditionalism despite the in-evitable new wave of Roman influence—a seventh-century counterpart to those who yearn for the Tridentine Mass in a post-Vatican II Church. Or one could interpret her position as a prophetic stance against what she sensed would be the replacement of the irresistible simplicity and dy-namism of the Celtic system by the growing opulence and uniformity of the Roman system. If there were a synod to debate today's greatest controversies, such as the question of women's ordination or inclusive language in the liturgy, we don't know where Hilda would stand, but she would take a stand. And while it would not necessarily be the right stand, the most popular stand, or even the winning stand, we know it would be one born of her experience, her innate wisdom, her prudence and holiness. And even those with whom she disagreed would call her "Mother" because of her wonderful devotion and grace. For above all, Hilda was a religiously motivated woman who brought all her talents and energies to the task of founding a monastery and furthering the work of the Church. She was one of many such women during the great age of conversion. Together with the countless Anglo-Saxon monastic women whose names never made it into this century, Bede's whole company of twenty lit all Britain by its splendor. If Hilda's light shines a little brighter than the others, it may be because it's the one we're most inclined to be looking at right now.

NOTES

1. Bede, *A History of the English Church and People*, trans. Leo Sherley-Price (New York: Dorset Press, 1968) (Hereafter abbreviated *HE)* *HE* 5:3.
2. Ibid., *HE* 3:8.
3. Ibid., *HE* 4:19.
4. Ibid., *HE* 4:25.
5. Ibid., *HE* 4:7-10.
6. Ibid., *HE* 4:6.
7. Ibid., *HE* 4:10.
8. Lina Eckenstein, *Woman Under Monasticism* (New York: Russell and Russell, Inc., 1963) 95.
9. Christine Fell discusses the differences between Bede's treatment of Hilda and that of Etheldreda in "Hild, Abbess of Streonaeshalch," *Hagiography and Medieval Literature: A Symposium,* ed. Hans Bekker-Nielson and others (Odense: Odense University Press, 1981) 86-87; Susan Ridyard identifies some of the elaborations of Etheldreda's piety in *The Royal Saints of Anglo-Saxon England: A Study of West Saxon and East Anglian Cults* (Cambridge: Cambridge University Press, 1988) 176–210.
10. *HE* 4:23.
11. *HE* 2:15.
12. *HE* 2:6.
13. *HE* 4:23.
14. *HE* 4:23. Christine Fell in "Hild, Abbess of Streonaeshalch," notes that Bede gives only three of the standard manifestations of holiness in his chapter on Hilda: Her mother's vision; Hilda's pious death; and visions of her contemporaries at the time of her death. 86–87.
15. *HE* 4:23.
16. Peter Hunter Blair outlines the progression of Augustine's mission in "Whitby as a Centre of Learning in the Seventh Century," *Learning and Literature*

in Anglo-Saxon England, ed. Michael Lapidge and Helmut Gneuss (Cambridge: Cambridge University Press, 1985) 3–17.

17. *HE* 2:9.

18. *HE* 2:9.

19. *HE* 2:13.

20. *HE* 2:20.

21. *HE* 2:20.

22. *HE* 3:3. According to Leo Sherley-Price, when Bede refers to the Scots, he is speaking of the people of Ireland, many of whom emigrated to the northern parts of Britain, *A History of the English Church and People,* 339.

23. *HE* 3:5.

24. *HE* 3:5.

25. *HE* 3:14.

26. Christine Fell, "Hild, Abbess of Streonaeshalch," 79–80.

27. Unless otherwise noted Bede's biographical information on Hilda is from *HE* 4:23.

28. Susan Ridyard, "Anglo-Saxon Women and the Church in the Age of Conversion," *Monks, Nuns and Friars in Medieval Society,* ed. Edward B. King, Jacqueline T. Schaefer and William B. Wadley (Sewanee, Tenn.: The Press of the University of the South, 1989) 108.

29. *HE* 3:24.

30. Sources used for information on double monasteries include Susan Ridyard, "Anglo-Saxon Women and the Church in the Age of Conversion,"; Bertram Colgrave, trans., *The Earliest Life of Gregory the Great by an Anonymous Monk of Whitby* (Lawrence, Kansas: The University of Kansas Press, 1968) 34–35.

31. Christine Fell, "Hild, Abbess of Streonaeshalch," 95; Susan Ridyard, "Anglo-Saxon Women and the Church in the Age of Conversion," 110–111.

32. The story of Caedmon is told by Bede in *HE* 4:24. Those who write of Caedmon's poetry as a means of instructing the laity include Susan Ridyard, "Anglo-Saxon Women and the Church in the Age of Conversion," 112–113; Peter Hunter Blair, "Whitby as a Centre of Learning in the Seventh Century," 22–25; and Joan Nicholson, "Feminae Gloriosae: Women in the Age of Bede," *Medieval Women,* ed. Derek Baker (Oxford: For the Ecclesiastical History Society by Basil Blackwell, 1978) 17.

33. *HE* 3:25.

34. The significance of the Easter debate is discussed by J. F. Webb, trans. *Lives of the Saints: The Voyage of St. Brendan; Bede: Life of Cuthbert; Eddius Stephanus: Life of Wilfrid* (New York: Penguin Books, 1965) 9–17; Peter Hunter Blair, "Whitby as a Centre of Learning in the Seventh Century," 17–22; Leo Sherley-Price, *A History of the English Church and People,* 23-24; Bertram Colgrave, trans. *The Life of Bishop Wilfrid by Eddius Stephanus* (Cambridge: Cambridge University Press, 1985) 157–158; Henry Mayr-Harting, *The Coming of Christianity to Anglo-Saxon England* (University Park, Penn.: The Pennsylvania State University Press, 1991) 103-113.

35. Henry Mayr-Harting, *The Coming of Christianity to Anglo-Saxon England,* 108.

36. Bertram Colgrave, *The Life of Bishop Wilfrid by Eddius Stephanus,* chap.10.

37. Ibid., chap. 54.

38. Ibid., chap. 60.

39. Bertram Colgrave, *The Earliest Life of Gregory the Great,* 103.

40. Bede's biographical information on Etheldreda is from *HE* 4:19.

41. *HE* 4:20.

42. Susan Ridyard, "Anglo-Saxon Women and the Church in the Age of Conversion," 119.

43. Bertram Colgrave, trans., *Two Lives of St. Cuthbert: A Life by an Anonymous Monk of Lindisfarne and Bede's Prose Life* (Cambridge: University Press, 1940) 1.

44. Aelfric, "The Passion of St. Edmund," ed. and trans., Kevin Crossley-Holland, *The Anglo-Saxon World* (Totowa, N.J.: Barnes and Noble Books, 1983) 208.

45. Gueranger, *The Liturgical Year: Time After Pentecost, Book III*, trans., The Benedictines of Stanbrook (Westminster, Maryland: The Newman Press, 1949) 221–222.

46. Wiliam J. Rolfe, ed., *Scott's Marmion* (Boston: Houghton, Mifflin and Co., 1884) 59.

47. William Cathcart, *The Ancient British and Irish Churches, Including the Life and Labors of St. Patrick* (Philadelphia: Charles Banes, 1894) 86.

48. Ibid.

49. Ibid., 232.

50. Monica Furlong, "Introduction: A Non-sexist Community," *Women Included: A Book of Services and Prayers, The St. Hilda Community* (London: SPCK, 1991) 6.

51. Ibid., 7-8.

52. Ibid., 8.

3

St. Frideswide:
Monastic Founder of Oxford

Rosemary Rader, O.S.B.

One of the best kept secrets of Oxford, England, is the story of its
founder, Frideswide (c. 680–727 C.E.). This may be partially explained by
the fact that for a variety of reasons no written records of Frideswide's life
have survived from her historical period, the seventh and eighth centuries,
and that there were deliberate attempts to eliminate her cult and destroy
her shrine after Henry VIII's break with the Roman Church in the sixteenth century.

Tradition indicates that Oxford developed around an Anglo-Saxon
monastic church at a spot presently occupied by Christ Church (which is
now the Oxford Anglican Cathedral but also still called Christ Church).
Tradition further claims that a princess, Frideswide, was the first head of
the church and monastery there. But beyond these bare facts it is difficult
to separate the truth from the legendary material in twelfth-century accounts of the life of Frideswide.

The foremost expert on the Frideswide material, John Blair, considers
three twelfth-century sources particularly worthy of consideration, asserting that the legends contain "elements which seem close enough to the
world of mid-Saxon England to command a degree of respect."[1] The first
is a brief account of Frideswide's life written around 1125 by William of
Malmesbury, an English historian;[2] the second, a longer narrative written
around 1110–1120 which Blair labels "Life A";[3] and the third, labelled
"Life B" by Blair, written around 1140–70 by Robert of Cricklade, Prior
of St. Frideswide's Priory.[4] Blair concludes that both Malmesbury and the
writer of Life A drew on the same earlier, lost source, with Malmesbury
condensing the earlier account and the latter expanding it. There are other

33

manuscripts dating from the thirteenth, fourteenth and fifteenth centuries, but they are chiefly summaries or abridgements of Life A and B.[5]

Malmesbury's brief account is as follows:

> In ancient times there was in the city of Oxford a monastery of nuns in which the most holy virgin Frideswide reposes. A king's daughter, she refused marriage to a king, consecrating her virginity to Christ her Lord. But the king had determined to marry the young woman and when he realized his entreaties and flatteries were in vain, he planned to take her by force. Upon discovering this, Frideswide fled into a wood. But since no hiding place could be kept secret from her lover and no lack of courage would stop him, he followed the fugitive. But she, hearing of the renewed ardor of the young man, found her way to Oxford in the middle of the night with God's help and obscure paths. By morning her determined lover had also hastened there, and the young woman, despairing of flight and too exhausted to go further, invoked God for help for herself and punishment for her persecutor. And as he and his retainers passed through the gates of the city, he was suddenly struck blind by the hand of heaven. After recognizing the error of his persistence, and beseeching Frideswide through his messengers, his sight returned as quickly as it had disappeared. Hence it came about that the kings of England were in dread of entering or lodging in that town since it is said to bring destruction, and they all shrink from the danger of putting it to the test. So this young woman, triumphant in her celibate victory, established a monastery there and, responding to her Spouse's call, died in that place. In the time of King Ethelred, the Danes being doomed to death because of the implacable anger of the English, took refuge in that monastery and perished in the flames along with the buildings. But soon the holy place was purified by the king's penance, the monastery was rebuilt, the former lands were returned and new possessions were added. In our times only a few clerics, who lived as they pleased, remained there. Consequently, Roger, bishop of Salisbury, gave the place to Wimund, a canon of outstanding learning and great holiness. Working diligently at the task entrusted, he there gathered together for God many canons to live according to a rule.[6]

Life A and Life B are longer and more representative of the typical *Vitae* which were compiled and circulated in the late eleventh and twelfth centuries. With the rapid multiplication of reformed monasteries and churches and the emphasis placed on education, there was a greater need for books for liturgy, monastic reading, and instructive and exhortatory manuals for both clergy and lay people.[7] The saints' *Vitae* reflected for their readers and hearers the heroism and perseverance of earthly but heaven-oriented individuals who served as symbols of what was possible with God's grace and human cooperation. The elaboration of fragmentary data from an earlier time was viewed as an effective contribution towards the edification, and ultimately the salvation, of aspiring candidates for eternal life. It seems fair to assume that these increments to sparse details were viewed not as distortions of the original facts, but as creative and continuous engagement of the present with past traditions of holiness.

Undoubtedly Frideswide's original *Vitae* underwent such changes from the eighth to the twelfth century. The following is a summary of the basic elements of Frideswide's life as recorded in Life A and Life B.[8]

Frideswide was the daughter of Didan, a king of Oxford, and his wife, Sefrida. She was educated by a woman called Aelfgifu, and so applied herself to her studies that in five or six months she knew the whole psalter, often repeating one of her favorite passages, that she "might dwell in the house of the Lord all the days of her life." Her mother died from a serious illness after which King Didan built a church in the village of Oxford, dedicating it to the Holy Trinity, the immaculate Virgin Mary, and all the Saints, and placed Frideswide in charge. Frideswide studied eagerly how best to serve God, how to avoid the pomp and glory of the world, and began generously to help the poor. Seeking an ascetic life, she wore a hairshirt and was sustained chiefly on barley bread, a few vegetables, and water. The English marveled at such virtue in one so young, and her father was gratified, knowing that his only daughter was imbued with the Holy Spirit.

Frideswide then asked her father to help her become a nun so that she might praise God's name forever. The king approved of his daughter's wish and requested Orgar, the bishop of Lincoln, to consecrate his daughter to God as a monastic, along with twelve other young noblewomen. The king had houses built for the monastic women, including a refectory, a dormitory, and a cloister. He assigned religious men to look after the nuns' needs and gave the community several estates, villages, and a third of the town of Oxford in order to provide food for the nuns.

Not long afterwards King Didan became seriously ill, distributed his wealth to the poor, and died. Frideswide, bereft of both parents, devoted herself more intensely to the things of the Spirit, and in order to obtain God's mercy, resolved to bend her knees a hundred times each day and mortify her flesh a hundred times each night. She was tempted by the devil whom she scornfully rejected as she pursued her filial duty undisturbed.

Algar, a prince of the area, decided to marry Frideswide and sent envoys to her with his request, threatening her if she refused. She fearlessly proclaimed her betrothal to Christ, King over all kings, and rejected the demands of her suitor. When threatened to be taken by force to a brothel, she reminded the messengers that one's body could not be degraded without one's consent. When the king's men persisted, Frideswide prayed to God for help. The men were struck blind, but Frideswide, wishing to return good for evil, knelt down and asked God to restore their sight. Her prayer being answered, the king's men returned to him and recounted all that had happened.

Algar was furious and set out for Oxford to capture Frideswide. But an angel appeared to her, warning her to go to the river, taking with her several other nuns. There she would find a boat and a boatman sent by God, and would be taken to safety. All happened as predicted, and Frideswide and her companions went into a certain wood called Binsey (in some accounts, Bampton) where they hid in a little ivy-covered hut near a swineherd.

Meanwhile the king, still intent on defiling the vessel consecrated to God, entered Oxford and was struck blind (the reason for later kings fearing to enter Oxford). The king (contrary to Malmesbury's version) remained blind the rest of his life and continued to plot ways of harming Frideswide. She and her companions remained at Binsey for three years working many miracles, three of which were given special mention. A blind girl had her sight restored after she washed her eyes with water in which Frideswide had washed her hands; a young man chopping wood on Sunday was punished by having his hand, which burnt like fire, stuck on the handle of the ax, but after Frideswide blessed it with the sign of the cross the hand was safely released; and a fisherman possessed by the devil was cured. But Frideswide decided that she and her companions were to return to their monastery in Oxford where she was received with much rejoicing because the townspeople had heard of her good works and miracles. A young leper ran to her, asking for a kiss in Christ's name. She made the sign of the cross, kissed him, and he was immediately cured.

Frideswide remained at Oxford continuing her good works but remained humble in spite of her being publicly acclaimed by the nuns and lay people for her good advice and edifying example. She became seriously ill and predicted that she would die on Sunday, October 19. She asked that her grave be dug on Saturday lest anyone would have to work on Sunday on her account. As her pain increased, she asked for the Eucharist and spoke encouragingly to those around her. She then had a vision of the holy virgin-saints, Catherine and Cecilia, sent to be her guides on the path to heaven. After her farewell to the nuns and townspeople gathered there, she died. On the way to her grave, a paralyzed man with crutches called on her for help and was cured. Frideswide was buried in St. Mary's Church on the south side near the Thames River. Soon after her burial, other miracles began to occur at her gravesite.

Life B adds information previously mentioned in Malmesbury's account, i.e., that the church remained as it was until the time of King Ethelred when it was partially destroyed by the English themselves because their enemies, the Danes, had fortified themselves there. The king rebuilt the church around 1004, enlarging it in such a way that Frideswide's grave was thereafter the center of the church. The destruction of the church, archives, etc., may account for the paucity of details about her life and that of her community of nuns.

What the later Middle Ages knew of Frideswide was undoubtedly derived from the twelfth-century accounts summarized above and from their later abridgments, with Life B as the favorite source.[9] The dates of her life are generally estimated between 680–727. Her name, Fritheswythe or Frithuswith, translated "the bond of peace" or "peace-strong," is consistent with Anglo-Saxon names. In order to clarify what appears to be Frideswide's unique role in the development of the monastic church, community, and early village at Oxford, it is necessary to place her within the context of the political and religious milieu of England during the seventh and eighth centuries. [10]

Frideswide's monastery in Oxford, where Christ Church now stands, was at the north end of an important crossing over the Thames River. It was a Mercian kingdom ruled by a non-Christian king, Penda. After his death in 655 the Mercians accepted Christianity, and by the time of Frideswide's birth (c. 680) Oxford was ruled by a local king or sub-king (*sub-regulus*), possibly Didan, Frideswide's father.

Monastic life had reached Anglo-Saxon England with Augustine's mission from Rome in 597 to convert the people to Christianity. It was, therefore, an important and integral part of early Anglo-Saxon Christianity. The seventh and eighth centuries in England witnessed the rise of many monastic foundations of both women and men, attested to by Bede's *History* with its frequent references to the development of these communities. They were generally established by Christian kings, queens, and other members of the nobility who provided the land, buildings, resources, and sanctions necessary for the maintenance and growth of the communities. These monasteries generally had authority over their churches and local areas, and Frideswide's monastic foundation seems consistent with the pattern of this period. The monasteries figured prominently in the Church's influence on the learning and religion of Western Europe. Both primary and secondary sources indicate that this was a time when men and women were engaging as equals in the challenge of a new religion and way of life, a source of amazement and sometimes disbelief to any who presume the anti-feminist stance of the later Middle Ages to be representative of roles, attitudes, and customs of Christian peoples throughout Christian history. Anglo-Saxon women were asked to undertake responsible leadership in activities of both Church and monastery. In her study of Anglo-Saxon history, Christine Fell concludes that "No woman could have been asked to take on so powerful a role as the early abbesses unless they were used to handling power, but Christianity is certainly not at this stage cramping their range of activity and responsibility."[11]

Many of the monastic communities in England were based on the Gallic pattern of "double monasteries," i.e., they included both women and men and were usually presided over by an abbess. Both Stenton and Blair suggest that Frideswide's monastery may well have been such, and that Life A's statement that Didan assigned religious men to serve Frideswide's community might reflect this.[12] Since Frideswide's community was established in the first quarter of the eighth century, it seems likely to have been a community of this type. Mary Bateson, after a comprehensive study of the phenomenon, considered it dubious that any monastery of women established at this period would not have seen the simultaneous establishment of an adjacent community of men.[13] Many of the famous English monasteries of this period were founded after this pattern, e.g., Whitby, Repton, Ely, Wimborne and Barking, among others.

It is difficult to assess whether the rule which Frideswide and her community followed was that of St. Benedict. At this time there was no universally prescribed rule for monastic life. As Mayr-Harting points out, "The Rule of St. Benedict was well known in the seventh century and was regarded by many as particularly authoritative, but it was not to reach its exclusive eminence in the West until the ninth or tenth century."[14] It seems fair to assume that the rules of the individual monastic communities followed a general pattern compiled from several rules mitigated by the circumstances and customs of the specific region.

In order to understand the role of Frideswide and other Anglo-Saxon women who founded and presided over religious settlements (church, monastery, small village), it is essential to identify the position and status of women in Anglo-Saxon society, realizing that this may have varied slightly from one region to another. Information about Anglo-Saxon women reached the later Middle Ages by hearsay (oral tradition), *Vitae,* sermons, essays on aspects of Christian life, charters, and chronicles.

Within the last twenty years there has been a renewed interest in the unique roles of Anglo-Saxon women whose leadership was strongest in the four centuries immediately following the West Saxons' acceptance of Christianity in 634.[15] Scholars agree that these women, often formidable personalities and generally noblewomen, were accorded a high status in society. Hollis views their relatively high social and religious status as a continuity of indigenous custom since Germanic society (the Saxons' origin) viewed women as responsible agents of the supernatural during pre-Christian times.[16] D. M. Stenton maintains that the evidence which has survived from Anglo-Saxon England indicates that "these masterful and independent" women were "more nearly the equal companions of their husbands and brothers than any other period before the modern age."[17] Lina Eckenstein, writing almost one hundred years ago about English and German women's monastic communities in the eighth and ninth centuries, asserted, "The right to self-development and social responsibility which the woman of today so persistently asks for, is in many ways analogous to the right which the convent secured to womanhood a thousand years ago."[18] What she neglected to emphasize, however, is that noblewomen of that period, whether within or outside the monasteries, generally experienced a less confining existence than many of their later counterparts. Hence, one can assume that Frideswide shared in the greater mobility and responsibilities of her social class, living at a time and place in history when Church laws, structures, and teachings about women were not yet so strictly regulatory and pervasive as they would become in the Anglo-Norman period and thereafter. C. H. Talbot claims: "Never, perhaps, has there been such an age in which religious women exercised such great power."[19]

Richard Southern supports the same view, positing that Frideswide lived at a time of tension and social convulsion arising from the conversion of the ruling families of England to Christianity, a conversion which brought with it a breach with the past regarding certain laws and customs governing marriage and landholdings:

> And yet, out of this turmoil and disaster, there emerged in an incredibly short space of time a new literature, poetry, history, sculpture, architecture, and missionary activity abroad—all of them closely connected with or emerging from the early religious communities founded by the saints of that time like St. Frideswide. . . . The second point, equally extraordinary and unexpected, is that women played a very large part in these new creations. I say it is extraordinary because it was preeminently a time of war, violence, and feuds—the worst possible time for women. And yet women, like Frideswide, emerged as organizers of joint male and female communities under the government of *women,* holding up the religious life of the community, administering large tracts of country, and encouraging complicated social and scholarly enterprises; responsible for large-scale enterprises to an extent never again possible for women in European history until the present day.[20]

D. Stenton was among the first to argue that the position of women in England in the late eleventh and early twelfth centuries (the period immediately following the Norman Conquest) underwent a radical change from Anglo-Saxon times, resulting in a sharp decline in English women's prestige.[21] Dietrich similarly asserts that if well-born English women of the late medieval or early modern period looked back on their Anglo-Saxon counterparts, they would undoubtedly have envied them their rights, the alternatives they exercised, and the power they wielded.[22] From the late eleventh century onward there was a significant decline in the number of materials about women's contributions to Church and society. Hollis concludes that the writers' concern to bring their accounts in line with more "orthodox" conceptions of the nature and role of women contributed to this decline.[23] Frideswide, whose archival materials were certainly destroyed in the fire which destroyed part of her monastery and church in 1002, may also have been one of the victims of later selective copying and preserving of what was considered "important" for posterity. As women's status and positions were gradually eroded, and men's activities (e.g., wars, bishoprics, alliances) were increasingly considered the only ones "historical" and noteworthy of preservation, much information on women's lives and activities was relegated to oblivion.

In trying to assess Frideswide's role in her own time and in later history, Southern concludes, "In historical matters we should never be unduly impressed by the size of the accumulation of fact, nor unduly depressed when it is small. It is not what lies on the surface that matters, but what lies beneath the surface."[24] So if there is little actual documentation about the particulars of Frideswide's life aside from the elaborations of the twelfth-century accounts, there is sufficient evidence of what lay beneath the surface, i.e., the importance of the Frideswide cult which developed. It seems likely that Frideswide's monastic church, where she was buried in about 727, survived until the fire of 1002. King Ethelred rebuilt it so that Frideswide's relics were now in the center of the church. There is no evidence of the demise of the monastic community founded by Frideswide, except for one sentence in a cartulary of St. Frideswide's monastery: "Some time after the glorious death of S. Frideswide, the nuns having been taken away, Secular Canons were introduced."[25] Not much is known about the type of community of these canons, but Blair concludes that by the 1100s (c. 1122) St. Frideswide's was reformed as a priory of canons regular following the Augustinian rule.[26] In 1180 the priory church was again rebuilt and Frideswide's body was placed with great ceremony in a new tomb more worthy of her remains, one of the many resurrections and reburials to which her bones were subjected in their afterlife history. A fourteenth-century account describes what happened prior to the translation of the relics. The canons feared that the Abingdon Abbey monks, who had charge of the church in the period between the expulsion of the secular canons and the installation of the Augustinians, might have stolen Frideswide's bones. After three days of fasting the Augustinians stealthily entered the church at night to excavate the grave. In great frustration they first discovered an empty stone coffin, but being advised that it had been the practice to place an empty coffin over the corpses of the saints in order to discourage graverobbers, they dug deeper and found a skeleton. Their torches went out but were miraculously rekindled, a heavenly sign to the canons that the bones were truly those of Frideswide. So they closed the grave leaving the body in peace. Soon after this, even more miracles occurred as people from many areas devoutly visited the grave. The solemn translation of the bones took place on February 12, 1180 with archbishop, bishops, clerics, other notaries, and people of the area in attendance. After the archbishop of Canterbury laid her bones in the new tomb the people smelled a delightful scent like refreshing spices. [27]

Not long after the translation, Prior Philip, possibly to popularize the tomb and so add renown to the community, wrote a book about her miracles. In the accounts, people from Oxford and the surrounding area are cured of innumerable ailments like deafness, dumbness, rheumatism, arthritis, ulcers, skin diseases, paralysis, nervous disorders, and blindness, the latter being most prevalent.[28] Besides her shrine at Oxford there was also a holy well at Binsey, said to have sprung up at Frideswide's request while she and her sister-companions lived there before returning to Oxford. The well's curative waters seemed particularly effective in restoring sight.[29]

Henry Mayr-Harting considers Frideswide's recorded miracles unique in that females outnumbered males two to one, and the women's healings were chiefly female problems and the psychological difficulties which could result.[30] Mayr-Harting asserts that the miracles reflect "the perennial dislocations and illnesses caused by sexual problems, compounded for women in their being regarded in that society as inferior to men and having far fewer alternative outlets for their energies and emotions."[31] He concludes that Frideswide's shrine was not only a sanctuary and a retreat but a positive influence on the position of women when they returned to their family or peer circle after having been cured.[32] Like other healing shrines, Frideswide's was a source of spiritual, emotional, and physical support and comfort to various segments of society. It seems plausible that women especially might be attracted to her shrine because she was a woman, a local, sainted woman to whom they could more easily relate. It is equally plausible that she was respected and loved for the goodness, holiness, sensitivity, and concern for others which is reflected in the legendary accounts of her life. Frideswide's body, like that of other saints after their death, was seen as a channel through which God's power could flow to heal the diseases, hurts, and injustices of a suffering humanity.

In 1289 Frideswide's bones were again officially moved into a more ornate shrine, the fragmented stone pedestal of which is in Christ Church today. From the corners of its canopy three stone faces appear through sculpted leaves of ivy and other foliage found in the area. Although rightly assumed to be depictions of Frideswide and her companions hiding from her pursuer in the woods at Binsey, the faces are also representations of the early Celtic "Green Man" or "Green Woman," a popular image incorporated into Christian Medieval and Renaissance art as carvings on tombs, shrines of saints, and cathedral architecture. These sculptures, human heads wreathed by vegetation, appear to be images of irrepressible life, of renewal, rebirth, and resurrection, an archetype of a conscious, vital life force.[33]

Frideswide's shrine gained renown beyond the Oxford region, for in 1398 Henry Beaufort, Bishop of Lincoln, ordered that Frideswide's day, October 19, be celebrated throughout the city and the university of Oxford, and that indulgences would be offered to those visiting the shrine or supporting it with gifts.[34] Chaucer, in his fourteenth-century *Canterbury Tales,* an account of a Christian pilgrimage, indicates that Frideswide's intercessory powers extended beyond the confines of her shrine at Oxford. In the *Miller's Tale* she is invoked as protectress of the Christians undertaking the pilgrimage: "This carpenter to blessen hymn bigan, And seyde, 'Help us Seinte Frydeswyde'" (Line 3449). The shrine attracted royal visitors like Henry III in 1264 and Catherine of Aragon in 1518. There is in northern France in the village of Bomy, a pilgrimage-shrine of St. Frewisse associated with a church, a hermitage, and a holy spring. This has been accepted by some as a transplant of the English Frideswide cult, and Blair argues convincingly that her cult may have reached Bomy from Oxford in the late tenth or eleventh century through verifiable links between English and Flemish churches.[35] In 1434 Archbishop Henry Chichele ordered her feast to be officially observed as patroness of the university,[36] and in 1481 when it was publicly announced that the pope had officially sanctioned the cultus of Saints Osmund, Frideswide, and Ethelreda, Frideswide's feast was elevated to that of three nocturns (9 lessons) in the divine office.[37]

Frideswide's shrine survived until the reign of Henry VIII and the Reformation when shrines were considered popish and tainted with superstition. As such they became a source of discord and were to be destroyed. In 1524 St. Frideswide's Priory was suppressed by Cardinal Wolsey, the Augustinian canons being sent to other communities of the order. As part of Wolsey's plan to reconstruct the buildings as Cardinal College, he destroyed parts of the original complex. In 1532, after Wolsey fell into disfavor, the king refounded the establishment as King Henry VIII College. In 1538 Frideswide's shrine was destroyed as one of the popish citadels of superstition, and the riches of the shrine and its treasury filled the royal coffers. Frideswide's bones, however, were buried and safeguarded by Catholics in the area. In 1546 the church became the Anglican Cathedral of the Oxford Diocese. Frideswide's festival was abolished in 1549, but her name remained in both the British and the Oxford Calendar of Saints. In spite of periodic attempts to purge the churches of saints whose authenticity was deemed questionable, Frideswide's name and legend have remained intact.

In 1552 Catherine, wife of a former Augustinian canon, Peter Vermigli, was buried near the former shrine, but in 1556 during the reign of the Catholic Queen Mary, her bones were dug up and buried under a dungheap while Frideswide's bones were interred in the shrine. In 1562

Queen Elizabeth ordered that Catherine be given a decent burial. James Calfhill, then canon of Christ Church, not wanting to desecrate the bones of either woman, settled on a compromise to this difficult situation. He buried the bones of Catherine and Frideswide together in the same tomb in the church where they still remain today, assuming that the periodic reshuffling of the bones over the years did not cause a misplacement or destruction of the bones thus identified.[38] On the floor of Christ Church one can view the black marble slab placed in the vicinity of the tomb, imprinted simply with the word, "Frideswide." Here Catholic abbess and Anglican wife repose together, symbol of the peace and harmony that can exist between different expressions of religion and states of life. Near the shrine stands the richly ornate fifteenth-century "watching chamber," used either to guard the shrine from thieves and vandals, or as sanctuary for the celebration of the Mass in honor of those buried below or for those requesting the intercession of the saint.[39] The major incidents of Frideswide's life are beautifully portrayed in the stained-glass windows designed by E. Burne-Jones in the 1850s and placed in the Latin Chapel of Christ Church. They portray the saint as compassionate healer, mystic, teacher, benefactor of the poor and needy, and generally as leader of monastic family and local community.[40] If such depictions of the Frideswide story carry the seeds of truth, they are evidence that for the clientele of her shrine she was a model of what it meant to be Christian while at the same time she influenced the development of religious forms of life prior to the Norman invasion.

Her story lives on today in various ways. Each year in Oxford on St. Frideswide's Day (October 19) there is a procession and liturgical celebration in Christ Church Cathedral, frequented by both "town and gown." And in the busy center of Oxford near the Gloucester Green coach station there is a bas-relief on the facade of what was in the 1870s through the early 1900s Central Boys' School. Over the main entrance are the stone representations of King Alfred on the right and Frideswide on the left, both in the process of instructing children. The Oxford newspaper explains that the two Anglo-Saxons were "very happily chosen because of their historical associations with Oxford, and because of the enthusiasm with which it is believed they worked in the cause of education."[41] The school was eventually closed, but another one now bears her name, as do three churches in the area.

In recent years there has been a renewed interest in Frideswide's history, possibly in part due to excavations in 1972 and 1985 in both the Tom Quad and the cloisters of Christ Church, which revealed a cemetery which began in the eighth or ninth centuries. Although these excavations do not provide direct evidence about Frideswide's monastic establishment, other excavations support the fact that Oxford was an early fortified town laid out as a major thoroughfare around some existing religious site, all of which is consistent with and adds credibility to the Frideswide story.[42] There has also been some distancing both in time and attitude from the Reformation climate of distrust of anything connected to Rome. H. G. Liddell, Dean of Christ Church in the 1890s, gave a homily on the anniversary of Frideswide's translation to the new shrine in 1180, reminding the congregation of her somewhat forgotten place in history: "And now, as we are approaching the close of the nineteenth century, we strive to repair the injustices done by our fathers of the reformation to her who must be regarded as the foundress, not only of Christ Church, but of Oxford." [43]

Parker reminds his readers that in order to understand and appreciate the Frideswide legend or any other legend, one needs to know the difference between legend and myth: "We have to treat legends . . . very differently from myths. They, as a rule, grow up around a shadow, while legends grow up around a substance."[44] For those who knew the legend, who prayed at Frideswide's tomb, and who experienced physical, spiritual, and emotional healing at her shrine, the substance was real and was demonstrable because of their faith in Frideswide's holiness. In the legendary accounts, the piety which governed her life and which was publicly expressed in her various activities *with* and *for* others, modeled a Christian way of life that far surpassed any truths expressed in theological subtleties and abstruse doctrines. For the individuals and communities whose faith was nurtured at her shrine, Frideswide was real, and the question was then as it must surely be even now, not "Did she exist?" but "How did the facts and legends of her life influence the people of her time and later?" Her existence is verified by facts, as few as they may be, but her historical role as one who made a difference in people's lives is the genuine and crucial issue, and here the legend speaks for her. One need only experience the silence of the Christ Church cloister, the simplicity of Frideswide's tomb, the regal chapter house, and the grandeur of Christ Church itself to realize that they stand today as eloquent memorials to Frideswide, "bond of peace," the eighth-century abbess whose leadership was the initial heartbeat of ecclesial, academic, and civic life in Oxford.

Notes

1. John Blair, *St. Frideswide, Patron of Oxford* (Oxford: Perpetua Press, 1988) 9. See also his "Saint Frideswide Reconsidered," *Oxoniensia* (hereafter cited as Oxon.) 52 (1987) 71–127. The former (hereafter cited as SFPO) summarizes the conclusions presented in the latter (hereafter cited as SFR). For an important new study describing the development and landscape of Oxfordshire from its Anglo-Saxon settlement to the beginning of the twelfth century, see John Blair, *Anglo-Saxon Oxfordshire* (Dover, N.H.: Allan Sutton Publishing Inc., 1994). I am deeply

indebted to Blair's critical analysis of the various documents on Frideswide's life and role in history. I am also grateful to the staff at the Centre for Oxfordshire Studies at the Oxford Library and the Bodleian Library at Oxford University.

2. *Gesta Pontificum Anglorum,* ed. N.E.S.A. Hamilton Rolls Series, Lii (London, 1870) 315. Malmesbury, in *De Gestis Regum Anglorum,* ed. W. Stubbs, 1 (Rolls Series, 1887) 213, writes that he consulted the Archives of St. Frideswide's Priory for his hagiographical material. He assuredly also heard parts of the Frideswide story from oral tradition.

3. British Library, MS Cotton Nero E 1: ff.156–157. A later, abridged version is contained in the British Library, MS Landsowne 436, ff. 101–104, a chronicle and collection of *Vitae* in an early fourteenth-century hand, written at Romsey Abbey.

4. Oxford, Bodleian Library, MS Laud Misc. 114, ff.132–140. For evidence of Robert of Cricklade's authorship see Blair, SFR, 80. A more detailed study of the twelfth-century sources and their interrelatedness is in Blair, SFR, 73–85. A fourteenth-century life contained in the *Legenda* of John of Tynemouth, a monk of St. Alban's, seems based on the Laudian MS. His work was arranged alphabetically in the fifteenth century, a copy of which is printed in Carl Horstman, ed., *Nova Legenda Anglie* (Oxford at the Clarendon Press, 1901) I. 457–461.

5. For a listing and brief summary of these accounts see Blair, SFR, 93–96. For the sake of clarity and brevity, I hereafter use Blair's designations of Life A and Life B. See also E. F. Jacob, *St. Frideswide, the Patron Saint of Oxford,* The Frideswide Papers, 1 (May, 1953) 12–14.

6. Translation my own. Cf. Blair, SFPO, 27–28 and James Parker, *The Early History of Oxford.: 727–1100* (Oxford at the Clarendon Press, 1885) 94. Parker, 92-3, includes a translation of the burning of St. Frideswide's Church as recorded in the British Library, Cotton MS Vitellius E 15. Cf. Blair's translation, SFPO, 18–19, and *The Anglo-Saxon Chronicle,* trans. with an Introduction by G. N. Garmonsway (London: J. M. Dent and Sons, Ltd., 1953) 134–135.

7. For a more detailed study of the influence reformed monasteries and their revival of learning had on hagiographical materials, see P. H. Blair, *An Introduction to Anglo-Saxon England* (Cambridge: The University Press, 1977) 356–363, and Thomas J. Heffernan, *Sacred Biography: Saints and Their Biographers in the Middle Ages* (Oxford: Oxford University Press, 1988) 231–299.

8. The Latin texts and their English translations are given in Blair, SFR, 93–116 and 74–79. My summary in the text is taken from my reading and translation of the original manuscripts, though Blair's text served throughout as a good check system.

9. Blair, SFR, 74. A listing of these later versions are included on the same page, f.n.7. Cf. Jacob, 4–5 and 12–14.

10. For detailed accounts of the early history of the Oxfordshire region, see Parker, entire book; F. M. Stenton, "St. Frideswide and Her Times," Oxon. I (1936) 103–112; Blair, SFPO, 13–18 and *Anglo-Saxon Oxfordshire*. Valuable sources for the general history of Anglo-Saxon England germane to this study are P. H. Blair; Henry Mayr-Harting, *The Coming of Christianity to Anglo-Saxon England* (London: B. T. Batsford, 3rd ed., 1991); J. Campbell and others, *The Anglo-Saxons* (Oxford: Oxford University Press, 1982); F. M. Stenton, *Anglo-Saxon*

England, 3rd ed., rev. by D. M. Stenton and D. Whitelock (Oxford: Oxford University Press, 1971); C. J. Godfrey, *The Church in Anglo-Saxon England* (Cambridge at the University Press, 1962); *Bede's Ecclesiastical History of the English People,* eds. B. Colgrave and R. A. B. Mynors (Oxford: Oxford University Press, 1969) and Kenneth Harrison, *The Framework of Anglo-Saxon History to A.D. 900* (Cambridge at the University Press, 1976).

11. Christine Fell and others, *Women in Anglo-Saxon England and the Impact of 1066* (London: British Museum Publications, 1984) 14.

12. F. Stenton, "St. Frideswide . . ." 107–108, and Blair, SFR, 14–15.

13. Mary Bateson, "Origins and Early History of Double Monasteries," *Transactions of the Royal Historical Society* 13 (1899) 139–198. Other informative studies of this phenomenon are Alex H. Thompson, "Double Monasteries and the Male Element in Nunneries," in *The Ministry of Women: A Report by a Committee Appointed by His Grace the Lord Archbishop of Canterbury* (London, 1919) 145–164; J. Godfrey, "The Double Monastery in Early English History," *Ampleforth Journal* 79 (1974) 19–32; S. E. Rigold, "Double Monasteries of Kent," *Journal of the British Archaeological Association,* 3rd Ser., 31: 27–37 and Stephanie Hollis, *Anglo-Saxon Women and the Church: Sharing a Common Fate* (Woodbridge: Boydell Press, 1992) 11–13, 75–81, 93–97 and 101–107.

14. *Coming of Christianity . . .,* 148.

15. I am particularly indebted to Hollis' excellent study of Anglo-Saxon women in the eighth and ninth centuries. Other useful resources are Lina Eckenstein, *Woman Under Monasticism: Chapters on Saint-Lore and Convent Life Between A.D. 500 and A.D. 1500* (Cambridge: At the University Press, 1986) 79–142; Dorothy Stenton, *The English Woman in History* (London: George Allen and Unwin, Ltd., 1957); Christine Fell and others, *Women. . . .*; D. B. Schneider, "Anglo-Saxon Women in the Religious Life: A Study of the Status and Position of Women in Early Medieval Society," Unpub. Ph.D. Dissertation, Cambridge University, 1985, and S. C. Dietrich, "An Introduction to Women in Anglo-Saxon Society (c. 600–1066)," in *The Women of England from Anglo-Saxon Times to the Present,* ed. Barbara Kanner (Hamden, Conn.: The Shoe-String Press, Inc., 1979) 32–56.

16. 2.

17. 28.

18. ix.

19. *The Anglo-Saxon Missionaries in Germany* (London: Sheed and Ward, 1954) xii–xiii.

20. Richard Southern, "Sermon Preached in Christ Church Cathedral on Sunday, 19th October, 1980," in *Friends of Christ Church Cathedral Oxford* (Oxford: Oxonian Rowley Press Ltd., 1980–1981) 26.

21. 28. See also Hollis, 2–7 and Eckenstein, 80 and 198–213.

22. 32–56.

23. 12–3.

24. 23.

25. British Library, Cotton MS Vitellius, E xv, trans. and quoted in Parker, 92.

26. SFPO, 19. For an historical account of events, benefices, and legal enactments relating to the monastery see S. R. Wigram, ed., *General and City Charters:*

the Cartulary of the Monastery of St. Frideswide at Oxford (Oxford at the Clarendon Press, 1895) I.

27. British Library, MS Landsowne 436, ff. 103–104, printed in Blair, SFR, 117–119 and discussed further in Blair, SFPO, 19–21.

28. Bodleian Library, MS Digby 177.

29. See G. E. C. Rodwell, "The Flight of St. Frideswide," in *The Journal of the British Archaeological Association,* 22 (March, 1916) 85–89.

30. "Functions of a Twelfth-Century Shrine: the Miracles of St. Frideswide," in *Studies in Medieval History Presented to R. H. C. Davis,* eds. H. Mayr-Harting and R. I. Moore (London: Hambledon Press, 1985) 193–206. The article is a provocative one concerned with the social function of the shrine and its miracles.

31. Ibid., 198.

32. Ibid., 202–203. Other studies of the Frideswide miracles are R. C. Finucane, *Miracles and Pilgrims* (London: J. M. Dent and Sons Ltd., 1977) 127–129; Benedicta Ward, *Miracles and the Medieval Mind* (Philadelphia: University of Pennsylvania Press, 1982) 82–88 and J. Charles Wall, *Shrines of British Saints* (London: Methuen and Co., 1905) 64–71.

33. For an analysis of the Green Man archetype found in folklore and religious art, see William Anderson's *Green Man: The Archetype of Our Oneness with the Earth,* photography by Clive Hicks (San Francisco: Harper, 1990).

34. Lincoln Diocesan Archives, Register 13, iv–2.

35. SFR, 119-127. Parker, however, (102–103, f.n.3) sees no connection between the two shrines.

36. *The Register of Henry Chichele, Archbishop of Canterbury: 1414–1443,* ed. E. F. Jacob, 46 (1945) III. 256.

37. *Breviarium Ad Usum Insignis Ecclesie Sarum,* eds. F. Proctor and C. Wordsworth (1886) III. 938–942.

38. See Blair's account and his translation of Calfhill's document in SFPO, 21–23.

39. For a chronological account of the fate of Frideswide's tomb see Francis Goldie, *The Story of St. Frideswide, Virgin and Patroness of Oxford* (London: Burns and Oates, 1881) and Warner.

40. Warner presents a thorough description of the architecture, furnishings, windows, and sacred objects of Christ Church Cathedral and their significance. Cf. Wall.

41. *Jackson's Oxford Journal* (Saturday, October 2, 1901) 5, Col.6.

42. See Blair, SFPO, 24–25, f.n.7.

43. *A Commemoration Sermon Preached in the Cathedral Church of Christ in Oxford on the Sunday after St. Frideswide's Day, 1880, Being the Seven Hundredth Year after the Opening of the Present Church* (1880, Nov. 1, Christ Church) 13, unpublished but catalogued in the Bodleian Library, Oxford.

44. 101.

4

Erentrude: Nonnberg, Eichstätt, America

Linda Kulzer, O.S.B.

In 1980 Benedictines across the world celebrated the fifteen hundredth anniversary of the birth of St. Benedict and St. Scholastica. At one of the gatherings marking this occasion, Joan Chittister, O.S.B., gave an address entitled, "Benedictinism: A Heritage That Empowers."[1] This concept of a heritage that empowers, is currently taking on special importance for Benedictine women across the world and has inspired this work on the life of St. Erentrude.

Around the year 700, Erentrude founded Nonnberg in Salzburg, the oldest Benedictine women's foundation on German soil (later Austrian) and one which in recent decades has gained fame as one of the sites of the movie, "The Sound of Music."

St. Erentrude, a Merovingian noblewoman, and the abbey she founded are of particular interest to American Benedictines who can trace a connection from Nonnberg Abbey to its daughter house, the Abbey of St. Walburg in Eichstätt. This Bavarian abbey is the founding monastery of several Benedictine women's houses in the United States.

ERENTRUDE'S LIFE AND THE FOUNDING OF NONNBERG

Much of what is known about Erentrude comes from the early accounts of the life of her uncle, St. Rupert, a missionary of Frankish royal blood invited to the Salzburg region by Duke Theodo. As a missionary bishop of Worms, he became interested in this area, an ancient Roman settlement that still bore the name Juvavum. Rupert's help in developing the salt springs found in this location resulted in the name of Salzburg. Theodo himself was baptized by Rupert, and many of his people responded to Christianity.[2]

Around the year 685, only two hundred years after the birth of St. Benedict, Rupert returned to Franconia to obtain more help for his work in Salzburg. Esterl indicates that "because Rupert was a friend of monastic living" he intended to set up monasteries.[3] Thus he returned from France with twelve young men and his niece, Erentrude. The Lectionary of Canisius states that he brought his niece along "in order that from both sexes luminaries of the Church might shine in this region."[4] With his twelve companions, he formed the first community of the famous Benedictine monastery of St. Peter at Salzburg. Both Duke Theodo and his wife, Duchess Regintrudis, were involved in suggesting the site of the women's monastery and in providing gifts of supporting properties.[5] The fact of its origin is reported by the oldest sources for Salzburg's history— the Indiculis Arnonis and its addition, Brevis Notitiae. Under the title, "Building of the Convent of St. Erentrudis in Juvavia and of the Lands Which Duke Theodo Gave It," the latter tells of the founding of the abbey.[6]

The monastery was built to the southeast of the town of Salzburg where the old Roman fortress once towered on the hill that later became known as Nonnberg (the mountain of nuns). Rupert dedicated the community to Mary the Mother of God and placed Erentrude at its head. Although the two communities in Salzburg were monastic houses, it is quite possible that they did not adopt the Benedictine rule until a later century.[7] The recent author and archivist, Sister Regintrudis Reichlin of Nonnberg, claims that the Rule of St. Benedict was introduced in Nonnberg very early. The old frescoes discovered in the convent church in 1857 indicate, however, that the Benedictine rule was definitely introduced after the year 1000. According to Dr. Paul Buberl, these frescoes were influenced by the school of Ravenna and originated around the middle of the twelfth century; however, Reichlin designates Nonnberg as "the oldest convent of Benedictine women on German soil."[8] Erentrude and her companions lived and worked here, apparently loved and appreciated by all. When she died on June 30, 718, her remains were placed in a grave in the rocks.[9] There is much evidence that she was honored by miracles soon after her death, and as early as the ninth century she was recognized as a saint.[10]

Beyond these facts taken mainly from early accounts of Rupert's life, very little actual evidence remains about Erentrude's life. Not until the beginning of the fourteenth century did Caesarius, a chaplain at Nonnberg, write the first biographical sketch of Erentrude. It consists of the traditions and information which he gathered from the stories told by the oldest nuns and the people of the area. In the beginning, Caesarius indicates that he is doing this writing at the order of the bishop as a result of his twenty-eight years of experience as chaplain at Nonnberg.[11] He sketches a thoroughly loving and attractive image of Erentrude in this narrative which is the foundation of what is now the common office of the saint. He describes her as coming from a Franconian-Merovingian royal house and having formerly been the superior of a group of women consecrated to God in Worms.[12]

Several sources hint at the possibility of strife in the Worms convent: "Erentrude experienced bitterness in Worms. This steeled her character and her shoulders became strong, but her special desire more than ever before was for the rest of mystical contemplation."[13] There is some suggestion that when her uncle asked her to come to Salzburg, a number of nuns came with her or later followed her to Nonnberg. Caesarius describes her life at Nonnberg:

> On the mountain, however, on which it is pleasing to God to dwell and on which the cornerstone, Jesus Christ, wished to be honored, she desired to love God not only with her voice and lips, but with her utmost heart. Resting at Christ's feet with Mary she perceived his words in contemplation, but she also went out with Martha in the service of the poor.[14]

The office of her feast praised her great love for children which she passed on to her spiritual daughters as a holy inheritance. It also cites her maternal goodness toward the poor and injured whose wounds she dressed. The accounts contain a number of references to her careful direction of her nuns and of the young women entrusted to her.[15] According to Caesarius, "she guided the daughters subject to her with all gentleness and wisdom." Finally, he quotes her favorite verse from Psalm 73: "To be near to God is my happiness. I have made the Lord my refuge."[16]

Theodo's wife, the duchess Regintrudis, became a nun in Erentrude's community after the death of her husband. A Franconian princess, she may have been related to Erentrude. Her name is entered in the necrology on May 26, the anniversary of her death, as "Regina Regintrudis, *piae memoriae*" with the addition of "*fundatrix nostra.*"[17]

The description of Erentrude's death given in the Bollandist account suggests that around 718 Rupert told her of his imminent death.[18] In response, she begged that she would be allowed to follow soon. Rupert is said to have died on March 27, 718. Erentrude died three months later, on June 30. The Lectionary of Canisius indicates that when she knew her death was near, she "ruminated" on these words from the psalms: "It is good for me to cling to God, to place all my hope in God." He indicates that she received viaticum, made a perfect confession, entrusted the nuns under her care to God, "and with torches lit went to meet her spouse full of good works and almsgiving."[19] After her death her reputation spread, and confidence in her intercessory power grew. People began talking about her miracles, and as a result Holy Virgil, a bishop who followed Rupert, allowed her to be openly venerated.[20]

REGARD SHOWN FOR ERENTRUDE SINCE HER DEATH

Erentrude's remains received unusual attention three centuries after her death. At that time because the convent and church of Nonnberg which had deteriorated from fire, and perhaps plundering, was rebuilt by Emperor Henry as a thank offering for a cure which he attributed to Erentrude's intercession. Around 1024, when the solemn dedication of the newly built church took place, Erentrude's remains were taken from her first tomb and transferred with great honor and reverence into the crypt of the new church.[21] Six hundred years later, on September 4, 1624, her remains were solemnly enshrined in a silver reliquary and placed beneath the altar in the monastic choir chapel. From that time until Vatican II, the transferal of her remains was commemorated each September fourth on the feast called the *Translatio Erentrudis*. Today, the abbey celebrates the feast of the Dedication of a Church on that day.[22]

It appears that at the time of the transfer of the relics in 1024, the name of the abbey may have changed from St. Mary's Abbey at Nonnberg to the Abbey of St. Mary and St. Erentrude. The new Romanesque church built at that time was called the "Church of Holy Erentrude, because through her holy life she blessed this place and because her burial site is here."[23] Today the abbey is referred to as St. Erentrude's Abbey at Nonnberg.

The transfer of her remains in 1024 appears to have been the scene of a rather dramatic miracle. Caesarius, the Nonnberg chaplain who wrote about her life and miracles in the early 1300s, tells what happened to Abbot Mazzelin on that occasion. The legend indicates that in 1024 Abbot Mazzelin of St. Peter's Abbey in Salzburg attended the solemn translation of her bones into the crypt of the new church. Since he admired Erentrude greatly, he wished to have a relic of her. Torn by this desire, he secretly took a particle of her body. Caesarius indicates that he took a chest bone.[24] To the astonishment of all present he was immediately struck blind. He admitted his theft and promised to resign as abbot and to live as a hermit on an adjoining mountain. He then regained his sight and kept his promise. After he died, a wagon drawn by oxen was supposed to bring his body to St. Peter's, his monastery, for burial. The animals, driven by a secret power, went to Nonnberg where he was buried in the church near St. Erentrude, the person he so honored. Archeological excavations show that there actually is a grave in front of the left entrance of her crypt, which could contain Mazzelin's remains.[25]

An examination of Erentrude's relics in 1924 revealed that she must have been short and slight. A lock of blond hair was found, which, according to an expert, Dr. Hella Pock of Vienna, could not belong to a person of southern or central Germany. The osteological examination showed that Erentrude was at the most fifty-five years old at the time of her death.[26] In artistic reproductions, Erentrude is generally shown in the garments of an abbess. In one hand she carries an abbatial cross and in the other hand a model of the Nonnberg church.

NONNBERG'S HISTORY AND THE EICHSTÄTT FOUNDATION

All available accounts of Nonnberg's history agree that in the course of its nearly thirteen hundred years of existence this community of monastic women has never been suppressed. There are many indications of truly difficult times when "Nonnberg too had concerns about the permanence of its venerable old house. Contrary to expectations, it was spared the worst."[27] Strong evidence of the continued existence of this abbey is in the lists of the successive abbesses since the time of Erentrude. Reichlin tells us that Kaerlind was the first successor of Erentrude and goes on to indicate the source of information about the early abbesses.

> The famous book of St. Peter's "Liber Vitae" saved the names of the next ten leaders of the Convent of Our Lady. It was produced at the occasion of St. Virgil around 784 by reason of an older dipthycon [a folding slate]. These nuns are Waltrat, Raegindrud, Imma, Hiltrud, Catestin, Rodrud, Maiginhilt, Hraitun, Heotrat, Catans.[28]

It was under the Abbess Ita in 1035 that Nonnberg founded a daughter house, the Abbey of St. Walburg, at Eichstätt in Bavaria. St. Walburga had been born in England in 710. Around 754 she and other English nuns responded to Boniface's call for help in evangelizing Germany, and she became head of a Benedictine abbey at Heidenheim. A century after her death there, her remains were moved to Eichstätt where her brother had been bishop.[29] A small community of canonesses was established there to honor her relics, but it dwindled until it almost ceased to exist. In 1035 Leodigar, Count of Lechgemund-Griefsbach, decided to use part of his fortune to rebuild the Church of St. Walburga in Eichstätt and to establish a community of Benedictine nuns there. With the help of Bishop Heribert he invited the nuns from Nonnberg in Salzburg to make a foundation at St. Walburg and introduce Benedictine observance there. A document drawn up on July 24, 1035 continues the story:

> At this time the niece of Leodigar, Imma, was blessed as first abbess here. She was a woman who led a venerable life, proved herself with good works, and had been strengthened by the teaching of the Abbess Ita in the Abbey of Holy Mary and St. Erentrudis in Salzburg.[30]

Others who helped form the new community of St. Walburg in Eichstätt were the remaining canonesses and some Benedictines from neighboring houses.[31]

However, it was the leadership coming from the monastery of Nonnberg founded by Erentrude in 700 that brought to this venture the oldest stream of Benedictinism in Germany. Here it met and blended with the spirit and ideals of Walburga and Boniface.[32] From this foundation in Eichstätt, Sister Benedicta Riepp and her companions ventured forth in 1852 to volunteer for the mission field in the United States. Today, forty motherhouses of Benedictine women of the Bavarian tradition look to her as their American foundress.

WOMEN'S SPIRITUALITY IN THE LATTER PART OF THE MEROVINGIAN ERA

Erentrude lived during the close of the Merovingian period, a period lasting from the middle of the fifth century to about 750. Her death in 718 occurred only thirty years before Pepin dethroned the last Merovingian king, the event which begins the Carolingian era.

To better understand Erentrude, then, we need to know something about the general attitude of Merovingian women toward Christianity. Suzanne Wemple makes these general comments:

> Like women in the early centuries of Christianity, women of Merovingian Gaul were the staunchest supporters of the new religion, converting their husbands, baptizing their children, building churches and nourishing the faith with monastic foundations.[33]

For more specific data about Merovingian women whose experiences were similar to those of Erentrude, we need to focus on what we can discover about women in monasteries during the Merovingian era. A spiritual literature of the sixth and seventh centuries appears invaluable for this particular study. It reveals a monastic spirituality seeming to have arisen quite directly out of the life and experiences of Merovingian women and consists of the biographies of two Merovingian saints, Radegund (521–587) and Balthild (600[?]–680), by nuns who knew them personally. This information is particularly valuable because it gives us actual records of Merovingian women's own experiences of spirituality.

Much of the information here is dependent on Wemple's research and assumptions.[34] She indicates that the lives of these two Merovingian women were very different, but that they both founded monasteries and developed "their foundations into enduring centers of spirituality and culture."[35] There are interesting similarities here with the life of Erentrude. Not only is she also a monastic foundress whose monastery at Nonnberg has endured to the present, but her life span, c. 668 to 718, overlaps Balthild's.

Radegund was a Thuringian princess who was captured in battle as a child in 531. She became the booty of Clothar, one of the Merovingian kings, and was forced into marriage with him at the age of twelve.

> Radegund exasperated the king by passive resistance. He complained that she acted more like a nun than a queen, immersed herself in charitable work, kept him waiting at meals, quit his bed to pray and wore haircloth under her royal robes.[36]

The murder of her younger brother by Clothar finally led her to leave her husband's court for good. She fled to Noyon and dedicated her life to God, then settled for some time at a villa her husband had given her at Sais. She turned this villa into a hospice for the sick and the poor. When Clothar tried to reclaim her as his wife and queen, she appealed to Bishop Germain of Paris, who persuaded the king to give Radegund her freedom and to help her establish a monastery at Poitiers. She lived in a cell adjoining that monastery until her death in 587.[37]

Two contemporary lives of Radegund were commissioned:

> The original "official" vita was written in about 587 by Fortunatus, poet, friend, and spiritual advisor to Saint Radegund. . . . The "second vita" as it was called was written some twenty years later by the nun Baudonivia, confidant, companion, and witness to the events of Radegund's life.[38]

The second Merovingian woman saint whose biography gives us valuable information about the spirituality of Merovingian women is Balthild. She was of Anglo-Saxon origin, captured on the coast of France and brought to Paris as a slave. King Clothar II (639–656) was attracted by her beauty and made her his queen. After his death she ruled Nuestria for eight years and was known to be especially concerned for the poor and the enslaved. She founded a monastery for men at Corbie and one for women at Chelles. Forced to withdraw from court around 664–665, she took refuge at Chelles and lived there under the Abbess Bertila until her death in 679 or 680. A nun at Chelles is believed to have written her biography a few years after her death.[39]

The book, *Sainted Women of the Dark Ages,* by Jo Ann McNamara provides an outstanding study of eighteen holy women who lived in the sixth and seventh century. She makes a claim for these women that provides a backdrop for the continued exploration of the spirituality of Merovingian women.

> They lived in a rough and brutal age, an age moderns have condemned as "the dark ages," but from the peril and suffering of their lives they shaped themselves as models of womanly power, womanly achievement, and womanly voices. They did not hide their lights under a bushel, but lit candles in the darkness and set them high upon a candlestick.[40]

This brief review of the lives of Radegund and Balthild makes it possible for us to reflect more closely on the accounts of their lives "as works that reflect truly female expressions of Merovingian life."[41] Wemple indicates that the exceptional aspect of these accounts is not that they were written by contemporaries, "but that they were written by female members of their communities, who sympathized with and understood female modes of spirituality."[42] Female values and ideals are introduced into hagiography as a result of these accounts by Baudonivia and the Chelles author. Prior to this time, the ideal woman saint had been represented as an asexual person who imitated male virtues, but here we find heroines who "relied on female attributes to achieve spiritual perfection."[43] Wemple puts this quite clearly:

> The prototype of the ideal nun that Baudonivia presented to her sisters was not, however, a self-effacing and sexless abstraction. In contrast to Fortunatus' portrayal of Radegund . . . Baudonivia described Radegund as an outgoing and emotional woman who was as concerned about the affairs of the monastery as about the development of the kingdom.[44]

Wemple points out that these women were still expected to practice the usual monastic virtues of humility and self denial. But an unusual theme was introduced into hagiography when these two saints were characterized as mother figures and peacemakers among the warring royalty. She indicates that it "represented the assimilation into religious life of the nurturing and mediatory roles women were expected to play as daughters and wives in Merovingian society."[45]

These writings did not urge women to transcend their natures, but they dignified the female role as a source of spiritual perfection. Care and service of others was the normal function of Merovingian women. The women biographers of Radegund and Balthild presented these activities as more than a means of self discipline and an exercise in humility. Rather, "They associated the care of others with prayer and identified it with the virtue of charity. . . . They exalted charity as the very essence of monastic life."[46] Wemple again calls attention to the way in which the women biographers here contributed to a new outlook:

> By recording the impulse of love in the religious development of Radegund, Balthild, and Aldegund, their biographers made an important contribution to monastic spirituality. They introduced a new motif into hagiography, providing an alternative to the male ideal of humility, penance, and renunciation of self.[47]

The accounts of the lives of these two women show how Merovingian women forged their own spiritual ideal by drawing on values associated with female identity and also how "under the influence of this ideal created by women a new form of monasticism arose representing a balance between the active and contemplative ways of life."[48]

How do Erentrude's life and spirituality relate to what has been explored thus far concerning the spirituality of Merovingian women? One of the legends about Erentrude's early life makes an interesting connection with Radegund. According to this story, born and raised in Franconia, Erentrude entered the convent of St. Radegund in Poitiers and took the veil. She received her education there, all the while remaining in touch with Rupert. This version states that after Rupert was called to be bishop of Worms he asked Erentrude to follow him to Worms, where she entered a convent.[49]

The likelihood of Erentrude's connection with other Merovingian monastic houses of that time helps us understand some of the descriptions of her. One statement speaks of her "maternal goodness toward the poor and the sick whose wounds she dressed and whose pain she sought to assuage." These activities of Erentrude and other monastic women of her era make it rather obvious that they did not live the strictly secluded life associated with later claustration of women religious. McNamara describes their activities in more detail:

> It [wealth] was also distributed among the troops of beggars, vagabonds and refugees who came daily to the monastery doors. The rule of claustration never prevented the nuns of this period from opening their gates to suppliants. Here, rather than in the spectacular baptism of kings, is where the real work of conversion took place.[50]

It is possible that the care of the sick as a spiritual work of mercy so characteristic of women religious took on an even more lasting form in Erentrude's newly founded monastery. There still exists today in Salzburg a health care facility (apothecary) which can be connected with the founding of the monastery of Nonnberg. Reichlin refers to the development of Nonnberg's apothecary from the time of Erentrude, who "according to legend loved to attend the sick and . . . had a special motherly concern for sick children."[51] She indicates some specific happenings in the history of the apothecary especially during the fourteenth, seventeenth, and eighteenth centuries.[52] In another publication Reichlin indicates what has since become of the community's relationship to the apothecary:

> Even though public health care and the modern condition of the apothecary took over many of the tasks formerly the exclusive right of the old con-

vents, there are opportunities enough even today for the nuns to follow St. Erentrude's example.[53]

It was pointed out earlier that care of and service to others was the normal function of Merovingian women. The women monastics of this time, however, "associated the care of others with prayer and identified it with the virtue of charity."[54] The central importance of charity among the women religious of the Merovingian era is well described by McNamara:

> The most direct impact of the saintly women [seventh century] on the secular public was as a living sermon, a model of the Christian life to be imitated by all. Thus charity in all its aspects was central to their efforts.[55]

Wemple has pointed out that as a result of the influence of charity as an ideal, "a new form of monasticism arose representing a balance between the active and the contemplative ways of life."[56]

This concept of balance between the active and contemplative lives appears as a theme in the descriptions of Erentrude's life:

> She desired to love God not only with her voice and lips but with her utmost heart. Resting at Christ's feet with Mary she perceived his words in contemplation, but she also went out with Martha in service of the poor.[57]

Earlier in Erentrude's life when strife arose among the women in the Worms convent, it was said of her that her "desire more than ever before was for the rest of mystical contemplation."[58] It seems clear that Erentrude shared with other Merovingian monastic women of her time a sense of the appropriate balance between the active and contemplative ways.

For Merovingian women, care and service of others was paramount. When these women integrated this ideal into their monastic life, it changed the tenor of monastic life up to this time. No longer were humility and self denial central; instead, for these women charity became the focus and purpose of their monastic existence. With charity as the governing ideal, the balance between the active and contemplative ways of life became much clearer. Erentrude's life and ideals were characteristic of the women of her age. With the Merovingian women of her time, she was devoted to the care of others. With the monastic women of her day, she devoted herself to the poor and the sick. With them, she viewed charity as that ideal which demands both union with others and with the God who created others. The accounts of her life indicate in a striking manner how a life centered in charity can result in a beautiful balance between the active and contemplative life. Her life and accomplishments provide a heritage for all Christians, but in a special way they provide inspiration for women. They are a model for women in an area where they frequently experience the most significant struggle of their lives: the never-ending concern for the appropriate balance between caring for others and caring for the longings of their own soul.

NOTES

1. The original address was given on June 19, 1980, for a Congress of Monastic Men and Women meeting at St. Benedict's Monastery and St. John's Abbey in Minnesota. It was reprinted in *Sisters Today* 52:2 (October 1980) 66.

2. Ulrich Schmid, "Rupert," *Catholic Encyclopedia,* 229.

3. Franz Esterl, *Chronik Des Adelignen Benedictiner-Frauen Stifter Nonnberg in Salzburg* (Salzburg: Duyle, 1841) 28.

4. "Ancient Lectionary of Canisius," Tome 6, *Acta Sanctorum Ordinis Benedicti* III ed. Mabillon (Paris, 1668–1701) 348.

5. Bollandists, *Acta Sanctorum,* vol. VII (Brussels: 1845) 533. See also Regintrudis Reichlein, O.S.B., *Stift Nonnberg zu Salzburg in Wandel der Zeiten* (Salzburg: Anton Pustet, 1953) 10–11.

6. Reichlin, *Stift Nonnberg,* 10.

7. H. Schmidinger, "Erintrude, Saint, Arindrud, Erendruda," *Dictionnaire D'Histoire et de Geographic Ecclesiastiques* vol. 15 (Paris 1963) 697.

8. Reichlin, *Stift Nonnberg,* 12.

9. Ibid., 10.

10. Esterl, 4.

11. Caesarius, "The Book of Miracles," *Acta Sanctorum Ordinis Benedicti* III, ed., Mabillon (Paris 1668–1701) 350.

12. Reichlin, *Stift Nonnberg,* 11.

13. Mabillon, "Ancient Lectionary of Canisius," 348.

14. Reichlin, *Stift Nonnberg,* 12.

15. Regintrudis Reichlin, O.S.B., "St. Erentraud am Nonnberg in Salzburg, Osterreich," *Benedictus Bote* 21 (1951) 236.

16. Reichlin, *Stift Nonnberg,* 12.

17. Reichlin, *Stift Nonnberg,* 13.

18. Bollandists, 533.

19. Mabillon, "Ancient Lectionary of Canisius," 349.

20. Esterl, 8.

21. Bollandists, 534.

22. Irmgard Schmidt-Sommer and Theresia Bolschwing, O.S.B., *Frauen vor Gott* (1990) 6.

23. Esterl, 8.

24. Caesarius, "The Book of Miracles," 351.

25. Schmidt-Sommer, *Frauen vor Gott* 7. It is interesting to note that the Venerable Mazzelin has a feast day on June 30, the same day as Erentrude. His life story is similar to the legend as quoted in the major sources. See Alexius Hoffman, O.S.B., *A Benedictine Martyrology:* Being a Revision of Rev. Peter Lechner's, *Ausfürliches Martyrologium des Benedictiner* (Collegeville: St. John's Abbey, 1922) 170.

26. Alfonso M. Zimmerman, "Erentrude (Ehrentraud)," *Biblioteca Sanctorum* ed. Pietro Palazzini et al Vol. IV (Rome, 1964) 1313.

27. Reichlin, "St. Erentraud," 238.

28. Reichlin, *Stift Nonnberg*, 13.

29. Emmanuel Drey, O.S.B., *Die Abtei St. Walburg* (1035–1935): 900 *Jahre in Wort und Bild* (Eichstätt: St. Walburg Abbey, 1934). English translation by Gonzaga Engelhart, O.S.B., *Spring and Harvest* (St. Meinrad, Ind.: The Grail, 1952) 13–22.

30. Anna Maria Brigitta, O.S.B., and Andreas Bauch, *Heilige Walburga: Leben und Wirken* (Abtei St. Walburg, 1979) 2nd revised printing, 1985. English translation by Gerard Ellspermann, O.S.B., *St. Walburga: Her Life and Heritage* (Eichstätt: Abtei St. Walburg, 1985) 38.

31. *Spring and Harvest,* 25–26.

32. Faith Schuster, O.S.B., *The Meaning of the Mountain: A History of the First Century at Mount St. Scholastica* (Baltimore: Helicon, 1963) 13.

33. Suzanne Wemple, *Women in Frankish Society* (Philadelphia: U. of Pennsylvania, 1981) 3.

34. Suzanne Wemple, "Female Spirituality and Mysticism in Frankish Monasteries: Radegund, Balthild and Aldegund," *Medieval Women: Peaceweavers,* eds. John A. Nichols and Lillian T. Shank. See also Wemple, *Women in Frankish Society,* chapter 6.

35. Wemple, "Female Spirituality," 41.

36. Frances and Joseph Gies, *Women in the Middle Ages* (New York: Crowell, 1978) 21.

37. Lina Eckenstein, *Woman Under Monasticism* (New York: Russell & Russell, 1963) 53–55.

38. Jane Tibbitts Schulenberg, "Saints' Lives as a Source for the History of Women, 500–1100," *Medieval Women and the Sources of Medieval History,* ed. Joel T. Rosenthal (Athens: University of Georgia) 291.

39. Wemple, "Female Spirituality," 40.

40. Jo Ann McNamara and John E. Halborg, with E. Gordon Whatley, *Sainted Women of the Dark Ages* (Durham and London: Duke University Press, 1992) 15.

41. Wemple, "Female Spirituality," 42.

42. Ibid.

43. Ibid., 43.

44. Ibid., 43–44.

45. Ibid., 43.

46. Ibid., 48.

47. Ibid., 48–49.

48. Ibid., 49.

49. Reichlin, "St. Erentraud," 236.

50. Jo Ann McNamara, "Living Sermons," *Medieval Religious Women: Peaceweavers,* eds. John A. Nichols and Lillian T. Shank (Kalamazoo, Mich: Cistercian Publications, 1984) 33.

51. Reichlin, *Stift Nonnberg,* 55.

52. Reichlin, *Stift Nonnberg,* 55–56. She indicates that during the fourteenth century Erentrude's successors had to care for a wider circle of needy. At that time

Abbess Margaretha I founded an establishment at the foot of the mountain near St. Edward's Church. It was the beginning of the later St. Edward's Hospital. The sick and the lepers enjoyed the special attention of the Nonnberg abbesses, who washed their feet in the St. John's Chapel, cared for them, and gave them gifts of money.

53. Reichlin, "St. Erentraud," 22.
54. Wemple, "Female Spirituality," 48.
55. McNamara, "Living Sermons," 32.
56. Wemple, "Female Spirituality," 49.
57. Reichlin, *Stift Nonnberg,* 12.
58. Reichlin, "St. Erentraud," 236.

5

St. Walburga:
Medieval Nun, Free Woman

Emmanuel Luckman, O.S.B.

Freedom is a constant theme in both the Old and New Testaments concerning God's gifts and life for his people. From Genesis to the last chapter of the Book of Revelations, God frees his people "that they may have life, and have it to the full" (John 10:10). Paul tells us in no uncertain terms that we are not children of the slave but of the free woman. For freedom, Christ has set us free (Gal 4:31-5:1). This Christ-centered gift of freedom characterized the historical life of St. Walburga of Heidenheim (c. 710–799) and imparted to this great "free woman" of the eighth century a spiritual wisdom that still has meaning for us, her spiritual sisters and brothers, more than a thousand years later.

Walburga's historical life eludes us because of the lack of coherent, factual information. Aside from honorary mention by Huceburc, the biographer of Walburga's two outstanding brothers, Saints Willibald and Wunibald, we have only miracle reports from the memories of the local people recorded by a priest one hundred years after Walburga's death.[1] According to these earliest accounts, we see Walburga acting in brave and fantastic ways. She tamed wild wolves with the wave of her hand; she cured the sick and dying upon request, and by prayer and supplication, she called upon her God to touch the heart of a gruff and uncivil porter and received in reply a full night's divine lighting for her astonished community. These and other adventures were some of the events in the daily life of Walburga. Legendary though these stories may be, we discern in them a woman remarkable both for her zeal and devotion to God and for her humble ability to place herself serenely in the background while great events were happening around her and because of her. Whatever the actual facts may be, Walburga of Heidenheim is without doubt one of the great women missionaries of the Anglo-Saxon, Benedictine, missionary movement to Germany. Little is known about her, and what is told tends to be shrouded in the mantle of legend and pious reconstruction. These later pious reconstructions, while edifying succeeding generations, seldom yield accurate pictures of the practical life of the early, missionary Benedictines to Germany or of the personalities and characters of these missionaries, especially the women. Legends, on the other hand, should not be entirely ignored or repudiated, as they characterize history, and interpret and reflect facts in the minds of the people.[2]

To convey an accurate picture of the lives and spirits of these medieval, Benedictine, missionary monks and nuns, we need to uncover not only the known facts of their earthly lives, the memories and legends about them which survived among the peoples but also to uncover an accurate picture of the Christian spirituality of the Anglo-Saxon culture in which Walburga lived for at least the first thirty years of her life. We need as well to take a closer look at the pagan, Germanic culture into which she came in the later years of her life, to challenge and transform it for Christ.

EARLY LIFE

Walburga was born in the year 710 into a noble and prominent Anglo-Saxon family in southern England. Her father was King Richard of Wessex, and her mother, Queen Wuna. Walburga was born during the golden age of Christianity in England. In 663, barely fifty years before her birth, differences between the Celtic and Roman churches were settled in favor of Rome at the historic debate at Whitby, the famous monastic settlement where St. Hilda was abbess.[3] At least two centuries before Walburga was born, the faith had spread through England and was maintained by groups of monks and clergy living as "ministers," preaching and ministering at erected crosses and other landmarks before founding churches which in time became parishes. Monasteries of monks and nuns of the Gallic pattern multiplied with saintly abbesses such as Hilda of Whitby and Etheldreda of Ely and hermits such as Guthlac of Crowland. The papal appointment to Canterbury of the Greek monk, Theodore, who was assisted by the African monk and abbot, Hadrian, succeeded in reforming the existing Church, founding new sees, and giving this new Christian land laws and discipline. Schools began to flourish. It was also during this period that the Northumbrian, Benedict Biscop, brought Roman ritual, chant, and Benedictine monasticism to Wearmouth and Jarrow, where the life and writings of Bede crowned a remarkable flowering of literature and artistic activity. It was during this time as well that the Gospels were lettered and illuminated at Lindisfarne. Under the direction of abbesses of particular energy and intelligence, flowering religious centers in the England of this time gained the reputation for being places of learning and culture, the equivalent of small, endowed universities today.[4]

From the seventh to the tenth centuries, foundresses and abbesses could assume powers usually reserved to bishops, abbots, and ordained clergy. Many of these communities, founded by noblewomen and daughters of wealthy landowners, consisted of adjacent foundations for both women and men called "double monasteries." Women governed these communities. As abbess a woman exercised both religious and secular power. Because the lands were held in the name of the community, the abbess was responsible for fulfilling the feudal obligations of a vassal and was responsible for the administration of the manors and fields upon which the sustenance of the monastic group depended. She also supervised the religious life of those living on the monastery property, the collection of tithes, and the choice of the village clergy. As abbess she naturally assumed responsibility for the spiritual life of the monks and nuns of her community.[5]

The great influence and prestige enjoyed by these early abbesses can be explained in part by the characteristics of religious experience and belief that preceded Christianity in the Celtic and Germanic countries.[6] As daughter of a king, Walburga inherited the natural self-assurance and confidence so common among her kinswomen. Her family background also served her well during her later years in Germany where she joined her uncle, Saint Boniface, and her two brothers, Willibald and Wunibald, in the mission field. This self-confidence, this "freedom of spirit," characterized Walburga from her childhood onward as accounts from Wolfhard record.

According to Huceburc, Walburga's family observed daily common prayers in front of a wooden cross erected on their land.[7] When Willibald fell seriously ill as a young child, his parents made a solemn promise to place him in a monastery should he recover. This stable round of daily communal prayer and the faithful keeping of the parents' promise upon Willibald's miraculous recovery are only two illustrations of life in Walburga's childhood home. Hers was an early childhood obviously penetrated by the power of strong Christian faith and a closely bound, loving family. This undoubtedly left a strong and enduring impression on the youthful mind of Walburga, influencing and strengthening her in the years to come.

An unforgettable event in the life of young Walburga was her father's decision in the summer of 720 to accompany Willibald and Wunibald on pilgrimage to the Holy Land. Accounts vary as to whether Wuna was still alive or had died sometime earlier, but the question seems to have arisen about what to do with ten-year-old Walburga. Even though there were many relatives suitable as foster parents during her father's long absence, Walburga herself asked to enter the abbey school of Wimborne. In these new surroundings, Walburga not only learned the literature and sciences of her day, but she was also surrounded by monks and nuns living the Rule of St. Benedict, many of whom were her blood relatives. The most notable of these relatives with whom Walburga lived her first years in the monastery and then joined on the mission fields of Germany was St. Leoba.[8]

EARLY MONASTIC LIFE AT WIMBORNE

Walburga spent the next twenty to thirty years in the Abbey of Wimborne under Abbess Tetta, a remarkable woman who undoubtedly shaped and refined the character of young Walburga. Highly gifted herself, Abbess Tetta had the reputation for being quick to size up and discern the abilities, and presumably also the lack thereof, of others. She was a strict disciplinarian yet governed her large community of reputedly five hundred nuns—not counting the monks, for it was a double monastery—wisely and firmly. Since she is frequently referred to as "saint" we can safely assume her spiritual gifts were as obvious as her intellectual and administrative ones. Tetta's double monastery was considered at the time to be one of the stricter observance, and it also had the reputation of being one of the most intellectual institutions in England or any other country at the time. The nuns of Wimborne were good Latin scholars; they also knew some Greek as was the custom, according to Bede, for monks and nuns of this time.[9]

Wimborne's nuns may have been quite adept at Greek and Latin and used their linguistic knowledge to deepen their reading of the sacred texts as well as their understanding of the early Church Fathers and the Councils. In the life of Leoba, we read that she "read with attention all the books of the Old and New Testaments and learned by heart all the commandments of God. To these she added by way of completion, the writings of the church Fathers, the decrees of the Councils, and the whole of ecclesiastical law."[10] We can safely assume that since Leoba lived in the eighth century, these writings dealt primarily with the Christological and Trinitarian controversies of the early Church and the various heresies that caused enough attention to find their way into ecclesiastical statements. This knowledge would serve Leoba, Walburga, and their companions well in the mission lands to which they were going.

It seems Walburga continued living at Wimborne for some years before embarking on the missions. The news of the death of her father in northern Italy undoubtedly had a great impact on her, leaving her without father or mother and with only her two brothers—both of whom were by this time living in Rome—as her closest relatives. If the adage is true that one becomes an adult at the death of the last parent, then we can assume Walburga reached her maturity in her late teens.

The date on which Walburga became a nun is unknown. While opinions vary, it seems most likely that Walburga waited until her brother Wunibald returned from Rome. She was devoted to this brother since they were close in age and grew up together in their parents' home. Willibald, on the other hand, had spent his life from early childhood in the English monastery until his pilgrimage to Rome with Wunibald and their father, and was therefore not as close to either sibling. After this pilgrimage and a stay in a monastery in Rome, Wunibald most likely returned to England for important business; and the future of his younger sister was reason enough to call him there. Walburga's royal dowry needed to be settled, and Wunibald, in Willibald's absence, was considered the head of the family. Wunibald returned to England about the year 727 when Walburga was approximately eighteen. Since he remained in England a year or two, Walburga undoubtedly was old enough to make the decision regarding her entrance into a monastery. The joy for both brother and sister at this time must have been immense, for now they had the consolation of being related not only by blood, but also spiritually, as members of the Benedictine family. This enabled them to retain their close bond of kinship in the years to come, working side by side on the mission fields of Germany where all three siblings eventually ended their earthly life.

MISSION TO THE GERMANS

As early as the seventh and the beginning of the eighth century, Christian missionaries had attempted to establish missions along the Saxon borders. St. Willibrord;[11] Sturm; the early martyrs, Ewald the Black and Ewald the Fair, are but a few of the early missionaries on the continent before the arrival of Boniface, Walburga, and her companions. Their work in Germany had been somewhat successful, contributing much to the moral and religious education of the people, but the area still lacked an organized, unified plan for the functioning of parishes and appointments of resident bishops. The earliest Celtic missionaries were itinerant priests and bishops who were more ascetics than pastors. They were, moreover, pronounced individualists who generally preferred to work alone. Even in foreign countries they tended to retain their own peculiar customs and seemed to have little understanding and regard for complex, ecclesiastical organization and hierarchical order. The Anglo-Saxon missionaries, on the other hand, were different. They possessed qualities the Celtic missionaries generally lacked: perseverance and endurance; adaptability; a talent for organization; an understanding of the necessity for order; a strong communal spirit; and a deep attachment to the center of unity, the bishop of Rome.[12] The Anglo-Saxons also brought with them to the continent their particular Christian culture still in the glow and vigor of its youth.[13]

Boniface set out in 723 to resume the mission work in Hessen, founding many monasteries to serve as nurseries of Christian culture, as centers of preparation for the missions, and as training schools for native clergy. Boniface kept in close correspondence with friends in England who supported his work by their prayers as well as by sending him books, church furnishings, vestments, and other necessaries. Moreover, many men and women of excellent education and high ideals came out of the English monasteries to take part in the missionary work. Boniface also founded monasteries for the nuns. Leoba presided over the one at Tauberbischofsheim, the central monastery for the missionaries newly arrived from England where they received their training in local customs and beliefs. From there, monasteries were founded in Kitzingen and Ochsenfurt (where Thecla was abbess), and in 751–752 the double monastery at Heidenheim near Eichstätt was founded.

The Anglo-Saxon missionaries experienced greater success than their Celtic or Frankish predecessors, both for cultural as well as political reasons.[14] The pagan Germans expressed their beliefs less by personal devotion, as the Celtic missionaries tended to do, than by collective communal celebrations. These celebrations took place in areas considered sacred, such as enclaves which were separated from the general world by forests, trees, and fountains. This cultural preference was fertile ground for the missionary monks and nuns whose communal ways of living and worshipping, in some ways already shared and honored by the Germans, provided pre-existing common practices guiding them in their relationships with their pagan neighbors.

The evangelization of the Germanic pagan required long and patient labor. Issues were not only cultural and political. The missionaries needed to deal also with an already existing heterodox form of Christianity planted earlier in the Germans' history by a Arian monk named Ulfilas.[15]

The conversion of the leaders of the various German tribes led to the conversion of the people, but the missionaries were unable to make ancient practices totally disappear. Thus arose the problem of the "Germanization of Christianity" about which many historians, especially those in Germany, have debated. Were the Germans converted to Roman Christianity, or did they retain the features of their old religious culture? Did the encounter of the two religions take place without one contaminating the other? These questions are still widely discussed and debated. For our purposes let it suffice to say that Walburga and her companions found a people still very pagan, yet not without some knowledge of the Christian God.

To evaluate the influence of both the Anglo-Saxon and the Germanic temper on Christian spirituality, we need to recall that the missionaries had agreed to the preservation of ancient customs. Without doubt Boniface and his co-workers fought fiercely against idolatry and destroyed or refashioned the various pagan shrines they found on their journeys. Yet they respected the localization of the cult and even certain rites. Pope Gregory the Great urged the Roman missionaries who were sent to England not to destroy the temples but to empty them of idols and to institute other solemnities to take the place of pagan feasts, for "it is undoubtedly impossible to suppress everything at once in hearts so uncouth; whoever wishes to climb a mountain only succeeds by advancing step by step and not in leaps and bounds."[16] In contrast to the methods of Charlemagne who forced his subjects into Christianity, the Anglo-Saxons adopted a policy of persuasion. Walburga and Leoba's enduring reputation as gentle and kindly women—an impression left in the minds and folk legends of the people—bears witness to the practical success of this "missionary persuasion" and its lasting, favorable effects.

Walburga and her companions likely perceived that both the Germans and Celts held similar views about women. Both societies held women in high regard, and in both, women had important roles in their religious customs and beliefs. Many abbesses and nuns living in the monasteries in the seventh and eighth centuries were venerated as saints both during their lifetime and after death. Perhaps more than in any other country, the sanctity of women occupied a great place in Germanic devotion.[17]

Walburga and her brothers were highly respected in Germany because of their royal lineage. To the Germans, the king was the proprietor of the sacred *(heilig)*, and it was understood that the king would exercise his magical power for the good of the tribe. To the German, the king represented God on earth, and his place of residence was described as one would describe heaven or paradise. Unlike the Celt, the German man was primarily a warrior; from the day he was born he was a trustee of power. Together with his companions, the *bersekir*, he put all his energy into achieving victory. He would kill to avenge himself of wrongs and preserve his dignity, considering vengeance a sacred right and duty. The German was also closely bound to his family. If excluded from this extended family, he was desacralized, became an outcast, and was left to perish alone in the wilderness—a cruel fate.

The Germans also had a great reverence for the Chair of Peter and the Prince of the Apostles from the beginning of the seventh century. The Germans saw St. Peter as the doorkeeper of heaven and the one who would lead them into paradise.[18] Together with Peter, other saints were venerated, generally those of royal descent whose relics were objects of both cult and "translation," the processional movement of their earthly remains to a more fitting and accessible location, usually churches and monasteries. To the German, the relics of the saints promised success and prosperity; and a country as newly converted to Christianity as Saxony could only progress spiritually and materially by possessing as many saintly relics as possible.

The more saints of whom a town could boast, the more powerful its influence and prestige among its neighbors.[19] Into such a world Walburga entered about the year 740, laboring together with Leoba and Thecla and their companion monks and nuns.

Walburga, it is believed, spent some time with Leoba in Taubersbischofsheim learning the necessary skills and languages to serve her on the missions. After these initial introductions, the missionaries were sent out in groups to various smaller mission outposts or to begin new foundations in hitherto uninhabited places. Life obviously was much different from what the English nuns were accustomed to in Wimborne, yet Walburga seems to have adapted well because nowhere is it recorded that the hardships of the missions were considered too overwhelming for anyone. Nor does anyone seem to have turned back and abandoned the mission frontier for the quieter, more settled, and perhaps more predictable life of Wimborne or any other English monastery. At least such accounts do not exist.

After the arrival of the Wimborne missionaries near the present-day city of Antwerp, the nuns traveled about three weeks by oxcart, on foot, and in small rafts down the rivers until they reached Thuringia. Walburga and her companions then separated into groups, each going to one of the three already existing monasteries founded by Saint Leoba. As monastic missionary training centers, they were designed to help the new arrivals adjust to the new land and customs, as well as to learn local dialects and without doubt the religious practices and Arian influences on Christianity in the area. Walburga went to Taubersbischofsheim where both Leoba and Thecla resided and remained there for the next year or two.

The life of Leoba gives us a relatively clear picture of what mission life was like for both the monks and nuns in Germany in the eighth century. We also learn that after Walburga set out on her own with some companions for a new mission station, she kept in contact with her friends and relatives— Leoba and Thecla.

Leoba's biographer informs us that the selection of a suitable location for a new mission monastery was always made with great care, requiring time, patience, and careful planning, and was accomplished only at the expense of many difficulties. The first settlements by the Anglo-Saxon missionaries were poor, straw-thatched huts located near rivers or streams. Monks and nuns worked together in these ventures as they were accustomed to do in the English double-monasteries. Together the monks and nuns worked to build their monasteries, churches, and schools, and began cultivating the land for their own needs. The missionaries not only worked to provide food and clothing for the native population in need, but also prepared and dispensed medicines, and offered education in arts and crafts as well as in reading and other fundamental skills. They also maintained hospitals and inns for travelers and guests.

These hostels or inns played an important role in the life of the Benedictine missionaries of the eighth century. In these inns missionaries, messengers, pilgrims, and wanderers not only found food and shelter for the night, but also took advantage of the exchange of information and knowledge. This practice of Benedictine hospitality also made possible the exchange of gifts and letters between missionaries, which was an invaluable source of mutual encouragement and instruction.

The nearness of Walburga to her two brothers after so long an absence must have been a source of great joy for the three siblings. Huceburc wrote that the exchange of conversation between the brothers and their sister was frequent and full of mutual devotion and pious fervor. Since the monasteries of Wunibald and Walburga were in proximity to one another, it is not surprising that when word reached Walburga that Wunibald lay dying in his abbey in Heidenheim, she was at his bedside almost immediately. According to Huceburc, Wunibald was never strong or robust physically, and the seven years spent in the primitive, missionary environment, coupled with ceaseless labor and austerities, exhausted what little strength Wunibald possessed. Both Walburga and their eldest brother Willibald were at Wunibald's deathbed and remained with him until he died. Walburga, as a member of the deceased abbot's family, then inherited the monastery at Heidenheim in accord with existing Frankish feudal law and became its first and apparently only abbess.[20]

Wunibald died on December 19, 781, and a few days later Walburga moved into the abbey. She brought with her many Anglo-Saxon nuns, among whom was their biographer, Huceburc. From this moment until her death, Walburga was considered the undisputed head of the now newly established double monastery of Heidenheim, and we can suppose Walburga patterned the abbey after what she had known in England and what had become expedient in the new mission land of Germany.[21]

Walburga's monastery seems to have flourished quickly; Wolfhard writes, "She [Walburga] gathered as soon as possible nuns consecrated to Christ"[22] and accepted into her community native girls, educating them as she and her nuns had been educated in England.

Walburga spent twenty years at Heidenheim, not only directing the work of the monastery, but also feeding the poor and caring for the sick with her own hands. She had the monastery built and enlarged to suit what she believed were the purposes of her mission.

Judging from the writings of Huceburc, a nun distinguished as the first historian of Germany, we can presume that in Walburga's monastery there existed a high and lofty atmosphere where true joy was combined with the conscientious and strict observance of the Rule of St. Benedict, great ascetical renunciation, and a remarkable desire—so strong in these early Benedictines—for learning and creativity. It seems Walburga was very broad-minded and a generous superior giving to the youngest member of her community, namely Huceburc, the challenge to develop her literary talents in spite of what Huceburc hints at as "the jealous reproaches of certain people."[23]

MIRACLE ACCOUNTS

Miraculous interventions by Walburga on behalf of her companions as well as for those whose life she came to convert to Christ provide us with some hints about her personality. These fantastic tales and legends shed light on the type of character she must have possessed and on her determination not only to trust in God to a heroic degree, but also to act on that trust. Whether the miracles attributed to Walburga are historical fact or pious legend can never be proved. The historical truth of the events is actually beside the point. What remains without question is the memory of a woman with outstanding character and unique sanctity. Varied accounts of courage and prudent, decisive action reach us about the nun Walburga after she leaves the enclosure of Wimborne for the open and unsettled territory of Germany.

Walburga's miracles were recorded and compiled by her biographer Wolfhard—a priest commissioned by Bishop Erchanbold to write down whatever he could learn about Walburga even though she had been dead for over a hundred years.[24]

Walburga's love of the poor and suffering drew many of them to her monastery where they received medicinal remedies, food, and clothing. From the manner in which Walburga's memory survived, she was also a source of Christian consolation, making all those who came to her monastery feel as St. Benedict advises, "as if they were Christ himself."[25] Walburga's charity, however, also moved her to actions that arouse our attention and questions, living as we do in a period after the development of canon law and the rules of monastic enclosure. In Wolfhard's account, Walburga kept vigil one night by the bedside of a dying girl. Fearlessly, she left her monastery at night, apparently alone, and set out for the home of the dying girl. On the way, wild dogs (wolves?) came to attack her, but she, trusting in God, was able to quiet them and make her way safely to the girl's home. Walburga watched at the patient's bedside throughout the night, and in the morning the daughter was restored to her parents in full health and vigor. They naturally attributed the remarkable recovery to a miraculous intercession by Walburga. The family offered Walburga presents, but she refused them and referred the miracle to God alone. Walburga returned to her monastery the way she came, alone.[26] This episode is an interesting indication of the character and spirit of Walburga for two major reasons. First, we know from the life of Leoba that the observance of enclosure in the English monasteries of this time was very strict.[27] Yet Walburga seems to have preferred the "spirit" to the "letter" of the Rule, which meant the preservation of charity and the furtherance of the kingdom of God. Perhaps in the monasteries of England during the golden era of Christianity, the people were converted enough to come to the monastery for help and instruction. In a still-pagan or at best an Arian land, there would be few if any "converted" people coming to the monastery; being "impelled by the Gospel of Christ," the missionaries were obliged to go to the people.

The second question would follow the first. Since the nuns were in mission territory, their rules of enclosure were obviously relaxed, making such "charity missions" not only feasible, but expected. Yet there seems to be no mention of an official relaxation of rules by any ecclesiastical or ab-batial authority of any kind in any of the accounts of early Benedictine women. Perhaps the most probable conclusion is that these early monks and nuns made their foundations and lived their monastic lives in the "spirit of the Gospel," long before canon law would regulate so much of monastic observance. Their models in both monastic observance and Christian living were the Desert Fathers and Mothers, many of whom left their self-imposed solitudes and enclosures to take part in councils and theological disputes, as well as to care for their neighbors. St. Benedict ad-monished the desert monk he found chained to a rock in a cave to unchain himself from his self-imposed bondage and bind himself instead to Christ.[28] Obviously, enclosure was considered a privilege and a means, not an end in itself. The monastery was meant to foster a spirit of prayer and recollection, and as we know from the life of Leoba, of study as well.

One other miracle account gives us yet another hint at the personality and free character of Walburga. She appears to have been not only coura-geous, pious, and intelligent, but also very self-possessed and sincerely humble. Perhaps the most insightful and provocative account of a miracle attributed to Walburga during her lifetime is the incident recorded by Wolfhard as "the Miracle of Light." On one occasion, Walburga remained in the chapel for some time after the Night Office, and when she went to retire, she found the hallways dark. She went to the night porter, a monk named Goumeraurd, and asked him to light a torch for her so she could find her way through the darkened passageways. He apparently refused her request rather rudely, obliging Walburga to grope her way to the dor-mitory in the dark. She did not become angry, but having made her way, finally, to the dormitory, she knelt in the center of the room and implored her nuns to pray "for our brother Goumeraurd." She then began her own prayer. Immediately, Wolfhard writes, the entire house was filled with a "light so bright and wonderful that its origin had to be from heaven."[29] Goumeraurd then felt the movements of grace, and finding his way to the dormitory, he knelt outside the door, publicly imploring pardon from Abbess Walburga. According to the account, the "light" continued to brighten the monastery until the morning office of Matins.

What can we conclude about Walburga from the brief, sparse accounts of her life? Wolfhard writes of Walburga's great, motherly solicitude for the nuns entrusted to her care, of her modesty, gentle spirit, heroic trust in God, and her readiness and willingness to suffer and endure any and all things for the glory of God and the furthering of his kingdom on earth. Walburga had the reputation of being a bearer of light and a liberator from distress until her last breath. She died on February 25, 779, and was buried in the floor of the abbey church in Heidenheim. One hundred years later, her remains were transferred to Eichstätt and placed in the altar of the "Little Church of the Holy Cross" just outside the city. They remain there to this day.

Posthumous miracles have occurred at the tomb of Walburga continuously since her death. As one of the most famous myroblytes, or oil-producing saints, Walburga continues to cure the afflicted more than a thousand years after her death with a non-aromatic fluid that flows from the stone on which her relics rest. This phenomenon recurs yearly from the date commemorating the translation of her relics to Eichstätt on September 8 through the anniversary date of her death and feast celebrated on February 25. Hundreds of miraculous cures were reported from the oily substance found on her bones at the time of her translation.

Significance

Walburga lived in a time when it would have been considered not only inconceivable, but heretical to consider Church and state separate. Born into noble surroundings, she chose the life of a nun as the way to God's Will. She lived in the shelter of a famous, well-established, highly developed, English monastery for most of her early life and was surrounded by noble and loving sisters. Joyfully she abandoned this security to build a kingdom for Christ in Germany, laboring alongside her brothers and sisters under primitive, often dangerous, and always difficult conditions. As a missionary to the Germanic people, she valued charity above all other virtues, and while accomplishing great things by the power of God, she managed to remain in the background unlike her more famous relatives and companions.

Her life reveals a spirit of dedication, of humility, of love, and of piety; yet the constant theme throughout her life is that of a spirit of freedom. Walburga was a "free woman" in the sense of the Apostle Paul, and her gift to others during her life and throughout the centuries has been the gift of freedom. In the legends told about her, Walburga is remembered not only as a holy nun, abbess, and missionary, but as a true disciple of Christ in whom the Spirit of God lived and moved with freedom.

Walburga of Heidenheim can teach us how to be faithful daughters and sons of our Heavenly Father, dedicated and heroic disciples of Christ his only-begotten Son, and missionary instruments of his Holy Spirit. She can also show us how to be true followers of St. Benedict, free men and women who seek not only to live entirely and exclusively for the kingdom of God, but also to share the freedom brought to us in Christ, be that freedom from illness, sin, weakness, or freedom for the prompting of the Holy Spirit and the building up of the kingdom of God.

The symbol of ears of corn with which Walburga is sometimes associated iconographically seems to have been borrowed, along with other details, from an earlier fertility cult—that of Walborg or Walpurg, the Germanic earth goddess.[30] The more enduring and authentic iconography of St. Walburga shows her with a small phial of oil and a copy of the gospels. She is also often shown with the abbatial staff.

What can Walburga teach us? Perhaps what Jesus meant when he said, "One thing only is necessary." Everything else follows.

NOTES

1. Huceburc of Heidenheim, *Vita Wynnibaldi Abbatis Heidenheimensis,* 108, 35, and the *Vita Willibaldi episcopi Eichstetensis* 1, 88.2–5. Andreas Bauch, *Quellen zur Geschichte der Diözese Eichstätt, Band 1, Biographien der Gründungszeit* (Regensburg: Verlag Friedrich Pustet, 1984).

2. Harnack, A.V., "Legenden als Geschichtsquellen," in *Reden und Aufsätze I,* Gießen 1904, 1-26, bes. 25.

3. See Bede, "Synod of Whitby," *History of the English Church and People* (London, England: Penguin Books, 1968) 187. This synod was held at the monastery by invitation of Hilda, who may have taken part in its proceedings.

4. Bonnie S. Anderson and Judith P. Zinsser, "Authority Within the Institutional Church," *A History of Their Own; Women in Europe from Prehistory to the Present,* vol. 1. (New York: Harper and Row Publishers, 1988) 185. St. Hilda (616–680), the grandniece of the seventh-century English king, Edwin of Northumbria, founded one such monastery and supervised two other monasteries in the course of her life. She made Whitby into a center of learning. Five of her community became bishops.

5. Ibid., 184.

6. Pierre Riche, "Spirituality in Celtic and Germanic Society," *Christian Spirituality, Origins to the Twelfth Century,* ed. by Bernard McGinn, John Mayendorff, and Jean Leclerq (New York: Crossroad, 1988) 163. The Celt was known as the religious person *par excellence* and lived among gods common to the entire Celtic society. Between the gods and the people were the heroes from whom the princely families were descended. The Celtic king's status approached that of the heroes: he was responsible for the material welfare of the people and

for the balancing of cosmic forces. At his enthronement rites he was invested with magical power conditional upon his moral and physical integrity. If he lost it, he was deposed. His wife played an important role beside him. In Celtic society, the women, whether they were virgins or mothers, had a privileged place which they maintained after that society's conversion to Christianity.

7. See Huceburc, *Vita Willibaldi,* 1. It seems that the only surviving children of Richard and Wuna were Willibald, Wunibald, Walburga, and one younger brother whose name has not been recorded in any surviving manuscript.

8. Elizabeth Alvilda Petroff, "The Life of St. Leoba, by Rudolf, Monk of Fulda," *Medieval Women's Visionary Literature* (New York, Oxford: Oxford University Press, 1986.) 106. Women from Wimborne went with missionaries to the Continent and stayed to administer religious communities and centers of learning established there. It was for the most part within the cloistered walls of the monasteries that women could be free of the intellectual limitations placed on them because of their sex. Being nuns in the cloister, they could then freely enjoy learning opportunities usually reserved for men.

9. Francesca M. Steele, *The Life of Saint Walburga* (St. Louis: B. Herder Book Company 1921) 53. See also Bede, *The History of the English Church and People,* 206, 313, 330. References to the knowledge of Latin and Greek by monks and nuns is peppered throughout Bede's work.

10. Rudolf, monk of Fulda, "Life of Leoba," *The Anglo-Saxon Missionaries in Germany,* trans. and ed. by C. H. Talbot (New York: Sheed & Ward, 1954) 215.

11. This saint is not to be confused with Willibald, the brother of St. Walburga.

12. Dr. Karl Bihlmeyer, revised by Dr. Herman Tuchle, "Anglo-Saxon Missions on the Continent. Willibrord and Boniface. Restoration of the Frankish Church," *Church History, Volume Two: The Middle Ages* (Westminster, Maryland: The Newman Press, 1963) 3–16. Indicative of these attitudes are the writings recording the missionary career of St. Boniface. He was consecrated "missionary bishop" of the Germans east of the Rhine without a fixed see on November 30, 722. On this occasion he took a special oath of obedience to the pope, similar to the oath taken by the bishops of the Roman province. This oath linked him with Rome and obliged him to an exact observance of her ordinances. Like all of his countrymen, Boniface was convinced that close contact with Rome was a necessary condition for the success of the Church in any land, and for the rest of his life he strove with the utmost conscientiousness to conform to Rome's wishes.

13. Ibid., 13.

14. Ibid., 16–17. Politically, the situation caused rival threats and bitter memories. The Saxons were once a very numerous Germanic people that had spread from the Elbe almost to the Rhine and from the Eider to the borders of Thuringia and Hesse. Expansion southward occurred after the extinction of the Thuringian kingdom in 531. The Saxons were bitterly opposed to Christianity, the religion of their political enemies, the Franks.

15. Ibid., 17. The first Germans converted to Christianity were those who made up the eastern group of Goths, Vandals, and Burgundians. By an accident of history they passed from paganism to a heterodox form of Christianity through the Arian monk Ulfilas, who taught the homoian Arianism condemned by the Council of Rimini in 359. Although we know almost nothing about the spirituality of the

Arian Germans, we can say that the strength of Arianism flowed from the national character of this religion. The Arian clergy were strictly submissive to the prince; a liturgy in the Gothic language brought together a faithful who, thanks to the translation provided by Ulfilas, had access directly to the Bible. The Burgundian and Vandal princes were concerned about theological controversies and tried by persuasion and force to convert the orthodox. The majority of their people remained faithful to their traditional beliefs and converted to the Catholic faith only when their leaders agreed to receive Catholic baptism in the sixth and seventh centuries.

16. See Gregory's letter in Bede's *History of the English Church and People,* vol. 1, 30.

17. Bernard McGinn, John Meyendorff, and Jean Leclercq, eds., "Celtic and Germanic Society," *Christian Spirituality* (New York: Crossroads, 1988) 173.

18. Bede, "The Synod of Whitby," *History of the English Church and People,* 192.

19. McGinn, Meyendorff and Leclercq, *Christian Spirituality,* 173.

20. Willibald would not have been eligible to inherit the monastery as he was then bishop of Eichstätt and had a living relative who also happened to be a Benedictine.

21. Andreas Bauch, "Die heilige Äbtissin Walburga," *Bavaria Sancta: Zeugen christlichen Glaubens in Bayern, Band I,* herausgegeben von Georg Schwaiger (Regensburg: Freidrich Pustet, 1970) 171. "Double monasteries at this time formed a strong juridical and domestic bond and unity perhaps never again to be repeated in the history of religious orders in the coming centuries. These double monasteries were generally composed of two distinct parts, that for the nuns and the other for the monks, with the church for common liturgical celebrations located between them. In the case of Walburga's monastery in Heidenheim, reconstructed models of the early, monastic settlements in Eichstätt reveal that the monk's monastery was to the north of the church and the nuns on the south. While sharing liturgical celebrations, the monks and nuns lived in separate houses and had separate refectories. The daily manual labor was shared by the monks and nuns, each doing their part to keep the monastery self-sufficient and organized," (translation is my own).

22. Wolfhard, *Miraculis S. Waldburgis,* 1. De luce coelitus effulgente in diversorio virginum, 539, 37–39. Andreas Bauch, *Quellen zur Geschichte der Diözese Eichstätt, Band I,* 254–257.

23. Huceburc, *Vita Willibaldi* 88.2–5 as interpreted by Andreas Bauch, "Die heilige Äbtissin Walburga," *Bavaria Sancta,* 172.

24. Wolfhard 4, *De translatione S. Walbirgae iussu Otgari episcopi Eystadium peracta,* Lib.I.C.5:MG SS XV.540,48–541:23. Andreas Bauch, *Quellen zur Geschichte der Diözese Eichstätt,* 260–265. The occasion of this commission by Erchanbold was itself indicative of Walburga's character and free spirit. According to the report by Wolfhard, Walburga appeared in a dream to Bishop Otkar of Eichstätt between 870 and 878 complaining in no uncertain terms about the neglect into which her tomb at Heidenheim had fallen over the century. She pointedly told him to tend to the proper care of her earthly remains. Accordingly, the good bishop arranged to have her bones transferred to the diocesan cathedral in

Eichstätt. The original intention was to re-entomb her remains next to her sainted brother Willibald, the first bishop of Eichstätt.

25. Rule of St. Benedict, ch. 53, "On the Reception of Guests."

26. Auctore Presbytero Wolfhardo, Lib. I. C. 3: MG. SS XV, 540, 8–39 *Miraculis S. Waldburgis* 2, "De curatione puellae moribundae."

27. Talbot, "The Life of Leoba," 207.

28. Gregory the Great. *Dialogues, Book Three,* ch. 16, translated by Odo J. Zimmermann, O.S.B., and Benedict R. Avery, O.S.B. (Collegeville: The Liturgical Press, 1949) xi.

29. Wolfhard, *Miraculis S. Waldburgis,* 1. De luce coelitus effulgente in diversorio virginum, 539.50–540.1.

30. Steele, *Life of Saint Walburga,* 151.

6

Leoba:
A Study in Humanity and Holiness

Catherine Wybourne, O.S.B.

Leoba of Bischofsheim[1] was the kind of person with whom one would gladly share eternity, or even a lifetime in community. She was a saint, but not the type whose sanctity makes heroic demands on others. She was ascetic, but she understood the value of an after-dinner nap. She had a gift for friendship and an insight into human nature which enabled her to understand, even if she did not approve, a novice's desire to dance on her novice mistress's grave. Yet, as her contemporaries recognized, there was more to Leoba than an engaging personality. She was learned, with an impressive grasp of Scripture, patristics, and law; she was brave, a pioneer of monastic life for women in Germany; she was an able administrator and a trusted counselor in both Church and court circles. Then as now, her name was linked with that of Boniface with whom, as friend and collaborator, she shared in the achievements of the Anglo-Saxon mission.

It comes as a surprise, therefore, to discover that the most important source for her life, Rudolf of Fulda's *Vita Leobae Abbatissae Biscofesheimensis*, found its way into the *Monumenta Germaniae Historica* series with the editorial disclaimer, "history will not gain much by it."[2] To be fair, Waitz was not interested in nuns, nor in saints as such, and only included the *Vita* because it shed light on Boniface's activities. For the modern reader, the *Vita* provides a glimpse of a woman who would have been remarkable in any age or place but whose gifts of nature and grace came to perfection in a setting at once familiar and remote: the pre-Carolingian monastery. To understand what she accomplished and its significance for later generations, it is necessary to examine not only the story of her life but also the distinctive features of the monasticism which gave it shape and scope.

MATERIALS AND SOURCES

Strictly contemporary sources for Leoba's life are few: a single letter from her to Boniface; a request for prayers from Boniface to Leoba and two companions, with a further businesslike note to her alone; brief references in a handful of letters from various members of their circle; a possible allusion in Willibald's *Vita Bonifatii*; and an entry in the Fulda necrology under the year 780.[3] Much the fullest record comes from Rudolf's *Vita*, completed in 836, nearly sixty years after Leoba's death.[4]

Rudolf was a pupil of Rhabanus Maurus—widely regarded as the most learned man of his day—and a considerable scholar in his own right. His sober narrative style and restrained treatment of the miraculous have commended him to historians. He says that he wrote the *Vita* in obedience to his abbot's command and dedicates it to Hadamout, not yet become abbess, in the hope that she will read it with pleasure and profit. He is refreshingly frank about his method and its limitations, admitting that he has not been able to find out everything. What he does record is based on the recollections of "venerable men who heard them from four of her disciples, Agatha, Thecla, Nana and Eoloba," and in particular, on notes made by the priest Mago, who had died five years previously without beginning his projected account of her life. Some things Rudolf can vouch for himself, notably two miracles at Leoba's tomb, and these he includes.[5] What he does not say is that he is writing in a well-defined hagiographical style intended to demonstrate Leoba's importance as spiritual patron and intercessor, as well as her more obvious role as exemplar of monastic holiness. In the process he reflects glory on his own monastery, which happily possessed the relics of both Leoba and Boniface.

Good hagiography is not necessarily bad history, nor is a consciously literary style evidence of distortion or falsification, but they do indicate that not every statement can be accepted at face-value. Rudolf writes with the preoccupations and presuppositions of a ninth-century monk, and it is worth considering how they affect the presentation of his material before examining the content of the *Vita* in detail.

Just as Willibald presents Boniface in heroic mode as another Paul, so Rudolf presents Leoba as another (but lesser) Boniface. Like Willibald, he omits much that we would like to know and leaves his chronology vague. Again like Willibald, he incorporates the work of others. The text reveals traces of several famous *Vitae*: Athanasius's Life of Anthony, Jerome's Life of Hilarion, Paulinus's Life of Ambrose, Constantius's Life of Germanus of Auxerre, the *Actus Silvestri*, and, most tellingly of all, Gregory's *Dialogues*.[6] Reference to Scholastica apart, all his borrowings are from *male* Lives. Tempting though it may be to wonder whether Rudolf secretly wished that Leoba could be more like a man, his borrowings often have little connection with his subject. All we can safely deduce from them concerns his preferred reading in the library at Fulda. More noteworthy is the way in which he tries to show that Leoba's life, and the monasticism in which she was trained, conformed to the Benedictine pattern of his own day. Sometimes this takes the form of "coloring" his history so that, for example, enclosure at Wimborne and perhaps Fulda, corresponds to ninth-century ideas on the subject. More often it is done through delicate allusions and analogy. Particularly striking is the way in which Rudolf treats Leoba and Boniface as a latter-day Scholastica and Benedict.

Leoba and Boniface regarded their friendship as perfectly natural; Rudolf sometimes gives the impression of being embarrassed by it. When describing Leoba's early life at Wimborne, he is at pains to assure us that the nuns had no dealings with men. He spiritualizes the relationship between her and Boniface, asserting that the latter "loved her not so much for her kinship with him on her mother's side as for her holiness of life and wise teaching."[7] It must be remembered that Rudolf was writing at a time when women no longer enjoyed the freedom or status of earlier centuries. Carolingian reform legislation, in particular, had assigned a much more circumscribed role to religious women than had been the case in Leoba's day.[8] A friendship so open to misunderstanding had to be interpreted and evaluated according to a safe role model, and what safer model could be found than that of Benedict and Scholastica? Boniface had been instrumental in establishing the *Rule of St Benedict* as the norm in monasteries throughout Germany. He was, therefore, the champion of the current orthodoxy: to link him and Leoba with Benedict and Scholastica was to disarm possible criticism by underlining the impeccably Benedictine character of Rudolf's subject. The Leoba/Scholastica parallel is not exact, but it constitutes a fascinating subtext with a genuine insight into the creative energy of monastic friendship placed at the service of the Church.

THE ENGLISH YEARS: C. 700–C. 748

Of Leoba's early years we know as little as we do of Boniface's. She was born near the beginning of the eighth century, certainly no later than 710, to English parents, Dynno and Ebbe. They were probably, as Rudolf says, of noble stock as were Boniface's parents. Her place of birth is unknown but was probably in the southwest of England. She was related to Boniface on her mother's side, and her father was among his friends. Everything we know about Boniface himself points to a West Saxon origin.[9] Hers was no ordinary birth, for her parents had given up all hope of offspring when Ebbe had a dream in which she saw herself holding a great church bell "which rang merrily." The symbolism was clear, the Scripture parallel plain: here was another Samuel who would do great things. An old nurse correctly interpreted the dream as signifying the birth of a daughter who was to be consecrated to God. This child was Thrutgeba, also called Leoba because she was "greatly loved."

Leoba's education was thorough, but it is impossible to determine where she received it. Rudolf remarks that she was an adult when she was handed over to Tetta, abbess of the renowned double monastery at Wimborne, but he may mean only that in her teens she was formally received into the community where she had been living since childhood. He definitely implies that the initial decision was made by her parents, which would not be surprising at a time when child oblation was common, especially in the case of girls; but Leoba herself must have ratified the choice later by profession. Some have suggested that she was educated at Minster in Thanet before becoming a nun at Wimborne, but the evidence is slight.[10] Since Leoba's family connections were concentrated in the southwest, it is arguable that any visits to Minster belong to a later stage in her monastic life.

Wimborne, as Rudolf describes it, is the perfect Carolingian nunnery, with an enclosure so entire it calls to mind the "glorious prison" of Marcigny in a later age. "The discipline there was much stricter than anywhere else," he remarks approvingly. The sexes were segregated behind high walls, with no clerics ever entering the nuns' part of the monastery except to celebrate Mass—a veto that extended even to bishops. The abbess directed the business of the house through a window, while the nuns themselves never went out, except for "a reasonable cause or because it would be of great advantage to the monastery."[11] It is clear that the abbess, rather than the bishop, decided these matters, but how trustworthy is Rudolf's description? Elsewhere, "a reasonable cause" was very liberally interpreted, and nuns were to be found away from home inspecting estates, attending synods, or going on pilgrimage. No one seems to have thought it odd, nor did their meeting monks and clerics often lead to scandal, although ecclesiastics sometimes worried that it might. According to Willibald, nuns as well as monks attended Boniface's lectures at Nursling.[12] Leoba may have been one of them since Wimborne is not far from Nursling, and the only surviving letter from her to Boniface reads as though there had been direct contact between them. At some stage as already mentioned, she may have spent time further away at Minster in Thanet, learning to write verses in the manner of Aldhelm. If so, Rudolf may not have known or may have deliberately suppressed the information because it was difficult to reconcile with his interpretation of life at Wimborne.

Despite Rudolf's assertion that the monastery was an old foundation, Wimborne was of comparatively recent origin, having been established early in the eighth century by Cuthburg, sister of Ine of Wessex. It was, therefore, still in its first vigor when Leoba entered. Rudolf mentions that the community at that time numbered about fifty, and he implies that the Benedictine Rule was followed. He says a great deal about the holiness of Tetta, the abbess, but makes no comment on the monastery's economic or political situation, not even to tell us that most of its members came from noble families. He says nothing about liturgy or the usual concerns of modern Benedictines except to remark that in time of need the Office was celebrated elsewhere than in church. A few letters in Boniface's collection enable us to conclude that the general level of learning and culture was high and that the house enjoyed an excellent reputation. Enclosure apart, Wimborne does not appear to differ markedly from other double monasteries of the time. What is remarkable is the role Wimborne was to play in the Anglo-Saxon mission, and that was largely the result of the friendship between Leoba and Boniface.[13]

It was while she was a young nun at Wimborne, sometime between 725 and 732, that Leoba sent her kinsman the only extant personal record of their friendship, a letter as poignant as it is graceful:

> To her most revered and dear Lord in Christ, her kinsman Boniface . . . Leobgytha, least of those who bear the light yoke of Christ, greeting: I beg you, of your kindness, to remember the friendship you once had in the West Country with my father, Dynno, who died eight years ago. Please would you pray for his soul and remember in prayer my mother Ebbe, your kinswoman, who is still alive but ailing? I am their only daughter. Oh, if only I might call you my brother, for there is no one living whom I trust and depend upon as I do you! I have sent you this little present, a trifling and unworthy thing, so that you may not forget my humble self now that you are so far away . . . . Dear brother, please shield me with your prayers from the darts of the enemy. And please would you correct the unpolished style of this letter and send me a few words of your own as an example? I long to hear from you.[14]

She concludes with some dutiful lines in praise of the Trinity which she asks Boniface to correct. In this letter we catch a glimpse of the weakening of the old kinship structures, and the special vulnerability of women without close protectors. Another letter from Denehard, Lull, and Burchard to Cuniburg shows that it was not only women who experienced a sense of loss and dependence.[15] In different degree, men too sought protection from standing alone without kith and kin. Boniface's circle of friends and helpers in Germany was very like the *comitatus* gathered round a secular lord, and the two letters support the idea of a complex web of relationships and dependencies existing alongside the formal structures of Anglo-Saxon monasticism.[16]

In later years, Leoba loved to recall incidents in her life at Wimborne. The story about the overly strict disciplinarian is given a pious gloss, but there is a sympathy and humor about the telling of it which suggest that it was a favourite anecdote. One of the nuns was virtuous but excessively severe. When she died, those who had suffered from her zeal vented their wrath by stamping on her grave and uttering curses. Tetta went to investigate this breach of monastic decorum and was shocked to discover that the level of the grave had sunk by about six inches. She interpreted this as divine judgment on the dead nun's harshness and reproached the younger nuns for their hardness of heart and unforgiving tempers. To put matters right, they devoted themselves to prayer and fasting for three days, at the end of which the grave returned to its normal condition. Clearly, feelings could run high at Wimborne, and there were no inhibitions about expressing them.[17] From this period also comes the charming story of the sacristan's lost keys which were eventually recovered from the mouth of a little fox, symbol of the devil himself. Both stories are used to illustrate the power of prayer, not only in Tetta, the holy abbess, but also in the community as a whole.

Leoba is, of course, the outstanding member of the community, and Rudolf's summing up of her fully merits Delehaye's despairing comment on this style of writing: "You ask for a portrait and you receive a programme."[18] The list of her monastic attainments and virtues is breathtaking. Like Boniface, she had a special love of Scripture, preferring to read and meditate on the Word of God above all other occupations:

> She had no interests apart from the monastery and the pursuit of sacred learning. She derived no pleasure from frivolous jests and wasted no time on girlish tales. . . . She committed to memory whatever she heard or read, and put it all into practice. . . . She was sparing in her use of food and drink and spurned dainty dishes. . . . She prayed continually. When she was not reading, she worked with her hands at whatever task she was given, having learned that anyone who does not work should not eat. She gave more time to reading and listening to Sacred Scripture than to manual labour, however. . . . She lived her life in such a way that she was loved with a pure affection by all the sisters. She learned from all and obeyed all, and strove to imitate and make her own the special gifts of each one. . . . Above all, she concentrated on the practice of charity, without which, as she knew, all other virtues are nothing.[19]

Does Rudolf make her just a little too good to be true, even for a novice mistress?

By the standards of her day, Leoba was already middle-aged, with many years' experience of monastic life, when the call to Germany came. It was prefigured by a dream in which she saw a purple thread issuing from her mouth and being gathered into a ball. The interpretation of the dream given by an old nun at Wimborne calls to mind Gregory the Great's conception of the relationship between contemplation and action, a conception which was to exert powerful influence on the monks and nuns of the Anglo-Saxon mission: "The ball she made by rolling the thread round and round signifies the mystery of the divine word which . . . turns earthwards through the active life and heavenwards through contemplation, now swinging downwards through compassion for one's neighbour, now springing upwards through love of God. By these signs God shows that your mistress [Leoba] will benefit many by her teaching and example, the results of which will be experienced in the far-off lands to which she must go."[20]

THE GERMAN YEARS: C. 748–C. 780

Historians have long acknowledged the prominent place of monasticism in the Anglo-Saxon mission. It is usually taken for granted that Benedictine monasticism is implied, but recent studies have shown that other influences were at work until quite late.[21] Boniface's commitment to the *Rule of St Benedict* is still something of a mystery. Levison simply assumed that he was "trained in the spirit of St Benedict" at Exeter and Nursling.[22] Yet the admission procedure at Exeter corresponds to that of Columbanus rather than of Benedict,[23] while Boniface's behaviour as a young priest at Nursling suggests that he retained some private funds, which would hardly have been the case had Benedict's Rule been observed in every detail. At least one of his monasteries in Germany, Fritzlar, had some un-Benedictine organizational features, and much has been made of his lifelong temperance, as though he were influenced by Irish ascetical ideas.[24] In fact, Boniface did not have much time for the Irish, especially not Irish bishops; but he appreciated the usefulness of monasteries as a scholarly backing to his missionary efforts. The synods of 742 and 743 recommended the use of the Benedictine Rule. Boniface became its advocate and doubtless intended Fulda to demonstrate what a Benedictine monastery should be. Soon after its foundation, an appeal to Abbess Tetta brought the first English nuns to Germany to contribute their share to the work of Benedictine transformation.

If, as generally assumed, all thirty nuns in that first group came from Wimborne, the home community must have been seriously depleted. Rudolf admits that Tetta was not overly pleased to receive Boniface's request, but it says much for the generosity and fervor of her community that the nuns were allowed to go. The names of some of the group are familiar: Cunihild and her daughter Bergit, who went to Thuringia; Cunitrude, who went to Bavaria; Walburga, later abbess of Heidenheim; Thecla, another kinswoman of Boniface, who went to Kitzingen and Ochsenfurt; and Leoba herself. A letter written by the priest Wiehtberht to the monks of Glastonbury, with the request that they forward it to Wimborne, speaks of his party having arrived safely and been well received by Boniface, but it is not certain that the nuns traveled with him.[25] Even the date of their arrival in Germany is a matter of conjecture. Rudolf links their coming to the sending of Sturm to Monte Cassino. Sturm was at Fulda in 745 but is known to have been in Italy by 748 and was still there in 749, so the nuns could have traveled anytime after 746. Contrary to C. H. Talbot's reading of the *Vita*, there are no grounds for thinking that Leoba was sent to undertake a second novitiate in Italy. Boniface simply asked Tetta to let Leoba join him as a comfort to him in his exile and the mission entrusted to him.[26]

Rudolf says that Leoba was given charge of "the monastery at a place called Bischofsheim, where there was a large community of handmaids of God." Does he mean that Leoba assumed direction of an established monastery, possibly linked to one of the communities in Gaul, or that she undertook the monastic formation of a group of completely inexperienced women gathered together by Boniface? He gives no indication that the monastery was a double monastery in the strict sense, although the name Bischofsheim (bishop's house) suggests that it was close to a clerical centre, in all likelihood a former residence of Boniface himself. Rudolf's main concern is to record the scale of Leoba's influence: "[The nuns] were trained after the example of their blessed teacher in the discipline of monastic life and drew so much good from her teaching that many of them became teachers themselves. Consequently, there was scarcely a monastery of women in those parts that lacked instruction from her disciples."[27] Bischofsheim was henceforth to enjoy special eminence as head of a loose confederation of monasteries.

The monasticism that Leoba took with her to Germany retained many of its Anglo-Saxon characteristics, at least during her lifetime. There was, first of all, the concern for sound learning. Leoba herself was an assiduous reader. Even when she was resting, the younger nuns were called upon to read the Scriptures to her, and woe betide anyone who made a mistake while she thought the abbess slept.[28] It is no exaggeration to say that, for Leoba, monastic life was pre-eminently the practice of *lectio divina*, that slow, prayerful absorption in the Word of God which encompassed the various duties of every day. There was the same common-sense approach to enclosure. Rudolf mentions nuns being away from the monastery for various reasons. Leoba's first miracle on German soil saw the whole village gathered together in the monastery church to witness the spectacular vindication of one who had been visiting her family. It would have been impossible for Leoba to build up the German monasteries had she been always at Bischofsheim. She is known to have visited Boniface and Lull and was the friend and confidante of Charlemagne's wife, Hildegard. In later years she sometimes went to pray at Fulda, a practice which recalls the Anglo-Saxon fondness for pilgrimages.[29]

It is more difficult to assess the liturgical and devotional temper of Bischofsheim. There was a typically Anglo-Saxon love of processions, of eloquent movements and gestures in prayer. There was the same readiness to fast and keep vigil, especially in times of danger. The Psalter was the best-loved prayer book, but there are echoes of the Marian devotion popularized by Aldhelm and found in a number of prayer collections, notably the Book of Cerne. On one occasion, Leoba stills a storm by invoking the Blessed Virgin Mary. It was, admittedly, a Marian devotion much less exuberant in expression than that found in some of the prayers deriving from Spain or Syria. Liturgical calendars from Regensburg and Fulda contain the names of Campanian saints, showing that the southern Italian influence on Anglo-Saxon worship continued in Germany. Pope Zacharias sometimes found it necessary to warn Boniface against accepting Gallican excesses, but not being clerics, Leoba's nuns are unlikely to have been touched by them.[30] Indeed, what we know of Anglo-Saxon "Gregorianism" suggests that Bischofsheim was neither more nor less "Roman" than any of the monasteries in England.

Perhaps the closest point of contact with the monasticism left behind in England was the apparent need for patronage. Rudolf makes much of Leoba's popularity with kings and princes, her good relations with bishops; but he leaves us in no doubt about the necessity of their good will. It was not so much a question of being dependent on the largesse of others for financial security—Rudolf makes no comment about the economic situation of Leoba's community beyond remarking that Charlemagne "loaded her with gifts," which was only to be expected of one in his position—as of receiving mutual support and recognition. The progress of the mission was not uniformly successful. Many areas remained half-pagan or heterodox for a long time.[31] In such circumstances, proximity to the powerful, whether prince or bishop, could be advantageous. Two of Leoba's disciples mentioned by name were obviously from local families. But it takes time for a monastery to become truly "naturalized," and there are hints that it was a struggle. Twice, Rudolf refers to Leoba's fixity of purpose, her deliberate turning her back on her native land and her kinsfolk: once when she was newly arrived in Germany and again when she met Boniface for the last time and he urged her never to abandon the land of her adoption or the task she had undertaken. The temptation must have been real.[32]

Some of Rudolf's miracle stories cast interesting sidelights on Leoba's character and the kind of problems she faced during the early years at Bischofsheim. The local populace was initially hostile but was eventually won over by her level-headed manner and Scholastica-like mastery over the elements. Her imperturbability and power rested on prayer and the use of sacramentals such as salt blessed by Boniface. As portrayed by Rudolf, Leoba's ability to cope with difficult situations was a measure of the extent to which she had realized her monastic vocation.[33]

Relations with her own community were warm and friendly. Rudolf's portrait of Leoba as abbess contains just as many stereotyped images as his portrait of her as an ordinary nun, but it does convey the impression of a real human being, and a very attractive one:

> She was a woman of outstanding virtue . . . and devoted all her powers to the work she had undertaken, that she might appear blameless before God and be a pattern of perfection to all who obeyed her. . . . She always took care not to teach others what she did not practise herself. . . . There was no pride or arrogance in her behaviour, no favouritism: she was affable and pleasant to all. . . . Always smiling and cheerful, she never broke out into unrestrained laughter. No one ever heard a bad word from her lips; the sun never set upon her anger. She always showed the utmost consideration for others in matters of food and drink . . . always practised the greatest discretion in her arrangements . . . never overdid watching or other spiritual exercises. Throughout the summer she and all the sisters under her used to take a rest after the midday meal, and she would never allow any of them to stay up late, for she used to say that lack of sleep dulled the mind, especially for reading.[34]

She was beautiful to look at, hospitable, approachable. The only quality that seems to be lacking is a musical voice, but doubtless that was an oversight on Rudolf's part.

Leoba's nickname in community, *Dilecta* or Beloved, shows that as abbess she had learned the difficult art of making herself loved rather than feared. One of the miracles in the *Vita* illustrates her compassion as superior by drawing on mother-child-feeding analogies. A nun called Williswind falls ill, and her malady increases to the point where she has to be sent back to her parents. Leoba visits her and restores her to health by feeding her milk from a little spoon which she herself ordinarily used. As Peter Brown has shown, such healing miracles are typical of the saint who is perceived as a spiritual patron rather than as a wonder-worker. Indeed, it is a striking feature of all the miracles Rudolf recounts that they are firmly anchored in experience of the natural order, into which divine grace has flowed through the holiness of Leoba.[35] Not surprisingly, the two miracles for which Rudolf himself vouches are similarly miracles of healing and reintegration. A pilgrim's fetters fall from him as he prays at Leoba's tomb, and another with some kind of palsy is cured after falling asleep and having a vision of being healed through the ministry of a "venerable old man wearing a bishop's robe and a young woman clothed in a nun's habit," obviously Boniface and Leoba. By the time that Rudolf wrote, Leoba and Boniface were being perceived according to the expected ideas about male and female saints: the bishop is "venerable," the nun somewhat incongruously "young."[36]

In 757, just before he set out for Frisia and martyrdom, Boniface and Leoba met for the last time. Not even the earnest exhortation Rudolf puts on the lips of Boniface can quite destroy the tenderness of the scene as Boniface hands his cowl to Leoba and charges her to continue the work they had begun. The Elijah—Elisha parallel springs to mind, as it is probably meant to do. So strong was the sense of a common purpose that it overrode all distinctions between male and female or ordained and lay.[37] There is the merest hint that Boniface was not quite sure about the attitude of his companions:

> He commended her to Lull and the senior monks of the monastery [Fulda] who were present, exhorting them to look after her with reverence and respect, and again stated his wish that after death her bones should be placed next to his in the same tomb, in order that they might await the day of resurrection together who during life had served Christ with equal zeal and devotion.[38]

Leoba's last years were marked by increasing involvement in monastic administration and court life. She regularly visited the monasteries with which she was connected, encouraging the nuns to make more and more progress in the way of life they had undertaken. But her wisdom and knowledge of ecclesiastical matters made her an invaluable counselor. Even the prickly Lull, who was not slow to order other nuns to keep to their cloisters, relied on her judgment and often consulted her.[39] As an old woman, her friendship with Hildegard, the saintly wife of Charlemagne, took her to court more often than she liked.

Finally, the time came for her to prepare for death, which she did in her customarily matter-of-fact way. Having done what she could to put the affairs of all the monasteries in order, she took the advice of Lull and retired to Schornsheim, about four miles from the episcopal see of Mainz. There she lived quietly with a few of her nuns, sometimes complaining when Lull was absent too long.[40] During her final illness she sent for an English priest named Torhthat, from whom she received viaticum. Did she, in her last hours, experience a sudden longing for her homeland or turn, like Bede, to prayer in her mother tongue? Rudolf's narrative is unusually sparing of death-bed details. All we know is that Leoba remained true to her promise to Boniface until the last. On September 28, in the year 780 or thereabouts, she died.[41] The monks of Fulda were reluctant to open Boniface's tomb, so they buried her on the north side of the altar he had erected in honour of the twelve apostles. A few years later the relics were translated to the western end of the church, and soon after Rudolf laid down his pen, their remains were moved again to Petersberg where they now lie.

LEOBA'S LEGACY

Leoba went to Germany at a time when Anglo-Saxon monasticism for women was no longer expanding at the same vigorous rate that it had half a century earlier. The English houses were not in any way decadent— Wimborne is proof of that—but they did not continue to flourish as the men's houses did. Nor, after the initial impetus given by Leoba, did monasticism for women in Germany develop in the same way as monasticism for men. New houses continued to be founded, but there were fewer for women than for men. In time the double monasteries died out until revived under very different conditions in the twelfth century. Historians tend to explain the disparity in terms of the limited financial resources available to women and the short-lived existences of the many "proprietary houses" founded for members of a particular family. Also significant is the fact that women's monasteries tend to do best in the unstructured conditions of mission territory. The situation in Germany changed dramatically during Leoba's lifetime. Within a very few years, Bischofsheim had become part of an established ecclesiastical order. Inevitably, rules and regulations multiplied. This fact is reflected in Rudolf's text and goes some way towards explaining the subsequent history of monasticism for women.

From the Council of Ver in 755 onwards, there was a change in the nature and scope of legislation for nuns. Emphasis on enclosure became more marked, and as time went on, the rules for women became much stricter than those for men. Some form of physical separation from the hurly-burly of worldly affairs had always been found desirable, for monks as well as nuns, but now enclosure for women acquired a new aspect. What had once been seen as a discipline that favoured a life of prayer and helped ensure women's autonomy now appeared more of a value in itself and somehow necessary to protect women from themselves. Under Charlemagne, control of enclosure no longer remained in the hands of the abbess but rested with the bishop—often a mixed blessing.[42] Abbesses were not henceforth in complete control of their monasteries' affairs: they were forced to rely on outsiders for the management of their estates. Educational standards in most communities fell, and nuns gradually ceased to have any say in many matters that concerned them.[43] Unseen and unheard behind their high walls, they were to become symbols of the hidden life of the Church.

Was Leoba, therefore, ultimately a failure—someone who impressed her contemporaries, but whose achievements now seem as insubstantial and irrelevant as her own halting attempts at Latin verse? Or was she someone who can still challenge us at both the personal and institutional levels? Every Benedictine will recognize the challenge of her sanctity, attained through the ordinary means of monastic life—prayer, reading, work, and obedience—rather than because of the extraordinary events of the Anglo-Saxon mission. Far from diminishing her humanity, being a nun integrated and developed the many gifts of mind, heart, and spirit with which Leoba was endowed. But there is another challenge which the Church as a whole is slow to admit. In Leoba's day, monastic life for women was not so very different from monastic life for men. The sheer number of women saints in the Anglo-Saxon calendars is evidence that women were regarded as responsible beings, capable of determining and maintaining the structures that would enable them to be faithful to their call. How ironic it is that Leoba and her companions would not be able to do in our day what they did in theirs without forfeiting the name of Benedictine *nuns*.[44] Might not the beautiful smile today be a little wry, though enchanting still?

NOTES

1. Leoba's baptismal name was "Thrutgeba." In a letter to Boniface, she calls herself "Leobgytha;" in the *Candidi Vita Eigilis*, "Liobgid" or "Leobgida," Boniface himself refers to her as "Leobgutha," see note 3 below. The Latin form is *Leoba* or, less correctly, *Lioba*. Although she is mentioned *en passant* in numerous books and articles about the Anglo-Saxon mission, there are still many gaps to be filled in, especially concerning the chronology of her life and work.

2. Rudolf of Fulda, *Vita Leobae Abbatissae Biscofesheimensis auctore Rudolfo Fuldensi*, ed. G. Waitz, *Monumenta Germaniae Historica*, Scriptores 15.1, (Hanover, 1887) 119. The text of Surio's edition, with some supplementary matter edited by Periero, may be found in *Acta Sanctorum* 47, Sept. VII (Paris and Rome, 1867) 698–718. There is an English translation in C. H. Talbot, *The Anglo-Saxon Missionaries in Germany* (Sheed & Ward, London and New York, 1954) 205–226. The chapter on Rudolf's *Vita* in S. Hollis, *Anglo-Saxon Women and the Church* (Woodbridge, 1992) only became available to me after this essay was written. Although we have worked along parallel lines, and in many places have come to similar conclusions, we disagree on key points of interpretation eg. Leoba's friendship with Boniface, enclosure, etc.

3. The best Latin texts are printed by M. Tangl, *S. Bonifatii Epistolae*, *Monumenta Germaniae Historica*, Epistolae Selectae I (Berlin, 1916). See also *Acta Sanctorum*, 47, Sept VII, 701, 704 and Migne, *Patrologia Latina*, 89, cols. 720–782. The translations in E. Emerton, *The Letters of St Boniface* (New York, 1973) must be used with caution. See also *Vitae Sancti Bonifatii*, ed. W. Levison,

Monumenta Germaniae Historica, Scriptores (Hanover, 1905). There is an English translation of Willibald's *Life of Boniface* in C. H. Talbot, *Anglo-Saxon Missionaries*, 25–62.

4. Rudolf's work can be dated precisely because he refers to the death of Mago five years previously (Fulda necrology 831) but says nothing about the translation of Leoba's relics in 837.

5. Rudolf, *Vita*, 122. Interestingly, there is no extant Life of Leoba by a nun of Bischofsheim.

6. See W. Levison, *England and the Continent in the Eighth Century* (Oxford, 1946) 76, especially note 2.

7. Rudolf, *Vita*, 126. The phrase "diligens eam" is a conventional expression of affection and friendship. Rudolf was sensitive to any suggestion of possible impropriety and rather labours the point that Leoba's later visits to Fulda took place during daylight hours and were always carefully chaperoned, see Ibid., 129–130.

8. Rudolf, *Vita*, 126. On the changing position of monastic women, see J. Nicholson, "Feminae Gloriosae: Women in the Age of Bede," *Medieval Women*, ed. D. Baker (Ecclesiastical History Society/Blackwell's, Oxford 1978) 15–29 and the comments of J. T. Schulenburg, "Strict Active Enclosure and Its Effects on the Female Monastic Experience," *Distant Echoes: Medieval Religious Women I*, eds. J. A. Nichols and L. T. Shank (Cistercian Publications, 1984) 51–86.

9. The literature on Boniface and the Anglo-Saxon Mission is vast, especially in German. T. Schieffer, *Winifrid-Bonifatius und die christliche Grundlegung Europas* (Freiburg 1954, reprinted Darmstadt 1972) is the most impressive biography to date. For Boniface's early years, see C. Holdsworth, "St. Boniface the Monk," *The Greatest Englishman*, ed. T. Reuter (Exeter, 1980) 49–67 and J. C. Sladden, *Boniface of Devon, Apostle of Germany* (Exeter, 1980) 5–17.

10. E. S. Duckett, *Anglo-Saxon Saints and Scholars* (New York, 1947) 397, assumed that Leoba was educated at Minster before becoming a nun at Wimborne because she refers to "my teacher Eadburg" in her letter to Boniface; so also L. Eckenstein, *Woman under Monasticism* (Cambridge, 1896) 134. The identification of the Eadburg in question with the abbess of Minster is not certain. It is more likely that Leoba was referring to a nun of Wimborne, see Rudolf, *Vita*, 124.

11. Rudolf, *Vita*, 127.

12. The evidence from other seventh and eighth-century monasteries suggests that Rudolf was exaggerating. Against the strictures of Aldhelm (largely to do with nuns' vanity) must be weighed Bede's generally positive picture in book IV of *Ecclesiastical History of the English People*, eds. B. Colgrave & R. A. B. Mynors (Oxford, 1969). Elfled moved around the estates attached to Whitby without attracting adverse comment and was accounted the best counselor at the synod on the Nidd, see *The Life of St Wilfrid*, 60, in *English Historical Documents*, ed. D. Whitelock, 695. For nuns attending Boniface's lectures, see *Vitae Bonifatii*, 10–11, and C. H. Talbot's comment on the general situation, *Anglo-Saxon Missionaries*, xii, "Never, perhaps, has there been an age in which religious women exercised such great power." Theodore tried to discourage double monasteries but failed; half a century later Boniface was quite realistic about matters, see A. W. Haddon & W. Stubbs, *Councils and Ecclesiastical Documents* (Oxford 1964) 3: 195, 354, 381.

13. The *Anglo-Saxon Chronicle* mentions the existence of Wimborne under the year 718, but the monastery was probably founded in 705. See the letter of Aldhelm printed in W. Dugdale, *Monasticon Anglicanum*, eds. J. Caley, H. Ellis & B. Bandinel (London, 1846) II, 89. Virtually all other information derives ultimately from Rudolf, *Vita*, 123–4. For general background, see H. Mayr-Harting, *The Coming of Christianity to Anglo-Saxon England* (3rd ed., London, 1991) especially chapters 9 and 10. The Anglo-Saxon monastery was destroyed by the Danes in about 1013, but the present Minster stands on the site of the old abbey church, by the Win and the Stour.

14. Tangl, 29. The date of the letter is disputed, but not later than 732.

15. Ibid., 49.

16 See H. Mayr-Harting, *The Coming of Christianity to Anglo-Saxon England*, 267-8.

17. Rudolf, *Vita*, 123–124. Historians often seem shocked by this story but it was not unknown for an acolyte to fling holy water at the back of a departing superior, "to drive the devil out," or for a novice to ask formal permission to murder a companion.

18. Delehaye, *The Legends of the Saints* (2nd edn, London, 1907) 26.

19. Rudolf, *Vita*, 124–125.

20. Ibid., 125. Gregory the Great's reflection on Rachel and Leah, that contemplation must bear fruit in action, was expressed many times in his letters: see the references given by H. Mayr-Harting, *The Coming of Christianity to Anglo-Saxon England*, 265. The Anglo-Saxon devotion to the person of the pope, often referred to as papalism, was really devotion to the memory of Gregory and his work for the English Church.

21. See J. M. Wallace-Hadrill, "A Background to St Boniface's Mission," *Early Medieval History* (Oxford, 1975) 138–154 and the excellent summary in C. Holdsworth, "St Boniface the Monk," in *The Greatest Englishman*, 49–67.

22. W. Levison, *England and the Continent in the Eighth Century*, 71.

23. Migne, *Patrologia Latina*, 80, col. 215.

24. Tangl, 40. Boniface always had a special horror of drunkenness, which he regarded as the characteristic Anglo-Saxon vice, Tangl, 78.

25. See L. Eckenstein, *Woman under Monasticism*, 136. The journey must have been hard and perilous but we have no account of it.

26. Rudolf, *Vita*, 125: "ad solatium suae peregrinationis atque ad auxilium legationis sibi iniunctae." This refers to Boniface's (papal) mission in Germany, not Sturm's (monastic) mission in Italy. Leoba had already been formed as a Benedictine.

27. Ibid., 126.

28. Ibid., 126.

29. Ibid., 127, 130. Boniface thought nuns risked their virtue by going on pilgrimage, but he was powerless to dissuade, see Tangl, 78.

30. The ornate blessings given by some bishops were a sore point with the pope, see Tangl, 371.

31. Boniface's letters are full of references to heathen incursions, backslidings, and the eccentric ministrations of half-crazed "holy men" like Adilbert. See Tangl, 59, 63, 108.

32. Rudolf, *Vita,* 126, 129.

33. See H. Mayr-Harting, *The Coming of Christianity to Anglo-Saxon England*, 262. Leoba was as much the archetypal Englishwoman as Boniface the archetypal Englishman. She could always be relied on in a crisis, see Rudolf, *Vita,* 127-8.

34. Rudolf, *Vita,* 126.

35. Ibid., 128. See P. Brown, *The Cult of the Saints* (Chicago: SCM, 1981) especially chapters 5 and 6 on "Praesentia" and "Potentia." Although his remarks concern late Antiquity, many of his insights are valid for the medieval period.

36. Rudolf, *Vita,* 130–1.

37. Boniface numbered many women among his friends and relied on them for books and other necessities as well as prayer and moral support. Never at any time does he give any hint of regarding them as inferior to men. See, for example, the tone of his letter to Eadburg, from whom he requested Peter's *Epistles*, Tangl, 35.

38. Rudolf, *Vita,* 129.

39. Lull excommunicated Abbess Switha for disregarding enclosure and allowing two of her nuns to go outside the house. All three were put on a bread and water penance for the rest of their lives. See J. T. Schulenburg, "Strict Active Enclosure," *Distant Echoes*, 68.

40. *Acta Sanctorum*, 47, Sept VII, 705. She was allowed the unique privilege of entering the enclosure at Fulda to pray beside Boniface's tomb, Rudolf, *Vita,* 129.

41. See Waitz's note to the *Vita*, 130: the year of her death has been variously ascribed to 779, 780 and 782.

42. There is a growing literature on this subject. In addition to J. T. Schulenburg's article already cited, see J. Luecke, "The Unique Experience of Anglo-Saxon Nuns," *Peaceweavers: Medieval Religious Women II*, eds. J. A. Nichols & L. T. Shank (Cistercian Publications, 1987) 55–65.

43. Contrast the tenth century, when English abbots and abbesses sat together to draw up the *Regularis Concordia*, with the twentieth, when only in 1993 were the nuns of the English Benedictine Congregation allowed to vote with the monks for the president of the Congregation although they had been members since 1623/5.

44. I am referring here to *moniales* in the juridical sense. The distinction between *moniales* and *sorores* is not one Leoba herself would have recognized, but it is one that Benedictine women currently live with. A monk is a monk, whether he lives an entirely contemplative life in a monastery or is pastor of a busy parish. The current Code of Canon Law, however, requires papal enclosure for contemplative nuns (667, para. 3), although in practice many communities have adopted a form of constitutional enclosure. Today, an individual nun might do many of the things that Leoba did, but not a whole community, because of the way in which *moniales* are defined.

7

Tetta, "Noble in Conduct" and Thecla, "Shining Like a Light in a Dark Place"

Deborah Harmeling, O.S.B.

The eighth century was a time of extraordinary vigor and vitality for women monastics both in Britain and Germany. In Britain established double monasteries were flourishing, and the Anglo-Saxon abbesses and their sister religious were held in high regard. In Germany the great Anglo-Saxon missionary Boniface was evangelizing and setting up new monasteries. Two women who are models of the established Anglo-Saxon monastic culture and the handing on of that culture to Germany are Tetta and Thecla. Tetta represents the established monastic tradition; Thecla represents that tradition passed on to a different time and place.

Important sources for the stories of Tetta and Thecla include the Boniface correspondence in which each one of the women is mentioned once (Tetta may be mentioned twice) and Rudolf of Fulda's *Life of Leoba*. In these sources, Tetta is the guardian of tradition, the model of the ordered, common life in the monastery. Thecla, like her namesake in the New Testament Apocrypha, *The Acts of Paul and Thecla*, is the one who responds to a call from outside the monastery and undertakes missionary activities. Tetta and Thecla both lived at a time when historical factors converged to open a window of opportunity that enabled Anglo-Saxon monastic women to partake in a great missionary endeavor. These favorable historical factors included the status of monastic women in Anglo-Saxon Britain and the particular esteem Boniface held for them; the importance of actual kinship and kinship as a model for male-female relationships to Boniface's mission; Britain's double monastery and minster systems; and finally the impact of the Carolingian reforms on the autonomy of monastic women. This window of opportunity was only open for about fifty years. Carolingian reforms in the late eighth and early ninth centuries and the monastic reforms of the tenth century, the Danish invasions, and the Norman Conquest of Britain closed that window. Monastic women who wished to travel and do missionary work had to wait until another monk named Boniface (Wimmer) appeared and another set of historical factors converged in the Germany and the United States of the nineteenth century.

In her article, "The Unique Experience of Anglo-Saxon Nuns," Janemarie Luecke closes by stating that the period from the 600s to the beginning of the Danish invasions "remains a unique episode in the history of Christian female monasticism."[1] Luecke presents evidence that the Anglo-Saxon culture and heritage esteemed the intellectual abilities of women and nuns and allowed them to participate prominently in social and political activities of the time. If the experience of Anglo-Saxon nuns as a whole is unique, the experience of the Wimborne Anglo-Saxon nuns is nothing less than astonishing. In the mid-700s some of them left their monasteries in Britain to become active partners with Boniface in his missionary work in Germany.

THE BONIFACE MISSION

First we need to know something of Boniface and his mission to Germany. Boniface was born Winifrid near Exeter in Devon between 675 and 680. He entered the Benedictine monastery at Exeter at an early age.[2] Later he transferred to the monastery at Nursling where he gained a reputation as a scholar. In 716 he set out for Frisia with the permission of his abbot. Receiving no support from local rulers or ecclesiastical authorities, Boniface returned to Britain. He then left for Rome in 718, determined to gain official backing from Pope Gregory II for his missionary activities. The Pope received him, changed his name to Boniface after the Roman martyr, and appointed him to spread the gospel in Bavaria, Thuringia, and Frisia. Spreading the gospel was a broad mandate that placed all of Boniface's activities within official Church ministry.[3] Boniface worked for about three years under the leadership of the local bishop, Willibrord. When Willibrord tried to persuade him to become his auxiliary bishop, Boniface refused. He saw his mission as a papal mission, and he would not confine his work to one area without the approval of the Pope. Boniface then sent a messenger to Rome to report and seek advice. The Pope called him to Rome and consecrated him a bishop in 722, giving him "a roving commission under the direct supervision of the Holy See."[4]

It was at this point that Boniface began to think of establishing monasteries. "He was conscious that the mere conversion of people and the provision of churches for them to worship in was insufficient. . . . A succession of teachers of caliber, imbued with a strong spirit of discipline, obedient to authority and motivated by the highest spiritual ideals [were needed]."[5] Boniface had kept his contacts with monasteries in Britain through correspondence with abbesses, abbots, nuns, and monks. They had provided him with books, clothing, money, and moral support during the early years of his work. The nuns at the British monastery of Wimborne, especially Leoba who seems to have been a relative, were part of his network of correspondents. In his capacity as bishop, he decided to request personnel from the Anglo-Saxon monasteries. In response to his plea for helpers, a group of thirty (one for every year of his mission) Anglo-Saxon nuns arrived in Germany around 748.[6]

We know the names of some of these women from the Boniface correspondence: Leoba, Walburga, Thecla, Cynehild. Otholon, a monk of St. Emmeran in Bavaria, rewrote and expanded Willibald's *Life of St. Boniface* between 1062 and 1066. In this *Life* he gives a list of the women who came from Britain and mentions the four women above, adding Cynehild's daughter Berthgit and Chunitrud.[7] We know that Leoba, Walburga, and Thecla were from the double monastery of Wimborne in Dorset, known then as the kingdom of Wessex. It is not known from what monastery Cynehild, Berthgit, or Chunitrud came. Because Cynehild is mentioned by name with Leoba and Thecla in letter 67 of the Boniface correspondence,[8] it may be assumed that she was from Wimborne also.

TETTA, ABBESS OF WIMBORNE

Abbess Tetta was responsible for forming these women in the monastic tradition and giving them permission to become part of Boniface's missionary enterprise. Tetta's birth date is unknown, but the date of her death is thought to be around 760.[9] She became abbess of Wimborne in the first half of the eighth century. Her baptismal name is thought to have been Cuniberg,[10] and the name Tetta to have been a familiar name or a nickname.[11] Some authors also identify her with Edburga.[12]

What is known about her life comes from Rudolf of Fulda's biography of Leoba, who was a member of the community at Wimborne. In this biography[13] Rudolf writes that Tetta was a holy virgin, the sister of a king, who was placed in authority at Wimborne.[14] He notes in the best hagiographic style of the time that Tetta was even more noble in her conduct and good qualities than in her state of life and she instructed more by her example of good deeds and conduct than by her words. He says she "maintained discipline with such circumspection [and the discipline there was much stricter than anywhere else] that she would never allow her nuns to approach clerics. She was so anxious that the nuns, in whose company she always remained, should be cut off from the company of men that she denied entrance into the community not merely to laymen and clerics but even to bishops."[15]

Rudolf goes on to tell two tales of Tetta's virtues. At Wimborne there was a sister who "because of her zeal for discipline and strict observance" was often appointed prioress and given other responsibilities. Her very zeal and, as Rudolf implies, her inflexibility and arrogance aroused great resentment among the younger community members. Instead of taking care to listen to her sisters, she was so stubborn and inflexible that she died without asking their pardon for any wrongs she might have done them. Her death and burial did not ease the hate and rage she had aroused in the younger sisters. In an amazing display of pique, they went to her grave, ranted about her cruelty, and "even climbed on her tomb as if to stamp upon her corpse, uttering bitter curses over her dead body."

Of course, Tetta heard of this and reprimanded the younger sisters "for their presumption." She then went to the grave and noticed that the ground had sunk about six inches. From this she understood that the dead sister had been punished by God with great severity. So she called the sisters together (probably all five hundred of them)[16] for what must have been quite a community meeting. She presented the community with a model for reconciliation. Reproaching the sisters for their cruelty, she reminded them of the Christian and monastic principle of being peaceable with those who are difficult; she advised them to lay aside their resentment and show their forgiveness; she asked that they join her in prayer for the dead sister, asking God to absolve her of all her sins. When they agreed to do this, she ordered them to fast for three days and give themselves in prayer for the repose of the dead sister's soul.

At the end of the third day, Tetta went with the whole community to the church and prostrated herself before the altar, praying again for the soul of the departed sister. As she prayed, the hole in the grave began to fill, and the grave became level with the surrounding ground. Rudolf writes, "By this it was made clear that when the grave returned to its normal state the soul of the deceased sister, through the prayers of Tetta, had been absolved by divine power."

In the second story, the sister who looked after the chapel went to close the door of the church before going to bed and "lost all the keys in the darkness." When she rose for Matins, she could not find any of the keys, so she lit a candle and searched all the places where she could have lost them. When she had searched several times, she went to Tetta and confessed her negligence. Upon hearing the story, Tetta observed it to be the work of the devil. She called the whole community together, and they recited Matins and Lauds in another building. Then they continued to pray. While they were at prayer, a little dead fox suddenly appeared at the doors of the chapel with the keys in his mouth. Tetta took the keys, and when the doors were opened, the community went into the church giving thanks to God. Rudolf draws the conclusion that the devil, because of pride, was transformed into a beast and "was unmasked as a fox through the prayers of the sisters and made to look foolish."

Given these examples of Tetta's leadership, strength of character, devotion to monastic discipline, and her insistence that her sisters never be in the company of men, we are surprised at her response to Boniface's request for personnel. Rudolf says that when Boniface wrote asking her to send Leoba to him to accompany him on his missionary endeavors, "the Abbess Tetta was exceedingly displeased at her [Leoba's] departure, but because she could not gainsay the dispositions of divine providence she agreed to his request and sent Leoba to the blessed man."[17] The canon law of Rudolf's time, no more than a hundred years later, required an abbess to obtain permission from the bishop if a nun wished to leave her monastery for any reason,[18] but Rudolf recognizes that Tetta had the authority to give this consent.

An additional mention of Tetta is found in the letter written by the priest Wigbert to the monks at Glastonbury. Wigbert writes in letter 101 of the Boniface correspondence, "Give my greetings to the brethren in the circle, . . . and tell my mother Tetta and her sisterhood of our safe journey."[19] If Tetta's baptismal name was Cuniberg, then she may also have been the person addressed in letter 49 from the Boniface correspondence. In this letter Denehard, Lull, and Burchard, assistants of Boniface, call themselves her sons and fellow countrymen and ask her "to keep us in communion with your holy congregation, and with the support of your prayers . . . we also wish it to be known . . . that if any of us should happen to visit Britain we should not prefer the obedience and government of any man to subjection under your good-will; for we place the greatest confidence of our hearts in you."[20] Tetta's feast is celebrated, according to different calendars, on either August 12 or December 17.[21]

THECLA, ABBESS OF KITZINGEN

What we know of Thecla also comes from the life of Leoba and the letters of Boniface. In letter 67, written sometime between 742 and 748, Boniface addresses Leoba, Thecla, Cynehild by name and asks prayers of them and the "dear sisters in Christ who live with you."[22] This letter was most likely addressed to them in Germany, perhaps at Bischofsheim where Leoba was abbess.

Thecla is also mentioned in Rudolf's *Life of Leoba* although mostly in passing. Rudolf says he depended upon the writings of others, "venerable men who heard [the facts of Leoba's life] from four of her disciples, Agatha, Thecla, Nana, and Eoloba."[23] Rudolf mentions Thecla again when a great storm arises at Bischofsheim. The people of the countryside entreat

Leoba to do something. Leoba urges them to join her in prayer at the foot of the altar, but after the storm continues, the panicked people demand more of her. Thecla, described as Leoba's kinswoman, says to her, "Beloved, all the hopes of these people lie in you; you are their only support. Arise, then, and pray to the Mother of God, your mistress, for us, that by her intercession, we may be delivered from this fearful storm."[24] After this encouragement, Leoba gets up and goes to the threshold of the church as if to confront the storm. After making the sign of the cross, stretching her hands to heaven and invoking the name of Christ three times, the storm abates.

In the *Passion of Boniface* written at Mainz between 1000 and 1050, Thecla is identified as founding the monastery at Kitzingen where "she shone like a light in a dark place."[25] Later collections of saints' lives give differing information about her. There seems to be a controversy about whether Thecla founded the monastery of Kitzingen and whether she governed the monastery at Ochsenfurt as well.[26] In the *Acta Sanctorum*, the Bollandists use the quotation from the Mainz biography of Boniface stating that Boniface settled Thecla near the river Moin, that she might shine as a light in Chizzingim [Kitzingen].[27] From this they draw the conclusion that the cult of Thecla is quite old. They also suppose that Thecla had noble and pious parents because she was related, probably on her mother's side, to Leoba. The Bollandists also point out that the Thecla who went to Germany is not to be confused with a Thecla from the monastery at Barking in Britain. The author of the article on Thecla in the *Acta Sanctorum* says that Thecla must have made such progress in holiness and learning under Leoba at Bischofsheim that she was first called to be abbess at Ochsenfurt. After the death of St. Hadeloga, the foundress and first abbess at Kitzingen, Thecla was appointed abbess there some time after 750.

The *Bibliotheca Sanctorum* states that Thecla was abbess of Ochsenfurt and then became abbess of Kitzingen but continued to reside at Ochsenfurt. At Kitzingen she was succeeded by St. Hadeloga. The author of the article in the *Bibliotheca Sanctorum* says this explains how her name became associated with Kitzingen.[28]

The monastery at Kitzingen was taken over by a secular ruler in 1544. In 1629 it was recovered by Archbishop Philip Adolp of Herbipolensis. In 1869 when the Bollandists were writing about Thecla, Kitzingen was a girls' school run by Ursulines. The congregation at Ochsenfurt apparently declined after Thecla either left it or died.[29] The *Bibliotheca* and the *Acta* agree that Thecla died somewhere around the end of the eighth century.

The author of the article in the *Bibliotheca* adds an obscure and unexplained note that Thecla came to be represented in art as caressing a lion, with a dark, transparent veil covering her head and the greater part of her body.[30] A check of the sources cited for this note indicates that someone has confused the Anglo-Saxon Thecla with the New Testament apocryphal Thecla. In *The Acts of Paul and Thecla,* when the apocryphal Thecla was thrown to wild beasts, "a fierce lioness ran to her and lay down at her feet."[31] This lioness fought off a bear and another lion for Thecla and then died. In the index to Baronius' *Annales,* the apocryphal Thecla is called a protomartyr who "commanded lions."[32]

Although the Anglo-Saxon Thecla's feast is celebrated in some places on September 27 or 28, by association with Leoba,[33] other martyrologies celebrate it on October 15.[34]

What we know of Tetta and Thecla leaves us asking for more information about them. What do they tell us of the women of their time and place? What is typical and atypical of their experience? What lessons do they have for us?

THE STATUS OF ANGLO-SAXON MONASTIC WOMEN

Tetta and Thecla, like Leoba and Walburga, were products of their time, a time in flux and, for women, unlike those times before and after. Literary, legal, and historical scholars differ on when Anglo-Saxon women began to lose their prestige and influence. None doubt that the Anglo-Saxon monastic women had a high degree of prestige and influence.[35] Some hold that in Anglo-Saxon Britain "women were more nearly the equal companions of their husbands and brothers than at any other period before the modern age. In the high ranges of society this . . . partnership was ended by the Norman Conquest. . . ."[36] Christine Fell goes further to say, "In the first enthusiasm for Christianity we not only see men and women engaging as equals in the challenge of a new religion and way of life, we see also women specifically asked to take a full and controlling part. No women could have been asked to take on so powerful a role as the early abbesses unless they were used to handling power."[37] Certainly Tetta, as the royal abbess of a double monastery in Britain, and Thecla, as an abbess in Germany, were used to handling power and making autonomous decisions. Stephanie Hollis presents a view that in Anglo-Saxon Britain "it might be more accurate to speak of a gradual erosion in the position of women, particularly monastic women, from at least as early as the eighth century."[38]

An important point in understanding the influence of the Anglo-Saxon monastic women is the fact that many Anglo-Saxon monasteries were royal monasteries. Wimborne itself was founded by sisters of the local king and was ruled by royal abbesses. There were political and social incentives for royalty to establish and endow monasteries. The political and social system of Anglo-Saxon times was land-based. The founding of monasteries allowed royal families to keep their lands and place their members in protected positions. There they could still be "heiresses to their parents' wealth, bringers of dowries and custodians of the children's estates."[39] Thus, the royal monastic women helped to preserve their families' estates and wealth. In addition, royal abbesses also came from backgrounds that gave them the training to be competent administrators, counselors, scholars, and teachers.

Anglo-Saxon monastic women were women of learning who composed and copied books. They could read and write Latin as the Boniface correspondence shows. "It is likely that, given what we know of the response of women to the intellectual challenge of Christianity and literacy in the eighth century, letters between members of different religious communities were commonplace. . . ."[40] In the 150 letters that make up the Boniface correspondence, there are sixteen letters from men to women, as well as two from Boniface written to all the brothers and sisters in a religious community. There are nine letters from women and one that seems to be from the leaders of three religious communities, an abbot and two abbesses. Christine Fell believes that this last letter is clearly the composition of one of the abbesses.[41] She suggests that the Boniface correspondence survived haphazardly and that it represents only a tiny fragment of "a vast Anglo-Saxon corpus of letters."[42]

Other evidence for the literacy of the Anglo-Saxon nuns is Aldhelm's work *De Laudibus Virginitatis*, written for the nuns at the monastery of Barking. Fell says this work was characterized by convoluted syntax and abstruse vocabulary. She notes that Leoba probably read Aldhelm's work and seems to have been influenced by his style and vocabulary. In his work, Aldhelm mentions that the nuns at Barking read Scripture, works on ancient law, the Gospels, the stories of historians, and the rules of grammar and metrics.[43] We have no examples of any correspondence of Tetta and Thecla, but as noble women of their time, they must have been able to read and write. What has survived of the Boniface correspondence portrays Anglo-Saxon monastic women who could think of going on pilgrimages, who were enthusiastic about Boniface's missionary work, who enjoyed writing and receiving letters, and who were eager for spiritual conversation and development.[44]

The Boniface correspondence also suggests that Anglo-Saxon nuns produced books, made clothing and altar cloths, and sent money to support the missionary activity. In his early letters, Boniface writes for books. In letter 35 he asks Eadburga, Abbess of Thanet, to copy in gold for him the Epistles of Peter, and in letter 30 he thanks her for her gift of books.[45] In letter 15 the Abbess Bugga promises to send him *The Sufferings of the Holy Martyrs*,[46] and other letters show that she sent clothing, incense, altar cloths, and money. Christine Fell notes that high quality Anglo-Saxon textiles and metalwork of the late eighth century have been found in the Abbey of Aldeneik in Luxembourg where Boniface visited. Although these are later than the Boniface mission, she believes they provide evidence for the quality of work that was probably done in the Anglo-Saxon monasteries.[47]

THE IMPORTANCE OF KINSHIP IN ANGLO-SAXON TIMES AND IN THE BONIFACE MISSION

Another aspect of the Boniface mission that is evident both in the correspondence and in Rudolf's *Life of Leoba* are the familial ties between the Anglo-Saxons in Britain and Germany. In Anglo-Saxon society, family was the primary social structure, and kinship the primary bond. Many of the correspondents in the Boniface correspondence were related by blood. Leoba was related to Boniface on her mother's side as she reminds him in letter 29,[48] and Rudolf says that Thecla was a kinswoman of Leoba. Willibald and Wunibald, missionary companions of Boniface, were the brothers of Walburga. Tradition holds that Boniface was their uncle.

Many of the women correspondents write to Boniface about the loss of male kinsmen, reminding us of the lonely and perilous state of a woman without kinsmen or family to support and provide for her in Anglo-Saxon times. Hollis suggests that the loss expressed in these letters referred not only to physical protection, but also to the loss of emotional solidarity.[49] She believes that the social primacy of kinship bonds made them the model for relationships between monastic men and women. It was the deep acceptance of each other as brothers and sisters in Christ, based upon familial experiences, that gives the Boniface correspondence its tone of mutuality, affection, and support. Hollis says, "The dominance of kinship as a relational model enabled the double monasteries to continue, and with them the friendships of monastic men and women."[50] The strength of these familial ties was one reason that Tetta could send her sisters to work with Boniface.

Finally, the Boniface correspondence shows the high esteem in which Boniface held the women with whom he corresponded and with whom he worked. According to Rudolf of Fulda, Boniface wanted to be buried beside Leoba with whom he shared his missionary ministry. "Boniface addresses monastic women as companions in the same spiritual endeavor."[51] He confides in Eadburga, Bugga, and Leoba as he would in a spiritual advisor or mentor and asks for their prayers and support. Hollis suggests that in letter 66[52] Boniface presents himself as a "participant in the ministry of all believers who confess to one another their shared human weakness and derive forgiveness and support from one another's prayers."[53]

THE DOUBLE MONASTERY SYSTEM

In contrast to the nuns on the continent, the Anglo-Saxon nuns of the eighth century "seem to have been relatively free of the trend to restrictive cloistering. . . . Although the early English houses were, in fact, enclosed, the enclosure seems to have been under the jurisdiction of the abbess (as in the case of Wimborne) and within the framework of the double monastery."[54] At the time of Tetta and Thecla, the royal double monasteries were flourishing in Britain. Wimborne itself was founded by Cuthburga, the sister of Ine, king of Wessex, probably around 705,[55] and its foundation was influenced by the double monasteries in Gaul. In fact, the enthusiastic spread of Christianity and monasticism from Britain to Germany was parallel to the earlier expansion of Christianity and monasticism from Gaul to Britain. Coulstock says that in the eighth century the debt of English monks and nuns to Gaul was repaid in Germany.[56]

The double monastery is an elusive and evolving institution in history. It was associated with Gaul in the seventh century, Britain in the second half of the seventh century, Ireland in the eighth century. In Spain, the fullest development of the double monastery was in the second half of the ninth century.[57] Although there may have been double monasteries in Germany before Boniface, little is known of them.[58] In Britain, Bede wrote about the most famous double monastery, Whitby, founded around 657 and governed by its first abbess, Hilda. There is no doubt that such institutions existed but they took many forms, and it is difficult to find a strict definition of one in the literature. One author defines the double monastery "as consisting of two communities, one of monks and one of nuns, established in the same place but not necessarily within the same boundary, observing the same rule, and together forming a legal entity under one authority."[59] Another author offers a broader definition with a specific limitation. "The association of the two sexes under particular conditions for a special purpose gives the double monastery its peculiar character. There is no promiscuous mixing of the sexes; the monastery is double, not mixed."[60] A 1919 report to the archbishop of Canterbury on the ministry of women noted that double monasteries provided communities of women with a "permanent staff of clergy vowed to the religious life who could perform for the sisters [sacramental] service . . . and of laybrothers who, while devoted to religious observances, could do work for which the nuns were physically unfitted."[61] The author of that report goes on to say that in the double monasteries the abbess was recognized as the head of the monastery, the nuns were seen as the persons for whom the monastery existed, and the men were "intended merely to fulfill the necessary duties for which the inmates of the cloister are disqualified by canonical and physical disabilities, and to supply assistance on occasion in the management of temporal affairs."[62]

Other historians indicate that the essential and original character of double monasteries was that a community of priests under a rule ministered to the spiritual needs of women under a rule, but as John Godfrey points out, nunneries made use of these types of male services without becoming double monasteries.[63]

To make matters even more confusing, there seems to be no typical Anglo-Saxon double monastery or even a typical Anglo-Saxon monastery before the ninth-century Benedictine reform. The Anglo-Saxon monasteries seem to have been prime examples of Benedictine autonomy and the importance of what we would call today the local charism. Even the vocabulary used to speak about these monasteries varies. The three words most commonly used in Latin texts of the time are *monasterium, cenobium,* and *ecclesia* but others like *cella, domus,* and *locus* also occur. Because of this, some historians are beginning to use the word "minster" from the Old English word *mynster* to refer to the Anglo-Saxon monasteries.[64] Sarah Foot suggests that all communal Anglo-Saxon establishments be called "minsters" because the usual translation "monastery" implies standards of monastic observance that were not observed and does not include the possibility that their members were engaged in pastoral work.[65]

THE MINSTER OR DOUBLE MONASTERY SYSTEM
IN ANGLO SAXON BRITAIN AND GERMANY

John Godfrey combines the idea of the double monastery with the idea of the minster in Anglo-Saxon Britain. He notes that there is little knowledge about what the men in double monasteries did, other than provide sacramental services. He proposes that in Anglo-Saxon Britain a double monastery, in addition to being a monastery, was a *mynster*, "an evangelistic and religious center for a district with pastoral responsibilities."[66] According to Godfrey, an establishment consisting primarily of nuns could not have undertaken the duties of a minster, attending to the spiritual needs of those on the minster estates in the surrounding district. The donors of the large monasteries, usually kings committed to the evangelization of their people, would not have supported and provided endowments for a monastery unless it was to be a Christian center for the district.

Godfrey emphasizes the pastoral character of the minster or double monastery, and this pastoral character is important for understanding what Boniface wished to achieve with his monasteries in Germany. It is also important to our understanding of what the mission to Germany meant to Tetta who was concerned for her sisters' welfare and had a particular concern about their interactions with men. Why would someone described as she is by Rudolf as "so anxious that the nuns, in whose company she always remained, should be cut off from the company of men" consent to sending her sisters to a mission outside the monastery and in the company of men? If Boniface and Tetta shared the same understanding of the type of monastery to be established in Germany and that type was the double monastery/minster model, Tetta's concerns about her sisters would be lessened. Thecla's work in Germany, as well as that of Leoba and Walburga, might have been understood by all concerned as that of establishing a center from which active ministry and evangelization could be done as well as the monastic Work of God. Although this is not what Godfrey suggests, Hollis argues that the double monasteries did allow women to exercise an active ministry in both Britain and Germany of the eighth century.[67] Coulstock says, "There is no doubt that the double monasteries under royal abbesses had their parishes, with their communities providing for pastoral needs."[68] This would explain Rudolf's story of people from the surrounding countryside coming to Leoba for help and protection when a violent storm arose.[69]

The information about the double monastery of Wimborne from Rudolf's *Life of Leoba*, was written about a hundred years after the Anglo-Saxon women came to Germany. Hollis speculates that although Rudolf does not disparage women or regard them as inferior, he is writing in a time when the local Church in Germany and canon law was moving toward "strict enclosure of religious, particularly female religious, . . . and the associated fears of contact between monastic men and women that brought an end to the double monasteries and with them . . . the egalitarian comradeship of the pioneering era."[70] Hollis also suggests that Tetta's ban on visiting clerics and bishops as indicated in the *Life of Leoba* may have allowed her to retain autonomous control of her monastery's affairs.[71] We know little of the double monastery in Germany. Rudolf does not speak of Bischofsheim as a double monastery. Heidenheim, founded by Willibald and then ruled by his brother Wunibald followed by their sister Walburga is the only double monastery that we know the Anglo-Saxons founded.[72] Yet the double monastery/minster was the system with which Boniface was most familiar, and it is most likely that it was the type of monastery he had in mind.

THE IMPACT OF CAROLINGIAN REFORM
ON THE AUTONOMY OF MONASTIC WOMEN

It is probable that we have little written information about these monasteries in Germany because the Carolingian councils of the eighth century stressed episcopal authority over monasteries and strict enclosure of monastic women.[73] At the same time, the double monastery was being viewed with suspicion, and few would be founded. The Anglo-Saxon spirit of pioneering encountered the Carolingian spirit of reform almost immediately in Germany so that by the deaths of Leoba and Thecla in the 780s or 790s, monastic women were in separate foundations, under episcopal rule, and strictly enclosed.

THE WISDOM OF THE ANGLO-SAXON MONASTIC WOMEN

What wisdom do the Anglo-Saxon monastic women, represented by Tetta and Thecla, have to give to monastic women and men of today? Through all the scholarly suppositions and assumptions, what stands out from the unique experience of the Anglo-Saxon women missionaries? These women were examples of the good zeal of which St. Benedict speaks. Their zeal was not only for their own progress in the traditional monastic way of life, but also for passing on that way of life, as they understood it, to others. These women were generous, responsive, and supportive. They were open to new ideas and new experiences while remaining grounded in their own monastic experience. Competent and strong, these monastic women could interact with the world around them and take risks. They were women who could leave the security of an established way of life, cross the English Channel, and head off into the thick forests of Germany. These women model for us the best of the monastic tradition of prayer, scholarly activity, and work. Their stories illustrate the vitality and the elasticity of our monastic heritage.

These Anglo-Saxon monastic women also show us the strength and power of mutual esteem, affectionate friendship, and shared values between women and men. Godfrey's work on the pastoral aspects of the double monasteries and Hollis' work on kinship as the model for male-female friendships give rise to wonderings about the day-to-day workings of the Boniface mission. The men and women of the Boniface mission have something to say to us today about the partnership of men and women in ministry.

The kinship model for male-female collaborative ministry is a fertile topic for future reflection and exploration. The Anglo-Saxon monastic women remind us that mutual esteem, affectionate friendship, and shared values form a basis for vital, collaborative ministry. With this basis, we can do great things for God and the Church, be noble in good conduct, and shine like lights in dark places.

NOTES

1. Janemarie Luecke, "The Unique Experience of Anglo-Saxon Nuns," *Medieval Religious Women: Peaceweavers,* eds. John A. Nichols and Lillian Thomas Shank (Kalamazoo: Cistercian Publications, 1987) 64.

2. John Cyril Sladden in his *Boniface of Devon* (Exeter: The Paternoster Press, 1980) suggests that Boniface was born in 680 and went to the monastery at Exeter when he was still under six years of age.

3. Ibid., 46.

4. C. H. Talbot, "St. Boniface and the German Mission" in *The Mission of the Church and the Propagation of the Faith: Papers Read at the Seventh summer Meeting and the Eighth Winter Meeting of the Ecclesiastical History Society,* ed. G. J. Cuming (Cambridge: University Press, 1970) 50.

5. Ibid.

6. Sladden, *Boniface of Devon*, 175.

7. Lina Eckenstein, *Woman under Monasticism: Chapters on Saint-lore and Convent Life between A.D. 500 and A.D. 1500* (Cambridge: University Press, 1896) 138–139. See also Willibald, *The Life of St. Boniface,* trans. George W. Robinson (Cambridge: Harvard University Press, 1916).

8. Edward Kylie, trans., *The English Correspondence of Saint Boniface* (New York: Cooper Square Publications, Inc., 1966) 148. A more recent translation of the Boniface correspondence with different letters is Ephraim Emerton, *The Letters of Saint Boniface* (New York: Octagon Books, 1973).

9. Alexius Hoffmann, *A Benedictine Martyrology* (Collegeville: St. John's Abbey, 1922) 268, gives the date of her death as around 760 while the *Bibliotheca Sanctorum* (Istituto Giovanni XXIII nella Pontificia Universita Lateranense Roma: Societa Grafica Romana, 1961) XII:442 places it as early as 745.

10. Alfons M. Zimmermann, *Kalendarium Benedictinum* (Wien: Herder & Co., 1937) 3:446.

11. Patricia H. Coulstock, *The Collegiate Church of Wimborne Minster* (Woodbridge: The Boydell Press, 1993) 55.

12. Ibid.

13. An English translation of Rudolf of Fulda's *Life of Leoba* is found in C. H. Talbot, trans., *The Anglo-Saxon Missionaries in Germany* (New York: Sheed and Ward, 1933) 205–226. Selections from this work are also reprinted in Barbara Bowe, et. al., *Silent Voices, Sacred Lives: Women's Readings for the Liturgical Year* (New York: Paulist Press, 1992) 378–390.

14. Tetta was probably the third abbess of Wimborne and may have been the sister of Aethelward. Coulstock, *The Collegiate Church of Wimborne Minster*, 55.

15. Talbot, *The Anglo-Saxon Missionaries in Germany*, 208.

16. A. Lindsay Clegg, *A History of Wimborne Minster and District* (London: The Outspoken Press, 1960) 23.

17. Talbot, *The Anglo-Saxon Missionaries*, 214.

18. Stephanie Hollis, *Anglo-Saxon Women and the Church* (Woodbridge: Boydell Press, 1992) 278.

19. Kylie, *The English Correspondence of Saint Boniface*, 114.

20. Emerton, *The Letters of Saint Boniface*, 77–78.

21. *Bibliotheca Sanctorum*, XII:442. See also Hoffmann, *A Benedictine Martyrology,* 268.

22. Kylie, *The English Correspondence of Saint Boniface*, 149.

23. Talbot, *The Anglo-Saxon Missionaries*, 205.

24. Ibid., 209–210.

25. Eckenstein, *Woman under Monasticism*, 138.

26. Sladden, *Boniface of Devon*, 176.

27. *Acta Sanctorum* (Paris: Palme, 1869) Oct. VII:59–64.

28. *Bibliotheca Sanctorum*, XII:182.

29. Ibid.

30. The author states that Giovanni Tritemio in his work *De Viris Illustribus Ord. S. Benedicti* (Colonia, 1575) III:172 was the first to give this information which was later picked up by Baronius in his *Annales Ecclesiastici* (Magnoza-Colonia, 1605) III:93–94.

31. *The Acts of Paul and Thecla* in *The Other Bible* edited by Willis Barnstone (San Francisco: Harper & Row, 1984) 452.

32. *Index Universalis Rerum Omnium Quae in Baronii ac Pagii* (Lucae: Leonardi Venturini, 1657) I:366.

33. *Bibliotheca Sanctorum,* XII:182.

34. Hoffmann, *A Benedictine Martyrology*, 26–61.

35. See Shelia C. Dietrich, "An Introduction to Women in Anglo-Saxon Society" in *The Women of England from Anglo-Saxon Times to the Present,* ed. Barbara Kanner (Hamden, Conn.: Archon Books, 1979) 36–38, for a brief bibliographical essay on the influence of Anglo-Saxon monastic women.

36. Doris Stenton, *The English Woman in History* (London. Allen and Unwin, 1957) 28.

37. Christine E. Fell, *Women in Anglo-Saxon England and the Impact of 1066* (Bloomington: Indiana University Press, 1984) 13.

38. Hollis, *Anglo-Saxon Women and the Church*, 7.

39. Coulstock, *The Collegiate Church of Wimborne Minster*, 53.

40. Christine E. Fell, "Some Implications of the Boniface Correspondence" in *New Readings on Women in Old English Literature* (Bloomington: Indiana University Press, 1990) 29.

41. Fell, "Some Implications," 31.

42. Ibid., 30.

43. Fell, *Women in Anglo-Saxon England*, 10–11.

44. Frederick Hockey, "St. Boniface in His Correspondence" in *Benedict's Disciples,* ed. D. H. Farmer (Leominster: Fowler Wright Books, Ltd., 1980) 107.

45. Kylie, *The English Correspondence of Saint Boniface*, 90-92.

46. Ibid., 49–50.

47. Fell, *Women in Anglo-Saxon England*, 116–117.

48. Emerton, *The Letters of Saint Boniface*, 59–60.

49. Hollis, *Anglo-Saxon Women and the Church*, 138.

50. Ibid., 143.

51. Ibid., 130.

52. Kylie, *The English Correspondence of Saint Boniface*, 147–148.

53. Hollis, *Anglo-Saxon Women and the Church*, 132.

54. Jane Tibbetts Schulenburg, "Strict Active Enclosure and its Effects on the Female Monastic Experience (ca. 500–1000)" in *Medieval Religious Women: Distant Echoes,* eds. John A. Nicholas and Lillian Thomas Shank (Kalamazoo: Cistercian Publications, 1984) 65–66.

55. Coulstock, *The Collegiate Church of Wimborne Minster*, 7, 34–41.

56. Ibid., 32.

57. Mary Bateson, "Origin and Early History of Double Monasteries," *Transactions of the Royal Historical Society*, New Series 13 (1899) 150.

58. Ibid., 184.

59. Sally Thompson, *Women Religious: the Foundation of English Nunneries after the Norman Conquest* (Oxford: Clarendon Press, 1991) 55.

60. Bateson, "Origin and Early History of Double Monasteries," 138–139.

61. A. Hamilton Thompson, "Double Monasteries and the Male Element in Nunneries" in *The Ministry of Women: a Report by a Committee Appointed by His Grace The Lord Archbishop of Canterbury* (London: Society for Promoting Christian Knowledge, 1919) 163.

62. Ibid., 164.

63. John Godfrey, "The Double Monastery in Early English History," *Ampleforth Journal* 79 (1974) 30.

64. Sarah Foot, "Anglo-Saxon Minsters: a Review of Terminology" in *Pastoral Care before the Parish,* eds. John Blair and Richard Sharpe, (Leicester: Leicester University Press, 1992) 215.

65. Ibid., 225.

66. Godfrey, "The Double Monastery in Early English History," 30.

67. Hollis, *Anglo-Saxon Women and the Church*, 13.

68. Coulstock, *The Collegiate Church of Wimborne Minster*, 66.

69. Talbot, *The Anglo-Saxon Missionaries*, 209–210.

70. Hollis, *Anglo-Saxon Women and the Church*, 272.

71. Ibid., 275.

72. Ibid., 274.

73. Schulenburg, "Strict Active Enclosure," 56.

8

St. Irmengard:
No Poor on the Isle of Chiemsee

Miriam Schmitt, O. S. B.

Saint Irmengard (c. 831–866), a ninth-century Carolingian princess, is revered today not only as the cofounder and first abbess of the Benedictine Abbey of Frauenwörth in Chiemsee, but also as our twentieth-century's latest intercessor among the canonized Benedictine women saints. Nearly eleven centuries elapsed between her brief lifespan on the isle of Frauenchiemsee and the long-awaited honor accorded her when she was "raised to the altars" by Pope Pius XI on December 19, 1928.[1] Like numerous medieval saints, Irmengard was acclaimed by Chiemgau's *vox populi* as the Bavarian "people's saint" shortly after her death, but unlike those who without the Church's formal canonization were eventually included in the Roman Martyrology, Irmengard's cult met untold obstacles in the intervening centuries prior to the Church's confirmation of her sanctity.[2]

Irmengard, similar to all saints, has a dual citizenship: her earthly life as a Carolingian Bavarian and her life beyond the grave as Chiemgau's saint and invisible patron. Her story must necessarily be appraised on both levels.[3] Except for one brief document, Irmengard left no annals or chronicles, no artistic illuminations, nor any writings of an autobiographical, literary, prophetic, or spiritual nature. Because these resources are lacking, puzzling questions remain unanswered regarding her life. Little is verifiable of her spirituality except for weighty inferences drawn from the three exhumations of her remains and the oral stories told and retold for nearly forty generations. Throughout the centuries she has continued to attract the needy and the poor. Her power to elicit the admiration of pilgrims today at the threshold of the twenty-first century is puzzling. Such ardent devotion can not be attributed to memorable legends, heroic accomplishments, or hagiographical *Vitae* about miraculous powers customary with many medieval saints. All these are non-existent. In this dual story, the people's still-lively veneration of Irmengard is in direct contrast with the scant records extant of her life.

To learn about the Carolingian monastic Irmengard of Chiemsee, and what caused her to be reverenced for more than a millennium in song, poetry, and art; venerated by countless pilgrims visiting her tomb; and prayed to by the nuns of Frauenwörth Abbey and the needy people of Chiemgau and Bavaria; we will consider Irmengard's ancestral and family background as a ninth-century descendant of Charlemagne, her mission as a nun of Buchau and abbess of Frauenwörth, and Bavaria's veneration of her as their saint.

IRMENGARD'S ANCESTRAL HERITAGE

Charlemagne (742–814) and Hildegard of Kempten, his second wife, were the paternal great-grandparents of Irmengard. Her grandfather, King Louis I, (778–840) the sole surviving son and legitimate heir of Charlemagne, inherited the Franconian Empire upon his father's death. Louis I, also called "Louis the Pious or the Debonair,"[4] married Irmengard, the grandniece of the famed Bishop Chrodegang of Metz. The royal couple was blessed with three sons—Lothar I, Pippin, and Louis the German—the father of Irmengard of Chiemsee. In 817 Louis the Pious divided the Empire among these three sons. A year after the death of his wife Irmengard in 818, Louis the Pious married Judith of Welfish descent, the older sister of Emma who later in 827 became the wife of the youngest son, Louis the German. Judith thus became both his stepmother and his sister-in-law. After the birth in 823 of Charles, Judith insisted that the Empire, divided earlier in 817 among the three sons of the first marriage, now be redistricted in 829 to include Charles the Bald as a legitimate heir. In compliance with her ambitious demands, the weak, vacillating Louis made his six-year-old son the Duke of Alemannien.

The series of intrigues precipitated by Judith's behavior toward the sons of Louis the Pious' first marriage resulted in continuous disputes, bitter family feuds and revolts, and considerable bloodshed over the division of the empire among the sons of the two marriages. The complexities flowing from Louis the German's dual relationship with the imperial family contributed in some degree to the eventual disintegration, not only of the eastern kingdom but also of the entire empire governed by his father, Louis the Pious, and his brothers.

Even though the Carolingian era seemed to focus on the spread and unification of the empire through military strength, it was also a golden age noted for its patronage of culture, religion, monasticism, and scholarship. The renaissance begun by Charlemagne came to fruition under Louis the Pious who fostered education, manuscript copying, theological writing, scriptural commentary, poetry, history, and Church and monastic reform.

IRMENGARD'S IMMEDIATE FAMILY

King Louis the German, known as the Bavarian Carolingian,[5] ruled the eastern part of the Franconian Empire and made Bavaria the center of his kingdom. He was noted not only for his sense of justice; fostering of scholarship, literature, and biblical interpretation; a deep piety and eagerness for the spiritual, but also for his competence as a builder of abbeys in Regensburg, Lorsch, and Frauenchiemsee. A year after founding Regensburg as his seat of residence (826), he married Emma, the daughter of Count Welf and the Saxon Eigelwich. Throughout the nearly fifty years they lived together, Louis the German loved and admired his virtuous wife, describing her as "my most beloved spouse, Emma."[6] Louis gave her the royal monastery of Obermünster in Regensburg where, it is said, she frequently distributed alms to the poor and needy, barefoot. Both Louis and Emma died in 876, only a few months apart—Emma in January and Louis in August. Louis the German was buried in the monastery at Lorsch whereas Emma was interred either at her abbey of Obermünster or at St. Emmeram in Regensburg.

God blessed their marriage with seven children—three sons (Carloman, Louis, and Charles the Fat) and four daughters (Hildegard, Irmengard, Gisela, and Bertha). Since no mention is ever made of Giscla, it is believed that she died in early childhood. Following the Frankish custom of equal partition among heirs rather than the Roman principle of transmitting an undivided empire,[7] Louis the German failed to maintain the unity of his eastern kingdom in his attempt to divide his realm among his sons. The three daughters (Hildegard, Bertha, and Irmengard) received royal monasteries from King Louis the German and were appointed abbesses of these minsters. During the Carolingian era, abbeys were frequently given to the daughters of royalty. Some historians conclude that both Charlemagne and Louis the German, in conferring cloisters on their sisters or daughters and appointing them as abbesses, eliminated the need to deal with sons-in-law as potential heirs in the further division of the empire.[8] Louis the Pious supposedly refused to let his daughters marry but kept them at court. Royal abbeys served not only as religious and educational centers, but also as protective bulwarks for emperors and kings and as places for the formation of their sons and daughters.

Theodrada, the daughter of Charlemagne, was given the Abbey of Münsterschwarzach on the Main River and appointed its first abbess. Upon her death in 844, Hildegard (828–856), the oldest daughter of Louis the German and Queen Emma, succeeded her great-aunt in ruling Münsterschwarzach as abbess. After founding the renowned abbey at Zürich and becoming its first abbess in 853, Hildegard immediately proceeded to construct Zürich's famous abbey church, but her untimely death three years later halted the construction temporarily. Both abbeys were bequeathed to Bertha, the youngest daughter of Louis the German. As abbess at Zürich, Bertha completed the magnificent construction of the abbey which the historian, Ratbert of St. Gall, praised in glowing terms.[9] Why Bertha, the younger sister, rather than Irmengard inherited both Münsterschwarzach and Zürich upon Hildegard's unexpected death is not disclosed. Irmengard, in 856, had undoubtedly already received the monastery of Buchau and probably Frauenchiemsee from her father, Louis the German.

LIFE AND MISSION OF IRMENGARD

In this familial and religious yet politically strife-ridden milieu, Irmengard began life around 831, probably at Regensburg, her family's city of residence. Christened Irmengard after her paternal grandmother and her aunt, the wife of Lothar, her name meaning "the powerful one," carried prophetic significance.[10] Originally, the name referred to the Germanic pagan deity, Irmin, whose name signified the might of divinity. Later, the name took on the Teutonic meaning, "public guard." Through her intense love of God, compassion for the poor, and her contemplative spirit, Irmengard Christianized and popularized the name, not only for Bavarians but also for all Germans.

Irmengard's birth coincided with the revolt of 831 to 833 during which her father and his two brothers, Lothar and Pippin, deposed Louis the Pious (Irmengard's grandfather) on Rothfeld, later renamed Lügenfeld, near Sigolsheim. Publicly humiliated, forced to don a garment of penance and become a Church penitent, the Emperor was imprisoned in a monastery dungeon by his own sons. Louis the German and Pippin later freed him from Lothar's grip. This intrigue of sons armed against fathers and of brothers against brothers, with vassals forced to take sides, happened repeatedly during the reigns of Louis the Pious and later of Louis the German.

It is not surprising that throughout the years, the question continues to emerge whether Irmengard felt called to mediate and make reparation to God for the involvement of her grandfather, uncles, father, and brothers in these bloody uprisings.[11] Was Irmengard's mission in life interconnected with her family's cultural and political affairs? Did she feel called upon to counteract through a life of prayer, fasting, and asceticism her family's violent, dynastic feuds, and the warfare they waged to acquire land and imperial power? Whether the gentle Carolingian princess felt called to intercede with God on her family's behalf is at best mere speculation.

HEIR OF BUCHAU MONASTERY

Nothing certain is recorded of Irmengard's early childhood. During the Carolingian era, at an early age, the daughters of royalty were frequently entrusted for their upbringing and education to the nuns at nearby Benedictine abbeys. In addition to the religious influence of Queen Emma, Irmengard may have been formed either by the nuns of Obermünster in Regensburg or more probably by those at Buchau on Federsee in Upper Swabia now Württemberg.

The royal cloister of Buchau near Saulgau was founded in 770 by Irmengard's paternal great-grandmother Hildegard, the wife of Charlemagne, and her sister Adelinde, Irmengard's maternal great-great-grandmother. Both were daughters of Hildebrand von Spoleto, a cousin of Duke Tassilo III who founded Frauenchiemsee that same year. Whether Buchau originally was a cloister for canonesses or a Benedictine abbey is uncertain.[12] Louis the German gave Buchau to Irmengard for her beneficial use. Most probably Irmengard never governed Buchau as abbess since her name is not included in their roster of abbesses. The historian, Hermann Tüchle, maintains that, during Irmengard's time, Buchau followed the Rule of Benedict.[13] He bases this conviction on Benedict of Aniane's reform of the Benedictines which occurred around 818 in the region of Bavaria.

DOCUMENTS DESCRIBING THE THREE CAROLINGIAN ABBESSES

The only surviving document testifying to Irmengard's life describes a transaction of goods between the monastery of Buchau and the abbey of Reichenau, signed at Bodman on April 29, 857.[14] At the request of Irmengard on behalf of Buchau, Louis the German negotiated with Abbot Folchwin of Reichenau for an exchange of land: two hides— approximately 160 to 240 acres[15]—on Bodensee (Lake Constance) in exchange for four *Kilstrionen* (possibly four tenant farmers on homesteads who were obligated to give tribute or pay rent) near Saulgau.[16] In that era, rental payment consisted of produce from the land. It is not possible to ascertain from the records whether this exchange was mutually convenient for both monasteries, or whether Irmengard was only accommodating Folchwin who desired to acquire the land nearer his abbey. It is also possible that Buchau may have needed a source of income or deemed it necessary to enhance its position in Saulgau.[17]

Even though it may not be a true reflection of Irmengard's place in the affections of her family, scholars have commented on the variant terms used by family members in referring to the three Carolingian abbesses—Irmengard, Hildegard, and Bertha—who were also sisters. In the document between Buchau and Reichenau, Louis the German twice refers to Irmengard simply as *"Irmingardae dilectae filiae nostrae"* (Irmingard, our beloved daughter).[18] The lack of extant documents relating to Irmengard's brief reign as abbess at Frauenchiemsee may be due to the destructive burnings there, not only during the Hungarian invasion in 907 but also in 1491 and 1572. Louis the German refers to Hildegard, however, as *"dilectissima filia nostra Hildegardis"* (our most beloved daughter Hildegard).[19] Her epitaph written by Ratbert of St. Gall reads, *"potens Christi clarissima virgo"* (most illustrious virgin powerful in Christ).[20] Bertha acted as mediator in 869 between King Lothar II (her nephew) and Louis the German (her father). Lothar's love for Bertha is conveyed in the words, *"Berta dilectissima patrui nostri gloriosi regis filia"* (Bertha, the most beloved daughter of our uncle, the illustrious king).[21] Louis, her brother, gives the purpose of his donation of goods in Alsace as *"pro amore dilectissimae sororis"* (out of love for our most beloved sister);[22] Also, King Louis, her father, at Queen Emma's request, gave Bertha a letter of protection, exempting her from the jurisdiction of the earls of the region.

FOUNDING AND REFOUNDING OF FRAUENCHIEMSEE

Founding of Frauenchiemsee by Duke Tassilo III

When or why Irmengard moved from Buchau to the scenic yet isolated isle of Frauenchiemsee as its heir and abbess is not known. Even though no documents exist concerning the founding of the twin abbeys on the two isles in Chiemsee, Herrenchiemsee for men and Frauenchiemsee for women, tradition has held that they were founded about 766 by Tassilo III, the last Bavarian duke of the House of Agilolfinger who ruled Bavaria from 748–788.[23] The church of Herrenchiemsee was consecrated on September 1, 782 by Bishop Virgil of Salzburg. Recent literature indicates the probability that Frauenchiemsee's church was likewise dedicated on this same date.[24]

Irmengard must surely have been aware of Charlemagne's role in the tragic downfall of Duke Tassilo III, Frauenchiemsee's founder, which occurred in 788, barely sixty years prior to her arrival.[25] Tassilo, accused of high treason and desertion of Pippin's army, was taken to Ingelheim for trial by the German Parliament. For this desertion which took place twenty-five years earlier, Charlemagne deposed Tassilo on October 25, 788, as the duke governing Bavaria and sentenced him, his wife, and family to death. At Tassilo's request for clemency, the death sentence was commuted, and he was blinded and banished to a monastery. Six years later at Charlemagne's orders, the duke was taken to Frankfurt for yet another trial. Once again Tassilo had to plead for forgiveness and renounce forever all claims to the dukedom for himself and his descendants. His grave inscription preserved at Kremsmünster, a monastery he founded where he very likely was buried, reads, "Tassilo, once a duke, then king, finally a monk."[26]

Tassilo continued to be honored at Frauenwörth on December 11, the anniversary of his death. The first painting after the fire of 1572 by Margaretha Leitgeb (1575) on a two-part wood tablet depicts the abbey's saintly cofounders: Tassilo in knightly armour on the left; Irmengard on the right, dressed simply as a Benedictine nun. Both wear a nimbus of sanctity round their heads.[27] A later painting of 1732, baroque in style, shows Tassilo as a Benedictine monk with a crucifix in his hand, a halo surrounding his head, and a two-winged angel carrying away his crown and scepter. The inscription reads, "Tassilo: King of the Lombards, Duke of Bavaria, our founder."[28] The early abbey prayer books included a prayer to blessed Tassilo. Jean Mabillon (1632–1707), an erudite Maurist historian, included him among the saints and the blessed of the Benedictine Order. A document written on the eve of the Secularization Act of 1803 mentions the liturgical vigil, *Requiem,* and sermon for the feast which was celebrated annually at Frauenwörth on December 10, the anniversary of his death, to honor Duke Tassilo III as their founder. The handwritten and still-extant sermons of 1751 and 1753 preached by Abbot Honorat von Secon are proof of this custom.[29]

Irmengard, First Abbess and Second Founder of Frauenchiemsee

After Tassilo's deposition in 788, Charlemagne as Emperor reserved the royal abbey of St. Maria in Frauenchiemsee for himself. Louis the German, having inherited Frauenchiemsee as King of Bavaria in 817, presented Irmengard with the challenge of rebuilding Frauenwörth. As its second founder, Irmengard may have assumed abbatial responsibilities by the mid 850s; but whether she introduced the Rule of Benedict for her followers during her reign can not be definitively established in the absence of documents.

Excavations in 1961–1964 by Professor Vladimir Milojcic, a Heidelberger archaeologist, indicate that the foundations of the church and the imposing Carolingian gatehouse *(Torhalle)* at Frauenwörth were erected during the mid-ninth century when Irmengard was abbess. Architecturally, the gatehouse resembles the King's Hall of St. Michael at Lorsch which Louis the German endowed; the church is similar to St. Emmeram and Obermünster in Regensburg. The gatehouse, cloister, and abbey church of

Frauenchiemsee were likely richly endowed by King Louis the German. The only architectural remains of this era are the gatehouse, the foundations of the minster, and the bronze door-knocker in the shape of a stylized lion's head.[30] The archaic and beautiful angels still visible in the frescoes of the gatehouse's Chapel of St. Michael are characteristic of ninth-century Carolingian art. These discoveries indicate that Irmengard, as an artist-builder like her sisters Hildegard and Bertha, possessed a keenly sensitive appreciation for beautiful architecture and art.[31]

Irmengard was known by the fisher folk of Chiemsee for her compassion towards the needy. Even though it may be a topos, their epithet, "During her [Irmengard's] lifetime, there were no poor on the shores of Chiemsee," fittingly summed up her generosity.[32] Irmengard undoubtedly remembered the almsgiving of Queen Emma, her mother, and modeled her charity on this example.

DEATH AND CULT OF IRMENGARD

The legend surrounding Irmengard's death on July 16, 866, is preserved on Chiemsee's wooden plaque, a painting dated 1607. The inscription addresses Irmengard as "venerable abbess" and "illustrious princess, daughter of the mighty King Louis the German" and continues, "Irmengard, in her final days, heard the voices of angels inviting her to heaven."[33] Death for Irmengard occurred during the year when her brother Carloman was in revolt against their father. Of the three necrologies of nearby abbeys noting her death, only Seeon mentions Irmengard as abbess. The obituary in the *Calendar of St. Gall* reads, "16 July: Irmengard, daughter of King Louis and consecrated nun of Chiemsee, has died, age 34."[34] The *Annals of Weingarten,* a Welfish monastery, records the year as 866; refers to Irmengard merely as a nun, not as abbess; and simply states, "Irmengard, the sister of the illustrious King Charles, died."[35] A belated handwritten entry made during the twelfth century in the *Necrology of Seeon* confirms her abbatial title but changes the date of her death, "Irmengard, abbess of Chiemsee, 17 July."[36]

In a 1077 document (there is question of its authenticity), Henry IV (1056–1106) revoked the gift of Frauenchiemsee made earlier to the Archbishop of Salzburg and thereby reconfirmed its long-standing rights and privileges as an imperial abbey.[37] The document's value lies chiefly in the mention made of Tassilo as founder, Charlemagne as ruler, and King Louis the German as successor, who gave the abbey to his daughter Irmengard and constituted her its first-known abbess.

Irmengard of Chiemsee's remains were placed in a white marble sarcophagus and buried in the foundation under the southwest column of the Carolingian Minster. Burying the remains within the structural foundation was considered equivalent to canonization in the early Church. It expressed symbolically the unique sanctity of the deceased and the lifelong support given to the Church by this "popularly acclaimed saint." In the early 1960s Milojcic rediscovered Irmengard's original grave and sarcophagus under the southwest corner of the minster. The description of the second exhumation in the diary of the reigning abbess was in accord with this discovery.[38] These excavations by Milojcic conclusively proved that the church's foundation already stood at Irmengard's death.

Irmengard's cult received impetus from her periodic appearances to the nuns of her abbey and her presence felt by Chiemsee's fisher folk. The persistent growth of Irmengard's cult was closely linked to her intercessory powers in response to prayers addressed to her on behalf of the needy, the poor, and the afflicted. The three exhumations of her remains—in 1004, 1631, and 1922—a process conducted only for saintly persons during this era, were significant steps toward Irmengard's eventual canonization as a saint honored by the entire Church.

THE SAINT-MAKING OF IRMENGARD

The First Exhumation

Irmengard's first recorded appearance to the nuns of Chiemsee occurred during the reign of Abbess Tuta, a century after Frauenchiemsee had recovered from the Hungarian invasion of 907. Abbess Tuta turned to Abbot Gerhard in neighboring Seeon for counsel and assistance regarding the exhuming of Irmengard's remains. This first opening of Irmengard's grave around 1004, described in the *"Kränzlein von der seligen Irmengard,"* is the most ancient testimony to the public cult of Saint Irmengard.[39] After examination and veneration, Gerhard reinstated the bones, except for the skull which he kept as a relic for Seeon. There it remained, unlabeled and forgotten, until the third exhumation in 1922 when a diligent search was conducted for it.

A lead tablet (now in Munich's National Museum) was placed in the grave by Abbot Gerhard.[40] On the frontal side of the tablet, the following message was carved along with the date of Irmengard's death and the first invocation to her as a saint: "In this grave rests Irmengard, a daughter of the powerful King Louis, an outstanding holy virgin. She has appeared to us in the time of Abbess Tuta. But many years previous she was our superior. She died on July 16." Around the tablet's edges, this Advent message was written: "Believe and rejoice always in the Lord. Again I say, rejoice." On the reverse side of the tablet, a cross was engraved with these words on its long beam: "Abbot Gerhard made this." Between the short lateral crossbeams these words were carved: "A—O, *Crux—Lux, Rex—Lex*" (Alpha and Omega, Cross and Light, King and Law). Around the edge of the tablet were these words from Philippians: "Let your goodness be proclaimed to all humankind. The Lord is near. Pray for us." This invocation of Irmengard is the first of many written petitions addressed to her as a saint.

Irmengard's remains were interred under the white marble memorial slab on which Abbot Gerhard had this epitaph inscribed in her memory:

> Under this white marble rests the noble virgin Irmengard, precious to God through her holy service. Blessed is Kaiser Louis, whose daughter she was. She was filled with unusual gifts and left Father and crown that she might consecrate herself to Christ and live on earth as God's bride. Here she led her lambs to the Lamb of God and consecrated to him these virgin companions. Her fatherland rejoices because of her, Bavaria is joyful because of such a noble Lady. God himself called her out from on high with the sweet words, "Enter, O Virgin, into the joy of your bridegroom!" May we also with her follow the snow-white innocent Lamb.[41]

In 1473 Abbess Magdalena Auer von Winkel had Gerhard's epitaph engraved on a red marble stone to replace the white marble slab. Three coats of arms representing Irmengard, the abbey, and Abbess Magdalena Auer were substituted for the final words of the original engraving.[42] Irmengard's symbol was that of the French fleur-de-lis (anachronistic as she was not French but a Carolingian of German descent). In his handwritten account of the event, Peter Frank, Frauenchiemsee's historian from 1467–1508, addressed her as "Saint Irmengard," and it is believed, added the words, "Now pray, holy Mary, to your Son."

Second Grave Opening and Translation of Remains

Abbess Magdalena Haidenbucher (1576–1650) governed Frauenwörth for forty-one years (1609–1650) during the first half of the seventeenth century. In her diary she recorded the story of Chiemsee during her abbatial term. During the Thirty Years' War (1618–1648), she provided a haven for many religious women who fled to Chiemsee for refuge. During these troubled times, Abbess Magdalena frequently prayed to Irmengard, yearning ardently to translate her remains to a more appropriate sacred space. Irmengard, as recorded in the diary, appeared to some nuns requesting the translation. Abbess Magdalena enlisted Abbot Albert Keuslin of St. Peter's, Salzburg, to place this petition for the translation of Irmengard's bones before Archbishop Paris Lodron of Salzburg under whose jurisdiction Chiemgau belonged.

The second exhumation of Irmengard's remains occurred on October 20, 1631.[43] When the original sarcophagus was opened, her body, with the lung and liver still preserved but the skull missing, was found lying in an orderly position. Since a considerable portion of her garment was still intact, it was clearly identified as a hairshirt. Irmengard's bones were transferred to a tin coffin and brought in festive procession into the church for veneration. As a reminder of Irmengard's generosity to the poor, the abbess distributed 210 loaves of fine wheaten bread to the people. A Worship of Praise, sung by the choir monks of Herreninsel, preceded a Requiem Mass at which the Lord Prelate of Herreninsel presided. Amid the festive pealing of bells, the bones of Irmengard were translated to a new resting place in the Chapel of the Apostles, now renamed Irmengard Chapel. The exhuming of the body, its translation to an altar or chapel, and the inclusion of the feast in a local church calendar prior to Pope Urban's decree in 1625 came to symbolize the official canonization of a saintly person.[44] Abbess Magdalena had this inscription written as a memorial:

> In this coffin lie the bones of the highly revered in God, the illustrious princess and holy virgin, Lady Irmengard, daughter of Louis of France, as the first church prelate of this worthy House of God and Cloister here at Frauenchiemsee, who died in the year 900, and through the Most Reverend in God, spiritual noble woman, Frau Maria Magdalena Haidenbucher, now Abbess of this Cloister, were transferred on 20 October, 1631.[45]

Ten years later Irmengard once again appeared to the nuns, this time lamenting that her bones lay in water. Upon careful scrutiny, the nuns discovered that ground water had seeped into the foundation of the Apostle Chapel. Again Abbess Magdalena's diary gives a full account of the translation of Irmengard's bones on August 28, 1641, back to the former gravesite.[46] The coffin, whose wooden cover showed Irmengard as a haloed saint, was placed in a higher grave away from water seepage and more accessible to pilgrims. The original site was then forgotten until its rediscovery in 1961. Irmengard's feast was introduced into the Benedictine Calendar of Saints as July 16. At Chiemsee the feast was celebrated with a Mass followed by the distribution of loaves of bread to the poor. The primary purpose for the second exhumation, the furthering of Irmengard's canonization process, was thwarted because of the immediate challenges which faced the abbey because of the ongoing Thirty Years' War.

Irmengard's Cult: 1625–1928

Pope Urban VIII, in codifying the saint-making process, prohibited in 1625 and reiterated in 1634 the public veneration and cult of any new saints not formally approved by Rome but exempted those venerated for centuries.[47] Nevertheless, between the second and the third exhumations, the cult of Irmengard took quantum leaps. The inclusion of her name and feast in numerous martyrologies, church calendars, directories, prayer books, and hagiographical writings is evidence of this. Expressions of gratitude for favors received rapidly abounded in votive pictures and artifacts left at Irmengard's tomb.

The first significant entries were made in 1655 by Gabriel Bucelin in *the Menologium Benedictinum sanctorum et beatorum* for Blessed Irmengard: July 16 as her feast and October 20 for the translation of her relics.[48] Bucelin briefly recounted Irmengard's holiness and the wondrous signs God had worked in her honor. Irmengard's relics, according to the diary of Abbess Scholastika Theresa von Perfall, were shown in the Church of Frauenchiemsee to Bishop Albrecht Sigismund von Freising on May 14, 1672.[49] Two of Blessed Irmengard's relics, a tooth and one small bone, were placed in a silver shrine at St. Peter's Abbey, Salzburg, in 1721.[50] These relics were vital in verifying Irmengard's remains in the third exhumation.

The handwritten prayer books compiled between 1711 and 1736 testify to the inspiration received by the nuns who visited the grave of Irmengard, their first known abbess.[51] The lengthy prayer tribute entitled "*Kränzlein der seligen Irmengard* (1711 and 1728) compares Irmengard to a burning lamp, a beautiful lily and a rose among thorns, a faithful turtledove, a paradisal vine, a loyal servant, and God's forget-me-not. The prayer addresses her thus: "You [Irmengard] were chosen to be our faithful spiritual Mother and Abbess. You governed this cloister well with honor and possessions, and so you may rightfully be considered our pious and true foundress."[52] The *Book of Ceremonies and Functions of Frauenchiemsee* listed for July 17, 1730 (no reason given for this change in date) a ritual description of the festive celebration of Blessed Irmengard on that date beginning with the pealing of bells, the pouring and sharing of wine, and the singing of the Requiem.[53]

Following Bucelin's example, the Bollandists both in 1725 and 1853 placed Irmengard in the *Acta Sanctorum* under the two dates, July 16 and October 20.[54] The entries by Bucelin and the Bollandists prompted various other groups to include Irmengard in their local calendars. In 1755, A. M. Zimmerman likewise included her in his Church Calendar, and in nearby Donauwörth, the Cloister of the Holy Cross in 1786 followed Bucelin's example.[55]

The first part of the nineteenth century undoubtedly seemed like a twofold death sentence pronounced over the cult of Irmengard. Because of the Secularization Act of 1803, the government confiscated Frauenwörth with its goods, archives, art works, church utensils, and vestments but allowed the nuns to live there until they died. The cherished lead tablet with its inscription by Abbot Gerhard was taken to the National Museum in Munich. The ban on Irmengard's cult by Pastor Johann Michael Maier von Breitbunn in 1809 undoubtedly caused the nuns even greater suffering.[56]

Maier forbade all veneration of Irmengard and confiscated all votive pictures, images, and gifts around the grave. Even the saint's halo on the painting gracing her tomb was removed in 1829. The enduring love for Irmengard could not, however, be wrenched out of the hearts of Chiemsee's fisher folk. Legend has it that the fishermen, as they plied their trade at night on Chiemsee, saw the minster's church wondrously lit on certain feasts, casting streams of light across the waters of the lake. Seeing this unusual brilliance, they remarked: "The Abbess [Irmengard] again processes about, making her rounds."[57] Even the death knell decreed by the government's confiscation of the abbey and the prohibition of the cult could not extinguish the people's love for Irmengard. Rather, like the mythical phoenix, it emerged from the ashes of the funeral pyre to renewed growth. Finally, in 1837, this dark night came to an end when King Louis reinstated Frauenchiemsee, their Benedictine life resumed, and the people were free once again to come and pray at Irmengard's tomb.

To lovers of Irmengard, it must have seemed like coming full circle when Petrus Lechner, prior of the Scheyern Benedictines, included Irmengard's name in his Martyrology of the Benedictine Order in 1855.[58]

In 1879, Archbishop Antonius von Steichele reinstated July 16 as Frauenwörth's feast, honoring Blessed Irmengard with a festive Mass rather than with a Vigil and Requiem.[59] Knowing the impact of images on the veneration of saints, in 1913 the archbishops of Munich and Freising approved a new picture of Blessed Irmengard, and her halo was restored. The newly rebuilt St. Hildegard's Abbey, Eibingen, included a Beuronese painting of her in their abbey church.[60] Monsignor Eugenio Pacelli (later Pope Pius XII) prayed at Irmengard's grave on July 24, 1921. The time was now propitious to initiate the proceedings for formal canonization, more than a millennium after Irmengard's death.

THE FINAL EXHUMATION

In the early years of the twentieth century, the question of public veneration with the celebration of the Eucharist and Office honoring Irmengard was still unresolved. In 1922, Abbess Benedikta M. Fensel obtained the help of Munich's Cardinal Michael von Faulhaber for the furtherance of Irmengard's cause for canonization. On July 13, 1922, the tomb was reopened for the third time and her remains investigated by Professor Ferdinand Birkner.[61] The stone sarcophagus was found without its cover. In it was the smaller tin coffin with the inscription engraved on the cover at the 1631 exhumation. After Birkner reconstructed the skeletal bones, he determined that they came from a less-than-robust woman in midlife who suffered from gout. Since the skull was missing, inquiries were made at St. Peter's Abbey, Salzburg, but without success. A further search led to the eventual discovery that the relic, a woman's skull, at the monastery of Seeon belonged to Irmengard. Both abbeys, Seeon and Frauenwörth, had forgotten that Abbot Gerhard, the primary investigator in the first exhumation of 1004, had removed this relic to his monastery. The teeth found in the grave as well as the eye tooth given to St. Peter's Abbey, Salzburg, matched the skull found in Seeon. Birkner concluded that the woman's skull venerated in Seeon belonged to Blessed Irmengard. Since it had been established once again that the remains were those of Irmengard, all was in proper order to proceed with the request for her canonization.

Canonization

During the Episcopal Conference at Freising and Fulda, Cardinal Michael Faulhaber, archbishop of Munich and Freising, in the name of the episcopate of all Germany, petitioned Pope Pius XI to approve the cult of Blessed Irmengard. Pius XI allowed the simple form of the canonization process laid down in the seventeenth century by Urban VIII (1623–1644). It is considered the "narrower back door 'equipollent' (equivalent) beatification or canonization for cults that were at least a century old at the time of Urban's decrees."[62] On December 19, 1928, Pope Pius XI canonized Irmengard as a saint, and her feast was officially set as July 16.[63] Cardinal Faulhaber relayed the news to Frauenwörth with the message, "For the history of this Diocese (Munich), this means an hour of grace." In his archdiocesan newspaper of February 2, 1929, Faulhaber extolled two unique qualities of Irmengard: her asceticism (fasting, penance, and watchful prayer) and her motherly charity to the poor.[64]

Frauenchiemsee observed Irmengard's canonization with a four-day festival, July 14–17, 1929. The festivities culminated in the celebration of the Eucharist *(Dilexisti)* with a proper oration honoring Irmengard at which Cardinal Faulhaber presided and of Vespers *(de Virginibus)* with its own proper *Magnificat* antiphon. Many people from Chiemgau and Bavaria joined Fraueninsel in the event, rejoicing that the *Bavaria Sancta* had been given a new saint as witness of its great Catholic past. Irmengard's relics were interred in a shrine of crystal glass and returned to the Apostle Chapel now renamed St. Irmengard Chapel. On July 13, 1931, Cardinal Michael Faulhaber recommended that Irmengard's skull be returned by Seeon and placed in the chapel dedicated to her honor at Frauenwörth Abbey.

SIGNIFICANCE OF IRMENGARD AS NINTH-CENTURY SAINT

In artistic creations, Irmengard is frequently depicted as a youthful saint in a Benedictine habit, wearing on her head either a Carolingian crown with the customary four half-circles or a simple halo. In her left hand she carries an abbatial staff or crucifix, and in her right hand she holds either a flaming heart or an octagonal tower. These symbols represent Irmengard as a woman of royalty, a builder, and a spiritual leader who used her temporal and spiritual influence not for herself but for others. The flaming heart signifies her deep love of God and compassion for the poor. Her identity, shaped by a life of contemplation hidden with Christ in God, exemplified humility, asceticism, and surrender to God. In her brief earthly sojourn as nun of Buchau and Abbess of Frauenchiemsee, Irmengard witnessed to a pursuit of peace and an unrelenting quest of non-violence in the midst of family feuds. Her influence as the refounder of Frauenchiemsee still continues as countless needy and distressed turn to her for aid in seemingly hopeless situations. Although the buildings constructed in the ninth-century during her brief reign as abbess have been destroyed and the cloister's possessions were lost through plundering invasions, devastating fires, and government confiscation; the memory of Irmengard's dual life will never be wiped out. She continues to be the light upon the lamppost shining brilliantly, enlightening not only her Bavarian and German people but also our planet most radiantly in its darkest hours. In the challenges facing us as Church at the threshold of the twenty-first century, may we trustfully turn to Irmengard, our recently canonized, Benedictine woman patroness, and say with the Chiemsee fisher folk: "Irmengard walks among us once again." As Christians alert to the signs of our era, we can confidently rely on St. Irmengard, "the people's saint," who keeps watch and intercedes for us as we embrace our prophetic Gospel mandate to hear the cry of the poor in our era.

NOTES

1. *Acta Apostolicae Sedis* 21 (1929) 24–26.

2. Since the label "cults" during the last decades has largely taken on a pejorative connotation in the media, it is necessary to define its usage. In this chapter, "cult" embraces the entire saint-making process beginning with the veneraton of the holy person and culminating in papal canonization. See Kenneth Woodward, "Saints, Their Cults, and Canonization," *Making Saints* (New York: Simon and Schuster, 1990) 50–86.

3. Karl Böck, "Irmingard," *Menschen und Heilige* (Donauwörth, 1985) 149–153.

4. For a more complete coverage of the Carolingian era, see A. Cabaniss, *New Catholic Encyclopedia* (New York: McGraw Hill, 1967) 7:657; 8:1018–1019; *The New Encyclopaedia Britannica,* 19th ed. *Micropaedia* (Chicago: Encyclopaedia Britannica Inc., 1990) 7:503–505; and Raoul van Caenegem, *Collier's Encyclopedia* (New York: P. F. Collier, 1993) 25–26. For a comprehensive view of

this era, see Pierre Riche, *The Carolingians: A Family Who Forged Europe,* trans. Michael Idomir Allen (Philadelphia: University of Pennsylvania Press, 1993).

5. See Hans Pörnbacher, *Sankt Irmengard: Die Heilige des Chiemgaus,* 3rd ed. (Anton H. Konrad, 1992) 10–12 for a brief résumé of Louis the German's character.

6. Ibid., 10.

7. James Bryce, *The Holy Roman Empire* (New York: Schocken Books, 1961) 77–79.

8. Maria Walburga Baumann, *Die selige Irmengard von Chiemsee: Jungfrau aus dem Benediktinerorden* (Munich: J. Pfeiffer, 1922) 22–23: Irmengard Schuster, *Die selige Irmengard von Chiemsee* (Chiemsee: Frauenwörth, 1966) 9; Herman Tüchle, *Lebensraum und Lebenkreis der seligen Irmengard* (Bad Buchau: A. Sandmaier & Sohn, 1966) 2–3.

9. Schuster, *Die selige Irmengard,* 10–12; Baumann, *Die selige Irmengard,* 21–22.

10. Baumann, *Die selige Irmengard,* 24–25; Charlotte M. Yonge, *History of Christian Names* (London: Macmillan, 1884) liv, 326–328.

11. Schuster, *Die selige Irmengard,* 6–8; Baumann, *Die selige Irmengard,* 25.

12. Schuster, *Die selige Irmengard,* 13; Baumann, *Die selige Irmengard,* 26–28, 30-31, holds that Buchau was founded as a Benedictine abbey but was already a cloister for canonesses by Irmengard's time; she never was abbess there, only a *monialis.*

13. Tüchle, *Lebensraum und Lebenkreis,* 3–4.

14. Baumann, *Die selige Irmengard,* 25–26, 122–126 gives an explanation and copy of the Latin with a German translation of the Buchau-Reichenau document; *Wirtembergisches Urkundenbuch,* I, 149f.

15. *Webster's New World Dictionary* defines a hide of land (the German *Huben*) as "varying from 80 to 120 acres." To understand the variations in measuring land during this era, see Wilhelm Störmer, "Frühmittelalterlich Grundherrschaft bayerischer Kirchen," in W. Rösener (Hersg.) *Strukturen der Grundherrschaft im frühen Mittelalter* (München, 1982) 388–392.

16. For an explantion of *kilstriones* (Latin) or *Kilstrionen* (German), see Ph. Dollinger, *Der bayerische Bauernstand vom 9. bis sum 13. Jahrhundert,* (München, 1982) 172–173.

17. *Das Bistum Konstanz* 4, *Das (Freiweltliche) Damenstift Buchau am Federsee,* im *Germania Sacra,* ed. Bernhard Theil (Walter de Gruyter: Berlin, 1994) 51.

18. Baumann, *Die selige Irmengard,* 25–26, 34, 122–123.

19. Ibid., 34.

20. Schuster, *Die selige Irmengard,* 10.

21. Baumann, *Die selige Irmengard,* 22, 34.

22. Baumann, *Die selige Irmengard,* 21–22; Schuster, *Die selige Irmengard,* 10–11.

23. Baumann, *Die selige Irmengard,* 33, 114 n. 28; Schuster, *Die selige Irmengard,* 14–15.

24. See H. Dopsch, "Das Salzfass," *Heimatkundliche Zeitschrift des Historischen Vereins Rupertiwinkel* 12 (1978) 81ff.

25. Magdalena Schütz, "Der Stifter—Bayernherzog Tassilo III, *Geschichte der Abtei Frauenwörth* (Chiemsee: Frauenwörth, 1982) 12–17.

26. Baumann, *Die selige Irmengard,* 16, gives Lorsch as a burial place whereas Schuster, *Die selige Irmengard,* 15–16, gives Kremsmünster.

27. For the significance of the wooden plaque, see Peter von Bomhard, "Die selige Irmengard von Chiemsee," *Bavaria Sancta: Zeugen christlichen Glaubens in Bayern,* trans. Georg Schwaiger (Regensburg: Friedrich Pustet, 1973) 3:81; Schütz, *Geschichte,* 12 (illustration of Tassilo); Schuster, *Die selige Irmengard,* 16, 39 (illustration of Irmengard).

28. Pörnbacher, *Sankt Irmengard,* 6; for the illustrations of Tassilo and Irmengard, see Schuster, *Die selige Irmengard,* 60–61.

29. The customs honoring Tassilo are described in Schuster, *Die selige Irmengard,* 16; Pörnbacher, *Sankt Irmengard,* 6; and Baumann, *Die selige Irmengard,* 110–111, n. 10.

30. Pörnbacher, *Sankt Irmengard,* 9, 31–32; Lothar Altman and Peter von Bomhard, *Frauenwörth,* trans. Christine McQueen (Munich and Zurich: Schnell and Steiner GMBH & Co., 1984) 4.

31. For a description of the *Torhalle* and St. Michael's Chapel with its frescoes, see Alois J. Weichslgartner and Wilfried Bahnmüller, *Frauenchiemsee* (Freilassing: Pannonia, 1991) 4–7; Bomhard, *Bavaria Sancta,* 7–9.

32. Schuster, *Die selige Irmengard,* 20, Baumann, *Die selige Irmengard,* 36.

33. Schuster, *Die selige Irmengard,* 22.

34. Ibid.

35. Ibid.

36. Ibid., 20.

37. See Baumann, *Die selige Irmengard,* 127–131, for a copy of the document in Latin and German; Bomhard, *Bavaria Sancta,* 71–72; and Schuster, *Die selige Irmengard,* 21.

38. Schuster, *Die selige Irmengard,* 22–24; Bomhard, *Bavaria Sancta,* 70–71; Weichslgartner and Bahnmüller, *Frauenchiemsee,* 2–4.

39. Baumann, *Die selige Irmengard,* 40–42.

40. For the quotes given on the lead tablet, see Pörnbacher, *Sankt Irmengard,* 18–22; Schuster, *Die selige Irmengard,* 23–24; and Baumann, *Die selige Irmengard,* 41–46.

41. The text is translated from Pörnbacher, *Sankt Irmengard,* 22.

42. Baumann, *Die selige Irmengard,* 46; Bomhard, *Bavaria Sancta,* 70.

43. For a detailed account see Baumann, *Die selige Irmengard,* 35–36, 56–71 and Pörnbacher, *Sankt Irmengard,* 24–27.

44. Kenneth Woodward, *Making Saints,* 65; Baumann, *Die selige Irmengard,* 60–61, 67–71.

45. Schuster, *Die selige Irmengard,* 29.

46. Baumann, *Die selige Irmengard,* 75–77; Bomhard, *Bavaria Sancta,* 83–84.

47. Baumann, *Die selige Irmengard,* 73–74; Woodward, *Making Saints,* 75–76; Bomhard, *Bavaria Sancta,* 83.

48. Baumann, *Die selige Irmengard,* 82–83.

49. Ibid., 83.

50. Ibid., 83–84.

51. Ibid., 132–139.

52. Ibid., 28–30, 140–157 (copy of the script).

53. Ibid., 84–85.

54. *Acta Sanctorum,* Joannes Bollandus et al, entries made July 1725, October 1853 (Venice, 1748) 4:121; 8:814, 1121.

55. A.M. Zimmerman, *Kalendarium Benedictinum* II (Metten, 1934) 460.

56. Bomhard, *Bavaria Sancta,* 85.

57. Baumann, *Die selige Irmengard,* 86–87.

58. Petrus Lechner, *Martyrologium des Benedictiner-Ordens* (Augsburg, 1855) 280.

59. Baumann, *Die selige Irmengard,* 88–89.

60. An illustration (follows p. 40) and an explanation of the Beuronese painting of St. Irmengard in St. Hildegard's Abbey Church is given in Baumann, *Die selige Irmengard,* 90.

61. For a more detailed account of the third exhumation and translation of Irmengard's remains, see Schuster, *Die selige Irmengard,* 19–20, 28–31.

62. Woodward, *Making Saints,* 75–76.

63. Bomhard, *Bavaria Sancta,* 86–88.

64. Pörnbacher, *Sankt Irmengard,* 31.

9

Hrotsvit: Medieval Playwright

Teresa Wolking, O.S.B.

As Western culture approaches the year 2000 to mark its second millennium, it is fitting to look back to the lives of some of the medieval monastic women who have lived and loved monasticism through these many centuries. One of these women is a well known playwright named Hrotsvit.[1] The name Hrotsvit means "loud cry" or "strong cry."[2] Writing in Latin, Hrotsvit refers to herself as *"clamor validum."* Hrotsvit, henceforth referred to by the familiar form of her name, Roswitha, was a tenth-century Benedictine canoness about whom little is certain other than her three books of writings.

A member of the Benedictine Abbey of Gandersheim in what is now Bavaria, Germany, Roswitha distinguished herself by using a remarkable classical education to produce poetry, legends, and plays imitative of Terence. Her works uniquely bridged the drama of Greece and Rome with Europe's later western drama, and her histories contributed measurably to the history of her native Saxony.

Although her family name is not known, it is presumed Roswitha was born to royalty in Saxony around 935. She joined the royal Abbey of Gandersheim in her early twenties, followed the Rule of St. Benedict in a life of prayer, study, and creative work, and died around 1000 in her late sixties.[3]

Gandersheim, one of the oldest of the eleven nunneries in Saxony, was founded in 852[4] by Duke Liudulf, the great-grandfather of Emperor Otto I, and was consecrated November 1, 881.[5] It was one of the so-called free abbeys, subject only to the pope and the king. In Roswitha's day, the Abbey of Gandersheim enjoyed a period of material prosperity and cultural and intellectual eminence. It provided a fine education with exceptional teachers and an ample, well-stocked library.[6] First established at

Brunshausen on the River Ganda in Eastphalia, the original abbey was surrounded by the Harz Mountains. A new abbey was soon built, and the town of Gandersheim grew up around the abbey which became a center of learning and civilization.[7]

Well-schooled teachers at the abbey imparted their love for learning. Roswitha was an avid scholar living amid the nuns and other canonesses who made up the abbey. Haight explains that canonesses lived the communal life of the monastery and participated in the recitation of the Divine Office. While regular nuns took perpetual vows of stability and conversion, canonesses were not required to take vows other than those of obedience and chastity. That provision allowed a canoness to receive guests, to come and go with permission, to own books and other property, and to have servants. Obviously Gandersheim was a refuge for women of nobility. Canonesses' convents were renowned for their learning and the excellence of their dedicated teachers.[8]

Living in the darkest period of Western cultural history but educated within Gandersheim Abbey, Roswitha honored her teachers, both of whom later became abbesses: Rikkardis and Gerberga II, niece of Emperor Otto the Great. She considered her Abbess, Gerberga, a major influence in her own development. Dronke thinks perhaps Roswitha also received some outside tutoring from the court of King Otto.[9] The authors with whose work Roswitha is acquainted are important in both medieval and ancient literature and include Christian writers of the time.[10] Roswitha is without doubt a literate, privileged, and unusual woman. Significant for her scholarship, her canon of works, her ensuing fame, Roswitha is a phenomenon of feminism from a thousand years ago.

Both Wilson [11] and Dronke[12] show Roswitha as deeply rooted in the Renaissance of Charlemagne and the Ottos. Beginning her writing perhaps at mid-century, first she wrote legends and plays, completed her histories in 973, and divided her work into three books, calling her legends, Book One; her plays, Book Two; and her histories, Book Three.

Her first book contains eight metrical saints' legends; her second consists of six plays in rhymed rhythmic prose; her third includes two historical epics, one of the house of Otto and the other of the Abbey of Gandersheim. Her dedicatory letters and five prose prefaces complete her legacy[13] and give significant insight into her self-identity, her impulse to write, and her religious spirit.

It was only in 1501, five centuries after her death, that Conrad Celtes discovered and edited her works for publication.[14] Since that time a wealth of serious scholarship has appeared to attest to Roswitha's literary importance. Her significance today rests with the present-day response to her as a Christian, a monastic, a woman, a scholar, and a genuine, self-assured person who knows both who God is in her life and who she is in God's plan. Her knowledge of double standards for men and women throughout the world of her experience is evident.

Roswitha's basic theme is faith in the resurrection mystery. Her basic gift is confidence in her personal human experience; she senses that God within impels her. Well-equipped with classic humanities' skills, disciplined in monastic living, steeped in Scripture and Psalmody, she is eager to give the gift she has received (Matt 10:8) and, therefore, acts as a grateful Christian—a catechist via her pen.[15]

A marvelously enterprising and independent spirit, an integrated religious woman, Roswitha considered her talents a gift that should not lie idle. Self-aware and self-secure, she worked in secret, eventually showing her work to her abbess, who heartily approved; later, Abbess Gerberga II assigned her to write the histories of the Ottos and of the Abbey.

Her audience at the time of her writing was probably her community members, well-educated and scholarly noblewomen for the most part. A few trusted churchmen surely gave her criticism and encouragement.

THE LEGENDS: "THEOPHILUS"

It is fitting to look more closely at a few of Roswitha's writings. Her eight legends deal with the Virgin Mary; Christ's ascension; a martyr of 760 A.D. named Gongolf; a contemporary martyr, Pelagius, whose story she learned from an eye-witness; a martyr bishop, Dionysius; a repentant priest, Theophilus; a repentant bishop, Basilius; and the virgin martyr, Agnes. Most of her legends are borrowed from apocryphal sources according to their translator, Sister Gonsalva: "As folk-lore and romance her sources are precious, and for the student of mediaeval literature and art, they form a valuable resort for interpreting the imaginations, hopes, and fears of the age."[16]

Both her fifth and sixth legends, dealing with the Greek saints Basilius and Theophilus, are the first literary treatment of the Faust theme in Germany, antedating Goethe (1749–1832) by 900 years. They both concern men who made a pact with the devil and sold their immortal souls for earthly gain. Both sinners repent and are saved.

Leaning on Paul the Deacon's Latin rendering of the Greek legend of Theophilus,[17] Roswitha's "Fall and Conversion of Theophilus, Vicar of his Bishop," opens with his parents at his baptism dedicating him for Divine Service. Consequently he was entrusted to the bishop for his early education in the "streams of wisdom issuing from the sevenfold font (the trivium and the quadrivium)"[18] Advancing step by step, Theophilus becomes a vicar and an exemplary shepherd to his flock. His life shows great devotion to the Blessed Virgin Mary. He refuses to become a bishop when asked, but later is separated from his flourishing parish. The devil enters the story here and uses this devastation to taunt Theophilus with loss of prestige, thus capturing his soul.

Theophilus tearfully visits a magician who takes him to a group of devil-worshipers where Theophilus signs a contract for his own destruction. At once adulation, wealth, distinction come upon him, and Theophilus enjoys the change. God, in his mercy, now touches his soul with remorse and with a desire for Mary's kindness. Forty days of penance in Mary's temple wins him her comfort and his reconciliation with the Church. But he wants his signed paper back. One day he wakes to find the contract on his breast. He dies three days later.

Roswitha's themes of fall and conversion, of sin and salvation extol the power of prayer and penitence and honor God as merciful and forgiving. In touching feminine fashion, Roswitha enters into her character in compassionate description of the agony Theophilus suffers and also in his joy as he rises to spiritual wholeness and holiness. She shows how a Christian's experience of sin can become a doorway to spiritual growth.[19]

The Plays: *Abraham*

All Roswitha's work is didactic, devotional, and, though poetic, highly moral. She gives as her reason for writing her plays the hope that her works will offset the evil influence of Terence's racier tales. Bonfante claims historians of theater have given Roswitha's plays attention chiefly because of their classical tradition in imitation of Terence.[20] She has written six short plays: *Gallicanus, Callimachus, Dulcitius, Abraham, Paphnutius,* and *Sapientia.* These all deal with early Christians in confrontation with paganism. They exalt virginity and accept the fact that martyrdom is a real possibility in the life of any true Christian.

Two of these plays, *Abraham* and *Paphnutius,* involve the Good Shepherd theme. They both are concerned with the redemption of a prostitute. *Abraham* relates the fall and repentance of Maria, who from the age of eight has lived for twenty years a holy life in her cell next to that of her uncle, the hermit Abraham. Then, tempted by a deceitful lover in the dress of a young monk, she loses her virginity and returns to the world to live among prostitutes as a harlot herself. After two years of searching, Abraham finds out where Maria is, disguises himself as a soldier, finds her, and pretends to seek her favors. Following a good dinner they retire to her bedroom; there Abraham reveals his identity, and Maria, ashamed and despairing, willingly yields both to Abraham's compassion and to God's mercy. Returning with Abraham to her cell in early dawn, Maria takes up once more her life of prayer and fasting. She repents relentlessly for twenty years, showing herself now a resplendent example of joyful penitence.

Benedicta Ward, S.L.G., in *Harlots of the Desert,* her recent study of repentance in early monastic sources, notes how Roswitha used details from Ephrem the Deacon's account of the life of Abraham for her play. The monk who sins, the disguise, the disposition of earthly goods, the effort to reclaim a soul are usual motifs; unusual is having a hermit educate a tiny girl.[21] Her story is but a door to the world of the spirit, and shows how one must read these early accounts by interpreting what is veiled beneath the story's words. In the tradition of Christian hagiography, each character stands for something more. Maria, according to Ward, is "an image of salvation;"[22] she needs to learn utter dependence on God alone for mercy.

Wilson's research claims that *Abraham* was the first of Roswitha's plays to be translated, and it still continues to be esteemed as one of her masterpieces; the German humanists favored it for the dramatic talent evident in the recognition scene in the brothel between Maria, the courtesan, and her aged uncle posing as a lover.[23] Without a doubt, Roswitha deserves acclaim as the first medieval playwright.[24] It is "diverting to find that the first woman of any importance in the history of Theatre in Europe is a Benedictine Nun," remarks Rosamond Gilder.[25] Alone, she bridges the gulf between Seneca and Latin tragedy of 65 A.D. and the French mystery play of the twelfth century of the Christian Era. It is ironic that Roswitha, a devout daughter of that Church which sought to destroy the theater, is yet the first woman of European theater.

All six plays show familiarity with the amenities of life in the world beyond the cloister and draw upon a wide variety of classical authors. Gilder recognizes Roswitha's humanness, her self-reliance, her conscientiousness, her hardworking attitude towards her writing, and her justifiable pride in her achievement, claiming that by her plays Roswitha "established herself as poet-laureate of Gandersheim."[26]

In his criticism of Roswitha's *Abraham,* Dronke amusingly comments how "at home" Roswitha was in the Terentian world. "Hrotsvitha is in fantasy a Mary," he says, but "sees herself in imagination as someone stronger—as an Abraham who temporarily pretends to be of that wanton world, but who has not really succumbed to it. Like Abraham, she enters the world of wantonness in order to challenge it, or at least to redeem from it what she—or Abraham—holds most dear."[27] Dronke seems to sense that Roswitha feels that, together, woman and grace can conquer the frightening world of men. He sees her playing games, both in the content and the language of her writings, with the scholars of her day, issuing, in her own way, a challenge to the masculine world.

In her plays, Roswitha directs all her power to touch hearts and uses all the feminine strengths to do so. Exhibiting sympathy, compassion, understanding, Roswitha balances with feminine traits all the abstract masculine thought processes learned from her classical training. Cardinal Gasquet

observes: "The *situation* in Terence's comedies almost invariably turns on
the frailty of women; in Roswitha's plays as invariably on their heroic ad-
herence to chastity."[28] Further, all six plays repeat the idea that women
have the capacity to change their own lives. Roswitha strongly believed
this.

THE HISTORIES: "PRIMORDIA"

The dark, tenth century of Roswitha's day marked the crumbling of the
Carolingian empire while the papacy was also in decline and for sale.
Feudalism was on the rise, and the Holy Roman Empire, in crisis, was suc-
cumbing to the transalpine influence of the German king Otto.[29] A short-
lived hope, the vision of a restored Roman empire of pope and emperor
ruling in harmony from the capital of the world—Rome, of course—was
foreshortened by the untimely death of Otto III in 1002 and of the Saxon
pope Gregory V two years earlier.

But those were also the days Cardinal Gasquet called the Benedictine
Ages because monasticism was flourishing, classical learning was being
fostered, and nunneries were assisting the efforts of the monks in copying
manuscripts. Ironically, the Church, even while trying to wipe out the in-
iquitous literature of the pagans, was at the same time beginning to preserve it and to act as guardian of the precious manuscripts which, in
Europe at least, were all that remained as a witness of past intellectual
glory. Gandersheim was a center of light and learning, an attractive oasis
for eager minds, a place of hope and peace in a world of danger and
damnation. Given the foresight of Abbess Gerberga and the talent of
Roswitha, all history benefits from the efforts expended to preserve and
produce Roswitha's two, historical epics.

True companion-pieces, *Gesta Ottonis* and *Primordia Coenobii
Gandeshemensis,* Roswitha's two histories are closely related, and both
are composed in graceful rhythmic hexameters. Together they form a family saga, for the establisher of Gandersheim Abbey was also the founder
of the Saxon Dynasty.[30] The *Gesta* sings the praises of the Saxon royal
family, especially the success of Otto the Great; the *Primordia*'s 594
verses recount the origins and building of the Gandersheim Abbey
founded by Liudulf and Oda, finished by Otto the Great, and supported
originally by the Saxon dynasty.

Liudulf and Oda had an eldest daughter Luitgard, who was chosen to
be the queen and wife of the famed King Louis of France. Their five other
daughters, perhaps for reasons that had political overtones, joined the
abbey, and the second-oldest daughter Hathumoda became the first abbess
of Gandersheim and governed her little community in a life of holiness the
first twenty-two years of its existence. Daughter Gerberga was second

abbess, also for twenty-two years. Youngest daughter, Abbess Christine, ends Roswitha's history of the abbey with her death in 919. The *Gesta* then pursues the history of the Ottos, concentrating on Otto the Great.

Visions, miracles, dreams, and marvels abound. But the most outstanding character described in *Primordia* is Queen Oda, mother of the abbesses and foremother of the Kings Otto—there were three. After her husband Liudulf died, Oda saw to it that the monastery being newly built was brought to completion under King Otto the Great. Lady Oda herself went to the monastery to live, and while her own daughter Gerberga was Lady Abbess, lived an exemplary life to the age of 107 in the enclosure.[31] The passage describing blessed Oda's presence is evidence of the discipline of the abbey during the days of Gerberga I. Oda always encouraged her children and grandchildren to bestow support upon the Abbey of Gandersheim. Roswitha's lines on Luitgarda, queen with King Louis, show the concerned generosity of the nobility towards the abbey.[32] While historians sense nuances and some creativity in the arrangement of certain facets of Roswitha's histories, one fact is undisputed: her histories offer an authentic source for the dynasty she illumines.

THE CRITICS

During the five hundred years between Roswitha's death and the discovery by Celtes of her manuscript, Roswitha's work was hardly remembered or discussed. She was without influence before the Renaissance. Attempts to prove her work a forgery were futile. The German humanities' scholars have been proud to proclaim her one of their own, albeit she was a woman.[33] She was among the learned women on the list of Lucretia Marinella in Italy of 1600.[34] She had enacted her own style and succeeded. Her plays were likely performed in her own day and certainly have been performed since 1888. Her "loud cry" to date has been heard and read in German, French, Italian, Russian, and likely some additional languages. Roswitha Day was celebrated on February 27 in Gandersheim in 1929. Her plays have been translated into English by Christabel Marshal under the pseudonym Christopher St. John, 1923; by Helene Homeyer, 1970; an acting version by Larissa Bonfante in 1979; and most recently by Katharina M. Wilson of the University of Georgia, 1984. In New York, the Roswitha Club took shape and published Anne Lyon Haight's *Hroswitha of Gandersheim* in 1965. Besides discussing her life and her times, this resource provides an annotated bibliography of her works arranged chronologically from 1494 to 1965.

Contemporary medieval scholars like Katharina Wilson and Peter Dronke constantly challenge and surprise readers with the wealth of scholarship they have unearthed and analyzed.

The catalog of acclaim reads like a litany of pioneering: Roswitha is the first-known dramatist of Christianity; the first-known Saxon poet, the first woman historian of Germany; her legends offer the earliest expression of the Faust theme; her dramas are the first performable plays of the Middle Ages; her epics are the only extant Latin epics written by a woman; and finally, she is the "first medieval poet to have consciously attempted to remold the image of the literary depiction of women."[35]

Dronke is a very sympathetic critic, sensitive to Roswitha's attributes and appreciative of her work, and remarks that "women write from inner need, ardent yet unfanatical, seeking solutions that are apt and truthful existentially."[36] Dronke compliments Roswitha's many-sided resourcefulness, and he likes her coquetry and considers this her distinction.[37]

While Roswitha wrote on the destiny of women in a society whose criticism of women was harsh, Frankforter notes that "Hroswitha of Gandersheim accepted the secondary role which her society accorded women, but she seems to have seen in the Christian dynamics of sin and salvation a destiny which gave women great worth and a basis for self-respect."[38] This same critic underlines Roswitha's emphasis on the reality of the Christ life, on the dignity it confers, and on Christ's power at work in women and in men.

Wilson notes in Roswitha's work a clearly didactic aim, but sees also that her works glorify God, giving her art a religious and moral worth. Roswitha's life and work was a pursuit of learning for Christian ends, much in the way that Jean Leclercq promotes a love for learning and a desire for God.[39]

As nothing human was foreign to Terence, so Roswitha in her contemplative solitude was united in communion with all humankind in every societal and cultural dynamic. This bond with the universal was sufficient for her characters to portray an individuality that is God's mark.[40]

CONCLUSION

In her own day, Roswitha was a creator, a scholar, a woman, a Benedictine, a canoness devoted to the Liturgy of the Hours, a royal historiographer, a poet and playwright, a witness to her faith. Today she is a gift for all Benedictine women.

For present-day monastics, Roswitha's love of learning continues to inspire and encourage scholarship, the kind Leclercq delineates as essential to monastics in keeping with the vocation to which they have been called. She challenges today's monastics to be vital witnesses to the reality of monasticism: single-minded living devoted solely to the honor and glory of God. She challenges them to go deep into the center of living, which is prayer. She herself is a sainted example.

She challenges Christians to know and live their faith, even unto martyrdom. She invites them, likewise, to reckon with the gifts and powers of women, to be accepting and grateful when God uses women, even as prophets. Christians today might pray to her for catechists who are warm, humane, faith-filled, intimate with Jesus, and zealous for souls.

For the contemporary Church, Roswitha encourages a renewed love for consecrated celibacy, an appreciation of the vowed life, and attention to Christ's message. The faith proclaimed through women like Roswitha witnesses to a world order which Jesus sought to bring about.[41] Her work addresses evangelization, education, the alienated, the marginalized, the sinner. Her thrusts are virginity, fidelity, penitence, and compassion. Though Roswitha lived in a dispensation different from that of Terence and the early Christian saints and martyrs, she was ever aware of the universal wisdom and values which permeated both worlds. As a Christian on pilgrimage, she saw the ripple effect of each person's life and work as assisting the gathering in of all God's people into the promised kingdom.

To this day, Roswitha is an honor to women, to the tenth century, to monasticism, to the Christian tradition.

Gandersheim's "loud cry" did not rend the temple veil, shake the earth, or cause graves to yield up their dead. But Roswitha's words certainly have raised many of her readers to a richer, fuller living of their faith.

There are moments in literature when the important thing is to suspect, to hint, to leap, and there are moments when the important thing is to conclude, to bring together, to bind. Roswitha did the latter well, most often concluding with a prayer. To conclude, then, using the model Roswitha provided in her work, let us pray:

> Today and every day, let us beg the Lord to pour out on our world the Spirit that gave life to Benedict, to Scholastica, to Roswitha, and all who preceded us in the monastic life. Let us ask the Spirit to lead us to our future in hope and joy and bring all of us together to everlasting life.
>
> Let us ask this in the name of Jesus, our Oneness. Amen.

NOTES

1. Variant spellings: Roswitha, Rosvide, Hrotsvitha, etc. The name used in this paper is that used six times in her writings by the poet herself. Anne Lyon Haight, *Hroswitha of Gandersheim: Her Life, Times, and Works, a Comprehensive Bibliography* (New York: The Hroswitha Club, 1965) 11.

2. Hrotsvit Latinizes the Saxon 'hruot=clamor and sui(n)d=validus.' Patricia Demers, *Women as Interpreters of the Bible* (New York: Paulist Press, 1992) 38.

3. Katharina M. Wilson, "The Saxon Canoness, Hrotsvit of Gandersheim," *Medieval Women Writers* (Athens: The University of Georgia Press, 1984) 31.

4. Peter Dronke, *Women Writers of the Middle Ages: A Critical Study of Texts from Perpetua (203) to Marguerite Porete (1310)* (New York: Cambridge University Press, 1984) 852.

5. Sister Mary Bernardine Bergman, O.S.B., *Hrotsvithae Liber Tertius: A Text with Translation, Introduction and Commentary* (St. Louis: Saint Louis University Press, 1942) 105.

6. Haight, *Hroswitha of Gandersheim,* 11.

7. Bergman, *Hrosvithae Liber Tertius,* 149.

8. Haight, *Hroswitha of Gandersheim,* 11.

9. Dronke, *Women Writers,* 296.

10. H. Homeyer, *Hrotsvithae Opera* (Munchen: Schoningh, 1970) 950–953 tabulates the numerous classical sources manifest in Hrotsvit's writings; Wilson, "Saxon Canoness," 31.

11. Katharina M. Wilson, trans., *The Dramas of Hrotsvit of Gandersheim, Matrologia Latina* (Toronto: Peregrina Publishing Co., 1985) 3.

12. Dronke, *Women Writers,* 56.

13. Numerous prayers are interspersed within Hrotsvit's creations; thirteen occur in her legends alone. Some are quite lengthy compositions detailing her religious beliefs.

14. Wilson, *Dramas,* 16.

15. Demers interpreting Wilson, 38. It is interesting here that Gerda Lerner, *The Creation of Feminine Consciousness from the Middle Ages to Eighteen-Seventy* (New York: Oxford University Press, 1933) 24, notes how third-century canonesses "devoted themselves to a life of common prayer and the preparation of other women for Christian baptism."

16. Gonsalva Wiegand, O.S.F., *The Non-Dramatic Works of Hrotsvitha: Text, Translation, and Commentary* (St. Meinrad, Ind.: Abbey Press, 1937) 5.

17. Wilson, *Dramas,* 19.

18. Wiegand, *Non-Dramatic Works of Hrotsvitha,* 159.

19. Homeyer, *Hrotsvithae Opera,* 147, and Wilson, *Dramas*, 19, both suggest that because "Theophilus" ends with a before-meal prayer, Hrotsvit's legends were probably read to the community members in the dining room.

20. Larissa Bonfante, trans., *The Plays of Hrotswitha of Gandersheim* (New York: New York University Press, 1979) x.

21. Benedicta Ward, S.L.G., *Harlots of the Desert* (Kalamazoo: Cistercian Publications Inc., 1987) 87.

22. Ibid., 88.

23. Wilson, *Saxon Canoness*, 35.

24. Ibid., 38.

25. Rosamond Gilder, "Hrotsvitha, the Strong Voice of Gandersheim," *Theatre Arts Monthly* 14 (1930) 331.

26. Ibid., 335.

27. Dronke, *Women Writers,* 80.

28. Cardinal Gasquet's introduction to *The Plays of Roswitha* , Christopher St. John, trans. (New York: Benjamin Blom, 1966) xii.

29. Father John Laux, *Church History* (Cincinnati: Benziger, 1932) 269 summarizes briefly to the effect that Adelaide in distress calls King Otto (963–973) to

defend her. He does, crosses the Alps, and then marries her on Christmas day 951. Pope John is impressed, makes Otto an offer: " Come to Rome and I'll make you emperor." Other churchmen supported the idea; they welcomed German aid—(at a price). Otto was crowned February 2, 962. Laux says, "Thus Otto transferred the Roman Empire to the Eastern Franks and began The Holy Roman Empire of the German Nation that lasted at least in name eight hundred and thirty-four years." 269.

30. Sister Hilda Obermeier, O.S.B., *Hrotsvitha, Gandersheim, and the Saxon House* (M.A. diss., The Catholic University of America, 1925) 31.

31. Bergman, *Hrosvithae Liber Tertius,* 105.

32. Ibid., 107.

33. Wilson, *Saxon Canoness,* vii.

34. Lerner, *Creation of Feminine Consciousness,* 262.

35. Wilson, *Saxon Canoness,* 30.

36. Dronke, *Women Writers,* x.

37. Ibid., 83.

38. A. D. Frankforter, "Hroswitha of Gandersheim and the Destiny of Women," *The Historian* XLI (1979) 314.

39. Katharina M. Wilson, "Hrotsvit and the Artes: Learning *Ad Usum Meliorem,*" *The Worlds of Medieval Women: Creativity, Influence, Imagination,* eds. Constance H. Berman, Charles W. Connell, Judith Rice Rothschild (Morgantown: West Virginia University Press, 1985) 5, and Jean Leclercq, *The Love of Learning and the Desire for God: A Study of Monastic Culture,* trans. Catharine Misrahi (New York: Fordham University Press, 1962) 57: "Learning is necessary if one is to approach God and to express what is perceived of Him; on the other hand, literature must be continually transcended and elevated in the striving to attain eternal life."

40. Jean Leclercq, "Solitude and Solidarity: Medieval Women Recluses," *Medieval Religious Women: Peaceweavers,* eds. Lillian Thomas Shank and John A. Nichols, Cistercian Studies Series 72 (Kalamazoo: Cistercian Publications Inc., 1987) 81.

41. Francis D. Kelly, *The Mystery We Proclaim : Catechesis for the Third Millennium* (Huntington: Our Sunday Visitor, Inc., 1993) 55.

10

St. Hildegard of Bingen (1098–1179) and Bl. Jutta of Spanheim (1084–1136): Foremothers in Wisdom

Hildegard Ryan, O.S.B.

*She [Wisdom] is a breath of the power of God
and a pure emanation of the glory of
the Almighty.
She is a reflection of eternal light
at play everywhere on the earth,
delighting to be with the children
of the earth.*[1]

St. Hildegard of Bingen and Blessed Jutta of Spanheim were the graced recipients of Wisdom or *Sapientia:* the essence of the thought of God immanent in our world and referred to above.[2] Wisdom is restless until it finds a dwelling place,[3] a fertile heart in which to take root and grow towards its own origin: the Creator of all life. Wisdom is the force behind the *obsculta*[4] of the Benedictine Rule, St. Benedict's call to his followers to "listen," and sets the scene for the only play which has no ending. There are two players: *magistra*—teacher or master—and disciple, and the scene is set for daily encounter with the paschal mystery in its stark reality. The disciple is called to incline the ear of her heart[5] to the teacher's instructions, to open her eyes to the light,[6] to run while the light remains,[7] to run while there is time to accomplish all the teachings of Wisdom by the light of life,[8] and to walk according to another's decisions and directions, in glad obedience.[9] When all this is accomplished, the disciple discovers that she is still at the beginning.

Hildegard of Bingen and Jutta of Spanheim, disciple and *magistra*, are twelfth-century foremothers in this paschal drama grounded in *Sapientia*. Blessed Jutta of Spanheim or of Disibodenberg, as she came to be known, was an anchoress and the sister of Count Meginhard of Spanheim. She encountered her disciple, Hildegard, when, as a child of eight years, Hildegard was placed in Jutta's care by her parents, Hildebert, Baron of Gut Bermersheim, and his wife, Mechtild.

In the *Life of Hildegard,* written by the monks Gottfried and Theodoric, we read that the child was secluded at Disibodenberg with this devout woman, Jutta, who taught her humility and innocence, the Psalter, psalm notation, and the playing of the ten-stringed lyre. We are also informed that Jutta was Hildegard's "venerable mother," who yearned over her, rejoiced in her progress, and perceived within her disciple "a leader, and a pathfinder of the ways of excellence."[10] "Venerable mother" is thus the title attributed to Jutta, one dedicated to God as an anchoress. The vocation of Jutta of Spanheim is described by Miriam Schmitt, O.S.B., a contemporary Hildegardian scholar, as one of intimate communion with God in a life of seclusion.[11] Perhaps it was in this secluded life of communion with God that Hildegard herself first experienced the spiritual struggle which would later be expressed in her *Ordo Virtutum*.

The life of a twelfth-century anchoress was characterized by three realities: prayer, fasting, and good works. This life was in keeping with the tradition of eremitic life through the centuries. Also in keeping with the tradition was the acceptance of disciples—in the case of Jutta, young girls entrusted to her formation. What Hildegard and her companions experienced of their *magistra* through six years in the hermitage and twenty-four years as a growing community under the influence of the re-established male Benedictine community at Disibodenberg is described by Hildegard in her *Vita*. She tells us that this woman of nobility, Jutta, *"was inundated with the Grace of God, like a river flooded by many streams. She never allowed herself rest from good deeds until she made a good end of this present life."*[12] Jutta is a graced woman and a source of life for her disciples, a foremother in Wisdom, upheld by a wisdom rule, which in itself, rested on the rock of listening, the *obsculta*. Again, we turn to Hildegard for a description of St. Benedict, the author of this wisdom rule:

> *[He was] a closed fountain in that he poured forth his teaching under the direction of God and fixed the exact keynote of his teaching neither too high nor too low, but right in the middle sphere so that everyone, the strong in mind or the intellectually weak, can readily drink from it according to his capacity.*[13]

Benedict, Jutta, Hildegard, and her companions were all participants in a traditional discourse of human relatedness:[14] ways of listening, acting, and speaking that have been tried and tested in the refining fire of Divine Wisdom. Within this tradition, Hildegard of Bingen progressed in holiness under the care of her "venerable mother," with one aim: to please God alone.[15] From the age of eight until the age of thirty-eight,[16] the year of Jutta's death, Hildegard pursued the "ways of excellence"[17] as part of a long procession of people who had already pursued[18] the same path.

Hildegard made her monastic profession at approximately the age of fifteen in what was by then the nucleus of a cenobitic community growing up around Jutta[19] and living under the wisdom Rule of Benedict. Hildegard received the veil, sign of her consecration, from Bishop Otto of Bamberg. There seems to be no doubt that it was a black veil, the symbol of lifelong profession; later, as abbess of her community, she exercised her autonomy by allowing her nuns different forms of dress. Part of this was the wearing of tiaras, crowns, and white veils on feast days, for she saw that the virginity of her nuns *"had no bright emblem—nothing but a black veil and an image of the cross."*[20]

During the years following her profession, the *Vita* speaks of Hildegard *"guarding her virginity with the rampart of humility"* and manifesting *"tranquillity of heart by her retiring silence and fewness of words."*[21] This description, in its traditional hagiographical style, can lead us far from reality. We know that Hildegard, in her own commentary on the Rule of Benedict, speaks of boredom which is inseparable from too long a silence, and reinforces the abbot's discretion in granting permission for converse with one another, no doubt as part of that great discourse of human relatedness.[22] In this description, though, the *Vita Hildegardis* echoes the sounds of a wisdom rule, as it does in two other instances. Firstly, patience is noted as the guardian of all progress in virtue, and secondly, physical weakness is that ever-present reality which brings humanity to look at the face of God and to wait upon the Lord.[23] Hildegard suffered frequent illness which, in her own words, *"wasted my body and sapped my strength."*[24] This sharing, through patience, in the suffering of Christ was a visible part of her existential wisdom which, after thirty hidden years as disciple relating to *magistra*, would produce the fruits of a totally Christo-centric theology grounded in the monastic tradition.

Sapientia, at home in the heart of Hildegard, brought about her spiritual birthing that included its multiple offspring, not least of which was her prophetic inspiration. Such inspiration came to life through the medium of visions in the tradition of the Old Testament: *"If anyone among you is a prophet, I make myself known to that person in a vision."*[25] Hildegard reinforces the sacred interaction between *Sapientia* and its visionary manifestation when she writes, *"Wisdom teaches by the light of love, and makes me glad to tell how I myself am regarded in this vision."*[26] She speaks of being called from the womb; of having visions from her third year of life on up to her fifteenth year when she realized her unique calling; and of concealing her visions from all but her venerable mother, Jutta, who in turn *"disclosed them to a monk whom she knew."*[27]

After Jutta's death in 1136, Hildegard was chosen to be abbess of the community.[28] Only then did this same monk and confidant of Jutta, whom we know as Volmar, order Hildegard to write down her visions *"till he could consider their true character and their origin."*[29] Her visions, committed to writing, revealed an understanding of *"the prophets, the gospels . . . of other holy men . . . of certain philosophers,"*[30] an understanding devoid of a comparable educational background[31] and one which prompted Bernard of Clairvaux to remind her of her infused knowledge, her anointing of the Spirit.[32] Her gift of prophecy, found to be of God and in accord with authentic Old Testament tradition, was *"approved and accepted by the greater masculine world"* when Pope Eugene III *"had her writings read publicly before many people"*[33] during the Synod of Trier:[34] *"Trusting in the grace of God he sent a letter containing his blessing and ordered me to diligently commit to writing whatever I saw or heard in vision."*[35]

Such prophetic inspiration, the offspring of Wisdom, became, in the life of this Benedictine foremother, a force working itself out in the history of the twelfth century. As all Benedictines are called to prophetic witness with whatever variety of expression is required by the needs of the Church and the world at a given epoch,[36] so Hildegard, as part of her Church and world with its religious, secular, historical, cultural, and sociological aspects, revealed the Wisdom of God in prophetic witness: in utterances, writings, theater, music, reform, natural medicine, harmony with all creation and in relationship with the earth. The Wisdom of God, in the spirit of this one Benedictine woman, was everywhere at play in her world, in her times, in her life.

The fertile setting for her prophetic activity was not the small dwelling place of Jutta, inadequate for a growing community, but rather a place revealed to her by the Spirit "where the river Nahe flows into the Rhine."[37] The area was Rupertsberg, named after St. Rupert the Confessor.

Opposition to the move from Disibodenberg to Rupertsberg came from the monks of St. Disibod who "could scarcely tolerate the thought of her going at all."[38] At this time, three illnesses witnessed to Divine intervention in the event. Hildegard, whose first opposition was from the monks, "fell into a long illness"[39] until the monks of St. Disibod realized that it was Providence who demanded their consent to the move. Opposition ceased on their part, but continued through an unordained monk, Arnold, until he, too, was stricken with what seemed like a fatal illness. After being carried to the Church of St Rupert and promising to cease further opposition, he was healed and contributed to the project, working by the labour of his hands to clear the chosen site. The Abbot of St. Disibod, Kuno, was also enlightened, even if it was through fear, by a second illness which oppressed Hildegard. The strangeness of her illness so filled him with terror that he, too, ceased any further opposition. The granting of one last permission concluded the argument,[40] and Hildegard and her nuns were permitted to establish their new monastery at Rupertsberg, while remaining dependent on the monks of Disibodenberg in all spiritual matters and for monastic profession.[41] It was here, in a new place revealed to Hildegard by the Spirit, that her prophetic inspiration and creativity began to overflow with a relentless energy that would disturb even the strongest forces of mediocrity and confront them with the *Sapientia* of God.

One of the most common errors when writing a biography is to ignore the source from which a being flows and to speak of a person in terms of accomplishments, to divide a life into orderly periods of time in which such accomplishments are achieved. Hildegard of Bingen, a woman whose entire being flows from Wisdom and is possessed by Wisdom, defies any such divisions. Scripture tells us that Wisdom is *"quicker to move than any motion. . ."*[42] and pervades and permeates all things. Her life epitomizes a oneness; an existential unity, immanent and tangible, of Wisdom in the fullness of prophetic inspiration and creativity. It is the Wisdom which Hildegard herself describes as "green like the first sprouts of the patriarchs and prophets who sighed in their tribulations for the Incarnation . . . and white like the virginity of Mary, and red like the faith of the martyrs, and brilliant blue like the lucent love of contemplation. . . ."[43]

Sapientia is the prophetic breath within Hildegard's being, manifesting itself in a multitude of colors. Firstly, her writings—the literary witness of her visions—include three major works: *Scivias,*[44] compiled with the help of her monk-scribe, Volmar, between 1141 and 1153, consists of three books concerning the Creator and creation, the Redeemer and redemption, and the history of salvation. *Sapientia,* finding its expression in visionary perception, reveals the living *logos* of God who in turn shines forth the *"holiness and goodness of the Father"*[45] in light. But the *logos* itself is Wisdom, the Word *"who was in the heart of the Father before all creatures."*[46]

The theology of *Scivias* is entirely Christo-centric, and the influence of the Johannine prologue is dominant: pre-existent unity with the eternal God, the life, death, resurrection, and return to glory of Jesus the Christ. One of the more evocative images of the *Scivias* depicts the dead Christ on the cross with life pouring from the wound at his side and filling a cup held by his spouse, the Church; the lower half of the image is marked by Christ's birth, sepulcher, resurrection, and ascension. The woman symbolizing the Church opens her hands in a gesture of adoration before the mysteries being renewed.[47] It is a profound revelation of one possessed by Wisdom and unified in vision.

Scivias, this book of knowledge revealed in the forty-third year of her life, is also rich in monastic theology and the tradition of a wisdom rule. There are references to the monastic values of stability,[48] humility,[49] Christ as shepherd,[50] listening,[51] vigilance,[52] and fear of the Lord.[53] Longing and desire,[54] reliance on God,[55] and faith in the presence of God everywhere[56] also echo within the monastic tradition. There is even a theology of correction.[57] Excerpts can be found on the nature of a monk's embrace of monastic profession and of his cowl as the symbol of the incarnation and burial of Christ.[58] For Hildegard, the origins of monastic life issue forth from the light of Divine Wisdom and are explained thus:

> The first light of day designates the faithful words of the apostolic teaching; the dawn, the beginning of this way of life which, following that teaching, first came about in solitude and in caves; but the SUN symbolizes the separate and well-disposed way I then brought about through My servant Benedict, whom I passed by in burning fire, teaching him to honour the Incarnation of My Son in the garment of His way of life and imitate His passion in the abnegation of his will.[59]

Liber Vitae Meritorum (The Book of Life's Merits) was written between 1158 and 1163; and *Liber Divinorum Operum* (The Book of Divine Works) between 1163 and 1173. The first of these was a treatise on vices and virtues in colorful Hildegardian imagery. The last of the great trilogy, a volume recounting ten cosmological visions, was near completion when the death of her scribe, Volmar, occurred.[60] Historically, Hildegard situates this work in 1163 "when the oppression of the See of Rome under Henry the Roman emperor was not yet ended."[61] She records the voice from heaven addressing her as a "wretched creature and daughter of much toil" and announcing that "the depth of the mysteries of God" have completely permeated her. It commands her to "transmit for the benefit of humanity an accurate account of what you see with the inner eye and what you hear with the inner ear of your soul."[62] The end goal for Hildegard is an adoration born of Wisdom and a reverence worthy of the God of Wisdom. The inner eye of her spirit, the inner ear of her soul grasped heavenly mysteries of the true and living light, mysteries such as the origin of life, the creation of the world and humanity, and the coming of Christ. But more than all this, it thrust forward into the ultimate in monastic prophetic witness: the completion of the cosmos and the end of time.

Woven into Hildegard's overall sapiential revelation is yet another creative masterpiece inspired by the wisdom of the Rule of Benedict in its exposition of the ancient monastic theme, struggle against temptation, with its origins in the inspired texts of the Old and New Testament literature. This masterpiece is *Ordo Virtutum,* the earliest discovered liturgical morality play.[63] It is a creative art form used in women's monastic communities through the centuries. This form of feminine expression addresses the realities of monastic living which place great emphasis on silence, work, prayer, personal and communal discipline.

Hildegard's radical creativity goes beyond any norms of composition which may have been typical of this period and reflects her prophetic, visionary, and apocalyptic expression. It is a play about virtues depicted as allegorical figures calling the penitent person to conversion. The images are both biblical and Christological, and the cries of the allegorical figures are those which originated in the earliest forms of monastic life. The fathers and mothers of the desert, those ancient *penitentes*, were called to and fro by opposing voices—good and evil. This ancient theme finds a parallel in Benedict's tools for good works or instruments for virtuous living: charity, humility, obedience, fear of God, hope, chastity, faith, renunciation, self-discipline, victory, discretion, and patience. Hildegard has created a masterpiece in monastic theology and in the subtleties of spiritual warfare. While the devil in scene one shouts, "What's the use of hard effort . . . look to the world: it will embrace you with great honour. . . ." the virtues reply, "Is this not a plangent voice of utmost sorrow?"[64] In scene three, the lamenting penitent is addressed by the virtues: "You who escaped, come, come to us and God will take you back."[65] St. Benedict, in chapter 4 of the Rule, the *"Tools of Good Works,"* reminds the monastic to be certain "that the evil you commit is always your own and yours to acknowledge"[66] and warns a little further on: "hate the urgings of self-will."[67] After many teachings on the virtuous life, his final word is "never lose hope in God's mercy."[68] Surely this is the underlying foundation of the *Ordo Virtutum:* "God will heal you. God will take you back. The good Shepherd is searching for his lost sheep."[69] St. Benedict's use of 1 Cor 2:9 with the promise of unheard of glory for those loved by God is echoed in Hildegard's royal nuptials[70] and the heavenly Jerusalem,[71] the destiny of one fashioned in the deep height of the Wisdom of God.[72]

The *Ordo Virtutum,* together with her cycle of songs, forms what Hildegard called the *Symphony of the Harmony of Celestial Revelations.*[73] Since her music is yet another expression of her profound unity with the God of Wisdom, her description is accurate. Wisdom enters into the human spirit, finds a home there, and gives birth to a new creation. Her antiphons and responsories, sequences and hymns reinforce this tangible unity of her spirit. The communion of saints, the procession of those who had gone before her in Wisdom, the Mother of God, the women and men who had been refined in the fire of God's love—St. Disibod, St. Rupert, St. Matthias, St. Ursula and her virgin companions, the martyrs—all are part of the one great movement toward the light of God's face enlivened by the Spirit of God.[74]

Not least among those worthy of her creativity is Boniface, English Benedictine monk, who was instrumental in the evangelization of the Teutonic peoples:

> O Boniface
> the living light saw you
> like a wise man
> who returned to their source
> the pure waters flowing from God
> when you watered the greenness of the flowers.[75]

Perhaps the "greenness" is the blood of martyrdom poured upon the earth and received by the earth which truly watered those waiting for the freedom of Christ.

Hildegard's musical creativity is a source of new life and an offspring of Wisdom. Dr. Greta Mary Hair, in her work on *"O Ecclesia,"* Hildegard's sequence for St. Ursula,[76] makes a suggestion which points to the essence of Hildegard's productivity and giftedness in this field, commenting that Hildegard may have invented her own musical mode with a vocal range especially suited to the registral disposition of her nuns.[77] This suggestion is made after considering a number of questions relating to the modal origins of her music. However, as Dr. Hair also points out, this does not deny the influences "absorbed through her musical experiences and environment which were intelligently and imaginatively woven into a musical style of her own."[78] Hildegard was a creator by the power of Wisdom everywhere at play in her world. For one so highly sensitive and receptive to the varying shades of light, it is not unusual to find a "new creation" at the touch of her hands or the sound of her voice. But what is a new creation? Surely it is something that frees the human spirit from bondage and calls forth a person's fullest potential. It is an act of Wisdom which "renews the world,"[79] a Wisdom that is "the breath of the power of God"[80] breathing into one's spirit the very life of the Creator-God.

While Hildegard's medical works, *Causae et Curae* and *Physica* cannot be called visionary, they are nevertheless the fruit of *Sapientia*. Within Wisdom "is a spirit intelligent,"[81] and within Wisdom is life and healing, harmony and perfect union. Wisdom teaches that the earth is Mother and in this capacity is fertile with healing properties. Hildegard, foremother in Wisdom, is conscious of a great harmony that exists in all creation, a oneness that knows there is nothing lacking or wanting in the order of creation. "Greenness is the living life of the fruitful earth."[82] and it is this greenness or *viriditas* which is the image Hildegard uses for spiritual fertility. Virtues are green with vitality, indolence is drought, good deeds are greening power, and its opposite is aridity.[83] Greenness is one with moisture, signifying holiness and unity with the Spirit.[84] Wisdom is everywhere at play, gathering all creation into the perfection of unity and harmony. Hildegard of Bingen, sensitively tuned to the cosmos, sees the *"Living Light"* shedding its rays on the relationship between human life and plant life, between the subtle workings of the mind and the functions of the body, between woman and man in the fullness of relationship, between all creatures and all creation. Hildegard is prophetess of unity and harmony taught her by *Sapientia* who proclaims: "He it was who gave me sure knowledge of what exists . . . the powers of spirits and human mental processes, the varieties of plants and the medical properties of roots."[85] In this knowledge, "God's deeds are established in such a way that no creature remains so incomplete as to lack anything in its nature."[86]

In the life of every prophet, there is a story of rejection and intense suffering. For Hildegard of Bingen, it took the form of criticism and impending excommunication. Because her nuns were exclusively from noble families, she was challenged as living in opposition to the gospel of Christ, the Christ of the poor and marginalized. But noble blood as a criterion for acceptance into the community brought other difficulties which challenged her at her most vulnerable level: that of relationship.

The situation concerned Richardis of Stade, whom Hildegard loved deeply. Richardis, a member of the Rupertsberg community, was in the grip of the temptation to fame because of the influence of her family. She was also the woman whose nobility of conduct, wisdom, and consecrated celibacy Hildegard reverenced. When Richardis accepted the position of abbess in a nearby community, Hildegard refused to "give her leave to take up her new task."[87] When Archbishop Henry of Mainz appealed on behalf of Richardis and her family, Hildegard responded with a prophetic letter stating the truth of the evil practice: "The spirit of God, full of zeal, says: pastors, lament and mourn at this time, because you do not know what you do when you squander offices, whose source is God, for financial gain."[88]

Hildegard was challenging the dark side of the Church and monasticism and addressing those issues which clouded the light of Divine Wisdom. Not only did she address and condemn practices such as simony, she also challenged the Cathar sect which had spread to the Rhineland by the mid-twelfth century. As prophetess, she contested and condemned its view that human procreation was evil and that body and soul were in an unequal partnership. As a woman in her sixties, she later preached against the sect in Cologne, reminding the clergy of the dangers of these false teachings and proclaiming the Church, mourning and weeping over such wickedness.[89] Inherent in her prophetic criticism is her respect for the priestly ministry and her great fear of the way the clergy besmirched the face of the Church with "the great filthiness of their lascivious lives and the great foulness of fornication and adultery."[90] In Hildegard's approach to preaching monastic reform, she could not reconcile participation in the crusades with the living of monastic life as did Bernard of Clairvaux.[91] She warned the monks of St Eucharius to "be vigilant in God" because she had seen, in a true vision, some monks who were "enveloped in the blackness of acrid smoke because of their habitually foul behaviour."[92]

As prophetic reformer, she undertook four preaching tours which included such centers as Bamberg, Trier, Cologne, and Zweifalten. She undertook the last tour when she was seventy-two years of age, a witness to the life force of the Spirit which fired her to confront everyone with the Wisdom of God.

In her letters as well, the truth of a prophetic voice rings out without compromise, especially in the case of Frederick Barbarossa. During the period of papal schism, Hildegard moves from initial praise of Frederick and the warmth of relationship with his family[93] into the uncompromising position of prophetic condemnation of one who has not only condoned division within the Church and been excommunicated but has instigated that division by electing three anti-popes.[94]

To Abbess Hazzecha of Krauftal, Hildegard speaks of the life force of discretion against the death force of Satan's subtleties and addresses an age-old problem always present in monastic life. The melody of death plays us: "Your sins can't be wiped out unless you trample down your body with tears and grief and with such immense labours that it withers totally."[95] The melody, on the one hand, echoes the Rule of Benedict, chapter 4:57, with its exhortation to "every day with tears and sighs confess your past sins to God in prayer." The second part is subtly removed from the spirit of the Rule where it focuses on a false and self-centered asceticism which, as Hildegard points out, leads to a physical breaking of bodily strength and a departure from reliance on the mercy of God. For every Benedictine, asceticism is obedience, and nothing is ever undertaken in the way of a penance without the permission and discretion of the abbess. Thus, the voice which speaks of "immense bodily labours" to eradicate sinfulness is the subtle voice of the devil.

Two other events in the life of Hildegard are important because they reveal a Wisdom which has matured through many decades of building upon the foundation of the *obsculta*, listening to the Rule. The foundation is a firm call to choose instruction from one's earliest youth, *"and till your hair is white, you will keep finding wisdom."*[96] The first event is the exorcism performed on Sigewize, a woman of nobility possessed by the devil. One of Hildegard's biographers, Theodoric, exaggerates the story with traditional hagiographical embellishment. Nevertheless, the important fact is the way Hildegard attempted the exorcism. Steeped in the richness of Benedictine monastic liturgy, she created a ritual of exorcism which was committed to writing and performed on Sigewize by the monks and was effective for a time. When Evil gripped her a second time, Abbot

Brauweiler entreated Hildegard to house Sigewize in her community to continue the exorcism. Again, Hildegard used the tried and proven formula, liturgical prayer and fasting, not only by the nuns of Rupertsberg but also by the people of the surrounding area. Prayer and fasting to rid her of the demon lasted from February 2nd, then the feast of the Purification of the Blessed Virgin Mary, until Easter Sunday, the day of the Resurrection. The exorcism was accomplished without sensation or miracles during the Easter Vigil. Only one physical spasm is recorded and after that a period of convalescence. Was the time chosen purely coincidental or was it symbolic that the former feast of the Purification marked the end of Christmastide and Easter Sunday the beginning of Paschaltide? This included the Lenten season with its emphasis on the temptations of Christ and his journey through the passion, death, and resurrection. The paschal mystery was lived out by a woman in bondage. Perhaps the nuns of Rupertsberg witnessed the first holistic approach to healing as Hildegard assisted the woman of nobility to unburden her spirit, loosen the bonds, and expose the wounds of the years within the one place where there is no escape from the reality of God, of self, and of others. This was only one instance of many as Hildegard's reputation for healing and exorcism spread throughout her world and challenged evil in its various forms.

The second important event is the interdict placed upon the Rupertsberg community after a man of nobility is buried in the convent cemetery. Miriam Schmitt describes this event as the most bitter experience and most crucial test of Hildegard's prophetic mission.[97]

Hildegard's stance as a prophet reaches its fulfillment in the challenge she presented to ecclesiastical authorities who ordered that an interdict be placed upon the Rupertsberg convent, forbidding the nuns to attend Mass, receive the Eucharist, or sing the Divine Office. The dead body of a man of nobility who had been excommunicated, then reconciled with the Church before his death, was buried in the convent cemetery[98] and was the subject of the contestation. When the Mainz prelates, "in the name of their archbishop who was residing in Italy as a result of his own intrigue,"[99] ordered the body to be exhumed and cast out of the convent cemetery, Hildegard's response was to take her abbatial staff and wipe out all traces of the grave that could lead to its being identified and desecrated.[100]

In this, as in all events, Hildegard, guided by her "true light," wrote to the Mainz prelates: "So we did not dare expose him . . . not at all because we make light of the advice of honourable men or of our prelates' command, but lest we seem to injure Christ's sacrament—with which the man was blessed while still alive—by woman's savagery.[101]

Hildegard and her nuns abided by the interdict, knowing at the same time that no external force, human or otherwise, could prevent their spirits from being uplifted in the praise of God. Their primary motive, to praise their God, could not be suppressed or stifled by an interdict which prevented external expression. In her letter to the prelates of Mainz, Hildegard gives us her theology of liturgical music when she writes that she heard the voice of her "Living Light" speaking of the "diverse kinds of praises" in Psalm 150. This text reinforced the power of praise whether it be spoken "in a low voice"[102] as they were forced to do, sung, played instrumentally, or expressed in dance. Again, this prophet of unity and harmony captures the power of the cosmic liturgy pulsating with every living breath.[103] This interdict was imposed upon her convent in 1178, the year before Hildegard's death.

Her last extant letter addressing this issue was written to Archbishop Christian of Mainz in 1179. A few months before her death the interdict was lifted, but we can presume that this prophetess gave her life for the truth which she could never deny. The words of Benedict were personified in her prophetic ministry: "While there is still time, while we are in this body and have time to accomplish all these things by the light of life, we must run and do now, what will profit us forever.[104]

When all was accomplished for her and she yielded up her spirit on the seventeenth day of September, a Sunday and the day of Resurrection, legend tells us that a bright light appeared in the sky at dusk formed by two rainbows of brilliant and varied colors. These rainbows widened to the size of a huge highway and reached to the four corners of the globe. At the apex where the two rainbows met, a bright light took the form of a circular moon which dispelled the darkness of night over the dwelling place of the Rupertsberg community.[105] Was this a confirmation of the way her prophetic light had always dispelled the darkness of her times?

Hildegard of Bingen, foremother in *Sapientia*, was a reflection, like Wisdom, of the eternal light at play everywhere in her world, in a drama that has neither beginning nor end. When one player finishes, another continues, and the play goes on, generation after generation, as Wisdom delights to be with the children of the earth and makes of them friends and prophets of God.[106]

Hildegard of Bingen, empowered with *Sapientia,* called aloud in the streets and raised her voice in the public squares.[107] Her words covered the earth like mist and morning dew[108] providing moisture, the basic nutrient of all fertility. Called to build her life on the foundation of the *obsculta,* Hildegard of Bingen ran to accomplish the work given her to do, while there was still light—the light of *Sapientia.*

NOTES

1. Wis 7:25ff (adapted).

2. This is the Old Testament theology which most influenced the Johannine Logos Doctrine and formed the life and foundation of Hildegard's Christo-centric theology.

3. Wis 1:15.

4. *RB 1980: The Rule of St. Benedict,* ed. Timothy Fry, O.S.B. (Collegeville: The Liturgical Press, 1981) Prologue 1.

5. Ibid.

6. Ibid., 9.

7. Ibid., 13.

8. Ibid., 43.

9. Ibid., 5:16. Cf. Sir 35:1.

10 Anna Silvas, O.S.B., trans., "Saint Hildegard of Bingen and *The Vita Sanctae Hildegardis,*" *Tjurunga* 29 (1985) Book 1:1,22. Hereafter quoted as: *Vita* followed by book and chapter numbers.

11. Miriam Schmitt, O.S.B., "Blessed Jutta of Disibodenberg: Hildegard of Bingen's *Magistra* and Abbess" *American Benedictine Review,* 40:2 (June 1989) 170.

12. *Vita* 2:1, 70, *Tjurunga* 30 (1986).

13. Hildegard of Bingen, *Explanation of the Rule of Benedict* in response to the congregation of the community at Hunne, that was seeking an interpretation of the Rule, *Latin Fathers, Vol. 197* (Belgium, Turnhott, publishers to the Pontifical Press) trans. Peter Damien McKinley, S.G.S (Unpublished translation).

14. V. G. Oderman, O.S.B., "Interpreting the Rule of Benedict: Entering a World of Wisdom" *American Benedictine Review* 35:1 (March 1984) 38.

15. *Vita* 1:1.

16. From the age of eight to fourteen when Hildegard made her monastic profession, the *Vita* says that she was under the discipline of Jutta. It is uncertain whether this period was one of tutelage or oblation. During the twelfth century, oblation was the custom whereby a child was formally placed in a monastic community with a view to becoming a monk or nun (cf. chapter three of the *Life and Miracles of St Benedict* by St. Gregory the Great).

17. *Vita,* 1:1.

18. Oderman, O.S.B., "Interpreting the Rule of Benedict,*"* 36.

19. Miriam Schmitt, O.S.B., "Blessed Jutta of Disibodenberg," 177.

20. Hildegard of Bingen, "Letter to Guibert of Gembloux," *Hildegard of Bingen: An Anthology,* eds. Fiona Bowie and Oliver Davies, trans. Robert Carver (London: SPCK, 1990) 40.

21. *Vita,* 1:1.

22. Oderman, O.S.B., "Interpreting the Rule of Benedict," 38.

23. Cf. RB 7:25 and Sir 18:30.

24. *Vita,* 1:1.

25. Num 12:6.

26. *Vita,* 2:1, *Tjurunga* 30 (1986).

27. Ibid.

28. Barbara Newman, *Sister of Wisdom* (California: University Press, 1989) 6 n14, comments that the title *abbatissa* appears only in a document addressed to her by Frederick Barbarossa in 1163. Other than that, Hildegard is referred to as *magistra* or *praeposita, mater, domina,* and *sponsa Christi.*

29. *Vita,* 2:1.

30. Ibid.

31. Hildegard, in her *Vita,* 2:1, declares that she had hardly any knowledge of literature because Jutta, her *magistra,* wasn't a scholar. She goes on to speak of her musical creativity—the composing of hymns and other melodies in praise of God and the saints—and reinforces her ignorance of chant notation.

32. Bernard writes that Hildegard has the inner learning and the anointing which teaches all things and adds: "What more can we teach or advise you?" Cf. J. Leclercq and H. Pochais, eds., *S. Bernardi Opera, Vol. VIII,* I Epistolarum 181–230, II Epistolae extra corpus 311–547 (Rome: Edit Cisterc., 1977).

33. *Vita,* 2:1.

34. The Synod of Trier was held between November 1147 and February 1148.

35. *Vita,* 2:1.

36. W. Weston, O.S.B., "The Prophetic Dimension of Monastic Life," *Contemporary Monasticism* (Fairacres, Oxford: SLG Press, 1981) 41.

37. *Vita,* 1:2.

38. Ibid.

39. Ibid.

40. The land was owned partly by the Canons of Mainz, and the estate with its oratory by Count Bernard of Hildesheim. Cf. *Vita* 1:2.

41. *Vita,* 1:2.

42. Wis 7:24.

43. Hildegard of Bingen, *Scivias,* trans. Columba Hart and Jane Bishop (New York: Paulist Press, 1990) book 3, vision 9:25. Hereafter: *Scivias* followed by book, vision, and chapter.

44. An abbreviation for: *Know the Ways of the Lord.*

45. *Scivias,* 2,1:7.

46. *Scivias,* 3, 8:15.

47. Jean Leclercq, O.S.B., *Regards Monastiques sur le Christ au Moyan Age* (Paris: Tournai et Croupe Maine, 1993) 222.

48. *Scivias,* 1,1:1.

49. *Scivias,* 1,2:3,5. Cf. *RB* 7.

50. *Scivias,* 1,2:32. Cf. *RB* 64 and John 10:10.

51. *Scivias,* 1,2:25. Cf. *RB* Prologue 1 and Rev 3:20.

52. *Scivias,* 1,1:2.

53. *Scivias,* 1,2:2. Cf. *RB* 7:10.

54. *Scivias,* 3,3:10.

55. *Scivias,* 1,1:5. Cf. *RB* 7:27 and 7:44.

56. *Scivias,* 1,1:5.

57. *Scivias,* 3,14:18. Cf. *Vita* 2:1—discipline imparted with "much love and motherly affection," *Tjurunga* 30 (1986) 71.

58. *Scivias,* 2,5:19.

59. *Scivias,* 2,5:20.

60. Volmar died in 1173, and the appointment of Volmar's successor was a source of difficulty, even conflict. In 1174, the monk, Gottfried, came to Rupertsberg from the Abbey at Disibodenberg. He began the *Vita Sanctae Hildegardis* and completed Book One. Books Two and Three were written by Theodoric of Echternach in the ten years after the death of Hildegard. The Cistercian monk, Guibert of Gembloux, who had begun a correspondence with Hildegard in 1175, became her secretary in place of Gottfried.

61. Matthew Fox, ed., and Robert Cunningham, Ronald Miller, Jerry Dybdal and Matthew Fox, trans., *Hildegard of Bingen's Book of Divine Works with Letters and Songs* (Santa Fe: Bear & Co., 1987) 5. Hereafter quoted as *Divine Works* with book, vision, and chapter numbers for the visions; title and page number for letters; and title and page numbers for songs.

62. Ibid.

63. Bruce Hozeski, "Hildegard of Bingen's *Ordo Virtutum,* The Earliest Discovered Liturgical Morality Play," *American Benedictine Review* 26.3 (September, 1975) 251.

64. Hildegard von Bingen, Sleeve notes, *Ordo Virtutum* by Sequentia, directed by Klaus Heuman,. recorded in France, June 1982 (Editio Classica, Deutsche Harmonia Munda, 1982).

65. Ibid.

66. *RB* 4:41.

67. Ibid., 4:60.

68. Ibid., 4:74.

69. Hildegard von Bingen, Sleeve notes, *Ordo Virtutum,* scene Three.

70. Ibid., scene Two.

71. Ibid., scene Four.

72. Ibid., scene One.

73. Sabina Flanagan, *Hildegard of Bingen, A Visionary Life* (London, Routledge, 1989) 106.

74. *Divine Works,* "De Spiritu Sancto," 373.

75. Fiona Bowie and Oliver Davies, eds., and Robert Carver, trans., *Hildegard of Bingen: Mystical Writings* (New York: Crossroad Publishing Co., 1990) 123. Hereafter: *Carver.*

76. Ursula is one of thousands of virgin martyrs whose name was added to the sanctoral cycle in the late ninth century. The legend of St Ursula and her 11,000 companions was substantiated somewhat when a mass grave was found near the Church of St. Ursula in 1106. Dr. Greta Mary Hair suggests that Hildegard's sequence and her other works, based on the legend of Ursula and her companions, may have been inspired by the excitement engendered by the discovery of this mass grave and by the attempts to identify the bones of the women in question. The visions of Elizabeth of Schönau was one such means employed in search of the truth. Janet Martin and Greta Mary Hair, "O Ecclesia: the Text and Music of Hildegard of Bingen's Sequence for St. Ursula." *Tjurunga,* 30 (1986) 41.

77. Ibid.

78. Ibid., 58.

79. Wis 7:27.

80. Wis 7:25.

81. Wis 7:22.

82. Fiona Bowie and Oliver Davies, eds., *Hildegard of Bingen: An Anthology,* 31.

83. *Divine Works,* 1, 2:18.

84. *Scivias,* 2:1:8.

85. Wis 7:17 and 20.

86. *Divine Works,* 3, 9:2.

87. Peter Dronke, *Women Writers of the Middle Ages* (Cambridge: University Press, 1984) 154.

88. Hildegard of Bingen, "Letter to the Archbishop of Mainz," *Women Writers of the Middle Ages,* trans. Peter Dronke (Cambridge: University Press, 1984) 154.

89. *Divine Works,* "Letter to Archbishop of Cologne," 285-287.

90. *Divine Works,* "Letter to Werner of Kircheim," 328-331.

91. Fiona Bowie and Oliver Davies, eds., *Hildegard of Bingen: An Anthology,* 6.

92. Bowie and Davies, "Letter to the Monks of St. Eucharius," 136. For the entire letter see *Divine Works,* 314–320.

93. Hildegard had gained Frederick's protection over both the convent at Rupertsberg and its possessions in the year 1158.

94. Victor IV in 1159; Paschal III in 1164; Callistus III in 1168. See *New Catholic Encyclopedia,* 1967 ed., s.v. "List of Popes," M. R. P. McGuire, 575.

95. Bowie and Davies, "Letter to Abbess Hazzecha of Krauftal," 137–139.

96. Ecclus 6:18.

97. Miriam Schmitt, O.S.B. "Hildegard of Bingen: A Prophetic Witness for her Times," *Benedictines* Vol. XLI:I (Spring-Summer 1986) 37.

98. *Divine Works,* "Letter to the Prelates of Mainz," 354–359.

99. The Archbishop was at this time engaged in mediation between Emperor Frederick Barbarossa and Pope Alexander III.

100. Peter Dronke, *Women Writers of the Middle Ages,* 196.

101. Bowie and Davies, "Letter to the Prelates of Mainz," 149.

102. Bowie and Davies, "Letter to the Prelates of Mainz," 150.

103. Ps 150:6.

104. *RB* Prologue 43 and 44.

105. *Vita,* 3:3, *Tjurunga* 32 (1987) 57–58.

106. Wis 7:27.

107. Prov 1:20.

108. Sir 24:3.

11

The Visionary Life of Elisabeth of Schönau: A Different Way of Knowing

Anne Beard, O.S.B.

Upstate New York.
August 1906.
Half-moon and a wrack of gray clouds.
Church windows and thirty nuns singing the Night Office in Gregorian
chant. Matins. Lauds. And then silence.
  Wind, and a nighthawk teetering on it and yawing away into woods.
  Wallowing beetles in green pond water.
  Toads.
  Cattails sway and unsway.
  Grape leaves rattle and settle again.
  Workhorses sleeping in horse manes of pasture.
  Wooden reaper. Walking plow. Hayrick.[1]

So begins Ron Hansen's modern-day novel *Mariette in Ecstasy* about happenings in the lives of the fictional Sisters of the Crucifixion when their
young novice experiences visions and then stigmata. The author could as
easily be describing a scene at the Benedictine monastery in Schönau,
Germany, where twelve-year-old Elisabeth entered in 1141. Monastic life,
based on the Rule of St. Benedict written in the sixth century, is essentially
the same everywhere and in every time—an ordinary round of work and
prayer lived in community and in pursuit of God under a rule and a prioress or an abbot.

What was different about Mariette in her monastic setting is similar to
what was different about Elisabeth of Schönau in hers. At age twenty-three,
Elisabeth began experiencing ecstatic visions and the great physical and
emotional pain that surrounded them. Throughout this chapter, excerpts from

Hansen's novel will be cited to help us imagine ourselves in Elisabeth's place and perhaps understand her better. The content and theological implications of her visions were basically conventional; her messages to the clergy and admonitions to the faithful, though sometimes unwelcome, were sound. It was the unique relationship of Elisabeth to her God—and its attendant pain and passion—that was new and different in her time.

Very little is known about St. Elisabeth. Born in 1129, she experienced visions from the time they began in 1152 until her death in 1165. She was never canonized. However, in 1584, Gregory VIII listed her name in the Roman martyrology where she is remembered for her exemplary monastic life, not her visions, and her feast is commemorated on June 18, the date of her death. There is no biography of Elisabeth save the comments of her brother Ekbert upon her death in *De Obitu Elisabeth* and information gleaned from the accounts of her visions. Anne L. Clark has written a modern-day, definitive study of her and her works in *Elisabeth of Schönau: A Twelfth-Century Visionary.*[2]

It is believed that Elisabeth came from a well-established family, perhaps of the minor nobility. Nothing is known of her parents except her father's name, Hartwig. She had two brothers, Ruotger, prior of the Premonstratensian house of Pöhlde, and Ekbert, who was a canon at St. Cassius in Bonn, an up-and-coming churchman before joining his sister at the double monastery in Schönau in 1155. He became abbot of Schönau in 1167. There was an unnamed sister in the family, and one of the nuns at Schönau was possibly a sister, cousin, or niece.

That Elisabeth's parents were perhaps indulgent with their children is suggested by a passage from the *Vita* of Ekbert by Emecho. Elisabeth, who was urged in her visions to encourage her brother to enter the monastic life, reportedly hesitated to communicate this revelation to Ekbert "because she knew that he had been delicately brought up since his infancy" and therefore feared "that he would not be able to endure the rigor of our rule in fasts, vigils, and abstinences."[3]

Elisabeth had three cousins or nieces, Guda, Hadewig, and Regelindis, all of the Augustinian house of St. Thomas of Andernach, to whom her brother Ekbert addressed *De Obitu*. Of her three great-uncles, all referred to in Elisabeth's visions, the most famous by far was Ekbert, bishop of Münster. Unlike Bishop Ekbert, whose soul Elisabeth once saw in a vision enjoying his rewards in heaven, Uncles Helid and Theoderic were seen by Elisabeth in purgatory, suffering for their earthly sins, Helid for his "unbridled utterances. For, although he was a God-fearing man, he used to joke a great deal."[4]

Her brother Ekbert was a major influence in Elisabeth's life, as she was in his. When Ekbert joined her at Schönau, Elisabeth was already suffering from the derision and doubt generated by her abbot's revelation of an apocalyptic vision she had had. Ekbert was a person whose judgment Elisabeth could trust. Without doubt, Ekbert believed in the importance of his sister's experiences, and he set about recording and editing the accounts of them from the time he entered until her death, and after. Clark notes, "One must picture Ekbert choosing an alternative life for himself, a life . . . which offered him the possibility of participating in an extraordinary spiritual phenomenon from which he could personally benefit."[5]

Two other people figured prominently in Elisabeth's life: Abbot Hildelin and Hildegard of Bingen. Abbot Hildelin was in charge of Schönau from the time it was founded until after Elisabeth's death. Though the nuns chose their own *magistra* (teacher) who probably taught them the customs of the house and guided them in proper Benedictine behavior, Abbot Hildelin was the overall authority in the monastery and, as such, was responsible for the nuns' spiritual lives. Elisabeth's earliest visionary experiences were evidently reported to the other nuns at Schönau and to Ekbert when he came to visit. Recounting them gave Elisabeth some relief from her agony, she said, but she would not reveal the contents of her visions to the abbot or to anyone else.

Sometime before August 1154, an angel appeared to Elisabeth in a vision, warning of a future disaster and calamitous punishment to occur on earth in a year when the Annunciation coincided with Good Friday, which was to happen the following year. Elisabeth kept this vision to herself until her angel confronted her, asking why she did not divulge her divine revelations to others and whipping her for her failure to do so. At this point, she handed over the accounts of her visions to Abbot Hildelin, asking that he not say anything about the apocalyptic prediction.

The abbot urged Elisabeth to pray for a sign about the vision, and when told that her angel had said to preach penance, took that as affirmation that he should reveal on a public preaching trip the prediction of earthly punishments to come. He traveled around, warning of imminent destruction in the absence of reform, and people were moved to acts of great penance during Lent 1155. But letters containing terrible prophecies supposedly based on Elisabeth's visions and attributed to Abbot Hildelin were read in a public forum in Cologne. This exposed Elisabeth to mockery and derision, especially when the predictions failed to come true, and Hildelin to threats against his safety. The response to the revelation of her prophecy aroused in Elisabeth a concern for her reputation, especially among the clergy. This was to haunt her all her days.

Thereafter, Abbot Hildelin played a major role in Elisabeth's visions and daily life. Masses offered by him gained the release of souls in purgatory, as promised in Elisabeth's visions, and the sacraments administered by him to Elisabeth sometimes released her from her agonies or hastened her recovery from her ecstasies.

Elisabeth wrote to Hildegard for advice and comfort about the apocalyptic episode. Hildegard responded at length about spiritual pride and then likened Elisabeth and others who perform the works of God to exiles sounding the mysteries of God like a trumpet: "A trumpet only renders the sound and does not produce it unless another breathes into it in order to bring forth the sound."[6] Elisabeth was reassured by Hildegard's response about her role as prophet.

As early as 1158, Hildegard and Elisabeth were both recognized as visionary messengers of God.[7] Hildegard was thirty-one years old when Elisabeth was born and lived fourteen years after Elisabeth died. She wrote books on medicine and natural history, hymns, a play, and numerous letters to religious and laity alike. She traveled and preached extensively. With the Church's approval, Hildegard began publishing accounts of her own visions later in life.

The nuns at Schönau obviously knew of Hildegard's work. When Elisabeth started having her disturbing visions, her *magistra* contacted Hildegard for advice. Prior to experiencing the episodes that make up her *Liber Viarum Dei* (Book of God's Way), Elisabeth visited Hildegard when instructed to do so in a vision.

Hildegard was suspicious of visionaries like Elisabeth who lost consciousness during their experiences. Hildegard insisted that in her own visions she continued to be conscious and her inner senses continued to function, which was "doubtlessly intended to countervail the tendency of many of her contemporaries to assess visions and locutions as lower forms of contemplation. Such sensual manifestations were seen as a product of the body's frailty when confronted by the Divine," write Kerby-Fulton and Elliott in their study of two letters between Elisabeth and Hildegard.[8]

Kerby-Fulton and Elliott also note that Elisabeth and Hildegard were "united by a mutual awareness" that they were living in a spiritually decadent time and that they had received divine mandates to help deal with the problem.[9] Confronted by the same historical situation, however, "their writings reveal more contrasts than likenesses."[10] Hildegard allegorized her visions, systematically exploring the elements of Christian faith, while Elisabeth described in detail what happened to her body and soul. Hildegard has been called a great theologian, a role that cannot be ascribed to Elisabeth. "While Hildegard acted as adviser to emperor and Pope, [Elisabeth] in humblewise influenced the clergy and the people."[11] History has given Hildegard more attention than Elisabeth, but Elisabeth's works were more popular than Hildegard's at the time, judging from the greater number of manuscripts copied.

In her intensely felt accounts of her visionary experiences, Elisabeth more closely resembles the mystics of the twelfth and thirteenth centuries who came after her than she does her contemporary Hildegard. Elisabeth's visions, however, differed considerably from those of the later mystics; where theirs were sensational and bizarre, hers were childlike and scriptural.

Interestingly, Elisabeth stood at the beginning of a time when people of faith were looking for a new interiority and affective spirituality. H. O. Taylor sees in the "gathering religious feeling" of Elisabeth's day, which poured itself into "passionate utterances," the new emotionalizing of Latin Christianity. "The Middle Ages imbued patristic Christianity with the human elements of love and fear and pity."[12]

R. W. Southern maintains that there was a gap in Benedictine life by the twelfth century—that the individual monk had been forgotten in the search for perfection in external routines. "Strangely enough, the characteristics of spiritual life that monastics and laity alike were looking for in a Church ever more dominated by clerics (and negligent clerics at that) were the very characteristics called for in the visionary writings of the two traditional Benedictine nuns, Hildegard and Elisabeth, and expressed in the intensely personal visionary experiences of Elisabeth."[13]

THE VISIONARY WORKS

> Frequently, indeed as if by habit, on Sundays and other feast days around the hours in which the devotion of the faithful especially burned, a certain suffering of the heart fell upon her, and she was violently disturbed, and finally she was quiet as if dead, such that sometimes no breath or vital movement could be discerned. But after a long trance, when she had gradually resumed her breath, suddenly she would announce certain most divine words in Latin.[14]

This is how Ekbert described what often happened to Elisabeth during a vision. On a Sunday or other feast day, usually around the time for Mass or Liturgy of the Hours, Elisabeth would suffer physical pain before entering a trancelike state. Recovering, she would utter words of praise for God or quote Scripture at length.

Over her lifetime Elisabeth's visionary experiences were recorded in four major works: a set of three chronologically arranged accounts, *Liber Visionum Primus, Secundus,* and *Tertius* (Visions—Books One, Two, and Three); in *Liber Viarum Dei;* in *Revelatio de Sacro Exercitu Virginum Coloniensium,* a collection of revelations about St. Ursula and the 11,000 virgins; and in *Visio de Resurrectione Beate Virginis Marie,* a short series of visions about the bodily assumption of Mary. The accounts in Book One and the first part of Book Two of Visions are the most autobiographical and expressive of Elisabeth's emotional reactions to her experiences: fear, joy, excitement, wonder, doubt. In them, she reports spiritual tedium and torments by the devil and describes visits to the otherworld.

Clark identifies three types of visions described by Elisabeth: the simple vision, ecstasy, and rapture. In all three types, visual imagery generally predominates.[15] The simple vision—seeing something or having something appear to her—is not like seeing with normal sight, Elisabeth says. In it she "sees with the eyes of her heart or of her mind, by seeing in her mind's gaze *(mentis intuitu)*, by seeing in or through the spirit."[16]

Ecstasy—what Elisabeth calls *in mentis excessu* or "in the spirit"—Clark describes as "a state of trance in which her mind has been withdrawn from its normal functions."[17] Although Elisabeth almost always experienced visions when in ecstasy, she did have visions in a nonecstatic state. She could approach ecstasy or hold back from it, and in many cases ecstasy began with physical suffering. In fact, ecstasy was often a release from suffering and could last for a long period, as could her recovery after the vision.[18]

When in rapture, Elisabeth was raised up to heaven and her spirit was separated from her body. She was accompanied on these occasions by a particular angel whom she later sees as the agent of her rapture. The angel becomes her steady companion and guide, first appearing as a boy but later becoming more fatherlike. These rapturous visions, which began about six months after her first vision, seemed to be the most difficult for Elisabeth to describe.[19]

Elisabeth apparently dreaded the physical suffering that accompanied the visions. Her angel once chastised her for trying to avoid pain. Later, the Apostle Peter tells her she will suffer less in her visions, and from that time on the reports of physical suffering in her accounts decrease.

The prophetic vision that was revealed by Abbot Hildelin and brought Elisabeth's experiences to light was originally appended to the first version of Book One. (Ekbert later dropped the account from an enlarged version of the book.) Shortly after the visions recorded in the first part of Book Two occurred, Ekbert came to Schönau to live, and the accounts of the visions as well as their contents changed. Although they were still recorded in diary form in Book Two, the visions contained fewer personal details, and Elisabeth began to ask her visionary guide questions of an academic nature. By the third book, all chronological notations were dropped, and the emphasis was clearly on the revelation rather than the person and her experience.

Elisabeth's remaining works—*Liber Viarum Dei, Revelatio,* and *Resurrectione*—were more literary than self-revelatory. Ekbert obviously played a large part in instigating Elisabeth's inquiries of her visionary guide and in recording the results, but however much Ekbert may have urged his concerns on Elisabeth, it was she who had the visions and reported in all honesty what she experienced.

With Ekbert's coming, too, Elisabeth began to recognize her role as prophet and acknowledge that her experiences had meaning for the moral improvement of the Church at large. She had undergone unforgettable experiences in her personal encounters with the Divine and had been entrusted by God with a message that she felt compelled to reveal. In time, she accepted her responsibility as a holy woman whom others sought out for advice and direction. Clark maintains that another side of Elisabeth's personality emerges in the *Liber Viarum Dei* in which she tackles larger questions of spiritual interest and begins to see herself as the creator of a literary product, a book.[20]

The *Viarum Dei* consists of ten sermons or admonitions addressed to Christians climbing the mountain of life to heaven by ten different paths: the contemplative life, active life, martyrdom, marriage, virginity, the way of the rulers, widowhood, the solitary life, the way of children, and the way of adolescents. Elisabeth's book resembles Hildegard's *Scivias* in a number of details, though Elisabeth treats of different groups and different spiritual paths to God while Hildegard in her more universal allegory speaks of personified virtues, such as patience and abstinence, leading to the moral life of an individual.

Outstanding in Elisabeth's work is her attempt to define a variety of Christian roles in the world and their religious significance. In this she reflected the growing current interest in religious groups and their relationships to each other. Caroline Bynum lists Elisabeth and Hildegard, along with Gerhoh of Reichersberg, Herrad of Hohenbourg (or Landsberg), and Anselm of Havelberg, as writers "trying to analyze the various orders or callings in the church—a kind of work unknown in the early Middle Ages."[21]

The sermons in *Viarum Dei* introduce two issues of particular concern to Elisabeth: the Cathar heresy and the negligence of the clergy and its effect on the people. Catharism first appeared in Europe in 1143 or 1144 in Cologne. By 1170 it was a main heresy, and by 1243 it had been destroyed. The Cathars denied that matter was part of God's design and believed that souls, created by God, were captured or stolen and imprisoned in human bodies made by Satan. It was the aim of the Cathars to release human souls from their bodies. They advocated extreme austerity and asceticism. They shunned all marriage, all foods that were produced by sexual generation, all material elements in worship. They denied the incarnation, the virgin birth, bodily resurrection, the sacraments, and the Trinity. Elisabeth, Ekbert, and Hildegard all attacked the Cathars vehemently.

In *Viarum Dei* Elisabeth condemned ecclesiastical leaders for their neglect of their flocks, for their public shows of piety and their private iniquities, for their willingness to buy and sell sanctification (simony), for their disregard of traditions, for their worldliness, and above all for their failure to combat Catharism.

> *Mariette sits at a library table in the scriptorium and concentrates on a*
> *great variety of holy relics that are arrayed before her like runes.*
> *"Just try," Sister Hermance says.*
> *She sheepishly smiles and peers at a tooth. "Whose is this?"*
> *"Mine," Sister Félicité says.*
> *"Whose tooth, I meant."*
> *"Oh. Saint Valentine."*
> *She judges it again and says, "I'm sorry, but it isn't."*
> *"But is it holy?"*
> *She regards Sister Félicité with regret. "It's not even human."*
> *"She might be wrong," Sister Genevieve says, but Sister Félicité holds*
> *the tooth tightly inside her hand for a while and then hurries from the room.*
> *Mariette handles a torn inch of yellowed hem and flatly says, "I have no*
> *idea.". . .*
> *Sister Marthe insists, "Touch [my relic]."*
> *Mariette hears the neediness in Sister Marthe's voice and gets up from*
> *the library table. "Everything else is real." . . .*
> *Sister Sabine is jubilant. "I have a portion of the true cross!"*
> *Mariette considers the milkmaid with sadness, but says, "Yes. You do."*[22]

Elisabeth's *Revelatio* about the martyrdom of St. Ursula and the 11,000 virgins came about as a result of the discovery of an ancient Roman cemetery near Cologne believed to be the burial site of the saint and her companions. The legend of St. Ursula had gained popularity through the publication of two Latin *passiones* on the subject, one of which was considered the definitive version of the story. *Revelatio* was Elisabeth's most popular work, largely because manuscript versions of the legend were disseminated along with the relics throughout Germany, France, and the Low Countries. The monk Roger at Forde introduced Elisabeth's manuscript in England.

According to legend, Ursula, the beautiful daughter of a Christian British king, learned in a vision that she was to be martyred for rejecting a marriage proposal from a barbarian king. She offered to accept the proposal if she were given 10,999 virgins and eleven ships to take a three-year rest before the wedding. At the end of three years, the ships were blown by a strong wind to the Rhine River. The company disembarked at Cologne and made a quick trip to Rome to visit the tombs of the saints and prepare themselves for their coming ordeal. They returned to Cologne where they were trapped by the Huns attacking the city and killed for resisting the men's advances.

With the discovery of the graveyard and its holy contents, Abbot Gerlach of Deutz asked Elisabeth to confirm the identity of the relics unearthed there, which included the bones of men and children, as well as women. Elisabeth felt forced by circumstances to comply. She was also encouraged in her work by a vision in which she learned that she was predestined to reveal the truth of the Cologne martyrdoms to the world. *Tituli,* or epitaphs, "collected" by Thioderic of Deutz, were passed along to Elisabeth; many were pure fabrications. Elisabeth's task was to fit the *tituli* of the martyrs into the already well-known and accepted legend.

The Ursula stories were probably the most controversial of Elisabeth's visions. Lina Eckenstein writes:

> The whole account which Elisabeth promulgated in good faith, and which her contemporaries had no hesitation in accepting as genuine, forms a most interesting example of mediæval religious romance. It teems with chronological and historical impossibilities: apart from these it bears the stamp of truthfulness. It is pure romance, but it is romance set forth in a spirit of conviction and with a circumstantiality of detail thoroughly convincing to the uncritical mind.[23]

One impossibility recounted in *Revelatio* was the story of Pope Cyriacus, a pope no one had heard of until Elisabeth had her vision. Given the epitaph *Sanctus Ciriacus papa Romanus,* Elisabeth told the story of a Briton, Cyriacus, who was the nineteenth Roman pope until, on the instruction of God, he resigned his post before the whole Church and joined Ursula and her virgins on their journey when they arrived in Rome. This action so astounded and angered the cardinals that they removed all evidence of the pontiff from Church records.

The revelations recounted in *Resurrectione* about the bodily assumption of Mary into heaven conflicted with tradition, too, in this case, the date of the assumption. On the feast of the Assumption, August 15, Elisabeth had a vision confirming that Mary had indeed been bodily assumed into heaven. A week later Elisabeth asks her guide in a vision when the assumption occurred. She is informed that it came forty days after Mary's death, or September 23. Though the date was at odds with the traditional Church calendar, Schönau and some other monasteries adopted the September date on the strength of Elisabeth's vision.

Elisabeth's overall message to her troubled times was that God and the saints were extremely interested in the affairs of the present world, that it was possible for everyone to have a deep person-to-person relationship with God and other members of Christ's mystical body, and that heaven was not an abstract state of mind. Her experiences and messages swelled the great surge of devotion for the humanity of Christ and for his human mother that was building among the faithful.

THE VISIONARY EXPERIENCE

> —*We talked about our childhoods. She dressed her dolls as Jesus and*
> *Mary, just as I did. She played in a habit just like the one that her sister*
> *Annie wore. She whipped herself with knotted apron strings. She rebuked*
> *temptations against chastity by lying naked on thorns.*
> —*She seems to me quite ordinary.*
> —*Well, that's the point, isn't it?*[24]

Physical mortification in Benedictine monasteries in the Middle Ages was common but not extreme. The Rule itself avoids the excesses of physical asceticism most associated with eremitical forms of monasticism. Jean Leclercq, writing in *The Spirituality of the Middle Ages,* refers to "the hidden martyrdom of the well-led monastic life"[25] that prevailed in times of prosperity. "Discretion in the sense of moderation still remained a characteristic of the asceticism in the Benedictine monasteries of the old tradition where the labor of mortification lies chiefly in the exact and careful practice of monastic observances."[26]

Clark states that Elisabeth's visions and trances over the years "occur in the context of ongoing undernourishment and other forms of physical mortification."[27] She undoubtedly participated with the rest of her community in common ascetic practices. In addition to her abstemious consumption of food, her brother Ekbert writes, she engaged in "extensive weeping, genuflections, and the tearing of her flesh by coarse garments and a harsh belt which cut into her sides."[28] H. O. Taylor states, "The bodily infirmities, from which [Elisabeth] was never free, were aggravated by austerities and usually became most painful just before the trances that brought the visions."[29]

Elisabeth's observance of ascetic practices was probably stricter than that of her sisters and may have led to some of her visionary experiences. She reports, "On the vigil of All Saints Day, at Vespers, I struggled in agony for a long time and while I was doubled over in violent pain, I tightly bound the sign of the crucified Lord to my breast, and at last coming into ecstasy I became quiet."[30] Then she was taken up into heaven and saw visions.

Her visions, and particularly the physical and mental suffering that preceded and followed them, initially must have come as a great shock and source of wonder and confusion to Elisabeth. "I languished in my whole body, and first the tips of my hands and feet, and then all my flesh, began to crawl, and sweat broke out all over me. My heart was made as if it had been cut in two parts by a sword."[31] She describes herself as disoriented and increasingly overcome by sadness: "Nearly all my senses were topsy-turvy inside me."[32] In her earliest accounts she speaks of her spiritual tedium and reports having visions of the devil "who appeared to her in frightening human and bestial shapes."[33] Elisabeth's suffering often led to pain and weakness; she was sometimes immobilized by paralysis.[34]

> *I have had an experience. . . . Jesus spoke to me. . . . Ever since I was thirteen, I have been praying to understand his passion. Everything about it. To have a horrible illness so I could feel the horrors and terrors of death just as Christ did.*[35]

Elisabeth stood at a point in spiritual history when mystics, particularly women mystics, would be caught up in the imitation of Christ. Bynum describes at length in *Holy Feast and Holy Fast* the significance of physical suffering to women in the High Middle Ages who, through the Eucharist, experienced physical union with Christ's crucified body.

Just as we cannot argue that Elisabeth's ascetic practices caused her visions or their accompanying pain and anguish, neither can we make a case for Elisabeth's identification with Christ's physical suffering as union with Christ on the cross. She did suffer in her own body with Christ on the cross, particularly during Lent:

> Then after a little while the brothers began to celebrate the office of the day, and when they had continued as far as the reading of the passion, I began to agonize and be pressed beyond every limit in such a way that I could tell no one. Indeed, my brother, if all my flesh were torn to pieces, it seems to me that I would endure it more easily. Finally, however, I came into ecstasy and again I saw the Lord on the cross, and then at that time he gave up the spirit.[36]

Although her spirituality was marked by Eucharistic piety and devotion to Christ's humanity, Elisabeth never saw herself as partaking of the divine within herself. Indeed, she always saw her life as being invaded by God, "the experiential basis," Clark maintains, "for a powerful sense of God as other."[37]

Kerby-Fulton and Elliott say Elisabeth was the handmaid of a "cold, uncompromising and chastising God."[38] Even Christ, whom she sees in one vision as a beautiful young virgin with her hair spread out over her shoulders, sitting in the middle of the sun and holding a golden cup, appears in another vision as if recently crucified: "And when to the whole world he brandished the cross on which he had hung, and the wounds of his passion dripping as if with fresh blood, he shouted with a loud and exceedingly dreadful voice: Such things have I endured for you, but what have you suffered for me?"[39] Elisabeth says, "There was no splendor or beauty in him." Elisabeth saw her suffering with the crucified Christ as no more than what she owed him, and her identification with it was a source of consolation for and understanding of the pain she herself suffered daily.

Bynum states, "We cannot understand medieval religiosity until we realize how different such probing and embracing of body as pain-pleasure is from most modern notions of body. . . . [I]t is helpful to remember how little medieval people could do to mitigate discomfort of any kind. Thus medieval metaphors and symbols express the *experiencing* of body more than the *controlling* of it."[40]

Elisabeth's suffering began before she started having visions and presumably before she began practicing extreme mortification of the flesh. In her first book she refers to the "arrows" of the Lord and various spiritual torments she continually suffered at the hand of God from the day she entered the monastery. She understood her illnesses, as well as any tribulations of the sisters of her community, as actions of God in her life. Her daily existence throughout her life was one of physical hardship.

Elisabeth's visionary life was not all pain and suffering. In her last days she goes into a trance twice. Afterward, when her sisters beg her to tell what she has seen, she says she knows she is about to die because she has seen visions that God's angel, many years before, had told her she would not see again until her death. "On being asked whether the Lord had comforted her, she answered, 'Oh! what excellent comfort I have received.'"[41]

Physicality and the Monastic Experience of God

The idea of body, along with its sensations and emotions, runs like a leitmotif through Elisabeth's visionary life. There was herself, in the flesh—a prophet and visible sign of God's presence in the world. There was the very real physical and psychological suffering that surrounded her encounters with the Divine. Through devotion to Christ's humanity she came to experience God in an intense, personal way. She could identify closely with Mary, the earthly mother of God, and she could not understand the Cathars who rejected the body as evil. As Caroline Bynum says, "All the religiosity of the period was animated in deep ways by the need to take account of (rather than merely to deny) matter, body, and sensual response."[42] God was known to Elisabeth through her humanity—not only through the Body of Christ, the Church, and her community, but also through her own body.

> We seem to mystify people who are slaves to their pleasures. We often work too hard and rest too little, our food is plain, our days are without variety, we have no possessions nor much privacy, we live uncomfortably with our vows of chastity and obedience; but God is present here and that makes this our heaven on earth.[43]

Elisabeth of Schönau lived the life of an ordinary nun, but her Benedictine upbringing did not prepare her for visions and great suffering. It *did* offer her an environment in which to experience God. She was trained in obedience, contemplation, detachment, openness to God's call—a lifelong search for God within herself and among others in her everyday life.

Elisabeth had every reason to believe that she would experience God in the monastery. That is where one goes to seek God—among the members of one's community and within oneself. As a Benedictine contemplative, she fits the definition of a passive ascetic given by Jan Kowalczewski.[44] Unlike active ascetics who conceive of God as transcendent and essentially separate from humans, passive ascetics see an essential link between the human and the divine and between the sacred and the profane. The passive ascetic attempts "to experience spiritual power and presence on earth in its most ideal form—. . . the monastery." It is passive mystics, says Kowalczewski, who "create environments which allow them to experience the sacred as immanent everywhere, but relatively more apparent in the monastery, the city of God on earth."[45]

Ambrose Wathen maintains that God is present in the cenobitic fraternity itself in its communal nature. "This is not to say that God is only present in the community, but that the congregation, the fraternity itself, its structures, its routine, its very being, is the sphere of God's presence for the monk. God is not present in spite of the community, but in the existence and action of the community itself."[46] He adds, "Each monk is in his own person a manifestation of God to others."[47]

Community for Elisabeth was vital. Her trances and illnesses seem not to have disqualified her for monastic office, as she was chosen *magistra* at Schönau after she began having her miraculous experiences. She seems always to have been surrounded by a community of supportive women. She had her visions for her sisters, and they in turn helped her through her suffering. They eagerly prayed for any intentions requested in her visions. "In her identification with her sisters, she uses the pronoun *we* as often as *I*."[48]

Elisabeth's sisters "took a great personal interest in her experiences, and she was greatly loved in her community. Her writings abound in homely details of everyday convent life: the joy of the sisters at seeing a rainbow, their anxiety and willingness to do penance for her when she was afflicted with evil visions, their concern because she was too ill to receive Holy Communion, their attempts to protect her physically during her ecstasies."[49]

A Different Way of Seeing

Contemplation of the kind practiced by Benedictines is a different way of seeing and knowing, says modern-day theologian Elizabeth Johnson. It arises from an experience of connection with the sacred at the very core of life. "The contemplative 'knows' God, not in an extrinsic, conceptual way, but from within, experientially."[50] The fascination with the mystery of God is endemic to religious life everywhere and at all times, says Johnson.[51] Such was Elisabeth's way of knowing; she pursued a life whose intrinsic, underlying explanation was religious experience.

Elisabeth brought to her spiritual life imagination, emotion, and feeling. Ekbert reveals how involving Elisabeth's visions were when he writes in *De Obitu* that her last days were characterized by a kind of "emotional detachment, so unlike the rest of her earlier emotionally volatile life."[52] That she experienced the Divine in her visions and suffering says something about the existential angst underlying all human search for meaning, by whatever name it is called. Life, fully lived, exposes us on all sides to doubt, to risks, to suffering, to the threat of death.

The search for God within can be frightening and painful. Openness to God the Unknown, to God the Mystery, takes a special kind of courage—a willingness to give up the illusion that one is in control and to trust in the Divine. Elisabeth was a saint in this: that she surrendered to the will of God and allowed herself to be used by God. "The overwhelming infinity of God is . . . an experienced presence of God to the contemplative."[53]

If we of the twentieth century are seeking the fullness of life that comes with an experience of God (and writers in many different genres attest to this yearning), perhaps we need look no further than ourselves in the flesh. William Johnston makes a case in *Being in Love* for a conversion to one's own body, which results in a turning in love to community and a turning away from sin. He calls this conversion to our bodies and the body of Christ "the key to the Christian religion." The Word was made flesh and dwelt among us—"we must grow in understanding this awe-inspiring mystery which gives the lie to every theory that matter is evil."[54]

NOTES

1. Ron Hansen, *Mariette in Ecstasy* (New York: Harper Collins, 1991) 1.

2. Anne L. Clark, *Elisabeth of Schönau: A Twelfth-Century Visionary* (Phildadelphia: University of Pennsylvania Press, 1992).

3. Ibid., 123.

4. Thalia A. Pandiri, trans., "Visions—Book Two," *Medieval Women's Visionary Literature,* ed. Elizabeth Petroff (New York: Oxford University Press, 1986) 166.

5. Clark, *Elisabeth,* 19.

6. Kathryn Kerby-Fulton and Dyan Elliott, "Self-Image and the Visionary Role in Two Letters from the Correspondence of Elizabeth of Schönau and Hildegard of Bingen," *Vox Benedictina* 2 (July 1985) 222.

7. Ibid., 204. From the annals of the Premonstratensian house at Pöhlde in 1158: "In these days, God made manifest His power through the frail sex, in the

two handmaidens [Hildegard and Elisabeth] . . . many kinds of visions apparent to them through His messages which are to be seen in writing."

8. Ibid., 206.

9. Ibid., 208.

10. M. Colman O'Dell, "Elisabeth of Schönau and Hildegard of Bingen: Prophets of the Lord," eds. Lillian I. Shank and John A. Nichols, *Peaceweavers*, Cistercian Studies Series 72 (Kalamazoo: Cistercian Publications, 1987) 88.

11. Lina Eckenstein, *Woman Under Monasticism* (Cambridge: Cambridge University Press, 1896) 277.

12. H. O. Taylor, *The Mediæval Mind: A History of the Development of Thought and Emotion in the Middle Ages* (New York: Macmillan, 1919) 3:361.

13. R. W. Southern, *Western Society and the Church in the Middle Ages*, The Penguin History of the Church 2 (London: Penguin Books, 1990) 231.

14. Clark, *Elisabeth*, 180–181.

15. An outstanding exception to the predominantly visual nature of Elisabeth's visions was a rapturous state in which she saw nothing, but heard "a great and dreadful voice," presumably the voice of God and not some other being with whom Elisabeth was familiar. Ibid., 88.

16. Ibid., 85. Modern visionary Caryll Houselander, writing in *The Rocking Horse Catholic* (New York: Sheed and Ward, 1955) describes her visions as not something "seen with the bodily eyes—but something intensely realized with the mind." Cited in Margot H. King, "The Incarnational Spirituality of Caryll Houselander: Selections from Her Autobiography," *Vox Benedictina* 1 (July 1984) 192. Of a later vision Houselander writes: "In the ordinary way I did not *see* anything at all; at least I did not see anything with my eyes. So far as my eyes were concerned, . . . I saw her *with my mind* . . . and vividly in detail, in a way that is unforgettable, though in fact it was something suddenly *known*, rather than seen." King, 204.

17. Clark, *Elisabeth*, 85.

18. Ibid., 86.

19. Ibid., 87.

20. Ibid., 95.

21. Caroline W. Bynum, *Jesus As Mother: Studies in the Spirituality of the High Middle Ages* (Berkeley: University of California Press, 1982) 90.

22. Hansen, *Mariette*, 146–147.

23. Eckenstein, *Woman Under Monasticism*, 283.

24. Hansen, *Mariette*, 61.

25. Dom Jean Leclercq, Dom François Vanderbroucke, and Louis Bouyer, *The Spirituality of the Middle Ages*, A History of Christian Spirituality II (New York: The Seabury Press, 1982), 117.

26. Ibid., 118

27. Clark, *Elisabeth*, 89.

28. Ibid., 89.

29. Taylor, *Mediæval Mind*, 3:460.

30. Clark, *Elisabeth*, 87.

31. Ibid., 82.

32. Ibid., 13.

33. Ibid., 89–90.

34. Ibid., 82.

35. Hansen, *Mariette,* 40.

36. Clark, *Elisabeth,* 103.

37. Ibid., 106.

38. Kerby-Fulton and Elliott, "Self-Image," 209.

39. Clark, *Elisabeth,* 105.

40. Caroline W. Bynum, *Holy Feast and Holy Fast: The Religious Significance of Food to Medieval Women* (Berkeley: University of California Press, 1987) 245.

41. Taylor, *Mediæval Mind,* 3:462.

42. Bynum, *Holy Feast,* 253.

43. Hansen, *Mariette,* 30.

44. Jan Kowalczewski, "Thirteenth Century Asceticism: Marie d'Oignies and Lutgard of Aywieres," *Vox Benedictina,* 3 (January 1986) 21–26.

45. Ibid., 26.

46. Ambrose Wathen, "Fraternity As an Aspect of the Experience of God in the Cenobium," *Monastic Studies* 9 (1972) 128.

47. Ibid.

48. Elizabeth A. Petroff, ed., *Medieval Women's Visionary Literature* (New York: Oxford University Press, 1986) 41.

49. O'Dell, "Elizabeth of Schönau," 91.

50. Elizabeth F. Johnson, "Between the Times: Religious Life and the Postmodern Experience of God," *Review for Religious* 53:1 (January-February 1994) 73.

51. Ibid., 16.

52. Clark, *Elisabeth,* 44.

53. George Maloney, *God's Exploding Love* (New York: Alba House, 1987) 56.

54. William Johnston, *Being in Love* (San Francisco: Harper & Row, 1989) 30.

12

Herrad of Hohenbourg and Her *Garden of Delights: A Pictorial Encyclopedia*

Gladys Noreen, O.S.B.

INTRODUCTION

Herrad of Landsbourg (1130–1195) has the distinction of being the first woman to compile an encyclopedia. This undertaking was accomplished while she was abbess of Mt. St. Odile Monastery at Hohenbourg, Alsace from 1165 to 1195. Unlike modern encyclopedias, the twelfth century pictorial encyclopedia was to be a compendium of all there was to know about the structure of the world as seen in the light of salvation history.[1] This work and other encyclopedias, summas, and specula were the rage of the time. Herrad's work, *Hortus Deliciarum* or *Garden of Delights*, demonstrates her organizational ability as well as her talent as an artist, poet, scholar, and musician and reveals many facets of the society in which she lived.

Although there is a scarcity of information about Herrad, it is known that she was born in 1130 and presumably became a student in the abbey school. There is no date available for her entrance into the monastic community; however, she became abbess in 1167 and died in 1195. Similarly, there is little information about Hohenbourg Abbey, and it is not known if her monastery was reserved for the aristocracy or if her social status afforded her preference when a new abbess was chosen. Both were practices in the twelfth century.[2]

POLITICAL, CULTURAL, AND RELIGIOUS SITUATION OF TWELFTH-CENTURY ALSACE

In an attempt to provide a sense of security in a changing world, the twelfth century was marked by a compulsive urge to collect and systematize all forms of knowledge. It was a medieval conviction that the unity and order of the world could be rationally comprehended. Authors of the period did not examine assumptions, and they often mingled theology, science, and superstition in their manuscripts. The writings were truthful in the sense that they presented a balanced view of civilization as the compilers experienced it.[3]

During the long reign of Frederick Barbarossa from 1152 to 1190, some semblance of peace was brought to Alsace, then a province of the Holy Roman Empire. This peace came about because both king and army were involved militarily in Italy.[4] In addition, the second and third crusades took place during Herrad's monastic years, but she makes no mention of them in her encyclopedia. Since Herrad found no reason to include any reference to them in *Hortus Deliciarum,* it might be assumed that the crusades did not directly affect the community at Hohenbourg.

Outside the monasteries, the life of most medieval women was consumed by work. They prepared meals, made soap and candles, spun wool, made linens and clothing, and helped with farm work.[5] Only women of the nobility were educated; no other women had leisure for the pursuit of learning. Some preferred to enter monastic life rather than live with "the servitude and violence which they might have met in marriage, especially those who had a marriage more or less forced on them."[6]

During the High Middle Ages, intellectual activity was almost completely confined to monasteries.[7] Abbey schools provided both a liberal education and a religious education based on Scripture. Often children of wealthy and noble families boarded in the monastery and were occasionally accompanied by at least one servant.[8] The study of both the fine and domestic arts was included in the education of girls and the inclusion of musical compositions in *Hortus Deliciarum* suggests that the study of music was also part of the curriculum.

For all intellectual and technical works, Latin was the exclusive language, though literary works were being produced in the vernacular, including German. This was a new phenomenon.[9] Herrad incorporated both Latin and German in her text, a feature that made the Latin more understandable to the nuns of her community since it reduced a foreign language to the vernacular.[10] The *Summarium Heinrici,* a condensed and reorganized version of Isidore's *Etymologies,* was also available. It was written between 1020 and 1100 and included ten books of text and an eleventh book written in the form of an alphabetical Latin-German glossary. A compendium of eleventh-century school knowledge, *The Volumnes,* included quotes from Priscian, Bede, and Cassiodorus. Major portions of this work are copied verbatim in *Hortus Deliciarum.*[11]

Within the Church, the Gratian reform was completed with the compilation of canon law in 1152. Pope Alexander II was then involved in a dispute with Henry II and Frederick Barbarossa regarding the spiritual juris-diction in their respective kingdoms. He convened the Third Lateran Council at which time clerical marriages were outlawed, eventually re-sulting in an exaggerated fear of women.

Three years after Herrad's death, Innocent III became pope and pro-ceeded to eliminate the few sacerdotal and liturgical privileges that had been granted to certain abbesses.[12] Generally, churchmen were hostile to-ward women, but men in civil society were even more so. One expression of this hostility was civil law prohibiting women from being licensed as physicians.[13] Nevertheless, one author claims that Herrad was a physi-cian.[14] It may have been possible for a nun to circumvent this law in the privacy of the monastery. We read of medieval women who were skilled in the use of herbs, salves, and ointments. And we read of nuns who had additional educational opportunities which gives us grounds for believing that Herrad may indeed have been a physician, albeit unlicensed.

Historically, the twelfth century is known as the time of the flowering of medieval Christianity.[15] On the one hand, it was a society marked by beauty, piety, order, and creativity, and on the other hand by violence and chaos. A comparison of the cultural level of convents of this period with those of the seventh and eighth centuries indicates an overall decline.[16] The flowering of the culture may have taken place, but in general, women were not included.

HISTORY AND SPIRITUAL LEGACY OF HOHENBOURG

The monastery at Hohenbourg was named for St. Odile, patroness of those suffering from eye disorders. Hagiography regarding her is sparse and varied. Legend has it that she was born blind in 720. Her father, Duke Eticho, distressed at fathering a physically imperfect child, sought to dis-pose of her. His wife, the child's mother, asked to be allowed to send the infant away, and her husband agreed to this arrangement. After being miraculously cured of her blindness, Odile returned to her parental home at Hohenbourg. In his joy over her return, the Duke gave her the family castle for a monastery, with Odile as abbess.[17] The details of her life are elusive, but she is mentioned in Herrad's writing as the founder of the monastery at Hohenbourg. A miniature *in Hortus Deliciarum* shows the Duke seated on a faldstool, giving a key to Odile. In the background is a mountain with the twin-towered church of the abbey.[18] There was also a monument at Niedermunster commemorating the founding of the abbey by St. Odile.[19]

The abbey was granted exceptional privileges, perhaps because the water there was believed to produce healing in diseased eyes. It became a center for pilgrimage. Documents of the period indicate that both

Charlemagne and Pope Leo IX may have been pilgrims there.[20] By request of Frederick Barbarossa, Relinda became abbess at Hohenbourg in 1141. The abbey had been in a period of decline and was in need of a dynamic leader. Relinda was a former member of Admont Abbey, an abbey known for its outstanding observance of the Rule of Benedict, for the scholarly achievements of its members, and as a center for education. Relinda herself was known for her scholarship and was sent to Berg monastery to reform it. Hohenbourg was the second abbey that she was asked to reform.[21]

Hortus Deliciarum gives no clear indication about the rule followed by the community of Hohenbourg. The portion of the manuscript that contained a spiritual rule was lost. It could be assumed that the abbey followed the Rule of Benedict since Relinda, the former abbess, was once a member of a Benedictine Abbey. But Herrad follows the Augustinian view that contemplation is a property of the soul but above all of the virginal life.[22] She founded a Premonstratensian priory near the abbey and later added an Augustinian foundation that included a church, convent, farm, hospital, and hospice. It is possible that she was an Augustinian canoness. There is no definitive evidence to prove whether or not she was a canoness or a Benedictine.[23]

HORTUS DELICIARUM (GARDEN OF DELIGHTS)

The reading of Scripture and other spiritual literature was an integral part of monastic life. The nourishment of one's faith life was the purpose of all intellectual pursuits.[24] For Herrad, the ongoing formation of her community was a responsibility she took seriously. With assistance from members of the community, she planned and executed an encyclopedia for this purpose. It was especially inviting to the reader because it was filled with hundreds of pictures, most of them in color and with accompanying texts. Herrad was truly a woman of medieval Europe. Her encyclopedia was an account of history based on biblical narrative, the accepted practice of the day. She displayed a wide range of knowledge of patristic writers and creativity in selecting and executing many of the miniatures.

An unusual name for an encyclopedia, *Hortus Deliciarum* or *Garden of Delights* may have been suggested by a text from Honorius who writes that paradise, or the garden of delight, is the Church. He comments further that Scripture and Christ himself are in that *Garden*.[25] The title could also refer to the beauty and variety of the manuscript. It contained both contemporary and biblical scenes, included quotes from numerous sources, and was filled with beautiful miniatures. In its beauty it was as profuse as a cultivated flower garden in bloom. The encyclopedia was similar in intent to the cathedrals built during the Middle Ages whose stained glass windows, statuary, and frescoes served as Bible and catechism for the illiterate. Although Herrad added text to her manuscript, the miniatures provided the same visual instruction for her nuns.

Numerous sources influenced Herrad's writing with both religious and secular themes addressed. There were excurses on the Trinity, on angels, and on the Incarnation, as well as on the cosmos and secular learning. The *Sentences* of Peter Lombard, +1160, was used in one section of the manuscript. *Sentences* includes the whole of Christian doctrine in one manual, using a compilation from older and contemporary sources. This manual was used in the schools of the West into the seventeenth century.[26] There are also quotes or references to *Speculum Ecclesiae,* Anselm *On the Sacraments,* and excerpts from Clement and Augustine. She quoted from St. Bernard of Clairvaux's *Parabola* once, and because of the allusions she made to Bede's cosmology, she must have had a copy of it at hand.[27] Among the sources repeatedly quoted is *Speculum Mariae* which has not been rediscovered.[28]

There were a number of artistic influences present in the manuscript. In the miniatures on the parables, there were Ottonian and Byzantine characteristics. The art was representative of the school of Echternach and Regensburg. This was just part of the enormous reserve accumulated in the field of art before Herrad's time. It is obvious that some of the women who worked on the encyclopedia were highly trained artists.[29]

Originally, the encyclopedia had 342 leaves. The leaves or pages were folded to make a folio and were not bound. The size of the leaves was perhaps 39 x 27.5 cm with 50 lines of text per page. The first letter of each text was illuminated in the brilliant red pigments often used by the rubricator.[30] Other than this lettering, there were no decorations or illuminations in the manuscript. Usually, the *Garden* had two columns of text per page consisting of dialogue, verse, prose, and songs. Any titles given to the miniatures were centered on the column and were done completely in red.[31] Every person and implement in the miniatures was identified in Latin or German, or sometimes in both languages. Included in the work are two musical pieces, *"Sol Ovilur Occasus"* and *"Primus Parens Hominum."* The musical staff used by Herrad had its origin in Italian music of the mid-eleventh century and was widely used in Germany in the twelfth century, the latter composition being a rare example of polyphony from that century.[32] The composer of this section, whether Herrad or another nun, was obviously an accomplished musician. Perhaps more than one composer was involved.

Although the nature of a Christian society was one of the great questions of the day, the reader of *Hortus Deliciarum* finds no reference to any of the great questions and situations of that era.[33] A commentary on such matters was not the intent of this encyclopedia. The manuscript gave evidence that the plan for the work was to coordinate a pictorial, dogmatic, and didactic history with a text that used numerous authorities known to Herrad.[34] There was a list of popes that concluded before 1185, which indicates that the major portion of *Hortus Deliciarum* was finished before that time. Five calendar tables and a genealogical tree of Christ were included. The encyclopedia showed internal evidence that more than one person prepared the text and the miniatures. Apparently, one master plan was accomplished by a number of women.

There were 636 miniatures in *Hortus Deliciarum,* examples of perfect and exceptional harmony. They were the complete opposite of the monumental paintings of the period but employed the same masterful use of color. Artists who drew the miniatures worked within a small format for a limited number of readers, especially before the advent of the printing press. Herrad's work included both illustrated Scripture stories and subjects of a more secular nature. All were complex and perfectly executed. This intricate art form produced delicate, inventive, and beautiful works of art. Those trained to paint these miniatures learned modes of expression that used a wide range of standard gestures, actions, objects. There were standing poses for figures, formulas for how to draw bed clothes and how to portray seated figures.[35] These standard forms can be seen throughout the manuscript.

The models used for the miniatures were drawn from twelfth-century daily life. The horses of the Exodus scenes had harnesses like those of Herrad's day. The sun god, Apollo, was shown riding in a medieval cart. Many of the people were clothed in the garb of the day.[36] There is a close similarity between a miniature of the Annunciation and a ninth-century Greek manuscript.[37] Although these nuns were cloistered, they had remarkable access to numerous sources. Quite possibly one of the nuns knew Greek. It might be presumed that if they had a Greek manuscript someone was able to read it. Byzantine influence is found in numerous miniatures. There are illustrations of the episode of the rich young man in the New Testament which was known only in that tradition. Another example of Byzantine influence is found in the portrayal of Moses as a figure having rays emanating from his head. In the art of the West at this time, Moses was illustrated either as horned or veiled, but never before with rays.[38] The last example of rare figures in Western art is found in the miniatures of Jesus with children. In one of them, he is healing a lunatic child; in the other, he is placing a child in the midst of his disciples. Both scenes are unusual because children were not subjects of miniatures in the West until after the thirteenth century. One inventive illustration concerns an ancient tradition that God captured the great leviathan, the representative of chaos. Herrad's unique miniature presents God capturing the leviathan using a hook which is Christ on the cross.[39]

In another clever miniature, the artist portrays the genealogy of Christ with the ancestors—according to Matthew 1:1-16—listed in six rows, forming a tree. Christ is at the top, and Abraham is at the bottom. An angel shows the stars of the heavens to Abraham, and God is portrayed as planting the tree. This tree is below ground, and Christ is at ground level. At the level of Christ, representatives of the Christian community are shown including kings, monks, martyrs, virgins, bishops, and popes. Noticeably missing from the scene are lay people. A bias against the laity is evident here and in a later miniature. In that scene, people from various life situations are attempting to climb the ladder of perfection. At the top is charity, portrayed by a young girl. Temptations and the devil are there to lure each one from reaching perfection. The first to fall is the married couple. The highest rung is occupied by a hermit who appears to be the only one to deserve a chance for the life held out by God. The nun fails to reach perfection because she was seduced by a priest. Similar precautions about the clergy were not peculiar to Herrad. Ivo of Chartres remarked about the problem, and drastic precautions were taken at the convents of Foncorult and Jully.[40] Nuns are also warned in the miniature to resist temptations from rich relatives or worldly pomp. Women occupy the lower rungs and are portrayed as being more susceptible to the evil one. Women are also used by Herrad to incarnate temptation. Of the six reasons for failing to attain charity, three had something to do with women.[41] And being a woman of her times, Herrad was influenced by the negative attitude of the Church and civil society toward women.

The following are some of the many examples of inventiveness in *Garden of Delights*. In the miniature of Job sitting on a dunghill, his wife, fittingly enough, stands near him holding her nose. In another, Christ stands beside the cross waiting for crucifixion, a depiction unknown in Western tradition at that time. There are two similar miniatures representing the activities of Peter and Paul. In one, a figure representing the synagogue sits in a tub of water with a veil covering her head. Peter is baptizing her and inscribing a cross on the veil. In the other, Paul is shown baptizing an Ethiopian woman who personifies the Church of the gentiles. There is no parallel to these symbolic baptisms. The Virgin Mary was usually portrayed in blue clothing, but Herrad gives her a green gown, retaining the brilliant red slippers from an older tradition.[42]

In another miniature, Matthias is elected to take the place of Judas in the apostolic group. The Eleven are seated on a bench with Peter and Andrew in the center. Matthias sits next to Andrew who is holding out a platter to Matthias. There are dice on the platter. To the left of the bench is the unchosen man, Joseph Barsabas.[43] The miniature on Wisdom depicts seven women, representing the arts, forming a circle around Lady Wisdom. According to the medieval interpretation of Aristotle, there were seven liberal arts. The seven figures are dressed in the style of the twelfth century, and each is robed in a different color, holding emblems of her power. Music is dressed in purple and holds a lyre, a zither, and a hurdy-gurdy; grammar is dressed in dark red and holds a book and a birch rod. Each figure is encircled by a sentence explaining the special nature of her power. In the lower part of the same picture are four men at desks engaged in reading and writing. They exemplify the poets. Black birds appear to be whispering in their ears.[44] These miniatures with their accompanying texts convey to the reader Herrad's extensive knowledge and her openness to learning.

The last two miniatures, which are full page, concern the monastery at Hohenbourg. On one page is the pictorial history of Hohenbourg, including the Duke and Odile. In the center is the figure of Christ with the monastery church on a mountain behind him. To the right is the figure of Relinda, and on the opposite page is a mirrored image of Herrad. The page with the figure of Herrad lists the names and portraits of the forty-six nuns, lay sisters, and novices of the community.[45] It was a fitting way to end *Hortus Deliciarum* whose original purpose was to provide "spiritual pleasure" for her sisters.

Herrad and the other nuns who assisted with the calligraphy, lettering, and miniature painting in this manuscript provided an example of the education received in the fine arts in the abbey. It has been noted that there are both linguistic uniformities and uniform inconsistencies, demonstrating that one plan was followed, even if many nuns were involved in carrying it out.[46] Only minstrels were omitted from the manuscript; they do not appear in the illustrations or as models in the text although they were a part of medieval life. There was widespread disapproval of minstrels in religious communities where they were seen as the ministers of Satan without the possibility of salvation. This was a prejudice of many of the nuns of that era.[47] Virgins were addressed in *Hortus Deliciarum* as snow-white flowers. The equation of flowers with virtue used during the High Middle Ages was equated with the ethical triad of humility, love, and chastity.[48]

Although Herrad was a contemporary of Hildegard of Bingen, no mention is made of Hildegard in the manuscript. Conversely, there is no reference to Herrad in any of the extant copies of authors of her time following her death. Unlike Hildegard, Mechtild, or Elisabeth of Schönau, Herrad is scarcely known. *Hortus Deliciarum* was not, strictly speaking, spiritual and was not in any sense a mystical writing. *Hortus Deliciarum* was a pictorial encyclopedia valued and used by a long-forgotten community of nuns.

The manuscript was preserved at Hohenbourg until the mid-sixteenth century when a fire at the monastery necessitated its removal. Fortunately, it was taken to the library in Strassbourg where tracings were made of much of it. In a bombardment of Strassbourg in 1870, the library and its contents burned.[49] Thus ended the existence of the original seven-hundred-year-old document. Only fifty-four percent of the folios were copied in full, another twenty percent partially, and twenty-six percent have disappeared.[50] One can imagine the immensity of the undertaking after seeing the brilliant colors of the surviving copies. A reconstruction has been done, using all available data.[51]

HERRAD OF HOHENBOURG'S SIGNIFICANCE TODAY

Herrad presented both religious and secular knowledge, giving the impression that there was nothing demeaning or superficial about learning. She seemed to know that God is Truth and that all knowledge draws one closer to that Truth. However, she was influenced by her culture's perception of women, lay people, and entertainers of her time, revealing the particular bias of her era.

The spiritual dimension of life was continually placed before her readers in the numerous miniatures depicting Bible stories. Herrad's familiarity with Scripture was a witness to the privileged place the Word had in her monastery. Books published today are often wordy and lack beauty. *Hortus Deliciarum* reminds the reader that artistic beauty touches the interior life in ways that words do not. In a time when many people only know or care to know their own language, Herrad's manuscript, written both in German and Latin, illustrates the value of understanding more than one.

Hortus Deliciarum was a work of love. Herrad was concerned about others, namely her community, when she compiled the encyclopedia. And she devoted many years to its completion. She and the other sisters who compiled it used their talents for the education and inspiration of those who were their life companions. Her commitment to the spiritual and educational enrichment of others is worth emulating today.

NOTES

1. J. Gurevich, *Categories of Medieval Culture,* trans. G. L. Campbell (London: Routledge and Kegan, 1985) 289.

2. Jean LeClercq, "Conversion to the Monastic Life in the Twelfth Century: Who, Why, and How?" *Studiosum Speculum: Studies in Honor of Louis J. Lekai, O.Cist.,* eds. Frances R. Swietek and John R. Sommerfeldt (Kalamazoo: Cistercian Publications, 1993) 203–204.

3. Margaret Labarge, *A Small Sound of the Trumpet: Women in Medieval Life* (Boston: Beacon Press, 1986) 221.

4. Norman F. Cantor, *Medieval History: The Life and Death of a Civilization* (New York: Macmillan Company, 1963) 467–473.

5. Will Durant, *The Story of Civilization: The Age of Faith* (New York: Simon and Schuster, 1950) 4:825.

6. LeClercq, "Conversion to the Monastic Life in the Twelfth Century," 205.

7. Jean Comby, *How to Read Church History,* trans. John Bowden and Margaret Lydamore (New York: Crossroads, 1985) 151.

8. Margaret Deanesey, *History of the Medieval Church* (London: Methuen and Company, 1925) 135.

9. Cantor, *Medieval History,* 411–412.

10. Rosalie Green and others, *Herrad of Hohenbourg, Hortus Deliciarum: Commentary* (London: Wartburg Institute, University of London, 1979) 71.

11. Ibid., 64–68.

12. Paulette L'Hermite-LeClerq, "The Feudal Order," trans. Arthur Goldhammer, ed. Christine Klapish-Zuber, *A History of Women in the West: Silences of the Middle Ages* (Cambridge, Mass.: Belknap Press of Harvard University Press, 1992) 2:243.

13. Durant, *The Story of Civilization,* 825.

14. Norma O. Ireland, Index to *Women from Ancient to Modern Times: A Supplement* (Westwood, Mass.: F. W. Faxon Company, 1970) 323.

15. Andre Vauchez, *The Spirituality of the Medieval West from the Eighth to the Twelfth Century,* trans. Colette Friedlander (Kalamazoo: Cistercian Publications, 1993) 84–85.

16. L'Hermite-LeClerq, "The Feudal Order," 243.

17. Hermigild Dressier, OFM, "Odilia, St.," *New Catholic Encyclopedia,* 10:642.

18. Green, *Herrad of Hohenbourg, Hortus Deliciarum,* 345.

19. Herbert Thurston and Donald Attwater, eds., *Butler's Lives of the Saints* (New York: J. P. Kennedy and Sons, 1956) 551–553.

20. F. L. Cross and E. A. Livingstone, eds., *The Oxford Dictionary of the Christian Church* (London: Oxford University Press, 1985) 991.

21. M. P. Heinrich, *The Canonesses and Education in the Early Middle Ages* (Washington: The Catholic University of America, 1924) 105.

22. Matthias Bernards, *Speculum Virginum* (Koln/Gras: Bohlau-Verlag, 1955) 195.

23. Geoffrey Webb, "The Person and the Place: Herrad and Her *Garden of Delights,*" *Life of the Spirit* 16 (1961-62) 476.

24. Vauchez, *The Spirituality of the Medieval West,* 155.

25. Webb, "The Person and the Place," 475.

26. Deanesey, *History of the Medieval Church,* 135.

27. Green, *Herrad of Hohenbourg, Hortus Deliciarum,* 92.

28. Bernards, *Speculum Virginum,* 81.

29. Green, *Herrad of Hohenbourg, Hortus Deliciarum,* 34.

30. Ibid., 1, 2, 32.

31. Ibid., 89.

32. Ibid., 87.

33. Cantor, *Medieval History,* 306.

34. L. Eckenstein, *Woman Under Monasticism* (London: Cambridge University Press, 1896) 245.

35. Green, *Herrad of Hohenbourg, Hortus Deliciarum,* 36.

36. Richard W. Bulliet, "Vehicles, European," *Dictionary of the Middle Ages,* 12:373.

37. Eckenstein, *Woman Under Monasticism,* 243.

38. Green, *Herrad of Hohenbourg, Hortus Deliciarum,* 117.

39. Ibid., 101, 154.

40. Bernards, *Speculum Virginum,* 169.

41. Chiara Frugoni, "The Imagined Woman," trans. Clarissa Botsford, *Silences of the Middle Ages,* ed. Christine Klapish-Zuber, 358.

42. Green, *Herrad of Hohenbourg, Hortus Deliciarum,* 124, 165, 180, 182, 189.

43. Ibid., 184.

44. Eckenstein, *Woman Under Monasticism,* 246.

45. Green, *Herrad of Hohenbourg, Hortus Deliciarum,* 228.

46. Heinrich, *The Canonesses and Education in the Early Middle Ages,* 190.

47. Labarge, *A Small Sound of the Trumpet,* 226.

48. Bernards, *Speculum Virginum,* 81.

49. Eckenstein, *Woman Under Monasticism,* 239.

50. Green, *Herrad of Hohenbourg, Hortus Deliciarum,* 18.

51. Rosalie Green and others, *Herrad of Hohenbourg, Hortus Deliciarum: Reconstructed* (London: Wartburg Institute, University of London, 1979) 1ff. Note: This volume contains the surviving material and the probable titles of the lost material.

13

Following the Lamb Wherever He Goes:
The Story of St. Lutgard[1]

M. Zita Wenker, O.S.B.

INTRODUCTION

Certain moments in the history of the Church are freighted with a significance that sets them in clear relief against the backdrop of less remarkable times. One such age, spanning the late twelfth and early thirteenth centuries, witnessed an extraordinary intensity of religious life. Although decadence, abuses, and dwindling numbers were widespread in the ancient Benedictine order by this time, the Cistercians, founded in 1098, experienced phenomenal growth in the twelfth century, especially in France. By the thirteenth century they were facing the consequences of their own success both in numbers and in wealth. Cistercians elsewhere were experiencing a new vitality. In addition, the new mendicant orders, the Franciscans and Dominicans, founded in the early thirteenth century, appealed broadly to enthusiastic recruits, particularly those who did not belong to the nobility.

Into this milieu appeared some remarkable women known as the *mulieres sanctae* or *mulieres religiosae*. These women were mystics who lived in the late twelfth and early thirteenth centuries in Belgium, particularly in the Rupel River basin. They too were drawn largely from more ordinary members of society. Some were beguines such as Marie d'Oignies, the protobeguine; others were recluses such as Julianna of Mont-Cornillon, to whom we owe the origins of the feast of Corpus Christi. Another, Christina *Mirabilis*,[2] defies easy categorizing by the astonishing feats of her life. Still others of these women were nuns, such as the Cistercians Alice of Schaarbeeck, a leper, and the three Idas (of Léau,

Louvain, Nivelles). An especially charming woman who was to achieve prominence among the *mulieres sanctae* was the nun Lutgard. History knows her as St. Lutgard of Aywières (1182–1246). Members of the Cistercian Order are prompt to call her their own, and indeed she is, having lived the major portion of her life in the Cistercian Abbey at Aywières. Yet Benedictines can also claim her, for from the age of twelve until she was twenty-four, she was a member of the Benedictine Abbey of St. Catherine at St. Trond, (Sint Truidin) midway between Louvain and Liège. Her story is a fascinating one that deserves to be better known.

Who was Lutgard? What is her story? What about her vocation, her spiritual progress, her achievements? The story of her life bears some similarity to the *vitae* of the other *mulieres sanctae* in that they all engaged in ascetic practices, received supernatural gifts, enjoyed mystical experiences, and exerted varying degrees of influence on their contemporaries. Yet even with the similarities, Lutgard emerges as an individual, an engaging personality, a flesh-and-blood woman who became a great mystic.

LUTGARD'S BIOGRAPHER, THOMAS OF CANTIMPRÉ

Lutgard did not write her own life. Her story comes to us in the *Vita Lutgardis*[3] by Thomas of Cantimpré (c. 1201–c. 1276), a Dominican friar who knew her personally and, he certifies, knew her very well during the final sixteen years of her life when he was her spiritual director.[4] This first-hand contact and close relationship with Lutgard establishes Thomas' authority as a biographer and assures his readers of his trustworthiness. It is not likely he would contradict the saint's own testimonies which he merely committed to paper. Thomas genuinely esteemed Lutgard. Nevertheless, his motives were not entirely altruistic. In a gesture of barely disguised, pious bribery he promised Hadewijch, Abbess of Aywières, to write the Saint's life in return for receiving her amputated little finger as a relic. Indeed, he had wanted her entire right hand, but Lutgard herself while still alive assured him her little finger would be quite sufficient.

Thomas of Cantimpré joined the young Dominican order around 1232, shortly after St. Dominic's death. He studied under St. Albert the Great at Cologne, and was a confrere of Blessed Jordan of Saxony, the second Master General of the Dominicans, as well as other influential early Dominicans. Cardinal Jacques de Vitry was his friend and mentor. His other works include *De Natura Rerum* (c. 1245) and the *Bonum Universale de Apibus* (c. 1256-1261). For our purposes, however, interest focuses on his *vitae* of women saints and in particular on that of St. Lutgard. (He also wrote the *vitae* of Christina *Mirabilis* and Margaret of Ypres, as well as the supplement to Jacques de Vitry's *Vita* of Marie d'Oignies.) Despite his first-hand contact with Lutgard, some critics accuse Thomas of excessive credulity, especially in his reporting of various marvelous and mystical experiences Lutgard had.

Is his word trustworthy? Does he exaggerate? Competent scholars accept his word, albeit with some qualifications. Simone Roisin states, for example, that by the time Thomas wrote Lutgard's *Vita*, his writings were very similar to other mystical *vitae* of the Cistercian milieu.[5] Elsewhere, however, Roisin confronts the issue of his credibility head on, and reminds us that Thomas was careful to insist on the importance of witnesses, usually naming the sources of his information. Many of the names he gives are of historical persons whose existence is indisputable. Also, he didn't relate any of Lutgard's predictions unless he could demonstrate that they were, in fact, realized. As Thomas saw it with his thirteenth-century understanding, these factors were sufficient to demonstrate his reliability as a careful biographer. His writings contain many nuggets revealing the life and mentality of thirteenth-century Benedictine and Cistercian nuns.[6] Contemporary scholar, Caroline Walker Bynum, regards Thomas of Cantimpré and Jacques de Vitry as theologians and "remarkable clerical biographers."[7] Similarly, Elizabeth A. Petroff calls these two clerics our "best witnesses to the early period of activity among Beguines in the Low Countries."[8] Less kindly, Roger De Ganck says that some clergymen "'kissed the ground' on which some *mulieres religiosae* walked, among them . . . Lutgard."[9] Just the same, De Ganck admits that the *vitae* are important sources for our knowledge of the *mulieres religiosae* movement.

So the text of Lutgard's *Vita* by Thomas, as it has come down to us, is eminently worthwhile, flaws and all. It is to his credit as a biographer that Lutgard truly comes alive under his pen. Whether it is the young girl pleased by fine clothes and the attentions of suitors or the enthusiastic, youthful Lutgard telling the Lord to "wait here for me—I'll be back as soon as I can" (cf. I,8) or the compassionate woman healing physical, moral, and spiritual ills or the feisty Cistercian ordering the Lord to grant her prayers for a certain individual or "blot me out of the Book of Life" (cf. III,15) or the aging Lutgard, accepting blindness with only one regret—no longer being able to see her beloved friends' faces, we recognize in her a real woman who loved and was loved, who was a woman of her times, and who contributed much in her own way. In passages where Thomas harangues on his pet themes, the voice changes, and it is clearly Thomas speaking of his own concerns.[10]

Thomas bases the three books of the *Vita Lutgardis* on the three states of the soul of those who seek God: beginners, those progressing, and the perfect. The choice provides him with a vehicle for unfolding Lutgard's story gradually, from Book One which is the emphasis of this essay and relates her earliest years and her life as a Benedictine, through Books Two and Three that deal with Lutgard the Cistercian, up to and after her death.

Someone picking up Lutgard's *Vita* for the first time may find the language problematic. Besides what seems to be excessive adulation on the part of the biographer, there is talk of the beloved, of doves and eagles, of crowns, oil, and inebriation. These sound foreign, overly pious, sentimental, and divorced from any relevance for our own times. It would be a short-sighted error, however, to reject Lutgard's *Vita* out of hand simply because of the language. On the level of the text itself there is much to learn of this fascinating woman, and once we realize that the language of the *Vita* is permeated with scriptural and liturgical overtones recognized by the original monastic recipients, entire worlds of new meaning open up for us. There is much more significance here than we may at first suspect. The language and imagery of the Song of Songs (also referred to as the Canticle of Canticles), in particular, so pervasive in the *Vita*, were thoroughly familiar to Thomas' readers. The monastic life itself prepared the readers to resonate with the language and images that were already well-known to them through their daily chanting of the *Opus Dei* (the Work of God or the Divine Office). The psalms, antiphons, responses, and other readings from Scripture that they lived with and prayed day in and day out, bathed them in biblical images. Texts became familiar, part of their very being. And the hours given over to *lectio divina*, that peculiarly monastic type of deliberate, reflective reading of Scripture, continued the process already begun in the liturgy. Medieval authors speak of "ruminating" Scripture, chewing it over slowly and attentively in the mind and heart as a cow chews her cud. A homely image perhaps, yet it illustrates the extent to which Scripture prayerfully reflected upon is assimilated into the person as nurturing food for the spirit.

From the twelfth century on, the Song of Songs was the most frequently commented on book of the Old Testament and enjoyed immense popularity, particularly among monastics. Although the Song of Songs had been commented on for centuries—from Hippolytus of Rome and Origen to Gregory of Nyssa and many others—it was in the twelfth century that such commentary came to full flower. St. Bernard's commentaries on the Song of Songs were especially popular.[11] Jean LeClercq in his classic, *The Love of Learning and the Desire for God*,[12] elucidates the reasons. For one thing, the Song and monastic commentary on it appeals to the whole person, especially the heart, not simply the mind as the scholastics are accused of doing. And it is the heart that needs this continual nourishment in order to keep at the monastic quest year in and year out. Perhaps the key to the Song's popularity, though, can be found in the similarity between the Song itself and the monastic life. In its quintessential form, monastic life is seeking God. And what is the Song, but a poem about the mutual pursuit of beloved and Lover? The Song serves as a metaphor for the whole quest of the monastic life. Both the Song, as a love poem, and monastic life itself find their completion in the fullness of love. For monastics, the fullest experience of this love comes only in eternity when the seeker finds and dwells with the One who is Love in Person. But even on the way, love is the atmosphere in which a monastic lives and moves. In such a milieu as existed in the twelfth century, then, language that may require explanatory notes today was eminently understandable because it was the language of everyday life and experience.

An Overview of Lutgard's Life: The Early Years

St. Lutgard was born in 1182 in Tongres in the diocese of Liège, the child of a "mixed marriage" in the sense that her parents were from vastly different social backgrounds. Her mother was from the nobility, her father a common burgher. This was unusual since burghers were "beneath" nobles. The very fact of her parents' marriage was indicative of the changes occurring in society. The *Vita* does not say how their marriage came about, but we glimpse some tensions between them in their plans for their daughter Lutgard. Perhaps because of his own more modest background, her father hoped all the more for a good marriage for his daughter. To ensure that end, he invested some money for her dowry from her infancy. Unfortunately for him, the merchant to whom he entrusted it proved incompetent, not only failing to prosper but even losing the initial investment. We could speculate that had Lutgard's mother favored a marriage for her daughter, some solution could have been found to the financial disaster. After all, the mother apparently had resources, and the young Lutgard enjoyed being "splendidly" clad, which presumes comfortable means. Mama, set on her daughter's entering religion, was willing to see to it that any monastery her daughter wished to join would open its doors to her. But if Lutgard preferred to marry, her mother threatened that she would only have a cowherd for a husband. The loss of the dowry very likely played a role in Lutgard's eventual entry into the convent. Although it is couched in pious terms, the monastery may have provided a haven for an undowried daughter. We know from the *Vita* that she had a married sister whose own dowry may have already severely strained the family resources. Lutgard herself, in her early years, was far from uninterested in marriage, and a number of knightly suitors sought her company. But Mama strongly encouraged her daughter to choose Christ instead. Eventually, Mama prevailed, and at the tender age of twelve, Lutgard was entrusted to the Benedictine Abbey of St. Catherine at St. Trond, most likely as a child-oblate.[13]

Her episodes with suitors didn't end with her entrance into the monastery, however, and one of them even took advantage of her visit to a married sister to ambush her on the way, attempting to force her submission. Lutgard fled and escaped his evil intent. Even in this early episode, her lifelong association with Jesus Crucified is presaged in the way Lutgard handles the prurient curiosity of the townspeople who had heard of the incident. They gather to watch her on her return, eager to seize on racy morsels for gossipmongering. Lutgard is mortified, but she remembers all the humiliations that Christ underwent for her. This remembrance enables her to hold her head high, unveil her face, and proceed unperturbed through their midst. The unruly crowd, disturbed by her action, dissipates. Thomas refers to this incident as a turning point in which Lutgard continued her progress toward the Lord "with even more powerful gifts" (I,7). And the incident was also an answer to a fervent prayer Lutgard had uttered long before in which she asked the Lord to send her a disgrace so that she might imitate the disgrace Christ suffered in the Passion.

LUTGARD, THE YOUNG BENEDICTINE

Even though Lutgard apparently entered St. Catherine's Abbey without great enthusiasm for the monastic life, she was nevertheless open to God's grace and the promptings of the inner life. Thomas alludes to this when he says that she already experienced inward stirrings of God at work within her, although at that point she could not have verbalized much about it. God's servant was being prepared. When the initial vision of Christ occurred, she was ready to respond wholeheartedly. The somewhat reluctant child-oblate possessed the potential for great holiness, indeed for the full flowering of the mystical life; and in God's good time, that would be revealed.

HER FIRST VISION OF CHRIST

Lutgard's dalliances, if such they were, ended abruptly with her first vision of Christ. Once when she was in the midst of a conversation with a young man, Christ himself appeared to her in human form and showed her the wound in his side, bleeding as if freshly inflicted. Christ exhorted her to no longer seek "the caresses of unseemly love" (I,2). Rather it was his wounded side that she was to contemplate and love. This direct intervention of Christ changed Lutgard's life forever. Lutgard was so profoundly affected by this vision of Christ that it marked her conversion toward a life of ever-greater loving intimacy with God, and ever-deepening love and compassion for God's people. So compelling was the vision that no longer could human lovers hold any attraction or interest for her. In fact, the next and last time the young man presents himself, Lutgard sends him packing in no uncertain terms.

THE AGNES PROPHECY: KEY TO UNDERSTANDING
LUTGARD'S LIFE AND PASCHAL VOCATION

After Lutgard's initial vision of the Suffering Christ in which she is invited into the mystical life, numerous other mystical or paramystical phenomena occur. Very early on there is the prophecy of an unidentified, devout noblewoman who calls Lutgard a "good sheep," truly a second Agnes (I,3). Here we have a play on words based on the similarity between the Latin *agnus*, lamb, and Agnes, the popular, early-Christian martyr. There is much more here than wordplay, however. There is a similarity between St. Agnes and Lutgard. For one thing, they both share the charism of virginity lovingly consecrated to the Lord. In addition, Agnes underwent the "red martyrdom" of shedding her blood for Christ. Lutgard's martyrdom is protracted and "white," embracing her entire monastic vocation and all the struggle entailed in the *conversatio morum*, that specifically Benedictine vow. Even so, Lutgard greatly yearns for physical martyrdom. She experiences an actual hemorrhage so severe that it catapults her into menopause at the tender age of twenty-eight, and its scars remain with her all her life. More than mere similarity is at issue here, however. The incident of the Agnes prophecy holds a key to understanding Lutgard's entire life and vocation. The centrality of Christ the Lamb becomes increasingly clear as one reads the *Vita*. Lamb references occur at numerous critical points, more often than a cursory reading reveals.

In a vision occurring during the liturgy, a lamb appears, embracing her in choir. The lamb is not merely a meek, gentle animal but is also a powerful symbol of Christ, the "Lamb of God." The vision of the lamb emphasizes the strong element of reparation and of suffering vicariously for others as Christ the Paschal Lamb did, so characteristic of Lutgard's special vocation. Readers of the *Vita* would immediately recognize the implications of this vision since "Lamb" was a word richly invested with meaning, familiar and recognizable from their immersion in the liturgy. The "Lamb" image powerfully parallels Lutgard's life with that of her Lord, Jesus Christ, the Lamb whom she follows "wherever he goes." In other words, Lutgard is united with Jesus Crucified, the Lamb of God, in his agony and death; and she is united with him too in his glory as the Risen Lord, the Lamb seated on the throne, holding the Book of Life. This is the paschal mystery which is at the very heart of Christian life. The reality of suffering, even death, cannot be denied. But it isn't the whole story. Suffering is not the end. For all Christians, including Lutgard and ourselves as well, there is always more; ultimately there is fullness of life and joy in eternity. As the mystery of death-for-life was lived out in Christ's life on earth, so too is it lived out in Lutgard's life, and in the lives of all who follow Christ.

After the woman's prophecy, then, Lutgard is ready to make the words of Agnes her own when the still-hopeful youth once again presents himself. This time she repulses him with the words, "Depart from me, fodder of death, for I have been overtaken by another lover" (I,3). It is far from coincidental that these words, originally attributed to St. Agnes just prior to her martyrdom, are uttered by Lutgard, the "second Agnes."

OTHER MYSTICAL PHENOMENA

Elsewhere in the *Vita* there are instances of other intense mystical experiences such as Lutgard being rapt in God, being caught up in ecstasy, experiencing intense mystical union with the Crucified One—even the so-called mystical marriage. For the rest of her life, she would grow and deepen in her loving response to God, and God's hand was clearly upon her, as subsequent events would testify.

Beginning during her early years as a Benedictine, Lutgard was favored with visions of other heavenly personages as well. The Blessed Virgin appears as a consoling, encouraging presence when rivals in the community deride Lutgard's fervor. Marian visions continue at various crucial points in her life. Blessed Catherine,[14] her monastery's patroness, appears to her and tells her that she will always grow in grace until she reaches "the most powerful merit among the virgins." St. Catherine, appearing to another woman, encourages her to seek out Lutgard as her mediator and mother since God will give Lutgard "a merit and place in heaven equal to mine" (I,9). John the Evangelist appears to her in the form of an eagle (the biblical symbol for St. John) that places its beak on her mouth and infuses her with celestial secrets and knowledge. The beloved disciple of the Gospel is given the charge of enlightening another "beloved disciple," Lutgard. For much of her life, Lutgard is in frequent contact with the inhabitants of the heavenly realm, including sisters from her own community who have died, relatives, friends, and saints. The boundaries between heaven and earth are often indistinct, and as she nears death, the frequency of heavenly visitations increases, the celestial beings seemingly overwhelmed with joy at her approaching entrance into heaven.

There is a distinct shift later in her life in regard to her visions of Christ as well. No longer is it the Suffering Lord who appears, crucified and bleeding, begging for her intercession for "my sinners" (in those wonderfully comforting words for all of us in that category). In a tender, consoling vision, after Lutgard has prayed and wept for many years for sinners, the Lord appears to her and wipes away her tears with his own hand. He tells her she can now "persist in prayer with a placid fervour of heart" which will be as effective with the Father on behalf of sinners as all her tears have been (II,41). Another time, after she had predicted her own death, she describes how she sees Christ's face in contemplation: "An indescribable brilliance appears to me in an instant of time as I see the ineffable beauty of His glorified Being as if it were a resplendence. Were this vision not to pass quickly from the gaze of my contemplation, I would not be able to endure it nor continue to live" (III,9). As her death approaches, Christ appears "with a countenance filled with joy" (III,11). And a few weeks before she dies, Christ again appears "with immensely dazzling clarity" (III,12).

OTHER EXTRAORDINARY GIFTS

Among the gifts Lutgard received during her early Benedictine years was the gift of healing all sorts of ills. This must not have been an easy grace to live with since she asked to be relieved of it. Her biographer refers to the crowds of people who flocked to her because of this gift. Lutgard considered that the exercise of the gift of healing hindered her prayers and infringed on her time for "dallying with" the Lord. If indeed crowds gathered around her, there was noise and confusion, not exactly an ideal monastic atmosphere.[15] Lutgard was so bothered by the crowds coming for healing, and thus preventing the prayer she much more ardently desired, that she asked the Lord to take away the gift and in exchange to give her something more useful for herself. The replacement gift the Lord bestowed on her at her request was a thoroughly monastic one, the grace of understanding the Psalter she prayed daily in the *Opus Dei*. But after a time, Lutgard felt she wasn't progressing as much as she had expected, and she questioned the value of this gift for one who was unlettered as she was. The Lord asked her what she wanted, and Lutgard replied rather abruptly and with great boldness, "I want Your heart." The Lord answered her, "No, rather it is your heart that I want." Lutgard readily concurs: "So be it, Lord, on condition that your heart's love is mingled with mine and I have and hold my heart in You." Thomas tells us that a correspondence of hearts, "the union of an uncreated with a created spirit" occurred from then on. This is very likely the first recorded instance of the so-called mystical "exchange of hearts." Lutgard's next words clarify for us the meaning of what takes place: "With You as my shield, [my heart] is secure for all time" (I,12). This expression, "exchange of hearts," conveys the fullness and intensity with which Jesus Christ, God Incarnate, permeates Lutgard's heart and soul. She, in turn, is fully open to him. Of course, no actual physical interchange occurs.[16]

The progression from the earlier gifts of healing and understanding Scripture to the exchange of hearts with Christ, may well be a vehicle

Thomas employs to demonstrate Lutgard's development and continuing maturation in her life of mystical union with Christ. Nevertheless, there is an abrupt, qualitative, quantum leap from the first two gifts to this utterly mystical one. One may inquire just what it was within Lutgard that inspired her to request such a gift. Other gifts she received during her Benedictine years, which may be called paramystical rather than actually mystical, included one instance of levitation. As did many of Lutgard's mystical experiences, this occurred in a liturgical context on the day of Pentecost while the nuns were singing the *Veni Creator Spiritus*. Her sisters in choir with her observed that she was elevated two cubits from the earth into the air. Her admiring biographer finds no wonder in this since her soul was already "more elevated than the world." Why shouldn't her body accompany this movement?[17]

Another unusual gift was her experience of a wondrous radiance of light surrounding her one night during prayer (I,11). Thomas tells us that this experience of celestial brilliance brighter than the sun lasted most of the night. The brilliant light enveloping her may have been the visual equivalent to the mystical exchange of hearts. The One who referred to himself as the "Light" (cf. John 12:35-36; 46) overflows even physically into her to such a degree that it is apparent to others, including some of the sisters who envied her a little. They could not help but see that God was favoring his special disciple. This marvelous, radiant light proved to be efficacious for Lutgard as well as for those who witnessed it. Despite their envy, the light had the effect of increasing the grace of their spiritual life. They were affected by it, almost in spite of themselves.[18]

Two other lesser phenomena are also found in Book One. The first is the instance of Lutgard's fingers dripping oil, so caught up is she in sweetness of spirit after prayer (I,16). This happened while Lutgard was visiting a friend, a recluse in Looz. Thomas refers to it as a "manifestation of grace" within her, a true spiritual inebriation. Here again, as with other mystical or paramystical experiences she enjoyed, there is imagery with many liturgical resonances. Oil is a rich, biblical image that implies anointing and blessing, abundance, an outpouring of spirit.[19] Lutgard was so interiorly blessed by God that it was manifested externally and physically through the oil. Interestingly enough, St. Catherine, the patroness of her Benedictine monastery, was also a myroblyte or oil-producing saint. This is far more than mere coincidence, especially in light of the earlier vision Lutgard had had of St. Catherine, and the martyr's words to her. Moreover, the oil-producing event for Lutgard occurred in the context of spiritual joy and fullness expressed in a wholehearted, mystic dance. Her whole being was so filled with joy that it overflowed into physical, bodily expression.[20]

The final paramystical phenomenon during Lutgard's Benedictine years consisted in a vision of a large golden crown being placed on her

head by the bishop during a rite of consecration, probably monastic profession (I,17). All the other nuns were given linen wreaths, but at least in
the eyes of two witnesses, (notice Thomas's "two witness" evidence)
Lutgard alone was given a golden crown. Once more, the Lord showed his
pleasure in her by honoring her above the others, presenting her with a distinctive, regal mark of deference. With the crown, once again we have a
symbol full of scriptural resonances.[21]

Lutgard's numerous gifts notwithstanding, not all her sisters found her
a comfortable companion in community. Ever so often her biographer lets
us know that there was envy and jealousy toward her and a cynical attitude
toward the genuiness of her piety. Nevertheless, at about the age of
twenty-four, Lutgard was unanimously elected prioress of her monastery.
Whatever negative attitudes there were toward her had apparently been
mollified. In her view, however, the election was a disaster because it took
away from her the possibility of seeking and serving God undisturbed in
a life of prayer and holy leisure. So disastrous did it seem to her, that on
the very day of her election, she resolved to transfer to another monastery
where no such indignity would be forced upon her. Just how long she
served as prioress before her transfer to Aywières is not specified, but it
was for some time at least since the incident of the amorous abbot, recently returned from a voyage, insisting on greeting all the nuns with a
kiss, occurred when she was prioress. Christ himself came to the rescue
and placed his hand between Lutgard and the abbot so that she wouldn't
sense the "contagion" of the man's unwanted kiss (I,21). This episode is
one of the times when the voice of Thomas takes over in a diatribe against
incautious clergymen using their influential status to take indelicate advantage of consecrated virgins (I,21).

TRANSFER TO AYWIÈRES: LUTGARD THE CISTERCIAN

Eventually, after advice from her friends, John of Lierre and Christina
Mirabilis, and a threat from the Lord himself to desert her if she failed to
go there, Lutgard transferred to the Cistercian Abbey of Aywières in the
French-speaking section of the country. This provided assurance against
having to face the unwelcome prospect of being elected prioress again
since she spoke Flemish and never really mastered French. It must be
noted just the same that her contacts with others, both inside and outside
her community, didn't seem to suffer from her linguistic limitations.

In her new life as a Cistercian (not totally new, of course, since
Cistercians also live by the Rule of St. Benedict), Lutgard's mystical development continued. Something new that occurred in her Cistercian years
was her undertaking of seven-year fasts. These were always at the behest
of the Lord or the Blessed Virgin, not some personal caprice of her own,

and were for specific persons or circumstances such as the prevalent Albigensian heresy that was wreaking havoc in the Church. She embraced them heartily, and at three different times in her Cistercian life she undertook such fasts on bread and beer or bread and vegetables. She became well-known as a powerful intercessor both for people still on earth and for those in purgatory. Her purgatorial intercessions—including securing the release of the most powerful pope of the Middle Ages, Pope Innocent III—are especially notable occurrences in her Cistercian years.

Her last eleven years were lived under the veil of darkness, in which she accepted physical blindness because God asked it of her. Her one regret at being blind was that she could no longer see the faces of her beloved friends, an understandable human regret. Five years before her death, Lutgard predicted the day (but not the year) of her death. The prophecy occurred in a liturgical setting. It was the Third Sunday after Pentecost on which the Gospel, "A certain man made a great banquet" (Luke 14:16), was read. Lutgard confided to her friend, the learned nun, Sybille de Gages, "On the Sunday when this Gospel is being read, I shall have been carried to the banquet of the wedding of the Lamb, having already died" (III, 6). But when the first year came and went and Lutgard was still alive, Sybille forgot about it until the day years later, June 16, 1246, when the dead Lutgard was laid out. Hearing the same Gospel read, Sybille recalled Lutgard's prophecy. Notice the images used in her prediction: she who had so vigorously fasted for twenty-one years was carried to a *banquet*, the banquet of the *Lamb*. Once more, Christ the Lamb is present, this time at the final consummation of the faithful, loving lamb who had followed the Lamb of God wherever he went. Her time for glory had arrived.

At the moment of Lutgard's death, the image of the great, mystic dance reappears, and Christ himself is there to accompany her soul to paradise. The joy is so palpable that a few of the nuns experienced an outpouring of jubilation. Her death brought her forever into that life of union with God for which all the events of her life served as preparation and pledge. Miracles occurred immediately—God's stamp of approval, as it were, on Lutgard, this great servant and lover of God. The date of her entrance into heavenly bliss, June 16, is the day her feast is now celebrated.

Theological Reflections on Lutgard's Visions of Christ

By far the most important visions in Lutgard's story are those of Christ himself. And the Christ who shows himself to her from the very first vision is the suffering, wounded Christ. This is significant in light of her own life in which she becomes deeply united with Christ in his Passion, bearing in her own body a share in his suffering. Frequently her sufferings and fastings are offered in a vicarious way for others' needs and intentions. She is very much an active, intercessory sufferer who suffers with Christ, and thus shares in Christ's redemptive action. Moreover, her visions of Christ often involve a direct showing of his wounded side. This fact is significant since four centuries before St. Margaret Mary (1647–1690) and one-half century before St. Gertrud (1256–1302), these visions of Christ's wounded side constitute some of the earliest evidence of devotion to the love of Jesus for humanity under the title of the Sacred Heart.[22] Of course, there is no question here of the so-called "devotion to the Sacred Heart" with the observance of the nine first Fridays. Neither is there any question of a sentimental adulation of a disembodied organ floating in some primordial protoplasm. Genuine devotion to the incarnate Heart of Jesus is a sacral synecdoche in which the Heart really stands for the whole Person, Jesus Christ. The essence for Lutgard is precisely the loving encounter with God-become-human, God who is Love Incarnate. The Gospel of John speaks of blood and water flowing from the lance wound in Christ's side (19:34), thus showing us the totality of Christ's offering of himself on our behalf. Christian tradition associates "side" and "heart" with the same mystery of God's immense saving love for humanity. By associating the two, we see simultaneously the extremity of suffering and the utter fullness of love for the Father and for all humankind that caused Jesus to accept that suffering in the first place.

GOD'S OUTSTRETCHED ARM

Closely allied with Christ's wounded side and heart is his outstretched arm, seen above all in the Crucifixion. Lutgard's vision of the Crucified Christ meeting and embracing her at the entrance to choir one night is a striking example of this (I,13). On the most literal level, the image is that of Jesus Crucified, suffering for humanity as he is stretched out on the Cross. But to Lutgard and to readers of Lutgard's *Vita*, Christ's arms outstretched on the Cross also recalled the many powerful images throughout salvation history of God's mighty outstretched arm, working wonders for God's people. The same God whose outstretched arm wrought marvels for the chosen people, especially as related in Exodus and Deuteronomy,[23] is here before Lutgard, living and active in her life and in the lives of all the faithful. Through the vision of Jesus Christ Crucified, Lutgard, and all who read of her, are swept up into the powerful action of the Lord throughout all time.

LUTGARD AND THE EUCHARIST

As is the case with many women mystics whose mystical life is deeply Christ-centered, Lutgard's mysticism is also profoundly marked by the

Eucharist. Christ himself, in a vision recurring "almost everyday during the sacrifice of the Mass," appeals to Lutgard: "Do you not see how I am offering myself up totally to the Father for My sinners? Therefore do I wish that you offer yourself up totally. . ." (II,9). Her self-offering parallels Christ's gift of himself to the Father, and it is at his behest that she does it. Lutgard habitually receives the Body of Christ every Sunday. Once, her abbess, the lady Agnes, misguided but most likely well-intentioned, forbids Lutgard to receive the sacrament every Sunday. As an obedient nun, Lutgard obeys but says in effect, "You'll be sorry." And the abbess is so afflicted by an "unbearable infirmity" that she is prevented from entering the church until she repents and lifts her interdict. In another episode, after receiving the Lord in the Eucharist, Lutgard is so plunged into a profound experience of God that she is unable to eat, but she recognizes her need for sustenance. So she bargains with the Lord, asking him to give her spiritual consolation to the bulimic nun, Elizabeth, who never gets enough to eat although she eats hourly, thus permitting Lutgard to eat in peace (II,19,20). On another occasion when Lutgard is not well, two angels are seen escorting her to the altar to receive the Eucharist since no one else will help her. Still another time, shortly before her death, it is the Blessed Virgin Mary herself and St. John the Baptist who render this same service (II,39).

Erotic Elements in Lutgard's Visions.

It is possible to see in the visions of Christ to Lutgard some erotic elements, especially in the vision of the Crucified Christ stopping her outside the door of the choir (I,13). Here, Christ reaches out one arm from the cross, extends it and embraces her, pulling her to himself and almost forcing her mouth to his open side. Is this a prelude to some sort of mystical ravishment? It seems to me forcing the issue to interpret it in an overly erotic way. Doing so runs the risk of missing the much deeper theological meaning of the gesture of summoning Lutgard to an intense communion with Christ's redemptive action. Whatever there may indeed be of the erotic is strongly subsumed by the intense experience of union with Christ in his saving work of redemption. Lutgard is actually invited to share intimately in this work by her loving adhesion to God, above all in the Person of Jesus Christ.[24]

Lutgard's Affinities for Today

There are a number of elements in Lutgard's *Vita* that bridge the distance between her century and ours. Some of them sound very contemporary indeed. We note for instance her having been born to parents of differing socio-economic status and the ensuing problems that relationship presented. She survived an acquaintance-rape attempt. As a nun at St. Catherine's, she met with slander and cynicism from others in the community who were less fervent. Throughout her life she was insecure enough to need reassurances from God and others, despite her very obvious mystical graces and spiritual gifts. She was a "transfer sister," moving from the Benedictines at St. Catherine's to the Cistercians at Aywières. And since these latter nuns were French-speaking and she was not, she was in some sense an alien in a foreign section of the country.

As a monastic, she lived in "liturgical time" with the cycle of the Church's seasons, feasts, and hours of the day providing the framework, the very atmosphere in which the whole of life was lived out. Lutgard was a woman of great compassion for others, sometimes manifested in her healing of various diseases or spiritual and moral maladies. Her compassion also took the form of admonishing well-known clerics who happened to need it. Other times her compassion was manifested by her strong sense of intercessory prayer. Both persons still living and those who had died appealed to her for intercession, always with positive results. They could be lowly lay folk in the poorest ranks of society or, just as easily, the powerful Pope Innocent III, who needed her intercessory prayer to be delivered from purgatory. She was able to listen to needs, bring them to the Lord, and then give thanks for the results that followed, as follow they did. She heard confessions and entrusted the inner anguish of a number of persons to God for forgiveness and restoration of wholeness. She served as a spiritual *amma* to many. Today we would call her a spiritual director and someone in the healing ministry. She was also a woman for whom relationships mattered a great deal. Because she had many friends—both women and men—it is easier for us today to recognize in her a real human being. We would call Lutgard a well-integrated woman. She lived in intimate, continual union with God, and this union made her all the more approachable to her contemporaries. Her many mystical gifts served to heighten her humanness rather than stifle it.

Conclusion

Much more could be said about St. Lutgard, the Benedictine of St. Catherine at St. Trond who became a Cistercian at Aywières; she deserves book-length studies, especially in English.[25] But even allowing for pious exaggeration, some of her own contemporaries have strong words of praise for her. Master Jordan of Saxony, the Dominicans' second Master General, refers to her as the "mother and nourisher of the Dominican Order" (III,3). And the dying beguine, Marie d'Oignies, in a prophetic spirit, attests: "Under heaven the world has no more faithful or more efficacious intercessor in prayers

. . . than the lady Lutgard" (II, 9). She was truly loved and esteemed by those who knew her well. Some of the prodigious happenings in her life seem to separate her from us today more effectively than do the centuries between us. Yet we can recognize in her a warm, loving, lovable human being; a real woman; a woman of intense prayer. She is profoundly associated with Christ in his Passion, yet she is never lugubrious. Throughout the *Vita* she retains a charm, freshness, and vitality that endear her to her readers. These qualities emerge from the text, shining as brightly in translation as in the original languages. Lutgard faithfully followed the Lamb wherever he went. With her whole life she sang the "joyful canticle of redemption"[26] that united her with her Beloved and made her a powerful intercessor for her brothers and sisters. St. Lutgard, both the Benedictine of St. Catherine at St. Trond and the Cistercian of Aywières, is our sister, our ancestor in the faith, our foremother in St. Scholastica and St. Benedict. Let us claim her.

NOTES

1. A brief version of this chapter was presented at the Twenty-Sixth International Congress on Medieval Studies, May 11, 1991, Kalamazoo, Michigan, in a session sponsored by the American Benedictine Academy. A related study is forthcoming in the *American Benedictine Review*.

2. For a starter, she dies and then comes back to life. She accepts atrocious sufferings for the sake of souls in Purgatory. However worthy her motives, she nevertheless does very strange things, such as sitting atop high trees and jumping into ovens. Christina is best understood in the tradition of "fools for Christ's sake." See Thomas de Cantimpré, *The Life of Christina Mirabilis*, trans. Margot H. King (Toronto, Ontario: Peregrina Publishing Co., 1986, rpt. 1989) especially #1, 5, 6, 7, 8.

3. Thomas de Cantimpré, *The Life of Lutgard of Aywières*, trans. with introduction and notes by Margot H. King (Toronto, Ontario: Peregrina Publishing Co., 1987; reprinted 1988, 1989). I am grateful to Margot King and Peregrina Publishing Company for permission to quote from her translation. See also Thomas of Cantimpré, *Life of Lutgard of Aywières*, trans. with notes by Martinus Cawley, O.C.S.O. (Lafayette, Or.: Guadalupe Translations, 1987) 1–88 in his *Lives of Ida of Nivelles, Lutgard and Alice the Leper*. Prior to the translations by King and Cawley, English language readers only had access to Lutgard's *Vita* through selected quotations in Thomas Merton's *What Are These Wounds? The Life of a Cistercian Mystic, Saint Lutgarde of Aywières* (Milwaukee: The Bruce Publishing Company, 1950).

4. Extensive information on Thomas of Cantimpré can be found in Simone Roisin, *L'Hagiographie Cistercienne dans le Diocèse de Liège au XIIIe Siècle* (Louvain: Bibliothèque de L'Université, Bruxelles: Éditions Universitaires Les Presses de Belgique, 1947) 51–53, and Index references on 294. See also the same

author's "La Méthode Hagiographique de Thomas de Cantimpré" in *Miscellanea Historica in Honorem Alberti de Meyer* (Louvain: Bibliothèque de L'Université, Bruxelles: Le Pennon S.A., 1946) 546-557. Briefer biographical data are found in Arjo Vanderjagt, "Thomas of Cantimpré," *Dictionary of the Middle Ages* (New York: Charles Scribner's Sons, 1989) 12:34–35 and in Simon Tugwell, O.P., *Early Dominicans Selected Writings* (New York and Ramsey, N.J.: Paulist Press, 1982) 107, n.27, 483.

5. Roisin, "La Méthode," 549.

6. Roisin, *L'Hagiographie*, 53.

7. Caroline Walker Bynum, *Holy Feast and Holy Fast, The Religious Significance of Food to Medieval Women* (Berkeley: University of California Press, 1987) 64, 115.

8. Elizabeth Alvilda Petroff, *Medieval Women's Visionary Literature* (New York, Oxford: Oxford University Press, 1986) 51.

9. Roger De Ganck, *Towards Unification with God, Beatrice of Nazareth in her Context*, Cistercian Studies Series 122. (Kalamazoo: Cistercian Publications, 1991) 350.

10. See for instance, King, *Life*, Book I, 21

11. For an English translation, see Bernard of Clairvaux, *On the Song of Songs*, I–IV, trans. Kilian Walsh and Irene M. Edmonds, Cistercian Fathers Series 4, 7, 31, 40 (Kalamazoo: Cistercian Publications, 1971–1980).

12. Jean Leclercq, O.S.B., *The Love of Learning and the Desire for God, A Study of Monastic Culture*, trans. Catharine Misrahi (New York: Fordham University Press, 1961, 1974) 106–109.

13. For an enlightening investigation into child oblation see John Boswell, *The Kindness of Strangers, The Abandonment of Children in Western Europe from Late Antiquity to the Renaissance* (New York: Vintage Books, A Division of Random House, Inc., February 1990) especially 296, 319–321, and chapters 5 (228–255) and 8 (296–321).

14. St. Catherine of Alexandria, her monastery's patron, was an early fourth-century virgin and martyr who was very popular in the Middle Ages. See F. L. Cross and E. A. Livingstone, eds, *The Oxford Dictionary of the Christian Church* Second Edition (Oxford: Oxford University Press, 1958, 1974, 1983) s.v. Catherine, St., of Alexandria, 253. Also, John J. Delaney, *The Dictionary of Saints* (Garden City, NY: Doubleday and Company, Inc., 1980) s.v. Catherine of Alexandria, 138.

15. Benedicta Ward, *Miracles and the Medieval Mind, Theory, Record and Event, 1000–1215* (Philadelphia: University of Pennsylvania Press, 1982, rev. ed. 1987) 64, 86, 116. In this volume Ward describes the noisy rowdiness that accompanied pilgrims at some medieval shrines where they kept all-night prayer vigils replete with many candles, some praying, and loud cheers when a particular saint produced the desired cure.

16. A. Deboutte, "Lutgarde et Sa Spiritualité," *Collectanea Cisterciensia* 44 (1982) 77. Deboutte states that no vision or any exchange of hearts occurs, "Mais le coeur de Lutgarde qui cherche son chemin vers Jésus et qui, dans la prière, aboutit au coeur de Jésus," 77.

17. King, *Life*, I,10. A cubit is about eighteen inches.

18. Later in her life as a Cistercian there is another episode of a brilliant light above her (II, 31). In a related phenomenon, a young nun was alarmed to see a "flame of material light" issuing from Lutgard's mouth as she chanted Vespers in choir (II, 18).

19. Some salient Scripture references to oil: Exod 30:25; Lev 10:7; Ps 23:5; 45:8; 92:11; Isa 61:3.

20. This mystic dance, known as the *tripudium*, is often found in hagiography. There are other instances of the mystic dance in Lutgard's *Vita*. Once it is at Jacques de Vitry's death when he appears to her in great joy. Another occurs at her own death when her entrance into Paradise is described in these terms.

21. Some crown references include: Pss 21:4; 89:20; Isa 62:3; Jas 1:12; 1 Pet 5:4; Rev 2:10.

22. Of course, veneration of Christ's heart and wounded side actually begins with John's Passion account (John 19:34) in which blood and water flow out from Christ's sword-pierced side, signifying the totality of Christ's redemptive offering of himself. Moreover, there are numerous instances in both the Old and the New Testaments of wound, wounded, or wounds: Jer 10:19; 15:18; Nah 3:19. Of sides: Lam 3:13. Of heart: Pss 33:11; 69:21; Cant 4:9; 6:12; 8:6; Hos 11:8; Matt 9:36; 15:32; 26:38; Mark 9:22; 14:34.

23. Some references to God's powerful arm are found in Pss 44:4; 77:16; 89:14, 22; 98:1; 136:12. God's mighty outstretched arm is referred to especially in Exod 6:1, 6; 14:16. Deut 4:34; 5:15; 7:19; 11:2; 26:8.

24. A similar episode occurs in I, 14.

25. The volume, *Hidden Springs,* (forthcoming from Cistercian Publications and co-edited by John A. Nichols and Lillian Thomas Shank) contains three essays on St. Lutgard. Regrettably, this volume was unavailable at the time of this writing.

26. The beautiful phrase of Benet D. Hill, O.S.B., in an Advent retreat conference to my monastic community, December 4, 1993. Used with his permission.

14

Mechtild of Magdeburg: Poet and Mystic

Johnette Putnam, O.S.B.

God has enough of all things, only he can
never have enough contact with the soul.[1]

Scant information is available about Mechtild's life. What is known
has to be carefully gleaned from her work *The Flowing Light of the
Godhead.* She was born in Saxony in 1209 and died at Helfta between
1282 and 1284. From her learning, her familiarity with medieval literary
genres, and her ability to express herself evident in her writing, we can assume that she was a well-born and well-educated medieval woman. Her
first mystical experience, which she describes as a greeting by the Holy
Spirit, occurred when she was twelve years old.

In 1230, at the age of twenty-one, she went to Magdeburg to begin the
life of a beguine under the direction of the Dominicans. For forty years she
led an intense spiritual life of prayer and severe asceticism. During those
years she received extraordinary spiritual gifts and spoke with the voice of
a reformer, severely criticizing the clergy and calling the Church to conversion because of its materialism, its moral and religious laxity. She de-
nounced abuses in the Church and the laxity of the clergy in strong terms,
calling the Church an "unclean, unchaste maiden" and referring to the
clergy as "goats" and "Pharisees."[2] She aroused the hostility of the ecclesiastical authorities because she not only urged reforms but also resisted
the censure she received concerning her writings. Wearied by her struggles
and in ill health, she sought refuge in the monastery of Helfta in 1270.[3]

THE HELFTA CONNECTION

The Benedictine women's monastery at Helfta was founded at Mansfeld in 1229, then relocated in Helfta in 1258. In 1251, when she was nineteen, Gertrud von Hackborn was elected abbess and began her enlightened leadership which lasted for forty years. A learned woman, she developed a strong monastic culture at Helfta by encouraging and fostering the development of her nuns' intellectual and spiritual gifts. She insisted on the rigorous study of Scripture and the liberal arts because she was convinced that if learning were abandoned, the Scriptures would no longer be understood.[4]

Abbess Gertrud deliberately set out to create an environment that would encourage the growth of the spiritual, intellectual, and creative gifts of her sisters. "She was so successful that during her lifetime Helfta became a center of mysticism in Germany and radiated influence in all directions."[5] By her wise and visionary leadership she fostered the growth of the literary and mystical gifts of her sisters. In this vital, monastic culture, through their mystical writings, Gertrud the Great and Mechtild von Hackeborn, the sister of Abbess Gertrud, were able to share with others the gifts God had given them for the Church. It is into this environment that Mechtild of Magdeburg, worn out both by ecclesiastical hostility and her illness, was received graciously by Abbess Gertrud and her sisters in 1270. Soon after her arrival, she became seriously ill and, before long, totally blind. With the assistance of the sisters at Helfta, she was able to complete her seventh and final book of *The Flowing Light of the Godhead,* dictating it to the nuns before she died. Although considered a saint by her contemporaries, she has never been officially canonized by the Church.[6]

HISTORY OF THE MANUSCRIPT

Beginning in 1250 Mechtild wrote on loose sheets which were collected by her spiritual advisor, the Dominican Heinrich von Halle. Halle arranged the text thematically rather than chronologically, thus making it impossible for future readers to follow Mechtild's spiritual development. Later, he translated Mechtild's original Low German text, which did not survive, into a Latin version so that Mechtild's writings would be available to a wider audience. Unfortunately, he blurred the power of the original text (he explains what he did in his prologue) cutting, smoothing, and softening Mechtild's words. The book's title, *The Flowing Light of the Godhead,* is taken from the words spoken to Mechtild by Christ, telling her that she was to be a witness to the light of the divinity "flowing into the hearts that live without falsehood" (1.1).

In 1344–1345, at Basel, Heinrich of Nordlingen translated the entire book into the High German spoken in the Rhineland. A copy of this translation was later sent to the Forest Sisters of Ensiedeln. From there it eventually went to the library of the Benedictine monastery at Einsiedeln. In 1860, Dr. Carl Greith visited Einsiedeln to search for useful material for his book, *The History of German Mysticism.* It was then that he found the only complete codex of Mechtild's book. He encouraged the librarian, Gall Morel, to publish the manuscript; it appeared in 1869, six-hundred years after it was written by Mechtild. It is this copy which was translated into English by Lucy Menzies in 1955.[7] A second English translation has been completed more recently in 1991 by Christiane Mesch Galvani.[8]

THE FLOWING LIGHT OF THE GODHEAD AS LITERATURE

The Flowing Light of the Godhead reveals that Mechtild is a gifted poet capable of composing in various literary genres of the Middle Ages. The dialogue of the prologue is written in the style of the minnesingers of medieval court life. The entire work is a collection of poems, love songs, allegories, letters, parables, and moral reflections. As a work of spiritual genius, it is in the tradition of bridal mysticism so prevalent among the medieval mystics, especially in Bernard of Clairvaux's *Commentary on the Song of Songs.*

Mechtild writes in the prophetic and contemplative vein. She is prophetic in her critique of the medieval Church and clergy, and contemplative in her recounting of the soul's journey to God. To describe this journey, she makes extensive use of the imagery, metaphors, and motifs of the culture of the medieval court: God and Christ are pictured variously as emperor, king, knight, and lord. The soul journeys to the imperial court of God, the heavenly palace, where Christ appears as a nobleman, gives her courtly garments, and speaks to her in courtly language. In the mystical dance of union originating in Neo-Platonism and transplanted to Christian mysticism by Pseudo-Dionysius, Christ as a noble youth joins with her and the virtues in the contemporary courtly custom of the spring dance (1.44).

From the Old Testament and New Testament, she borrows the metaphor of wine to portray the inebriation of the soul in the highest state of mystical union and the image of bride-soul and Bridegroom-Holy Trinity (1.22). It is evident in her work that she was familiar with the writings of Bernard of Clairvaux, William of Saint-Thierry, the Victorines, David of Augsburg, Hildegard of Bingen, and Gregory the Great. Though not noted for its theological content, *The Flowing Light* is rich in sound, mystical doctrine and in an understanding of God's unconditional, compassionate love for us in our condition of unlimited, human frailty.[9]

In addition to being regarded as an excellent poet, Mechtild is credited with two original accomplishments: she was the first mystic to write in the vernacular rather than in Latin and the first in the history of Christian mysticism to record a personal vision of the Sacred Heart.[10] This devotion was more richly developed by Gertrud the Great of Helfta and popularized in the eighteenth century by Margaret Mary Alacoque.

INFLUENCES ON MECHTILD OF MAGDEBURG

Contemporary scholars are becoming increasingly aware that spirituality and mysticism have been affected in their development by the social and cultural currents of their times. They are convinced that spiritual life does not grow in a vacuum as if the soul were "alone with the Alone," isolated and unaffected by the realities surrounding it.[11] It is abundantly clear in the life of Mechtild of Magdeburg that her spiritual life and mysticism were deeply influenced by the social, cultural, and political currents of the thirteenth century.

Between the eleventh and the fourteenth centuries, Europe expanded rapidly, creating a new European social, cultural, and political order. The social change, though more geographically limited, possessed characteristics similar to the economic and political realignments of our own period as we face a developing new world order. Like us, the people living in the High Middle Ages, that time of unprecedented growth and change, groped toward the new as they released their hold on the old. And like us, they, too, experienced the uncertainties and instability of a changing world order. These new social, political, and economic currents were accompanied, particularly during the thirteenth century, by a period of unusual religious fervor during which the sense of the sacred was pervasive in the culture and evoked new spiritual and mystical movements which deeply affected Mechtild's life.

Perhaps the most significant change during this period was the social and economic phenomenon of the new growth of the towns. This urbanization affected not only society but the Church as well. The crisis of cenobitism, for example, occurred as the Benedictine communities began to lose their significance and their influence in a rapidly urbanizing society. This, in turn, was a significant factor in the rise of the new religious orders of mendicant Franciscans and preaching Dominicans, and further enabled the continuing expansion of the Cistercians. The spirituality of these new religious orders would affect Mechtild through her experience as a beguine and as a member of the monastery of Helfta.

THE SOCIAL STATUS OF WOMEN

These social changes had a detrimental influence on women's lives. With the rapid growth of the towns, the number of women in the population became significantly higher than that of the men. This shortage of marriageable men left a growing number of women in an insecure social and economic situation. At the same time, the position and influence of women in the Church and in the monasteries began to decline. With clericalism growing both in the Church and in monasticism, and with various forms of human deprivation occurring as a result of the imposition of papal cloister on women's communities, male dominance asserted itself more strongly. A striking example of this changing social situation is women's struggle for decades to be accepted by the Cistercian Order.[12] It is clear in the autobiographical sections of Mechtild's writings and in her manner of expression that she was profoundly affected by the social status of women in the Church and society. Like Hildegard of Bingen and Theresa of Avila, she too defers to clerical authority in a way that is demeaning to herself. She does this by assuming—in spite of her noble lineage, education, and spiritual gifts which far surpassed those of many of her male counterparts—the role of an unlettered, uncultured, sinful woman who should not be speaking of spiritual things:

> I was the simplest of all creatures who have ever appeared in the spiritual life. . . . All I knew about God was through the Christian faith alone. . . . Unblessed creature that I am! To all this came powerful love and provided me with these miracles. . . . Then I said: "Alas, merciful God, what have you seen in me? You know that I am a fool, a sinful and poor being in body and soul. You should bestow those things on wise people so that you might be praised." After that, I, poor, trembling creature, went in humble shame to my confessor and told him of these words, desiring his instruction. He instructed me to cry in shame, that a wretched woman should have been commanded to write this book straight from the mouth and heart of God (4.2).

We can discern deference to religious authority as well as true humility in these passages, but also some honest artifice in order to be heard, in order to speak in a voice different from the prevailing one and to avoid the charge of "emotionalism" and of female "hysteria," that "commodious and ill-defined vocable which allows us to classify all one wants to discredit in a woman."[13]

This cluster of factors—social, political, economic, and religious—led women to find a new avenue for the expression of their creative and spiritual energies: a new religious women's movement, the beguines.[14]

RELIGIOUS CURRENTS: THE BEGUINES

One of the most amazing and effective spiritual influences of the High Middle Ages was the mystical revolution sparked by the women's religious movement known in history as the beguines. These profoundly religious women were neither nuns nor recluses, but members of a religious movement that was nonmonastic in its origins and apostolic in its lifestyle.

They lived in beguinages, single apartments or numerous apartments grouped together in settlements in the middle of towns. They were most numerous in the Low Countries, the Rhineland, and northern France. Their spiritual life included many of the elements of thirteenth-century medieval spirituality, but these elements were more intensely lived and expressed by these remarkable women.

The beguines embraced a lifestyle without the voluntary canonical vows of poverty, chastity, and obedience. Their contemplation focused on the divine humanity of Christ and flowed over into the service of the poor; the uneducated, sick, and suffering humanity. They maintained close ties with the Dominicans and Cistercians from whom they received and to whom they gave spiritual benefits. Supporting themselves principally by weaving and spinning, they gave their surplus income to the poor. They gathered daily for community prayer, the Divine Office and Eucharist, and for the study of Scripture accompanied by theological reflection.[15] Modeled on the Community of Jerusalem, they were the medieval equivalent of modern "base communities."[16]

The beguines' spiritual life followed the popular religious currents of this period, only more intensely. "The Eucharist they regarded as the culmination of a mystical marriage between the bride-soul and the heavenly Bridegroom, Christ. Identification with Christ in his suffering often took the form of an intense asceticism, prolonged fasts, self-mortification, and accompanying visionary and ecstatic states."[17] In their piety they focused on the humanity and passion of Christ, and in their simple way of living they embraced the apostolic ideal of poverty of the new orders, the Franciscans and Dominicans.

As a beguine for forty years of her life, Mechtild immersed herself in beguine spirituality. Her writings reveal the intense world-denying asceticism, the simplicity of life, the devotion to the humanity and passion of Christ, the bridal mysticism, and the Eucharistic piety of the beguines. Beguine spirituality was not, however, the sole influence on Mechtild's spiritual life. Underlying beguine piety were the spiritual movements of the new orders of Franciscans, Dominicans, and Cistercians. These various movements shaped Mechtild's religious orientation, as well, and aroused the religious fervor of the thirteenth century. Among the three, it was, however, the Cistercian spirituality which most attracted Mechtild and influenced her in her manner of relating to God.

CISTERCIAN SPIRITUALITY: BERNARD AND BRIDAL MYSTICISM

Christian spirituality and Christian mysticism have their foundation in the words of Jesus, "Abide in me as I do in you" (John 15:4). The desire and promise of Jesus in his Last Discourse to abide with us is the basis of all spirituality and mysticism: "I pray . . . that all may be one as you Father are in me, and I in you; I pray that they may be one in us . . . as we are one—I living in them, you living in me, that their unity may be complete" (John 17:20-23).

The Cistercians developed a spirituality based on St. Augustine's theology of the spiritual life which was in harmony with this promise of Jesus. In his theory, Augustine had fused the experience of God witnessed objectively through the reality of the Church's incarnating Christ in community and subjectively in the inner experience of the individual "I" in which God is personally comprehended. This fusion became the theological basis for the various forms of Christian mysticism. On its foundation, the intensely affective spirituality and mysticism of the Middle Ages was built, "illumined by a new flame, the fire . . . of passion and love, [and the] dispassionate theorizing of Platonic thought was abandoned."[18]

By basing their spirituality on Augustine's theology of the spiritual life, the Cistercians were able to develop a deeply affective spirituality in the tradition of bridal mysticism. They dwelt on Christ's humanity and were concerned with the inmost cell of the heart where God abides. Their spiritual goal was to attain union with Jesus through a personal compassion with the Son of Man. The Cistercian worships Jesus as the Beloved worthy to be loved. With the Cistercians, eros reappears in mysticism, that nuptial eros of heart seeking heart. Bernard of Clairvaux's sermons on the Song of Songs are the most intimate outpouring of this type of bridal mysticism. Its essence is a love union in the spirit, an "exchange of love," the inmost union of the "I" and "Thou."[19]

Bernard's mysticism is the preeminent example in the Middle Ages of love mysticism. With Bernard, "there came a moment in the West when love became equated with the very essence of the spiritual life, when *contemplation* came to be defined as *amor*. . . . What the Greeks had cautiously spiritualized, Bernard applied in its full erotic power to the relation between God and the soul: 'No sweeter words can be found to embody that sweet interflow of affections between the Word and the soul than bridegroom and bride.'"[20]

This way of going to God is not, however, an easy way, for it requires total conformity of one's will to the will of God. The moral demands of love mysticism require much abnegation and ascetic discipline. This demand is best expressed by John of the Cross in his sixteenth-century work, *The Ascent of Mount Carmel:* "In order to arrive at possessing everything, desire to possess nothing" (I.13,11).

The metaphor which Bernard uses is that of the sexual union between Bridegroom (God) and bride (the soul). Since love resides in the will, the mystical union, according to Bernard, is achieved through a harmony of the will of the soul with the will of God. In Bernard's experience of this union, the coming of Christ, the Bridegroom's presence, is revealed by interior signs of an intensely affective nature: "Only by the warmth of my heart . . . did I know he was there. . . ." (Sermons on the Song of Songs, 74.6).

We see, in Mechtild of Magdeburg, the various currents of German medieval spirituality and mysticism: self-transcendence through extreme asceticism, devotion to Christ's humanity, affective spirituality. Influenced by Bernard's mysticism through her Cistercian contacts as a beguine, Mechtild is an outstanding example of the tradition of love mysticism. She, too, uses the mystical themes and images of the Song of Songs and is among the earliest to report a mystical experience of the love of the Sacred Heart.

CARL JUNG AND MECHTILD OF MAGDEBURG: LOVE, CELIBACY, AND THE INNER MARRIAGE

Carl Jung, the most prominent psychologist of the twentieth century, was intensely interested in examining the phenomenon of Mechtild's love mysticism from the perspective of his own discipline of psychology.[21] Jung located the reality of love in the relationship between the ego and the inner contrasexual archetype: anima/man, animus/woman. In Jung's thought, this relationship moves eventually to a more inclusive and extensive state of consciousness which draws one ever nearer to universal love.

In his study of the mystical traditions of East and West, Jung found support in the experience of the mystics for the possibility that "the anima or animus may be met and embraced directly in a more immediately psychological and hence spiritual manner."[22] Mechtild of Magdeburg was for Jung a powerful witness to that possibility in her experience of the inner marriage with the inner contrasexual, the animus, in a religious love affair.

In the mystical experience of the feminine celibate, Mechtild, the loved one, is "more than an image of empirical man."[23] It is rather the image of the incarnate God, the youthful figure of Christ cast in her poetic imagery in the role of a courtly lover with the Trinity in the background. As a result of her encounter with Christ, she is drawn into the "flow and light and heat of the Trinitarian God."[24]

In this state of heightened consciousness, Mechtild experienced the inner marriage with the inner contrasexual. In Jung's understanding, "the marriage of the ego with the anima or animus gives rise to a sense of unity with the source of light and life—in Mechtild's terms, the Trinity; in Jung's, the energies of the Self."[25]

In need of a literary genre which could best express this profound inner experience and which was in harmony with her artistic gifts, Mechtild turned to the love poetry of the minnesingers. She describes her first "meeting" initiated by the young Christ:

> "Now . . . I am aroused
> I must go to see her,
> It is she who bears both sorrow and love,
> In the morning dew —embracing tenderness—
> Which first enters the soul" (1,44).

Clothed in humility, chastity, and desire, she goes into the woods to meet her lover and is invited to dance with him. After the dance, her lover suggests,

> "Come at midday to the shade of the well into
> the bed of love; there you shall be refreshed
> with Him" (1,44).

She then begins a lengthy dialogue with her senses that try to convince her not to enter into the final meeting but to find consolation in noble virtues. Mechtild rejects their suggestions, even about sharing in the joys of Mary's maternity:

> "That is a childlike love,
> Suckling and rocking a child;
> I am a fully grown Bride,
> And I wish to go to my love.
> I must go to my lover's side" (1,44).

To the insistence of the senses that she cannot abide the intense fire of the glory of the Godhead, she replies that all are made for such love because all are of the same nature as the divine lover:

> "Fish will not drown in water,
> Birds will not sink in air
>
> . . . .
> God has given to all creatures
> The gift of making use of their talents.
> How then can I fight my nature?
>
> . . . .
> I should forfeit all to go to God
> Who is my Father by nature,
> My Brother by his humanity,
> My Bridegroom by love,
> And I am his since the beginning of time" (1,44).

And in haughty disdain for the advice of the senses, she enters the sacred space which she describes in this way:

So the dearest one goes to the fairest in the secret chambers of the innocent Divinity: there she finds her love's bed and love's dress prepared for God and man. Then our Lord says: "Stay, Lady Soul . . . you are so much a part of My nature that nothing can be between you and Me" (1,44).

Christ then confirms that she has always been his by nature and that, therefore, only their love can satisfy her deepest desires. To this she replies:

"Lord, now I am a naked soul,
And you, in Yourself, a beautifully adorned God.
Our communion
Is eternal life without death" (1,44).

And then Mechtild describes her inner experience of Christ's intense love, the inner marriage:

Then ensued a blessed quiet,
According to both their wishes.
He gives Himself to her and she to Him,
And only she knows what happens to her at this moment,
And that is good enough for me (1,44).

Through this experience of intense, intimate love, Mechtild begins, as Jesus has promised (John 17:20-23), to participate in the flow, life, and light of the Trinity.

Mechtild depicts, in her experience of the Triune Godhead, God's desire to "create the human in order to complete itself through intercourse with creatures, and in so doing to break the sterility of its previous splendid . . . isolation . . ., sundering the unfruitful self-sufficiency of Trinitarian life":[26]

Then the Holy Spirit played with the Father in great Gentleness and dissolved the Holy Trinity saying, "Lord, dear Father, I wish to give You Your own kind counsel, namely that We will no longer be unfruitful. We will have a created kingdom, and the angels shall be fashioned after Me, so that they will be one spirit with Me, and the other shall be mankind. For, dear Father, that alone is joy which is shared with great love and untold bliss in Your presence" (3,9).

The Father responds enthusiastically:

"We will become fruitful so that man will love us in return and recognize in some measure our great glory. I will make Myself a Bride who shall greet me with her mouth and wound me with her glance. Then first will love begin" (3,9).

And so what begins for Mechtild as a lover's meeting with the noble youth Jesus Christ ends with her inner marriage with the Trinity:

> "My Son will embrace you,
> My Divinity will infuse you,
> My Holy Spirit will lead you always further
> In blissful vision
> According to your will" (7,37).

It is true that the medieval mind would not perceive Mechtild's mystic experience of union with the inner Christ in Jungian terms as the union of the ego with the powerful animus figure through which the true self emerges. This understanding is, however, congenial to the modern mind conditioned by contemporary, therapeutic culture.

MECHTILD'S SIGNIFICANCE: CELIBACY AND CONTEMPLATION

Celibacy is a transcultural reality not limited to the Christian West but practiced in certain non-Christian Eastern traditions as well. Since the celibate life is not bound to a particular culture or religion but has a broader human significance, there must be an archetypal basis for its practice in such disparate cultures, religions, and historical periods.

In the experience of the inner marriage, celibacy finds its universal meaning because it bears witness to the interior wellsprings of all love. The true celibate, then, may not simply be the one who lives a celibate life style, but the one who moves deeply into a contemplative relationship with the inner sexual opposite (Sophia for the male celibate; Christ for the female celibate) through which a transformation of energies takes place in a gradual transcendence of self as an isolated individual. This movement makes possible a more extensive and inclusive relationship to the world which goes beyond one's individuality to a true personhood in universal love.

Mechtild's experience of the inner marriage frees the celibate life from falsely being characterized by our hedonistic culture as repressed sexuality. It deepens our appreciation of its potential to bring the human person to an inner unity through the total surrender of the will/self (ego) to the Will/Self of God (animus). Mechtild experiences this marriage as the fullest realization of the self:

> Ah Lord, love me much, and love me deeply and for a long time;
> For the more deeply you love me, the purer I shall become
> the more you love me, the more beautiful I shall become,
> the longer you love me, the holier I shall become here on earth (1,23).

Mechtild teaches us through her life and poetry that contemplation is essential for sustaining celibacy because celibacy, like marriage, is for relationship. Since the paradigm of all human relationships and human community is the Trinitarian relationship of Persons who cannot not pour themselves out in the unconditional gift of themselves mutually, One to the Other, contemplation, by its very nature as a relationship, must then flow out into the service of others in unconditional love.

Celibacy not sustained by contemplative prayer severs the celibate's relation to the animus—in theological terms, the Pauline Christ—and leads to "depression, lethargy, withdrawal, encapsulation in security systems which at the same time become the object of one's rage and finally physical illness as the incarnate symbol of the inner wasteland."[27] Without contemplative prayer, celibate life becomes meaningless because it gradually loses its *raison d'etre,* a loving relationship with God from which flows compassionate service to others. Sustained by contemplative prayer, the celibate becomes vivified by a passionate exchange of love with a passionately loving God:

> God has enough of all things, only he can
> never have enough contact with the soul (4,12).

It is this understanding of celibate love and the inner marriage, her poetic rendering of it, and the courageous example of her life that are Mechtild's most significant contributions to humanity and to the development of Christian life throughout the centuries.

NOTES

1. Mechtild of Magdeburg, *Flowing Light of the Divinity,* ed. Susan Clark, trans. Christiane Mesch Galvani (New York: Garland Publishing Inc., 1991) 4.12. All subsequent quotations from this work will be noted in the text with chapter and section number as given here.

2. John Howard, "The German Mystic: Mechtild of Magdeburg," *Medieval Religious Women,* ed. Katharina M. Wilson (Athens: University of Georgia Press, 1982) 154.

3. M. F. Laughlin, "Mechtild of Magdeburg," *New Catholic Encyclopedia* 9:546.

4. Jeremy Finnegan, "The Women of Helfta," *Peaceweavers, Medieval Religious Women,* II, eds. John A. Nichols and Lillian Thomas Shank (Kalamazoo: Cistercian Publications, 1987) 212.

5. Howard, "The German Mystic: Mechtild of Magdeburg," 155.

6. Laughlin, "Mechtild of Magdeburg," 9:546.

7. Lucy Menzies, trans. *The Revelations of Mechtild of Magdeburg (1210–1297 or The Flowing Light of the Godhead)* (New York: Longmans Green

and Company, 1953) xxii–xv; Cf. Howard, "The German Mystic: Mechtild of Magdeburg," 157.

8. Mechtild von Magdeburg, *Flowing Light of the Divinity,* ed. Susan Clark, trans. Christiane Mesch Galvani (New York: Garland Publishing, Inc. 1991).

9. Menzies, *The Revelations of Mechtild of Magdeburg,* xxv–xxix; Cf. Howard, "The German Mystic: Mechtild of Magdeburg," 156–159.

10. Howard, "The German Mystic: Mechtild of Magdeburg," 159.

11. Louis Dupre and James A. Wiseman, eds., *Light from Light: An Anthology of Christian Mysticism* (New York: Paulist Press, 1988) 17–18.

12. R. W. Southern, *Western Society and the Church in the Middle Ages* (Baltimore: Penguin Books, Inc., 1970) 315–317.

13. Francois Mollet-Jarvis, *Jeanne Guyon* (Paris, 1978) as quoted in Dupre, *Light from Light,* 20.

14. Southern, *Western Society and the Church in the Middle Ages,* 321.

15. Richard Woods, *Christian Spirituality: God's Presence through the Ages* (Chicago: Thomas More Press, 1989) 194–196.

16. Dennis Delvin, "Feminine Piety in the High Middle Ages: The Beguines," *Distant Echoes: Medieval Religious Women,* I, eds. John A. Nichols and Lillian Thomas Shank (Kalamazoo: Cistercian Publications, 1984) 186.

17. Fiona Bowie, ed., and Oliver Davies, trans., *Beguine Spirituality: Mystical Writings of Mechtild of Magdeburg, Beatrice of Nazareth and Hadewijch of Brabant* (New York: Crossroads, 1990) 27.

18. Joseph Bernhart, "Introductory Essay on Mysticism," *Theologica Germanica* (London: Victor Gallancz, Ltd., 1950) 49–50.

19. Ibid., 55–61, passim.

20. Dupre, *Light from Light,* 14.

21. John P. Dourley, *Love, Celibacy and the Inner Marriage* (Toronto: Inner City Books, 1987). This discussion on Jung's treatment of Mechtild of Magdeburg is found in Ch. 2 of Dourley's book. I am indebted to him for this analysis of Mechtild of Magdeburg's mystical experiences in the light of Jungian psychology.

22. Ibid., 28.

23. Ibid., 29.

24. Ibid., 31.

25. Ibid.

26. Ibid., 34.

27. Ibid., 41.

15

Mechtild of Hackeborn: Song of Love

Alberta Dieker, O.S.B.

Mechtild of Hackeborn (c. 1241–1299), a thirteenth-century visionary and passionate lover of God, has been called God's nightingale and the saint of the common life by countless admirers throughout the centuries. In our own time, Mechtild of Hackeborn has been overshadowed by her contemporary, Mechtild of Magdeburg, a lay beguine who lived her final years at Helfta, along with Gertrud the Great, Abbess Gertrud of Hackeborn, and Mechtild herself. Yet there is something compelling in the life of this comparatively unknown saint that can speak to monastic women today as vividly as it spoke to nuns and lay women alike in the late Middle Ages.

Mechtild was born into the aristocratic family of Hackeborn in 1241 and joined the Benedictine community,[1] then located at Rodarsdorf, as a child oblate when she was seven years old. She had accompanied her mother to the abbey to visit her older sister, Gertrud, already a professed member. Although she was very young, Mechtild was convinced of her vocation and begged to stay, even going from one nun to the other, asking to be allowed to remain with them. Her mother consented, probably with some reluctance, and left the child behind when she returned to the Hackeborn court and estate.

LIFE AT HELFTA

Three years later, in 1251, the nineteen-year-old Gertrud of Hackeborn was elected abbess of the Monastery of St. Mary's. She led her community in this ministry for forty years until her death in 1291. Under her leadership, the community grew until lack of space and a diminishing water supply necessitated the move to Helfta where the Hackeborn family donated land for a more permanent and adequate monastic environment. Under Abbess Gertrud's wise governance, Helfta rapidly became a center of learning and spirituality renowned for its emphasis on feminine culture.

In *The Women of Helfta*, Mary Jeremy Finnegan writes that Gertrud was noted for her affectionate kindness toward all her sisters, regardless of rank or relationship. "At the same time, the Abbess Gertrude maintained a high level of intellectual achievement among her charges. Free from any morbid distrust of learning, she was known to say that if the study of letters should be neglected, soon the Scriptures would no longer be understood and monastic life would begin to decay."[2]

The writings of the three Helfta mystics, according to Lina Eckenstein, "were looked upon by their contemporaries as divinely inspired" and "among the most impassioned books of the age," reflecting "the qualities which make early mysticism attractive—moral elevation, impassioned fervor, intense realism and an almost boundless imagination."[3]

During her life, Mechtild shared her visionary experiences of God with her confidant and friend, Gertrud the Great. It is not surprising therefore that during Mechtild's final illness, Gertrud and a companion, at the order of the abbess, recorded the account of her visions. Mechtild was greatly distressed when she learned that her visions had been written down, but when she was assured by Christ that this was the will of God and her superior, she was at peace.[4]

The original *Book of Special Grace* was written in Latin, and by the mid-fourteenth century was circulated on the continent in an abridged form in the vernacular. A Middle English version, *The Booke of Gostlye Grace*, was evidently translated and adapted from the German.[5] The fact that at least four manuscripts of the abridged *Booke* are extant in British libraries indicates that the work was widely read in England, as well as on the continent, by nuns and aristocratic women alike. "The importance and influence of the *Booke* in the English mystical tradition are assured of some status because it belonged to the class of newly available writings of Continental women mystics. As such it might have contributed to the foundation of a vogue for female mysticism."[6]

While Helfta was the home of mystics—and from all accounts, a Benedictine community devoted to the *Opus Dei* and communal life—it was not removed from the daily life of the time and problems familiar to communities of women of that era. Political rivalries and petty warfare between landholding families involved the monastery as well. In 1284, Gebhart, brother of one of the nuns, attacked the monastery, invaded the cloister, and scandalized the nuns by "behaving in an outrageous manner."[7] Ten years later, the monastery suffered damage in a war between rivals for the imperial office.[8] Even with the patronage of the Hackeborn family, Helfta incurred debts and was often in need of funds.

Church politics also affected the community. The monastery was placed under interdict in 1296, "greatly afflicting it on account of certain pecuniary matters."[9] The episcopal see was vacant, there were rival claimants to the office and benefice, and perhaps double taxes placed upon the nuns. The imposition of an interdict meant that no Eucharist, sacraments, or public worship could be conducted in their monastery, nor could bells announce the time of prayer, a severe punishment indeed for a devout and young community. This interdict, the occasion for one of Mechtild's visions, illustrates her acquaintance with Scripture, her detailed imagery, and her intimacy with Jesus, her Beloved. On the feast of the Assumption, as she prayed and wept over their deprivations, the Lord appeared and assured her that she would see wonderful things that day. In the vision that followed, Mechtild saw the Lord and his Mother leading the community procession into the church for the celebration of the Eucharist. Jesus carried a red and white banner embroidered with gold and silver roses, and when he arrived within the church, he vested for Mass in a red chasuble with pontifical ornaments. "St. John the Baptist was to read the Epistle and this because he was the first who exulted even in the womb for the joy of the Blessed Virgin, but St. John the Evangelist was to read the Gospel because he had been the guardian of the Glorious Virgin." Mary "stood at the right of the altar clothed in garments brilliant as the sun, having on her head a crown studded with all manner of precious stones."[10]

The Lord promised Mechtild that, as long as the interdict continued, he would bless the sisters with special favors. She complained that the nuns were being deprived spiritually because of a disagreement over earthly goods and asked if the Lord did not feel compassion for them. He replied, "And why should I have such compassion? If I were taking My bride into a banquet in a hall adorned with flowers, and perceived that her robe was in some disorder, would I not take her aside and remedy the fault with My own hands in order to take her in afterwards in more fitting guise?"[11]

MECHTILD AS A MEMBER OF HELFTA

Mechtild's visions indicate a great devotion to choir and common prayer. She was chantress (cantor) and choir director, gifted with a beautiful voice and unusual musical ability. Therese Schroeder-Sheker calls Mechtild a "maiden in love, with a voice heard in heaven, so finely tuned that she becomes a harp. . . . When she creates during long years a completely purified body of images, memories, feelings, desires, hopes, it is woven from the non-material substance of song. It is definitely her path to the Risen Christ."[12]

Mechtild, like the other Helfta mystics, was formed by the liturgy. On one occasion, she saw the Blessed Mother in choir, bowing with the community. When she was so weak that her voice failed, an angel stood beside her and sang for her. She must have had a remarkable ability to use her special talents and her intense spirituality in the context of community. Besides directing the choir, she taught the women who came to the monastery and corresponded with those who sought her advice. She was particularly concerned about the members of her community, family, and friends who were near death and was sometimes favored with visions of their eternal joys. Once, when Mechtild was praying for a dying sister about whom she had some concern, the Lord asked her, "Who is the mariner that, after having happily brought his goods safely into port would throw them into the sea?"[13]

All this she accomplished in spite of delicate health, especially during her last thirty years. She suffered from headaches, possibly migraines, but still managed to be an integral part of community life. The ability to balance her life of prayer, study, and the work of her community was indeed a special grace. Mechtild died around 1299 at the age of 57.[14] Her feast is celebrated on November 17.

In spite of the difficulties experienced by her community and those which arose from Mechtild's own sensitivity, she maintained a spirit of optimism and confidence. Filled with trust in Jesus, she spoke in the language of a lover. She considered not only creation but also each trial as a gift from God with a purpose.

COURTLY IMAGERY IN MECHTILD

Mechtild's popularity, especially with aristocratic women, was undoubtedly due to this optimism and the rich imagery of her visions. As Theresa Halligan notes, " There is a certain amount of explicit spiritual guidance, but the emphasis is on the magnificent pageantry of the celestial courts and the bliss of intimate concord with God."[15] In her visions, she saw Jesus as the king or lord surrounded by the splendor of a medieval court. She pictured the clothing, the banners, the processions in an array of color and movement. In the comparatively sheltered life of the abbey, she retained the vivid memories of courtly life and related them in detail, not only in the accounts of her visions, but also in her letters.

Mechtild's images are passionate, sensuous, and surprising in one who left her wealthy, aristocratic home at an early age. She portrayed the clothing and jewels befitting a lover and his beloved; she used personal, passionate love images and homely, playful images of lovers enjoying each other's company.

The words that Mechtild wrote to an unnamed correspondent might well be applied to the nun herself: "He [Jesus] clothed Himself for the love of you with a rose-coloured vestment, which love dyed for Him into the

Blood of His own Heart. A garland of roses also He placed upon His head, set all round with goodly pearls, the drops of His own precious Blood. The gloves upon His hands were so perforated that He could keep nothing in them, but poured out upon you all that He had so long hidden from the world."[16]

Finnegan comments on the symbolic garments, richly colored and adorned with jewels and golden ornaments, which frequently figure in Mechtild's accounts of her visions. Jesus once appeared as the King of Glory, dressed in a golden robe embroidered with doves. His red mantle, symbolizing the passion, was "open on two sides to indicate that the soul has free access to God."[17] Mary, as Queen of Virgins, wore a golden mantle, embroidered with doves, each with a fresh lily in its beak. Love was personified as a beautiful maiden, dressed in a green robe covered with lattices, each bearing the image of Christ the King. The dove, the lily, and the lattice through which the lover peers, are well-known love images in the courtly tradition.

Not only canonized saints but also former members of the Helfta community who had died graced Mechtild with their celestial visits. It is written that on one occasion, Mechtild of Magdeburg appeared to her, surrounded by ineffable glory and brightness. The latter asked to know something of her magnificent adornment and received the reply, "You cannot understand, for I now wear as many ornaments as there are threads in an earthly vestment; and all these have I received freely from the Lord my Spouse."[18]

On the day when the exposition of the holy veil, with its image of Christ, took place in Rome, Mechtild was granted a vision. Lina Eckenstein, relates it:

> On a mountain overgrown with flowers she beheld our Lord seated on a throne of jasper decorated with gold and red stone. The jasper which is green is typical of the power of eternal divinity, gold represents love, and the red stone the sufferings which He endured through love of us. The mountain was surrounded by beautiful trees covered with fruit. Under these trees rested the souls of the saints, each of whom had a tent of cloth of gold, and they ate of the fruit with great enjoyment.[19]

The sins of those who approached the image of the Holy Face with special prayers were transformed into jewels of glowing gold. Some saw their sins changed into golden necklaces, others into festive golden rings, still others into lovely golden shields "while those who had purified their sins by bodily suffering, beheld them as so many golden censers, for bodily chastisement before God is like the sweetness of thyme."[20]

In this vision of Christ, Mechtild revealed her awareness and appreciation of each of the senses as a means to know and love her God. The smell of thyme and incense, the sounds of musical instruments, and the array of colors and jewels formed a sensual feast that must have been almost overwhelming. Certainly Mechtild was not afraid to acknowledge and use her senses as a gift and a means of spiritual development.

LOVE IMAGERY IN MECHTILD

Especially bold are the love images that pervade Mechtild's writing, reflecting an acquaintance with the *Minnesong* tradition. A striking example of these love images is the morning offering, in which the Lord invited Mechtild to salute him as a "sweet Lover, from whom all joy, all good, and all happiness have flowed in heaven and on earth."[21] She offered her heart as a rose, blooming in beauty and fragrance, to delight the Divine Heart. She offered her heart also as a goblet from which her Loved One could drink of his own sweetness, and as a pomegranate, to be eaten and transformed into Love Itself.[22] Here the sense of taste, the flavour of the pomegranate, and the sweetness of the chalice, combined with the scent and beauty of the rose, are all gifts to be shared by lovers in the courtly tradition.

Mechtild used the symbol of the love knot to exemplify the transformation of hearts affected through praying the Psalter. As the community prayed the *Miserere,* Mechtild saw the Lord take from the heart of each nun a twisted knot which he placed in his own bosom.

> When the psalms were finished and the sisters ceased prostrating, there approached two princes of the heavenly court bearing a golden tablet, which they placed in front of our Lord; and as He undid the knots which He had placed together in His bosom, there appeared on the tablet in the form of precious stones the words of all the psalms and prayers which the community had just offered up; these stones were of wonderful variety, and not only shone with unwonted splendour, but gave forth also a most sweet sound.[23]

Is it surprising that, in the visions granted a musician, even the stones should give forth beautiful music?

The necklace, too, appears as a love symbol. At the Mass offered for the Abbess Gertrud one month after her death, Mechtild was granted a vision of her sister surrounded by heavenly princes who were singing and playing on cymbals. When Mechtild asked what reward she had received for the pain she had suffered in her right hand, she replied, " With this hand I embrace my Beloved, and it is a priceless joy to me that Jesus deigns to use this arm as a necklace, and is pleased that it should embrace Him."[24]

In a letter to an unknown correspondent, Mechtild used the gold ring and entwined fingers to illustrate the relationship between Christ and his beloved daughters:

The Lover of your soul holds your hand in His, His fingers entwining yours, that He may show you how He works in your soul and how you ought to follow Him by imitating His example.[25]

She went on to explain the significance of each finger:

The ring finger signifies the fidelity of His Heart, caring for us like a devoted mother, bearing our burdens and sorrows and protecting us from every misfortune. Join this finger also with His and acknowledge your great want of fidelity to this sweet and faithful Lover.[26]

Mechtild combined courtly imagery with the mystical imagery of the *Song of Songs*, and applied it to the cross of Christ which she saw as a bridal couch. She wrote to a spiritual daughter, "His lordly couch was the hard cross which He mounted with such joy and burning delight as never bridegroom enjoyed on couch of ivory or silk."[27] She further explained that the Lord awaited his bride on this couch of love with unutterable desire. The beloved must, on her part, utterly renounce all delight and approach him on his bed of sorrow and contempt and unite herself to his side, wounded by love.

HEART IMAGERY IN MECHTILD

There is the lover's pledge, full of optimism and hope, which Mechtild sublimely applied to the heart of Christ as she advised her correspondent to open it with the key of love:

Even as a king, who has not as yet brought his bride into his house, leaves a city or town full of wealth, and even his friends, as pledges that he will come and take her; so has the Bridegroom, your Lover, given in pledge His most precious house, namely, His own Divine Heart.[28]

Mechtild further admonished her friend that if anything troubled her she should receive it as if it were a chain of gold which God had placed around her in order to draw her to the love of his Son. If she needed humility or any other virtue, she was to open with the key of love "the precious casket of all virtues, even the Divine Heart of Christ."[29]

In one of her visions, Mechtild not only sees Jesus, a harp emerging from his heart, but also hears a voice telling her that the harp is the body of Jesus himself; the strings are all chosen souls, bound together by his love. He then gives Mechtild his own singing voice, surrounding her with his song and the music of the strings, issuing forth from the movements of his fingertips. Here, notes Schroeder-Sheker,

> The languages of love, alchemy, poetry, psychology, and mysticism collide with and eclipse any stagnant notions of religious limitation, loss of identity, or loss of freedom. Her experience is individual and shimmering.

The same writer calls Mechtild

> one of the most faithful, who literally lives from the leaven of the perfectly tuned strings sounding in His perfectly formed hands. His sung holy words are a new eucharist, suspended and offered in melody, Mechtild's most highly developed sensibility.[30]

In a striking and dramatic vision, the passion of Christ is compared to a wedding feast with its profoundly sensual rituals of banquet, dance, bridal garments, song, and marriage bed. Jesus reminded Mechtild that divine love drew him from his Father's bosom and caused him to serve thirty-three years seeking for her:

> And when the time of my wedding was at hand I was sold by my own heart's love as the price of the wedding banquet, and I gave myself for bread and meat and drink. I myself was the kithara and organ at the banquet by means of my gentle words.[31]

Jesus' three falls on the way to his crucifiction were the wedding dance after the banquet: his wedding garments, given to the soldiers who crucified him, were white and purple and scarlet; and his crown of thorns replaced the festal garland of roses. "Then fastened by the cruel nails I stretched out my arms for your dear embrace, singing on my bed seven songs of marvelous love."[32]

Devotion to the Sacred Heart of Jesus was fostered by the nuns of Helfta, especially St. Gertrud. Mechtild, too, saw Jesus' love in visions of his heart from which a trumpet or a harp emerged, sending out sweet and consoling music. One Sunday, when the community was singing the *Asperges Me* at Mass, Mechtild asked the Lord to bathe and cleanse her heart:

> Straightway the Lord with love unutterable, bending to her as a mother would to her son, embraced her saying: "In the love of my divine heart I will bathe thee," and He opened the door of His heart, the treasure-house of flowing holiness, and she entered into it as though into a vineyard.[33]

Within the garden was a river of love and trees bearing twelve kinds of fruit, representing virtues. There were fish with golden scales, palm trees surrounded by angels as if by a wall. For Mechtild and other medieval mystics, the Sacred Heart was a heart of beauty and gentle love rather than the bleeding, suffering heart of later centuries.

NATURE IMAGERY

The surroundings of courtly splendor were not the only setting in which Mechtild describes her experience of relationship with God. Nature imagery abounds in her encounters with the sacred. On one occasion she saw herself as a rabbit in the arms of Jesus. Like the rabbit, which never closes its eyes in sleep, the lover is always aware of the presence of the beloved.[34] She offered to another the advice given her by Christ:

> Be like a trusty little dog who always returns to its master even after frequent rebuffs. If she is wounded by a word, she should not withdraw impatiently, or if she does so for a moment, let her return, relying on my mercy, which for a single sigh pardons everything.[35]

Birds appear in Mechtild's writings—black birds indicating the presence of evil and doves and larks as harbingers of love. In one passage she mentions having offered special prayers, after which she was favored with this vision:

> Then the Angel presented with much reverence and joy to God, in what appeared to be a snow-white cloth, the prayers that had been offered, represented as living larks.[36]

Some went straight up to heaven, some lingered, but all were dispersed around a smiling Lord.

MUTUALITY AND PLAYFULNESS

Mechtild was also acquainted with the daily work of a household. In a practical vein, she consoled a nun who was concerned about not going to confession before receiving communion:

> When a powerful king is coming to lodge, one cleans the house immediately. But if he is so near that there is no time to throw out the dirt, one hides it in a corner till later. So, if one has the sincere desire to confess her sins and never to commit them again, they are erased from God's sight.[37]

Overwhelmed by the Lord's bountrous gifts to her, she asks Christ in culinary terms if they are really fitting to one who considers herself unworthy of entering his kitchen and washing his platters. When the Lord asks where the kitchen is, she is speechless, so he replies:

> My kitchen is my heart which, like unto a kitchen that is a common room of the house and open alike to servants and masters, is ever open to all and for the benefit of all. The cook in this kitchen is the Holy Ghost, who kindly without intermission provides things in abundance and by replenishing

them makes things abound again. My platters are the hearts of saints and of chosen ones, which are filled from the overflow of the sweetness of my divine heart.[38]

A playful example of one of Mechtild's constant themes, that all can share in the merits of the Savior and make them their own, is illustrated in a vision in which the Virgin Mary offers a pair of dice to Mechtild, to be given to the person for whom she has promised to pray, so that she might play with Jesus. Mary, in explaining the dice image, tells Mechtild, "When a husband casts dice with his wife, he likes to take from her in game her rings, her jewels, the pretty ornaments she has made for herself; for her part, she claims for herself everything that belongs to her beloved."[39]

CHARACTERISTICS OF MECHTILD

Mechtild of Hackeborn was not a reformer nor a serious critic of her Church and her times as were her contemporaries, Hildegard of Bingen and Mechtild of Magdeburg. This may explain why she has not enjoyed a revival today. Neither can her writings be brought forward to champion any cause. One might well ask if they have any value beyond their brilliant descriptions and delightful stories.

Yet Mechtild's writings reveal a woman of deep faith and a uniquely liturgical spirituality, who was devoted to the common life and community prayer in her own monastery. From all accounts, she was able to balance her personal prayer life and enrich it *with,* not *in spite of,* the regular observance and liturgical practices of a growing and vibrant community. As a talented musician, God's nightingale and *Domna Cantrix*, she was able to lead and train her community in the music required for liturgical prayer. In a large monastery of possibly one hundred members, there must have been nuns with varying degrees of musical ability, always a challenge and a trial to the gifted musician. Here again, Mechtild achieved a balance and harmony in keeping both with her own remarkable gifts and the liturgical needs of her community.

The warmth and sensitivity of Mechtild's experience of God and her passionate love of Jesus as a person can serve as an antidote to a cool, rational, and impersonal approach to spirituality. There is no puritanical fear of the senses, no hint that the body is an evil to be shunned. Colors, sounds, smells, touch, the intertwining of fingers, the music of trumpet and harp, the glitter of jewels, the smell of roses and thyme, the taste of pomegranate and wine, all mingle in glorious array in Mechtild's visions of God.

Her God was Mother as well as Father, displaying such feminine characteristics as offering food, smoothing a dress, filling kitchen platters, and tidying a room. When Mechtild prayed for a sister who was discouraged, Jesus offered this assurance:

> Why is she troubled? I have given myself to her for the fulfillment of all her desires. I am her father by creation, her mother by redemption, her brother in the sharing of my kingdom, her sister by sweet companionship.[40]

Important in Mechtild's spirituality is the meaning and beauty she associated with everything around her. Plants, animals, stones, colors, numbers, each had its own particular meaning as a virtue to be cultivated or an attribute of God to be loved and admired. Nothing was without significance in her life and surroundings. Always, the mystery of a loving God pervaded her writings.

In the current, throwaway world where even human life is cheap, acquaintance with Mechtild and the other medieval mystics could help to revive a sense of mystery, an awe regarding all creation's wonders. The ability to find beauty in all things, to find peace in chaos and uncertainty, is a special gift. Seeing everything in creation as something significant and precious in itself, reflecting and mirroring God, could help to redeem and save the world in a material as well as in a spiritual sense. St. Mechtild of Hackeborn can speak to us today, this nightingale who sings an unending canticle of praise to God. Her spirituality and mysticism is a reminder to us of feminine beauty and harmony in the age-old, yet ever-new context of Benedictine life.

NOTES

1. While some writers designate the Helfta community as Cistercian, Sr. Maximilian Marnau points out that it was not a member of the Order of Citeaux, though the Cistercian influence was present. The spiritual directors of the community were the Dominicans of Halle. See Margaret Winkworth, ed. and trans., *Gertrude of Helfta, Herald of Divine Love* (Mahwah: Paulist Press, 1993). Introduction by Marnau, 10.

2. Mary Jeremy Finnegan, *The Women of Helfta, Scholars and Mystics* (Athens, Georgia: The University of Georgia Press, 1991) 11–12.

3. Lina Eckenstein, *Woman Under Monasticism* (Cambridge: University Press, 1896) 328–329.

4. Theresa A. Halligan, ed., *The Booke of Gostlye Grace of Mechtild of Hackeborn* (Toronto: Pontifical Institute of Medieval Studies, 1979) 37.

5. Ibid., 52.

6. Ibid., 58.

7. *The Life of St. Mechtildis* (Rome: Vatican Press, 1899) 135. Quotations from this volume have been slightly modified to change archaic language and the pronouns "thy," thine," "thee," and "thyself" to forms of "your," "yours," "you," and "yourself." Verb forms have also been adapted when appropriate.

8. Ibid., 205–206.

9. Ibid., 211.

10. Ibid., 211–212.

11. Ibid., 214.

12. Therese Schroeder-Sheker, "The Use of Plucked-Stringed Instruments in Medieval Christian Mysticism," *Mystics Quarterly* 15 (September 1989) 136.

13. *Life,* 95.

14. The date of Mechtild's death is uncertain, probably 1298 or 1299. See Halligan, *Booke of Gostyle Grace,* 36.

15. Ibid., 41.

16. *Life*, 222.

17. Finnegan, *Women of Helfta,* 49.

18. *Life,* 149.

19. Eckenstein, *Woman Under Monasticism,* 345.

20. Ibid.

21. *Life,* 55.

22. Ibid., 55–56.

23. Ibid., 75–76.

24. Ibid.,183.

25. Ibid., 219.

26. Ibid., 220.

27. Ibid., 222.

28. Ibid., 223.

29. Ibid., 224.

30. Schroeder-Sheker, "The Use of Plucked-Stringed Instruments," 134.

31. Quoted in Finnegan, *Woman of Helfta,* 51.

32. Ibid., 51–52

33. Eckenstein, *Woman Under Monasticism,* 344.

34. *Life,* 68.

35. Finnegan, *Women of Helfta,* 48.

36. *Life*, 115.

37. Mary Jeremy Finnegan, "Idiom of Women Mystics," *Mystics Quarterly* 13 (June 1987) 70.

38. Eckenstein, *Woman Under Monasticism,* 346.

39. Quoted in Finnegan, *Women of Helfta,* 53.

40. Quoted in Finnegan. "Mechtild of Hackeborn: *Nemo Communior."* in *Peaceweavers: Medieval Religious Women,* eds. Lillian Thomas Shank and John A. Nichols (Kalamazoo: Cistercian Publications, 1987) 218.

16

Gertrud of Helfta:
A Woman God-Filled and Free

Jane Klimisch, O.S.B.

Our present era, the late twentieth century, is enjoying a Gertrud-of-Helfta renascence. However, the rebirth of interest in Gertrud is not confined only to this one medieval feminine saint; Gertrud is being reborn alongside Hildegard of Bingen, Hadewijch of Antwerp, Julian of Norwich, and other holy women of an earlier time. The expanding interest in Gertrud's life and works has flowered in new translations of her two major works[1] and in a fair amount of secondary literature.

In his *Life of Moses,* Gregory of Nyssa (+394) states that only one thing is really worthwhile and precious, namely, to become God's friend.[2] The writings of and about Gertrud of Helfta attest to this fact: Gertrud was an intimate friend of God. These are not wild words if one recalls Moses speaking to God on the mountain top as friend speaks to friend (see Exod 33:11) or if one remembers the words of Jesus to his disciples: "I do not call you servants any longer . . . . but friends" (John 15:15).

Like Bernard's affective rather than exegetical motive in addressing his monks on the Song of Songs,[3] this account, detailing and savoring Gertrud's friendship with God, aims to rekindle the fires of love from the glowing embers of Gertrud's life in those who read and relish her story. This aim is reinforced by the words Gertrud heard from the Lord as she responded to the mandate to write an account of God's gifts to her. The Lord spoke thus:

> If anyone with devout intention desires to read this book for the good of his [sic] soul, I will draw him to myself, so that it will be as if he were reading it in my hands, and I will take part in his reading. . . . Moreover, I will breathe forth over him the breath of my divinity, and he will be renewed by my Spirit within him.[4]

245

It is hoped that this essay will lead readers to Gertrud's own words and, in turn, to fresh outpourings of the Spirit from her Divine Friend.

THE WORLD OF GERTRUD'S TIME

Gertrud of Helfta in Saxony, who was born in 1256 and died in 1302, blossomed and matured in an era congenial to grace. In the larger world of her time, European universities were flourishing. Strands of classical languages and Aristotelian philosophy were woven into the fabric of liberal education. The study of theology opened new doors to those faithful seeking understanding. It was the era of Thomas Aquinas; the beginnings of polyphonic music; and the soaring Gothic churches of Reims, Chartres, and Notre Dame built of stone and stained glass. French troubadours and German minnesingers celebrated in song and dance the joys of earthly and heavenly love.

Yet, for all these signs of life, the thirteenth century had a shadow side as well. The Christian-Muslim wars known as the crusades were still raging, albeit in their final hour. Battles among feudal knights were commonplace although feudalism was waning. Cataclysmic events such as the Great Schism within the Church, the Hundred Years War, and the virulent Black Death were still in the offing.

Essentially, then, Gertrud of Helfta's era was one of peace and security. The Abbey of St. Mary at Helfta, where Gertrud was destined to grow from childhood to maturity, reflected this outer serenity. Its peacefulness, however, transcended that of the society at large. For it was an outgrowth of a deep and beautiful relationship with God with which the Helfta community was blessed.

THE BENEDICTINE/CISTERCIAN MILIEU OF HELFTA

Like a tender sapling, five-year-old Gertrud was planted in the good monastic soil of Helfta in 1261. Whether she was brought there by her parents or as an orphan is not known. However, she was born January 6, 1256, on the feast of the Epiphany, when the Christian world sang of the star in the East drawing all peoples into its radiance.

The Helfta Abbey was situated in the eastern Germanic region of the Holy Roman Empire near the city of Eisleben on property which had belonged to the family of the reigning abbess, Gertrud von Hackeborn. Abbess Gertrud (with whom Gertrud of Helfta is often mistaken) governed the abbey from 1251–1291 in an unusually enlightened and affirming way. As a child, Gertrud was blessed, indeed, to have this gracious and benign older woman as her spiritual mentor.

Although some Cistercian usages had been adopted by the Helfta Abbey, it designated itself Benedictine and not Cistercian. Often labeled

Cistercian, Helfta was never affiliated (accepted by the General Chapter) with that order. During that era, the Cistercian order was unfavorably disposed to the further inclusion of monasteries of women under its jurisdiction. The nuns of Helfta, however, received significant Cistercian influence from the sermons of Bernard of Clairvaux (1090–1153). They followed the Rule of Saint Benedict, but their spiritual directors were Dominicans. And it is likely, too, that the spirit of Francis of Assisi influenced them along with that of the German Rhineland mystic, Meister Eckhart (1260–1327), whose home was not far from Helfta.

Bernard stands out among those spiritual influences shaping Helfta. In his addresses to the monks of Clairvaux, Bernard made the point that it was not so much his desire to explain words as to influence hearts.[5] His sermons were suffused with biblical allusions and themes which, through God's grace, had molded his life. The seed of his affective, biblical spirituality found good ground at Helfta.

The daily monastic round at Helfta itself was also formative in the finest sense. A well-ordered community, its identifying features were a vibrant liturgical life, a regime of rigorous study, manual and intellectual work that served both monastic and neighborly needs, and the daily *lectio divina* which led to peaks of contemplation.

PROVISION FOR LIBERAL EDUCATION

Abbess Gertrud of Hackeborn was a person of exceptional prudence, discretion, and wisdom. She insisted on a well-equipped library so that all the nuns, especially the young, could diligently pursue their studies. She required that formative studies include not only Scripture and patristic writings but also rhetoric, literature, and philosophy.[6]

Under Abbess Gertrud the Helfta community became known as a center of culture and learning as well as a place of prayer and spiritual growth. The younger Gertrud was swept up into the orbit of learning. Her biographer says of her: "Gladly and eagerly she gave herself to the study of liberal arts."[7]

PRIORITY OF LITURGICAL PRAYER AND EUCHARIST

The Spirit breathes "according to person, time, and place"[8] says Gertrud's confidant as she writes of Gertrud's spiritual gifts. From her major work, *The Herald,* we gather that communal prayer at Helfta was centered in the Hours and the Eucharist. Liturgical seasons and feasts marked *kairos* time for the Helfta community. In accord with the daily horarium prescribed in the Rule of Benedict, the hours of the Divine Office gave a rhythm to each day, as did liturgical feasts to the entire year. Cyprian Vagaggini describes the atmosphere at Helfta:

The liturgical calendar is the actual calendar not only externally but even internally in a life of this kind. The precise characteristic is seen in Gertrude, too, who in fixing the time of the mystical graces of which she speaks, does not consider the year except in reference to the feasts and liturgical cycles, nor the day except in reference to the hours of the *Opus Dei*. It is a matter, therefore, of a picture of life in which the liturgy dominates not only qualitatively but even quantitatively.[9]

Daily Eucharist was not a prescription in the Rule of Benedict, but its importance in the Helfta horarium stemmed from the tradition of the Church at this time. It was in the Eucharist, as well as in the Divine Office, that Gertrud often experienced the mystical touches of God, the "hidden manna" beyond imagining described in *The Herald*.

MONASTIC FAMILIAL RELATIONSHIPS

The Helfta community, numbering about one-hundred sisters, was unusually large for its time. Four names stand out among its members. *Gertrud of Hackeborn* (1232–1291) was elected abbess at the age of nineteen and served the community for forty years in this role. Much of the joyful exchange among the nuns was due to the "good ground" cultivated by this abbess who governed for so long a time. *Mechtild of Hackeborn*, Gertrud's younger sister, served as mistress of novices and teacher of singing. Her lifetime, from 1241 to 1299, coincides closely with that of Gertrud of Helfta who, according to tradition, was Mechtild's dearest friend. Mechtild was in charge of the nuns' choir; in revelatory writings she is referred to as Christ's "nightingale." *Gertrud of Helfta* (1256–1302), whose epithet later was "the Great," was the namesake and fortunate disciple of Abbess Gertrud. The younger Gertrud enjoyed the friendship of many of the Helfta nuns who often besieged her with requests for spiritual instruction and advice. *Mechtild of Magdeburg* (c. 1210–1282) came to Helfta after living as a beguine for many years. Both as a writer and a holy person, she was a powerful model for the younger Helfta nuns.

The beautiful location of the monastery, with its streams and abundance of fruit trees, enhanced the grace-filled community life at Helfta. It mirrored the warm relationships these nuns enjoyed among themselves.

Was this thirteenth-century monastery of women, therefore, a Garden of Eden? Undoubtedly the Helfta nuns shared in Christ's sufferings as all Christians do in their journey of faith. In the Helfta writings there are references to fatigue, illness, the rigors of daily manual labor such as cleaning, baking, laundering. Gertrud experienced a high degree of mutual love at Helfta, yet community living gave her many opportunities for patience and forgiveness. Because of certain money matters, around 1298, a canonical interdict deprived the Helfta nuns of the sacraments for a time. This community trial brought profound sadness to them.

On the whole, however, Helfta was marked by serenity, joy, and a remarkable sense of oneness in Christ. As a result, the community radiated a strong and happy influence in all directions, even beyond its own walls.[10]

SPIRITUAL GIFT-SHARING THROUGH DIALOG AND WRITING

The "overflow to neighbor" was first evident within the abbey itself. Intimate friendships, spiritual colloquies, and corporate works were its immediate signs. One example was the collaboration of Gertrud and Mechtild of Hackeborn in writing the *Book of Special Grace,* a description of Mechtild's dialogs with God. The fact that all but Book Two of *The Herald* was compiled by anonymous Helfta nuns other than Gertrud points to vast amounts of prior spiritual exchange on a deep rather than a superficial level. Even Gertrud's personal dialogs with God seem not to have been unique to her. Other such dialogs are described within the Helfta writings. In a question-and-answer session concerning Gertrud, "Someone" asks the Lord what pleases him most in Gertrud. (The question has obviously not been posed by Gertrud herself.) The reply is, "Her freedom of heart." The questioner considers the reply inadequate and presses on until God gives a fuller explanation.[11] Dialog with God and with their sisters in community were trademarks of this unusual group of Helfta women.

Their dialog, however, was not confined to the abbey enclosure. Enclosure did not mean for them an airtight enclave basking in its own spiritual gifts. The manna received in friendship, contemplation, and ecstasy was to be shared with others who hungered for the true Bread of Life.[12] According to *The Herald,* the Spirit gave Gertrud a persuasive and gracious speech telling her to assist others, both within and outside the monastery, in their journey of faith.[13] Helfta became known for welcoming nonmonastic neighbors who sought spiritual companionship, material provisions, or whatever gift matched their need. Gertrud herself, in frail health and often lacking sleep, was at times driven to near exhaustion as she attempted to respond to all the needs of others. She admits to taking to her bed on one occasion to escape the tumult of visitors.

THE WRITINGS OF GERTRUD OF HELFTA

Her own words provide the finest access to the spirituality of Gertrud—directly in the Second Book of *The Herald* and indirectly (at times through direct quotations) in the remaining portions. A brief review of the Gertrudian corpus will be helpful at this juncture.

Gertrud's two major works are *The Herald of Divine Love* and the *Exercises.* Now, seven centuries after their appearance in Latin or in later translations, these two works are enjoying fresh translations from the original Latin. The original Latin title of *The Herald* is *Legatus divinae pietatis.* A commonly known title, *Revelations,* is a misleading designation. The original Latin as well as recent translations of the title far more accurately express the content of the work and the intent of Gertrud's partner in dialog. *The Herald* contains five "Books" within it, but only Book Two has been written by Gertrud. Entitled "The Memorial of the Abundance of Divine Sweetness," Book Two was begun, as Gertrud herself says, "under a most violent impulse of the Holy Spirit"[14] on Maundy Thursday in 1289. Gertrud was then thirty-three. Her writing is thus the result of a direct and irresistible divine mandate. Gertrud was reluctant to write about her experiences. God answered her reluctance and aversion with the assurance that her divine gifts had been given to her for others. Gertrud then took up the task, beginning with the story of her call from being a tepid religious to a Spirit-led person. Her own encounters with the Lord are then spun out humbly and gracefully. What results, however, is not really an independent account. It is considerably strengthened in credibility by the "cloud of witnesses" who have authored Books One, Three, Four, and Five. Book Two stands out, however, for the grace-filled flow of its style.

Gertrud's second major work, *Spiritual Exercises (Exercitia spiritualis),* is a collection of meditations and prayers based on Scripture and the liturgy and composed for the benefit of the Helfta nuns. The work differs from the personal and dialogic tone of *The Herald.* Gertrud presents seven themes meant to lead the reader to a retreat experience and union with God. The fifth experience has a temporary ring as she recommends that a day be regularly set aside "to be at leisure with the God of love."[15]

The Helfta style of writing, and Gertrud's own, is enthusiastic, the root meaning of which is "God-filled." The writing is descriptive, pictorial, laden with adjectives and comparisons, abounding in images, and suffused with scriptural and liturgical echoes. The latter appear not only as citations and quotations but saturate the writing.

As for Gertrud, she reflects the Helfta style but in a way unmistakably hers. Her single-mindedness shines out in one basic theme: God's goodness, love, and generosity. *What* she says is more important to her than a self-conscious striving for the *way* she says it. Her writing is affective, exuberant, even breathless. The reader senses that she can hardly contain herself. She describes her God-inspired writing thus:

> You [God] imparted this instruction so excellently and so sweetly that, without any effort, I wrote of things which I did not know before, as though

it were a lesson long since learned by heart. And you acted with such moderation that after I had written the daily task it was impossible for me, even with the exertion of every effort, to find any more of those words which next day presented themselves with such fluency and abundance, and without difficulty of any kind.[16]

At times, Gertrud is addicted to superlatives. She pushes language to its boundaries in an attempt to express the inexpressible. This effort may account for words which appear overemotional, flowery, and even grandiose. She is in good company. Paul spoke of having been caught up into paradise and hearing ineffable things which "cannot be put into human language" (2 Cor 12:4). And Augustine declares helplessly at the outset of his epic of spiritual conversion: "What can anyone say when he speaks of Thee?"[17] In Gertrud's defense, let us note that her Latin does not always translate successfully into English. For Gertrud, the frequently used word *dulcis*, for example, had shades of meaning: something strengthening and satisfying as well as smooth and soothing. Yet there is only one English equivalent, "sweet," to reflect these meanings. The recurrence of this word and other thirteenth-century expressions may sound out of harmony with today's taste. If her readers can dig beneath the peculiarities of the genre, however, and make contact with the solid core beneath, they will be amply repaid.[18] Gertrud's finest "style" comes from her life itself and her desire to share its riches with others. In her own words, she tells God that she wrote her works so that "others reading these pages may rejoice in your sweet love and be led to experience it in themselves . . . so they [the readers] . . . may be led to taste within themselves that hidden manna (Rev 2:17), which it is not possible to adulterate by any admixture of material images and of which one must have eaten to hunger for it forever."[19]

THE MYSTICAL SPIRITUALITY OF GERTRUD

The "lived" quality of Gertrud's writings leads us to consider certain aspects of her spirituality and their meaning today. In our time, readers of the Gospels are urged to aim primarily at meeting the living Jesus within and beyond the text. In the same way, the aim in reading Gertrud's writing is to discover the interaction of Gertrud and the Lord as it occurs in dialog, vision, and the wordless movements of her heart. The Benedictine theologian, Sebastian Moore, states that theology or the study of God (and one could add spirituality) is the weaving of the Jesus story with human autobiography, or "allowing my story to be opened up and to flower in the Jesus story."[20] To discover this interweaving of the divine and human story in Gertrud's life is the task and joy of all who read her works.

We will examine three such interweavings, from among many in Gertrud's life, for closer reflection: Gertrud's initial conversion, the encounters linked with the *Esto mihi* Sunday, and the two visits of the Lord on Christmas feasts.

Some writers on mystical experience point out that Gertrud seems not to have gone the usual route which begins with a purification or "dark night" experience. Yet Gertrud herself claims that her life immediately preceding her conversion was, in its darkness, the preparatory action of God for the graces which would follow. It is good to recall that at first Gertrud found the monastery a "land of unlikeness" where she felt she did not belong. Her early childhood was truly a hatching experience within the dark monastic egg. Later on, she became wrapped up in study which occupied her mind, captured her energy, and nurtured her vanity. By the age of twenty, she was tense and melancholy. She began to see herself as a nun in name only.

Then, on January 27, 1281, shortly after her twenty-fifth birthday, Christ intervened. Of this event she says, in part:

> I was in my twenty-sixth year. The day of my salvation was the Monday preceding the feast of the Purification of your most chaste Mother, which fell that year on the 27th of January. The desirable hour was after Compline, as dusk was falling.[21]

She speaks of God dispersing "the darkness of my night." She then describes a youth of sixteen who stood beside her, "handsome and gracious," who spoke these words in a courteous and gentle voice: "Soon will come your salvation, why are you so sad? Is it because you have no one to confide in that you are sorrowful?" And later, the youth added: "I will save you. I will deliver you. Do not fear."[22] References to salvation stand out. Little wonder, then, that Gertrud opens the second chapter of Book Two thus: "Hail, my Salvation, Light of my soul!"[23] Gertrud's astounding conversion experience may easily take its place alongside the "take-and-read" event in Augustine's life or the voice and blinding light which radically changed Saul of Tarsus to Paul, the Apostle.

The *Esto mihi* meetings with the Lord, which are special in Gertrud's view, also carry a salvific note. A paraphrase of the *Esto mihi* Introit might simply be: "[Christ Jesus], be to me the one you wish me to be!" And it is not these words alone which affect Gertrud profoundly. Here and elsewhere she refers to singing. The chant itself becomes a meta-language conveying to her that which is beyond words.

In the two Christmas encounters, so noteworthy for Gertrud, she is invited to hold and embrace the Word-made-Flesh, the incarnational hinge of salvation. Salvation and presence are the essence of these peak encounters. Incarnation and salvation (the complete paschal mystery) become all that Gertrud hopes to spread abroad through her life. In this identification with the One "in whom God was reconciling the world to himself" (2 Cor 5:19), Gertrud's life becomes an *inchoatio vitae aeternae,* an obscure beginning of the life of glory.

UNION WITH CHRIST THROUGH LITURGICAL WORSHIP

One need not read far into *The Herald* to discover how deeply Gertrud was immersed in liturgical worship. In a recent work, the Jesuit, Peter E. Fink, proposes that "every spirituality can and should intersect with the liturgy of the church."[24] Gertrud's life exemplifies this kind of confluence of liturgy, spirituality, and mystical experience. Cyprian Vagaggini asserts: "The most complete case history of the perfect marriage between liturgy, liturgical spirituality, and mysticism seems to be that of St. Gertrude."[25] He notes that her "mystical invasions" (his term) were in no way in conflict with communal participation in liturgy nor was liturgical participation an impediment to mystical experience. On the contrary, liturgical and mystical life were mutually nourishing and sustaining.

The monastic environment in which Gertrud's multi-faceted spirituality developed included the Eucharist, the Hours, feasts and fasts, liturgical seasons, and sacramental celebrations. The entire liturgical year was Gertrud's most important "calendar" as it was for all the Helfta nuns. Eucharistic piety of this era was strongly centered in the Mass. Gertrud cherished the Eucharist in its fullness as a sacred act, but she writes most frequently of communion. It even appears, at times, that she detaches communion from the complete liturgical action. Apparently the Lord overlooked this liturgically lopsided point of view and met Gertrud where he found her. After all, Gertrud herself insists in her writings that God tailors the way of communicating the Divine Self to the person, time, and place.

Gertrud cites other often-overlooked facets of liturgical worship: processions, seasonal colors, chants, the aroma of incense. She also finds the sitting, standing, and bowing connected with ritual charged with meaning even though, when she is fatigued or ill, she cannot always fully participate in them.

Through all the facets of liturgy, Gertrud experiences the presence of the Divine Being who is alive, real, and life-giving. In this divine companionship, she senses an immediacy, a fullness, and something like the annulment of time. But "presence" is not to be practiced by itself. It comes as awareness and awe, and then blossoms into mutuality and dialog. The patterns of dialogic address and response which abound in liturgy become the pattern, too, of God's mystical companionship with Gertrud.

FREEDOM OF SPEECH IN GERTRUD'S GOD-RELATIONSHIP

In *The Herald* one reads expressions such as "it was there that I heard these words;" "suddenly you appeared, saying . . .," or "I received your blessed response in these words." The narrator is Gertrud describing the way the Lord appeared and spoke to her.[26]

The question arises how Gertrud actually heard the voice of the Lord Jesus which she confidently repeats. A current writer wonders "whether mystics who 'hear' Jesus speaking to them . . . are not putting words into his mouth in a way that allows him to 'do his thing' in them. Is their dialogue a form of 'Christo-drama'"?[27] In an early work on mysticism, Evelyn Underhill states that mystical automatisms in their highest form have to do with that transformation of personality which is the essence of the mystical life. "They are media," she says, "by which the self receives spiritual stimulus, is reproved, consoled, encouraged and guided on its upward way."[28]

Mystical messages are heard by Gertrud either in an immediate way ("I heard the words") which mystics know well but find it difficult (or do not bother?) to explain, or as a distinct interior voice, perfectly articulated and remembered, but recognized only within the mind ("the Lord gave me to understand").[29] At still other times, Gertrud is "instructed" with wordless images alone[30] or with a combination of images and dialog.[31] Sometimes mystical communication takes place in the depths of silence. (Some favored persons refer to interior locutions as "loud thoughts.")

Gertrud's mystical voices from God are best left in the realm of mystery. Gertrud declares: "I have never found a human friend to whom I would dare to tell all I know; the human heart is too small to bear it."[32] Divine voices were an important gift in the lives of many saints, among them Joan of Arc, Catherine of Siena, Blessed Henry Suso, and Teresa of Avila. The human words of Gertrud, however, either as questions or responses to what she has heard, are worth exploring further.

In an early work, Thomas Merton devotes a chapter to what he calls the gift of "free speech." His first focus is on Adam speaking familiarly with God in the garden. To Merton, this familiarity implies the oneness of Adam with himself, with God, and with the world around him. Merton describes the original Greek term, *parrhēsia* (free speech), and its later usage in the New Testament and in patristic writings. He concludes that the gift of free speech may come to us "in the terrible yet healing mercy by which God gives us the courage to approach Him exactly as we are."[33]

Did Gertrud of Helfta receive the gift of *parrhēsia?* Other mystics such as Gregory of Nyssa and Isaac of Nineveh point out that both the term and the gift were important in the vocabulary and spiritual life of the early Church. Little has been written on *parrhēsia* in the English language. The interesting overtones it possesses in Christianity do, indeed, invite deeper research on the subject. The term has had a splendid history in the spirituality of the Eastern Church and, with various meanings, in both the Pauline and Johannine works of the New Testament.[34] Gertrud's liberty of heart, which the Lord found most pleasing in her, might well have been the supernatural basis for the gift of free speech *(parrhēsia?)* which she seemed to enjoy with her Divine Friend. This gift emerged sometimes as a reverent audacity, protest, or boldness, and at other times as gentle courtesy. It was threaded through with a sense of her own weakness coupled with an astonishing strength received from God. The gift flowered in the ecstatic paean known as *jubilus,* a high form of giving thanks for graces.[35]

An awesome sense of divine presence always preceded the "free speech" with which she addressed or responded to God. Gertrud states that at the end of a day of solitude and silence, prayer and reflection, she realized "that You had come and were there present." In fact, she claims: "However much my mind wandered away or sought pleasure in temporal things for hours or days at a time . . . when I came to myself again, I always found you there."[36]

SIGNIFICANCE OF "HEART" IN GERTRUD'S PIETY

What did the heart of Jesus mean to Gertrud? In what way did her experience of that heart differ from that of the seventeenth-century Visitation nun, Margaret Mary Alacoque?

Gertrud of Helfta's devotion grew from her mystical colloquies with the Lord, from Mechtild of Magdeburg's vision of the heart of Christ as the focus of divine love and compassion,[37] and from her spiritual exchanges with her intimate friend, Mechtild of Hackeborn. Important, too, was Gertrud's sense of an intimate connection between the heart of Christ and the Eucharist, and her saturation in the prophetical Scriptures wherein Jeremiah and others speak of the everlasting love found in God's heart (see Jer 31:3) and of the human heart as an organ of knowing: "I will give them a heart to know me" (Jer 24:7). Gertrud absorbed the biblical meaning of heart as reciprocal love and experienced her own heart as an indwelling center. "In the heart of Gertrud you will find Me," later monastics would sing in a vesper antiphon for her feast. But as the Lord dwelt in *her* heart, so she dwelt in *his* in the phenomenon called "an exchange of hearts." The wound in the side of the risen Christ became a door for her to enter the divine heart in a faith-filled way.[38] Gertrud also knew the Lord "by heart," so to speak. Her own heart became for her the highest operation of her intellect and the seat of her faith. Gertrud also linked the divine heart with the Latin concept of *pietas.*[39] This word denotes love of the tenderest and most self-giving kind. For Gertrud, it was the tender, loving heart of God that kept drawing all creatures into its embrace.

Pre-Vatican II devotion to the Sacred Heart promoted by Margaret Mary Alacoque was focused largely on reparation. For thirteenth-century Gertrud, the focus is that of compassion and reciprocal love. Gertrud relates that at one time she asked the Lord for a practice in memory of the Passion. He replied that she could pray with outstretched arms as an image of the Passion. Perhaps to avoid singularity in doing so, Gertrud reminded the Lord that such a practice was not the custom at Helfta.[40] The Helfta customs undoubtedly stemmed from a focus on the compassionate rather than the suffering heart of Christ.

The compassionate heart of Christ was understood and practiced by the Helfta nuns in their loving concern for others, near and far. A question is sometimes posed whether or not Gertrud was involved with the "world" at all or in tune with its needs. Or did she just pass through the world without engagement? Her credibility as a Christian mystic hinges on the answer. The writings which accompany Book Two of *The Herald* give ample testimony to Gertrud's outstretched hand and compassionate heart in responding to the needy both within and outside the monastery. One of the nuances in her active devotion to the heart of Christ is found in the word *suppletio*[41] which she uses frequently. For Gertrud, this word came to mean the way a compassionate God *supplies,* through us, what is lacking. When Gertrud encouraged those in trouble or counseled them in their darkness, she *supplied* them with new life.[42]

Finally, Gertrud was known and cherished by God for her "freedom of heart" which gave God ready access to her. According to the testimonial in Book One of *The Herald,* the Lord said of Gertrud: "I have always found her ready to receive my gifts, for she permits nothing to remain in her heart which might impede my action."[43] Gertrud's "freedom of heart" suggests a clear and spacious path within her for the overtures of God.

GERTRUD'S RELEVANCE FOR BENEDICTINES TODAY

In what sense might Gertrud inspire and give life, especially to monastics of today? We will cite four points based on what has already been stated in this chapter:

1. Gertrud's writings provide a description of friendship and intimacy with God based on *faith as relationship:* "Know that I am with you always; yes, to the end of time." (Matt 28:20).

2. Gertrud's deep *immersion in the Church's liturgy* calls us to renew our faith and joy in it. For it is here that we "speak the truth about what throbs in our hearts and shapes our world."[44] It is here that we are empowered to become more fully God's friends and God's own people.

3. Gertrud models for us the beauty and power of *dialogic prayer* found first in the liturgy as address and response and then mirrored in her mystical encounters with God. This ancient dialogic pattern of Christian prayer is meant to nourish both intimacy and common purpose. Moreover, Gertrud was also profoundly affected by the "I (We)-You" usages which abound in liturgy. She was at home addressing God in the vocative. This kind of familiarity that uses "you" is reflected in an eighteenth-century Hasidic poem which rejoices in seeking God as "You" and being sought by the same vocative.[45]

4. A renewal of Gertrud's *"heart knowledge"* of God would return us to our earliest biblical tradition of the heart as an organ of knowing. It would, in turn, move us to pray for understanding hearts (see 1 Kgs 3:9) so needed in our world today.

CONCLUSION

I hope that the *suppletio* which Gertrud extended to others will also supply what is lacking in these words about her. This chapter has only scratched the surface of her great life.[46] Moreover, as Bernard stated in his commentary on the *Song of Songs,* "the language of love will be meaningless jangle, like sounding brass or tinkling cymbal, to anyone who does not love."[47] The key to unlocking the love language in the *Song* or in Gertrud's writing is love itself. And in this we are always lacking. Carl Jung once wrote in a letter: "What infinite rapture . . . lies dormant in our religion. We must bring to fruition its hymn of love." The words in this chapter and those which surround it have this single and beautiful aim: the ripening of love.

NOTES

1. The two recent translations referred to are these: Gertrud the Great of Helfta, *The Herald of God's Loving-Kindness Books One and Two,* trans. Alexandra Barratt (Kalamazoo: Cistercian Publications, 1991) and Gertrude of Helfta, *The Herald of Divine Love,* trans. and ed. Margaret Winkworth (New York: Paulist Press, 1993). For the most part, the Winkworth translation is being used in this chapter. The German spelling, Gertrud, is being adhered to except when the name appears in a title or quotation as "Gertrude."

2. Gregory of Nyssa, *The Life of Moses* (New York: Paulist Press, 1978) 137.

3. Bernard of Clairvaux, *On the Song of Songs* (Sermon 16.1), trans. Kilian Walsh, O.C.S.O. (Spencer, Mass.: Cistercian Publications, 1971) 114.

4. *The Herald,* trans. Winkworth, 47.

5. Bernard of Clairvaux, *On the Song of Songs,* 114.

6. Hubert van Zeller, O.S.B., in *The Benedictine Nun: Her Story and Aim* (Baltimore: Helicon, 1965) says that "the literary and the monastic life need not

necessarily go together, but it is a healthy sign when they do: when they no longer try to go together there is stagnation—on the monastic side at least." 109.

7. *The Herald* I:1, 52. For further description of the Helfta literary and spiritual environment, see Elizabeth Petroff, *Medieval Women's Visionary Literature* (New York: Oxford University Press, 1986) 207–230 and Caroline Walker Bynum, *Jesus as Mother: Studies in the Spirituality of the High Middle Ages* (Berkeley: University of California Press, 1982) 170–262.

8. *The Herald* I:1, 54.

9. Cyprian Vagaggini. O.S.B., *Theological Dimensions of the Liturgy,* trans. Leonard J. Doyle and W. A. Jurgens (Collegeville: The Liturgical Press, 1976) 749.

10. Note a resemblance here to the Greek discourse on friendship which manifested a readiness to share in the concerns of the entire citizenry. True Christians likewise extend their concern to the needs of the Kingdom. See *Men in Dark Times* by Hannah Arendt (New York: Harcourt Brace Jovanovich, 1968) 24–26, and "Religious Life in the Future" by Richard Rohr, O.F.M. in *Origins* 18:15, September 22, 1988, 239.

11. *The Herald* I:11, 72–73.

12. Cf. *The Herald* II:24, 135.

13. *The Herald* I:1, 54.

14. *The Herald* II: Prologue, 94.

15. Gertrud the Great of Helfta, *Spiritual Exercises,* trans. Gertrud Jaron Lewis and Jack Lewis (Kalamazoo: Cistercian Publications, 1989) 73.

16. *The Herald* II:10, 110. See also Sister Mary Jeremy Finnegan, "Similitudes in the Writing of Saint Gertrude of Helfta," *Mediaeval Studies* 19 (1957) 48–54, and the Bynum work cited in note # 7.

17. Saint Augustine, *Confessions,* trans. Vernon J. Bourke (New York: Fathers of the Church, Inc., 1953) 7.

18. Michael Casey, "Gertrude of Helfta and Bernard of Clairvaux: a Reappraisal," *Tjurunga* 35 (September 1988) 3–23.

19. *The Herald* II:24, 135.

20. Sebastian Moore, "Four Steps Towards Making Sense of Theology," *Downside Review* 111, April 18, 1993, 79–100.

21. *The Herald* II:1, 94–95.

22. *The Herald* II:1, 95.

23. *The Herald* II:2, 96.

24. Peter E. Fink, S.J., *Worship: Praying the Sacraments* (Washington: Pastoral Press, 1991) 157.

25. Vagaggini, *Theological Dimensions of the Liturgy,* 716.

26. *The Herald* II:1, 95; II:5, 102.

27. Sebastian Moore, 98.

28. Evelyn Underhill, *Mysticism* (New York: Noonday Press, 1955) 272.

29. *The Herald* II:9, 108.

30. Cf. *The Herald* II:11, 111.

31. Cf. *The Herald* III:9, 163.

32. *The Herald* II:23, 131.

33. Thomas Merton, *The New Man* (New York: Farrar, Straus and Cudahy, 1961) 96. Scott Russell Sanders, "Telling the Holy," in *Parabola* (Summer 1993) says: "Stories about a time when we spoke easily with the starlings and sycamores, with mountains and mountain goats, with our Creator in the garden, arise, I suspect, not from a memory of what was, but from a longing for what might be." 7.

34. W. C. Van Unnik says, "in Paul, the real power of 'freedom of speech' is not only that the gospel is proclaimed, but that the Lord of the Gospel is revealed" 476. Van Unnik's work is "The Christian's Freedom of Speech in the New Testament," in *Bulletin of the John Ryland University Library of Manchester* 44 (1962) 466–488. An entry by Pierre Miquel, O.S.B., in *Lexique du Désert: Etude de quelques mots-clés du vocabulaire monastique grec ancien* cites patristic uses of the term *parrhēsia*. A rich source in English is that of Stanley B. Marrow, S.J., *Speaking the Word Fearlessly: Boldness in the New Testament* (New York: Paulist Press, 1982).

35. Gertrud the Great of Helfta, *Spiritual Exercises,* 93–121.

36. *The Herald* II:3, 98. See also Ralph Harper, *On Presence: Variations & Reflections* (Philadelphia: Trinity, 1991).

37. Richard Woods, O.P., *Christian Spirituality: God's Presence Through the Ages* (Chicago. Thomas More Press, 1989) 19.

38. *The Herald* II:23, 130–131. Compare also John 20 where Jesus invites Thomas to "put out your hand and place it in my side" (v.27).

39. See Gertrud the Great of Helfta, *Spiritual Exercises,* 65–67.

40. Two historical works on devotion to the Sacred Heart are those of Louis Gougaud, *Devotional and Ascetical Practices in the Middle Ages,* trans. G. C. Bateman (London, 1927) and Ursmer Berlière, *La Dévotion au Sacré-Coeur dans l'Ordre de S. Benoît* (Paris: Desclée, 1923). See also Gerard S. Sloyan, "Piety Centered on Jesus' Sufferings and Some Eccentric Christian Understandings of the Mystery of Calvary," *Worship* 67:2 (March 1993).

41. S. Maximilian Marnau, Introduction to *The Herald of Divine Love,* trans. Winkworth, 36–37.

42. *The Herald* I:8, 66.

43. *The Herald* III:11, 73.

44. John Carmody, "When people's concerns meet Jesus Christ, church lives," *National Catholic Reporter* 29:42 (October 1, 1993) 2.

45. This most famous Hasidic poem spins out eight stanzas on variations of "Lord of the world, . . . I shall sing you a song of you: You, you, you! . . . Where I wander—you. Where I ponder—you. Only you, you again, always you! You, you, you." Quoted in John M. Oesterreicher, *The Bridge,* III (New York: Pantheon, 1958) 126.

46. Why the epithet "great?" To distinguish her from Gertrud of Hackeborn with whom she is often confused? Or to exult in the "great things" God did for her as well as for Mary of Nazareth?

47. Bernard of Clairvaux, Sermon 79:1.

17

Dame Gertrude More (1606–1633): The Living Tradition

Jeremy Hall, O.S.B.

Just over three centuries intervened between the death of Gertrud the Great of Helfta in 1301 and the birth of Gertrude of Cambrai in 1606. Though momentous events, profound changes, and powerful personalities crowded the centuries that separated them chronologically, the perennial monastic bond and spiritual tradition that perdure through the ages united them. And that the first Gertrud was inspiration for the second is evident in a number of prayers and "fragments" found in Gertrude's breviary after her death.

Moreover, as will be seen in the following pages, Gertrude of Cambrai was instrumental in a monastic endeavor that traced the sources of their shared spirituality, preserved a great deal of the best sources from the intervening three centuries for English-speaking readers, and may well serve monastics of our own day who seek to intensify, revitalize, or reclaim their monastic lives, personal or corporate.

Gertrude (Helen) More, daughter of Thomas More's great-grandson, was born March 25, 1606, in Low Leighton, Essex. Her mother died when Helen was five, and her father Cresacre took upon himself the education of his intelligent, lively, and witty daughter.

For several years after Helen became an adolescent, Fr. Benet Jones, a Benedictine friend of the family and Helen's spiritual counselor, had spoken to her and to her father about a possible monastic vocation. No young person then in England could have any experiential knowledge of Benedictine life; following the dissolution of all monastic houses in England during the Reformation, any person seeking to live a religious life had either to join or to establish a community abroad. Father Jones was a member of the recently restored (1619) English Benedictine Congregation, successor to the centuries-long presence of the Order in England from the end of the sixth century to the dissolution of the monasteries in the middle of the sixteenth, a presence that has indelibly marked English spirituality. The monasteries of the Congregation were centered in what is now northeastern France and were committed to secret and hazardous service on the English mission during the years of persecution.

The Congregation had hoped for several years to establish a community of contemplative Benedictine nuns, and it was the foundation of such a community that Father Jones proposed to Helen's consideration. Lacking any experience of monastic life, Helen had misgivings, but at the age of seventeen she left England for the continent; two of her More cousins and four other young Englishwomen accompanied her. Helen was recognized as the leader, and the dowry her father provided was to finance the new foundation. They arrived at Douai in Flanders, site of the Benedictine monastery of St. Gregory, in the summer of 1623, and were joined there by Catherine Gascoigne, another young woman from a distinguished Catholic family in England. In the fall they went on to their destination, a partially restored house in the city of Cambrai.

The nuns were to be under the authority of the English Benedictine Congregation rather than the local bishop, and to be formed in the Benedictine spiritual tradition rather than in the "new movements" then current. To provide the necessary formation for the young women, the help of three members of a Benedictine convent in Brussels was secured. That house had been founded by an Englishwoman about a quarter of a century earlier and was not affiliated with the Congregation. After several months of formation, on the last day of 1623, Helen received the Benedictine habit along with the other eight, and chose Gertrude as her religious name. A year later (January 1, 1625) the same group of novices' proclaimed the traditional vows as Benedictines, members of the Convent of Our Lady of Comfort (later Our Lady of Consolation), and Sister Gertrude became Dame Gertrude, using the customary title in the Congregation.

However, not all had gone well during that year. Sister Gertrude was uncertain of any real vocation when she left England but followed the recommendation of her confessor. Throughout her novitiate year she was unsure that she wanted to, or even that she could authentically, profess vows that would bind her for life. Honest efforts to resolve the difficulties before profession were unsuccessful; though deeply troubled, she did make profession. That did not end her problems.

She was not the only novice to find the novitiate a severe struggle, nor were the novices' difficulties engendered only within themselves. The three Benedictines of the Brussels community had been formed, as was common in the Counter-Reformation climate, in the new currents of spirituality, especially Jesuit spiritual practices. These were properly designed to sustain and deepen the spiritual lives of religious engaged in the demanding involvements of "the active life." Included were formal discursive meditation that engaged the senses, imagination, and intellect in order to elicit the response of the will; frequent and detailed examination of conscience; sustained spiritual direction and frequent confession. The young Benedictines somehow recognized that theirs was a different call, and that a central cause of their sense of dislocation and frustration derived from unsuitable formation for the life they were to live. Further, they did not receive appropriate assistance from the chaplain or appointed confessors.

The novices wrote, therefore, to the president of the Congregation, Fr. Rudisind Barlow, who took the matter seriously. In July of 1624, in the middle of the novitiate year, he sent them a spiritual guide, Fr. Augustine Baker, who was destined to have a profound influence on Dame Gertrude, upon the Cambrai community, and well beyond it.

Father Baker seems to have had unique preparation for helping young monastics serious about seeking God. He came to the Cambrai community at the age of forty-nine, having experienced both struggles with faith and a deep hunger for God, times of real devotion and then extended periods of aridity in which no one seems to have helped him effectively, subsequent periods of laxity, and a final conversion that bore fruit in lasting fidelity in prayer. Thus he knew experientially the intensity of desire for an authentic prayer life, periods of faithful and fruitful prayer; he knew, as well, the pitfalls and the pain of the journey. Hence he could be perceptive and compassionate with the young religious.

Trained as a lawyer and having worked with a group of England's best historians, he had the tools to help in the formation of the English Benedictine Congregation and also to do very extensive research into the pre-Reformation history of Benedictines in England. He had extensive knowledge of the living tradition of English monasticism, its roots and its development. Having read widely and well in the classics of Christian spirituality (especially the mystical tradition), from the desert fathers to his contemporaries, with access to transcripts and the ability to translate for others, Father Baker brought a wealth of resources to the community.

However, his position at Cambrai was rather an ambivalent one, for the community already had a chaplain and appointed confessor. He was simply to be available as a spiritual teacher and guide for anyone who wished to ask his counsel. The response of the nuns varied. Sister Catherine Gascoigne became a quietly devoted disciple and remained so. Sister Gertrude not only kept her distance; she apparently led the opposition. Meanwhile her problems escalated, nor did her profession end her frustrations and confusion.

She did try to resolve them by extensive reading, including all the writings of Gertrud of Helfta, and by conferring with others—but not with Father Baker. Nothing seemed to help, and she was seriously tempted to transfer to another community.

Finally she did go to speak with Father Baker late in November after her profession. He seems to have quietly overlooked her earlier opposition and, with striking acuity, understood her complex personality quickly:

> She was very merry, yet very much subject to sadness. She had a timid, scrupulous conscience, yet had much courage, boldness, and even hardiness. She had a propensity to extroversion, and yet a strong one also to introversion. So that in some respects none was more scrupulous and timid, and in others none freer and bolder; none more merry and cheerful, and yet none more prone to sadness or easily cast into it; none more inclined to extroversion, and yet none had a greater call to, or more aptitude for, true introversion, but as yet she knew not how to do it. And indeed, none but the Divine Spirit could teach her this, or bring about a reformation of her life.[1]

He recognized that, though she had become a problem for herself and her community, she willed to do better, and tried sincerely. But she did not know how to achieve what she longed for. "What she needed," he wrote, "was to be brought into a simplicity of soul which is the immediate disposition to union with God, and that can be done only by the Divine working with the soul's co-operation, aided by Divine grace."[2] Aware that she had a profound "propensity," as he called it, for God, and a genuine capacity to love, he proposed a way of prayer that quite simply by-passed formalized methods and opened her heart to simple and direct acts of love. Instead of trying to overcome her faults by self-analysis and violent measures, he proposed that she gently do what she could, and trust God for the rest; love would overcome or transform what she seemed powerless to conquer. Instead of frequent examinations of a conscience that tended to scrupulosity, he taught her that living her "way of love" would of itself reveal to her depths of her own being that such examinations could never reach.[3]

This "way of love" was total openness to God's call and full and loving attention to the divine inspirations that flowed from it.[4] She would discern those inspirations with increasing clarity, and respond with corresponding freedom and joy. Only the Holy Spirit could reveal to each person the fullness of his or her unique call, and inspire the responses it should elicit. And thus, when one is truly centered in God, it is she who can best determine (within the demands and boundaries of her monastic commitment) how she is to live and to pray. For another to impose his or her own insights or practices as the way she is to follow would be a violation of her deepest being.

Father Baker followed this teaching faithfully in helping Dame Gertrude with the two principal elements in the spiritual life: prayer and asceticism. With regard to prayer he wrote:

> No rule can be laid down to limit a soul to one or other particular way of prayer. But the soul must watch closely herself and her call from God, what suits her best, and to what she is most drawn; she must also seriously pursue prayer one way or another, and then she will not fail to see how she should behave therein. . . . All that I did was to advise her, urge her, to perform her mental prayer one way or another, and never to desist either for aridity, or obscurity, or any difficulty whatsoever.

Since none of the first three types of prayer he discussed (vocal, discursive meditation, prayer of immediate acts) appeared to suit her, she should try affective acts "in the manner that experience would show to be best for her."[5]

Prayer must be accompanied by asceticism in any genuine spiritual life, for it "enables us to pray well by combatting self-will, the only impediment to perfect prayer and actual union with God." His instructions to Dame Gertrude on asceticism were simple but demanding: 1) do all that divine or human law obliges, including following divine inspirations, 2) abstain from anything forbidden by those laws or inspirations, 3) bear as patiently as possible all afflictions experienced in body, mind, or spirit, from whatever source they come. In his judgment these were enough for anyone, and allowed for freedom to follow inspirations in all non-obligatory matters.[6]

It is immediately evident that in both these matters crucial to contemplative life, prayer and asceticism, Father Baker insured for Dame Gertrude the liberty of spirit proper to one fully responsive to the Spirit.

In all these areas of spiritual direction for Dame Gertrude, Father Baker echoes not only the best of the contemplative tradition in the Church, but also the Rule of St. Benedict. Characteristically, he uses "divine inspirations" as key to its interpretation. Quoting the Prologue, "Our eyes being opened to the deifying light, let us hear with attentive ears what the Divine voice daily admonishes us. . . and never depart from the guidance of God," he wrote: "These words. . . express the drift and end of the external observances of the Rule which follow and are, as it were, founded upon the Prologue. And that scope or end . . . is that we should observe the impulses, light and guidance of the Holy Spirit."[7] In this context he commented especially on monastic obedience and the role of the abbot. Although he did not explicitly draw an analogy with spiritual direction, the implications are clear.

And so, one may ask, having finally broken through her resistance to Father Baker and having asked his assistance in truly seeking God, how did Dame Gertrude respond to his directions for the eight years he remained at Cambrai? And what was the effect upon her and her community?

Much of the answer is implied in Father Baker's account, but Dame Gertrude spoke for herself in various writings discovered only after her death, and never meant for publication.[8] These are in three parts. The first, titled "Confessiones Amantis," is a collection of fifty-three "confessions" patterned on St. Augustine's and largely based upon biblical texts used in liturgical prayers throughout the Church year. In them she addressed God in the kind of intimate, affective prayer that Father Baker had suggested. Unable, as she said, to do the discursive, methodical meditations so strongly promoted in her time, she produced these deeply personal ruminations on sacred texts, typifying the monastic *lectio, meditatio, oratio*— and eventually, *contemplatio*. They were well named "Confessions of a Lover," and were chosen by Evelyn Underhill as more illustrative than the writings of such great figures as St. Teresa or St. Augustine, of ". . . how intensely actual to the mystic is the Object of his passion, how far removed from the spheres of pious duty or philosophic speculation, how concrete, positive and dominant such a passion may be." Underhill spoke of her as "that remarkable mystic" and quoted at some length from these "confessions."[9]

The second part of her writings is a collection of "Fragments" of varied lengths, consisting of reflections and prayers. The third, her "Apology," is a fairly lengthy exposition and defense of Father Baker's teaching and of her experience of living by it.

It is in these writings of Dame Gertrude, ranging from critical evaluations of some spiritual teaching and practice to intimate prayers, that one sees at first hand her intelligence, good judgment, insight, wit, and courage—and, most abundantly, the transformation of her spirit's capacity into a single-hearted love of God.

She wrote of life in the convent as all but intolerable for the first two years at Cambrai, and of her desire to flee or shake off the burden.[10] She wanted urgently to relate to God and not be "as I was then, such a stranger to Him" (A, 227). Asking questions of those better formed and informed did not really help, nor did her extensive reading in "spiritual books." By contrast, when she finally sought Father Baker's help, it was almost immediately strikingly effective:

> I found myself in fifteen days so quieted that I wondered at myself. This change took place as soon as I had received from him some general instruction . . . as that I must give all to God without any reservation . . . of any inordinate affection to any creature—this I found myself willing to do—and that I must use prayer twice a day, which I found myself capable of. And although I found little of that which is called sensible devotion, yet

I found that with a little industry I was able to use it with much profit, and that it did make anything very tolerable which happened to me" (A, 273–274).

In another context she expanded this account:

On my going to Father Baker, almost in a desperate state, he told me my way must be by prayer. For this he gave me some instructions . . . and referred me for the rest of that point to God. He having done this . . . I found presently that course of love which I so much desired. . . . God did make all things that were necessary for me to know so plain that I wondered to see such alteration in my soul. Yea, by my saying the Divine Office . . . God did so enlighten and instruct me that no industry of mine own could have attained such knowledge for my only purpose of loving God and humbling myself" (A, 228).

What struck her at first in Father Baker's instructions was that "they were grounded upon God (not upon him)." This was a decided contrast to her previous experiences with authoritarian confessors and directors, and it provided the foundation for trust, simplicity, humility, and free obedience. Furthermore, she recognized the wisdom and charity in his directives about her failings. Whereas her previous confessors had "no other advice than to overcome all things by force and violence," Father Baker encouraged her not to be disheartened, but rather to turn to God, be patient with herself, quietly strive to overcome all inordinate affection for created things. By following this counsel, she observed that various faults "which, in spite of my desire, I could not at first reform, fell off, little by little" in God's time and by God's grace—and she grew in true humility (A, 222). In this same vein she commented, in numbers of contexts, on the radical difference between a forced, external obedience, often demanded of the young and inexperienced, and the freely given, internal obedience expressive of spiritual maturity. Referring to (and remembering) confessors, directors, and superiors who demanded total subjection to their authority in the name of fostering humility, she gave vent to her outrage: "O misery, that all this should be fathered upon holy obedience, the most noble of all virtues. . . . O my God! was this thy meaning when we vowed ourselves to Thee?" (A, 247) And again, in contrast, she referred to Father Baker's schooling in prayer, in true liberty of spirit to follow the leading of the Holy Spirit.

In one of her Confessions (#31) she prayed her gratitude for Father Baker's help, asking God's blessing upon him whose instructions "have made Thy yoke so sweet and Thy burden so light to me who . . . found it so grievous and heavy . . . whereas afterwards, on my being put into a course of prayer and mortification by him, my greatest obligations seemed to be most desirable burdens. For all Thy benefits be Thou by all praised forever."

Her prayer (in addition to the Divine Office) involved two daily half-hour periods given to her "way of the heart": loving openness and response to the presence of God, concentrated but not formally structured at prayer time, and then overflowing into the rest of her day. She trusted that God would then lead her according to the divine will, increasingly the focus of her own will. Father Baker called this the way of "sensible devotion"; she called it the "way of love," and prayed frequently, "Let me love or let me die." This was to be her way to holiness. She had tried every way proposed to her previously to no avail.

Those means, especially formal meditation, which had been urged upon her as it was upon most religious of the time, though impossible for her, were undoubtedly suited to others. This perception of the gift of the Spirit leading each person to the way of prayer suited to his or her original gifts of nature, and of the inner call and inspirations by which to guide one's life, was of paramount importance to her. In this context she criticized the practice of imitating a particular saint as a model of life, way of prayer, or specific activity. To do that, she believed, is ultimately to follow one's own choice. Rather, the way to spiritual progress is "to observe what it is that God exacts of them and enables them to do, and not what others do, or can do or have done. For as we all differ in face, so do we differ in the manner of our interior exercises" (A, 238–239). If the person is as faithful as she can be, God will faithfully increase the light of grace; progressively the person will recognize the Spirit's leading and be strengthened to follow it.

Her own experience affirmed this judgment. Her way of prayer made her "capable of understanding what was necessary for me in a spiritual life," of recognizing any "impediment between God and my soul," and "makes me abhor to do anything in the world for any other intention than out of regard for God, and because God would have me so do." She found that she was humbled in and by her prayer. When crosses came God showed her how to respond. "And thus I see that God doth so temper everything He layeth upon me that it is as much (and no more) as I am able to bear and is [appropriate] for me." She believed it was God who overcame all temptations in her and it would be presumptive to test her strength beyond what "obedience and necessity provide for me. This I find to be enough" (A, 273–274).

At the end of her "Apology," deeply grateful for the gift of God she had known, she addressed those who shared it.

> O you souls who are capable of prayer, be grateful to our Lord, for it is the greatest happiness that can be possessed in this life! For, by it, it is easy to

pass through all things, howsoever hard and painful. By it we come to be familiar with God Himself and to converse in Heaven; by it all impediments will be removed between God and our souls; by it we shall receive light for all that God would do by us; by it we shall come to regard God in all and wholly neglect ourselves; by it we shall know how to converse on earth without prejudice to our souls; and, in fine, by it we shall praise God, and become so united to Him that nothing shall be able to separate us for time or eternity from His sweet goodness. Oh, let Him be all in all to us, Who only can satisfy our souls" (A, 287).

The fullness of this gift and practice of prayer in her own life is suggested in her "Confessions:"

> What shall I say of a soul that hath tasted how sweet our Lord is?. . . . Thou dost admit her, longing and sighing after Thee alone, to, I know not what, nor can I express the unspeakable joy and delights which Thou sometimes admittest her to. . . . Yet out of Thy care of her Thou suddenly turnest away Thy face; whereat, till she love Thee for Thyself, she will become troubled and impatient. . . . If she bear this, making Thy will her law above all the desires of her heart. . . . Thou wilt assuredly return" (#18).

This is her only text that expresses "mystical experience" as commonly understood; she did not seek "extraordinary experiences" nor did she write of them.

Dame Gertrude refers to and reflects on the Rule of St. Benedict in numbers of places. The conclusion of Benedict's chapter on humility serves well to conclude any account of her search, her struggle, the fruit of her total emptying of self and transformation in Christ and his Spirit:

> Now, therefore, after ascending all these steps of humility, the monk will quickly arrive at that perfect love of God which casts out fear. Through this love, all that he once performed with dread, he will now begin to observe without effort, as though naturally, from habit, no longer out of fear of hell, but out of love for Christ, good habit and delight in virtue. All this the Lord will by the Holy Spirit graciously manifest in his workman now cleansed of vice and sin.

And Dame Gertrude did "quickly arrive." She was to die in but a few years, at the age of twenty-seven.

Dame Gertrude was nineteen years old and had been a religious about two years when Father Baker directed her to a way of prayer that changed her life; a change that affected her relationships and role in the Cambrai community as surely and deeply as it changed her relation to God. In 1629 the community decided it was time to assume authority for their own lives and release the Benedictine nuns from Brussels who had filled those roles since the community's founding. Dame Gertrude and Dame Catherine Gascoigne were the community's choices for Abbess. Both were under canonical age and the Congregation had to refer the matter to Rome; Dame Catherine was chosen, perhaps because she was six years older.

The two differed markedly in personality, and in earlier years would have had a difficult time working together effectively. Now, however, Dame Gertrude became assistant to Abbess Catherine, assumed the responsibility of cellarer, and directed the lay sisters. The community had grown by twenty-four members, and demands upon community leaders had grown proportionately: adequate income and housing were a real problem. The monastic cellarer, with responsibility for all the material goods and needs of the community, is described by the Rule of St. Benedict in terms very like those used of the Abbot: mature, wise, humble, steady, attentive to the needs of each member and the community as a whole, and solicitous as a parent for all. And the cellarer is to be obedient to the Abbess—something Dame Gertrude had not been noted for in her first two years at Cambrai. Now the two collaborated wholeheartedly, and the fruitful relationship lasted for the four years remaining to Dame Gertrude.

Several other significant events marked 1629 for the community. Dame Gertrude's younger sister, Bridget, joined the community, as did Abbess Catherine's sister, Margaret. The latter was the first to die in the community, and Bridget was to become prioress of Cambrai's foundation in Paris. In that same year, Father Francis Hull was appointed Vicar of the community by the Congregation. He has been described as "rigid, small-minded and somewhat obtuse." He caused great suffering to the community, and certainly to Dame Gertrude by trying to shatter her trust in the way of prayer that had brought her such inner peace and spiritual growth. He sought to impose his own activist and highly structured approach upon her and all the community. Seemingly jealous of Father Baker, he criticized his teaching and his direction of the nuns, and eventually incited the Congregation to formally examine Father Baker's orthodoxy in the Chapter of 1633.

In preparation for that examination, the Congregation required both Abbess Catherine and Dame Gertrude to submit a written account of their prayer, and the community had to turn over all its manuscripts dealing with Father Baker's teaching. One suspects, however, that the best testament to both the quality and the efficacy of his efforts were the persons of the Abbess and Dame Gertrude: the Abbess who had been faithful to his direction from his earliest days at Cambrai, and Dame Gertrude who had ultimately been so transformed in following that direction. Regarding this time of trial for the community, the Abbess later testified to the quality of Dame Gertrude's sustaining presence. "It cannot be imagined," she declared, "how great a comfort and encouragement she was to us all in these times of our difficulties, her example and words were so moving and efficacious and proceeding from a heart so inflamed with Divine love and God Almighty's honour that if a soul were even so much dejected as that she was ready to fall or faint, they were of force to raise her up again and move her to confidence and courage."[11]

Father Baker was to be completely vindicated, but the last time Dame Gertrude saw him was just before he left for the Chapter meeting at Douai. A week earlier, on the feast of Mary Magdalen, she had written in her "Confessions," reflecting on Matthew 6:5 ("They have received their reward"): "Let me live as long as it pleaseth Thee, or die in the very beginning of these my desires to love; send sickness or health, sudden or lingering death, poverty or abundance, good fame or that I be by all the world despised; and, in fine, in all do with me as is most for Thine honour" (#53).

That act of total oblation was to be her last entry. She fell ill the day she met with Father Baker, July 29, but did not know the cause. On the first of August she was taken to the convent infirmary, and it soon became apparent that she had an intensely painful and loathsome form of smallpox. She bore all the attendant suffering in complete serenity, even having to forego receiving the Eucharist because the disease so severely affected her throat. Several days before her death the Abbess thought it best to tell her that the illness was critical. Dame Gertrude responded, "God hath given me peace in my soul and what can one desire more. . . . I have nothing at all to do but to leave myself wholly to his disposition." From the feast of the Assumption until her death two days later, none of the community could be with her except the infirmarian and her cousin, Dame Ann More, because the disease had become so infectious. She died August 17.[12]

> God Almighty had chosen her for a foundress and leader of this little flock gathered together in His name and for His service. By her temporal means we had our beginnings, but much more was she enriched with gifts and spiritual graces, sufficient not only for herself, but also to help and bear up the community . . . managing the temporal affairs . . . and in promoting of the spirituality of it with as great zeal as can be imagined. . . . No mother could be more dear and tender of her only child than she was of the whole community.

This was the testimony of a member of Dame Gertrude's beloved Cambrai community.[13]

Manifestly Dame Gertrude and the community had cause for deep gratitude to Father Baker, but he had reason for enduring gratitude to them as well. Their esteem for him and response to his teaching (except for some early rejection such as Dame Gertrude's), the stimulation offered by minds and spirits like hers and Dame Catherine's, and the witness their very lives were to the validity of his direction—these must have been a source of joy to him. Members of the community requested him to write treatises for them on aspects of the life of prayer, and his ready response made these nine years at Cambrai the most fruitful, in spiritual writing, of all his career. Not only did the community urge this production; they preserved the whole body of this writing as well as notes on his conferences to the community. Further, beginning the year before Dame Gertrude's death, they followed his example of translating and transcribing others' work, in this instance some conferences of Bishop Francis de Sales, who had died a decade earlier. Thus began a tradition of scholarship that would characterize what has been called "the Cambrai school."

The community's support of Father Baker at his "trial" in 1633 has already been noted; it, too, must have meant much to him. After that examination and vindication of his work, Father Baker was assigned to the monastery at Douai for four years, during which time he wrote *The Inner Life of Dame Gertrude More* and edited her writings. He was then sent back to the English mission in 1638. Avoiding persecution for several years, he died there in 1641 at the age of sixty-six. In his final illness and death he was cared for by the mother of a nun of Cambrai.

Shortly after Father Baker's death a woman who was to be among the most influential persons in preserving his writing entered the convent of Cambrai. Most extant early copies of his treatises were transcribed by Dame Barbara Constable for other monasteries, for missioners, for lay men and women in England. However, many others of the Cambrai school, both monks and nuns, edited and circulated his manuscripts, of which there are between two and three hundred extant,[14] having survived the destruction of English monastic life in that part of the continent during the French Revolution.

Father Baker was highly regarded by many after his death, was almost immediately given the unofficial title of "Venerable," and the General Chapter of 1653 authorized the publication of his writings on prayer and spirituality. But opposition was again raised by some members, and again he was supported by Cambrai. In 1655 the president of the Congregation demanded that the nuns submit every Baker manuscript in their possession so it might be "purged of error"; the accusations were that he taught too much liberty of spirit, weakened obedience, and slighted regular monastic observance. It became a very difficult situation for the nuns, but Dame Catherine very quietly but very firmly refused to hand over any of the community's manuscripts. The opposition ceased following the death of two of Father Baker's opponents, and a digest of some forty of his treatises was prepared and published as *Sancta Sophia* by a Benedictine disciple, Fr. Serenus Cressy, in 1657.[15]

Finally, the last recorded act of Dame Catherine was an appeal to the Congregation president for "a new and very ample confirmation" of Father Baker's work as "the greatest treasure that belongs to this poor community."[16] Dame Catherine died in 1676, having retired three years earlier from the position of abbess to which she had been elected in 1629. In Dame Gertrude and Dame Catherine the trust in, and loyalty to, Father Baker spanned nearly fifty years and would continue through this community's heirs to the present day.

The Cambrai community continued its quiet but influential life until the forces of the French Revolution invaded the territory and finally the city of Cambrai itself in 1793. In October of that year the nuns were given fifteen minutes to evacuate the convent and were transported to Compiegne, where they were imprisoned. A number of the community and their chaplain died in very severe prison conditions; sixteen survivors, after a year and a half of imprisonment, were finally able to get passports for England in the spring of 1795. After two temporary locations, they settled at Stanbrook, near Worcester, in 1838. And so the circle of life was completed. The little group of young women who had left England to establish Benedictine life in a foreign land in 1623 came home in the persons of another generation two centuries later. There, in Stanbrook Abbey, the memory of Dame Gertrude as foundress and Dame Catherine as first abbess are revered.[17]

In the final chapter of his *Rule*, St. Benedict describes it as "this little rule that we have written for beginners," and in the same breath he invites his daughters and sons to "set out for the loftier summits" and suggests the guides who will lead them "along the true way" to those summits. "For anyone hastening on to the perfection of monastic life," he recommends holy reading of Scripture, the lives and teachings of the Fathers, the Rule of St. Basil. Twice in the brief chapter he directs this counsel to those who are serious about seeking, who want to "hasten," and who long for the ultimate goal of monastic life; and twice he promises that with the grace of God they can truly hope to reach this goal.[18]

Father Baker, Dame Gertrude, and the Cambrai community purposefully "set out for the loftier summits," following Benedict's prescription. A survey of the writings to which Father Baker referred in his works, many with great frequency, is indicative of the breadth and depth of his familiarity with the best guides "to the loftier summits." Besides Scripture and the Rule, he cites the "Lives of the Desert Fathers," Cassian's "Conferences," Dionysius the Areopagite, Gregory of Nyssa and Gregory of Nazianzen, Gregory the Great, and Augustine among the early masters. Of a later time he cites or quotes Bernard of Clairvaux especially but also Hugh and Richard of St. Victor, Catherine of Siena, Francis of Assisi and the "Fioretti," Aquinas, Bonaventure, and Angela of Foligno; then another pair of favorites, Tauler and Suso, as well as Ruysbroeck and the *Theologica Mystica* of Harphius. Nor did he neglect his sixteenth and seventeenth-century contemporaries: the Spanish Carmelites (especially Teresa and John), Francis de Sales, Abbot Luis de Blois, and the two Capuchins (Barbanson and Benet Fitch) to whom he refers frequently and with warm approval.

Understandably, however, he had a marked affinity for the English mystics of the fourteenth century: primarily *The Cloud of Unknowing* by an unknown author and *The Scale of Perfection* by Walter Hilton, but others as well. Merton observed that the special quality of these English mystics, good sense and moderation, "is perhaps due above all to the fact that it developed out of the English monastic tradition."[19]

Father Baker promoted this quality and range of sources among the Cambrai community as a matter of course: "Good books," he told the nuns, "are a necessary good for your souls." At the same time he remarked on the quality of the convent's library as "good and choice" and said that many of its holdings were irreplaceable.[20] Seeking to improve it further, in June of 1629 he wrote to Sir Robert Cotton, whose library, including a rich collection of pre-Reformation manuscripts Father Baker had consulted earlier (and which eventually became the nucleus of the British Library),[21] requesting that Sir Robert provide for the nuns any manuscripts or books in English that would be helpful for contemplatives. He also asked for Hilton's *Scale* in Latin for use by those of the community who had command of it. If Dame Gertrude is representative of the community's response to Father Baker's promotion of classical sources, his efforts were very effective. Even in her very personal writing she refers to many of them, kept excerpts from favorites, and recommended her own list with "all the works of Father Baker" in first place.

However, neither Father Baker nor the Cambrai community were concerned only with the availability of quality spiritual reading for themselves. The English Catholics who had fled to the continent were eager for a deepened spiritual life, especially according to their own tradition. There was also a constant illegal exchange between Catholics in England who had secretly preserved manuscripts and books through the Reformation years, and Catholics on the continent who urgently wanted copies. And the reverse was also true; many manuscripts went out from the scriptoria of English religious houses on the continent back to their homeland. Books were smuggled into England in surprising numbers as well.[22]

Both because Father Baker's own love of the English spiritual masters was embraced by the community and because English Catholics were so eager for sources in their own spiritual tradition, nuns and monks of the Cambrai school devoted themselves especially to preserving and promulgating those texts. The impact of this dedicated work has been evaluated by the English Benedictine historian of this century, David Knowles. When, in the general renewal of the older religious orders among English Catholics in the Low Countries and France, "the English Benedictine Congregation renewed its life with communities of men and women in what was truly a second spring of vigour, the English mystics became once more an influence, so that for a space of fifty years or so there was what may be regarded as a kind of prolongation of the spirituality of the fourteenth century."[23]

The Cloud of Unknowing and the *Letter of Privy Counsel* had long been read by English Catholics seeking to live the contemplative life. Father Baker encouraged the Cambrai nuns to read it annually. He wrote a lengthy commentary on it which was frequently printed along with the text and is available in Abbot Justin McCann's last edition of the *Cloud* in 1943. After the Reformation Cambrai became the principal manuscript source; no printed text was available until 1871.[24]

Walter Hilton's *The Scale of Perfection* is another fourteenth-century work highly esteemed by Father Baker and translated by him into the English of his time. Merton judged that, of all the works of the English mystics, it "comes closest to being in the tradition of the Fathers, embracing the whole scope of the active and contemplative lives."[25] Published initially in 1494, the latest edition in Father Baker's time was 1533. It was not published again until 1659, when the Benedictine, Serenus Cressy, edited a modernized version. Again there is a direct connection to Cambrai: Father Cressy was chaplain in the house of Cambrai nuns founded in Paris by Dame Gertrude's younger sister, Dame Bridget. She herself became a scribe there and was probably responsible for a number of manuscripts now at Colwich Abbey in England, where the Paris community finally established themselves.

Yet another English text of the time is Julian of Norwich's *Revelations of Divine Love*. Father Baker had modernized and transcribed some portions for the nuns of Cambrai; Father Cressy published the long text. The history of the *Revelations* is a complicated one, but the latest edition concludes that, apart from extracts, "we owe the long text to the piety and learning of Augustine Baker and his spiritual school."[26]

These are the principal works made available by this Cambrai school under Father Baker's inspiration. There are many others extant, more or less complete, ranging from patristic times to Father Baker's contemporaries. They are spread about in monasteries of the English Congregation, in the British Museum and several French libraries, and elsewhere. The work of the school was not only transcription, however. The two Cambrai nuns whose original work is known are Dame Gertrude herself and Dame Barbara Constable, whose writing gives evidence of wide reading and fine discernment. Her knowledge of Latin served in translations and in effective use of liturgical and patristic texts.

It is surely worthy of note that in the history of the Cambrai group's study and writing, in an age very alert to any hint of "heresy," they were with one exception apparently never under suspicion. That one exception was the charge, within his own Congregation, that Father Baker's work was tainted by a kind of Illuminism; he was, as has been noted above, completely cleared of any such charge. That none were apparently ever "infected" by Jansenism, Quietism, or Illuminism in that age must surely be credited in great part to their immersion in the classical tradition, the deep main stream of spirituality in the Church.

Although Dame Gertrude More and the nuns of Cambrai did not have extensive opportunities for formal education, they did have superior spiritual formation. With this as foundation, nurtured by an intense but balanced monastic life, and recognizing as they did the needs of their time, they provided a remarkable monastic legacy. In reflecting on that fact, one is reminded of the wit and warmth of a recent abbess of Stanbrook Abbey (and hence a daughter of Cambrai), Dame Laurentia McLachlin, addressing this very subject in terms of her own community's life and work:

> If work of this sort is required of us, the very best, both in matter and form, is expected from a Benedictine house. . . . The idea that Benedictines are essentially brainy must be dismissed as a myth, if not a calumny. But the life does encourage serious thought as well as knowledge of the Church's actual needs, and if opportunities occur in the way of writing, talent in such direction should be fostered. . . . With regard to such work of the house, there is a providence that visibly directs it, and in consequence supplies the means for carrying it out. Most activities are started quite unconsciously and if they grow into anything it is by the blessing and under the guidance of God.[27]

Although recognized as a scholar, she disclaimed the title and said that any knowledge she possessed resulted quite simply from "living the life": an overflow of monastic *conversation.*

Is all this merely a matter of historical interest or has it significance for our time? There would seem to be some resonance of Gertrude's age with our own, of her Benedictine life with ours, of the impact of her community's decisions about identity and direction with questions before Benedictines today.

In the first place, both Gertrude and today's Benedictines have lived in relative proximity to a major Church Council concerned with the reform or renewal of religious life: the Council of Trent ended in 1563 and the Second Vatican Council in 1964. Both called for change and, inevitably it seems, polarization to a greater or lesser degree followed; communities then and now had to work their way through a challenging time in the Church's history.

Following each Council the call to action seemed to be heard, at first, more distinctly than the accompanying call to prayer. In both instances it seems that a subsequent dissatisfaction (not with action but with activism) opened the way to a renewal of prayer. Dame Gertrude found that in an era when new modes of prayer abounded, only a way suited to her call in monastic life made spiritual freedom and growth, even real community life, possible. And hers was a simple contemplative prayer, true to the tradition of monastic life.

After Vatican II also, a great variety of "prayer types" were offered to an interested public, perhaps inviting a sampling rather than a focused approach. The time seemed characteristically attracted to the "new," the "original." But "original" has the more profound meaning of returning to origins, a living tradition, renewing life from its roots. That was the vision, the motivation, of Augustine Baker, Gertrude More, and the whole Cambrai foundation. For them, contemplative prayer and life was their native land. To many others it was suspect. It was assumed that contemplation and action were opposites; that would seem to be the perception of many today as well. But Father Baker wrote that before Dame Gertrude began her way of prayer, "her head and senses were often more busily employed than they should have been" and that even afterward she was scarcely less active.

> All the business that the house could afford for all its members was hardly enough to satisfy the activity of her mind. . . . There was nothing concerning the house of any importance, great or little, but she had her head or hand, or both in it, but more the former. None conversed more at the grate than she did, for her own or others' recreation. None was more given to asking or hearing news about things outside; but for things within there was no need to ask, for none knew more than she.[28]

And it is to be remembered that she was assistant to the Abbess, cellarer and responsible for the lay sisters of the community.

Moreover, Dame Gertrude wrote that, while no member of a religious house should be overburdened, "no employment which religious women have in religion can hinder them after they have a good entrance into prayer; because if they pray not at one time they can easily pray at another, or, best of all, pray with the work itself, and make the work their prayer."[29] Nor was contemplative prayer a matter only for nuns and monks. In his recent study of English Benedictines of Father Baker's generation, David Lunn concludes: "Augustine Baker advocated a style of prayer that could be lived in any walk of life but refused to be confined to any closed system."[30]

Again, in Dame Gertrude's time and our own, many regard the contemplative as escapist, elitist, unproductive, even selfish. This school of Cambrai could itself refute that charge—at least in the realm of service to generations of both students of the spiritual tradition of the West and those who seek to live it. But they served their own generation as well as its heirs. A paper preserved in the archives of the city of Cambrai, for instance, states that the presence of the nuns was of great advantage to the city. Many visitors from England (presumably more permanent exiles as well as the many who travelled for brief stays in the Lowlands) wanted to live near the nuns.[31] Apparently these nuns had some qualities of life esteemed as gift by their contemporaries.

Today an abundance of books on the market promote "simplicity" of life style in face of the consumerism and artificialities of recent culture. Dame Gertrude wrote a good deal about simplicity: a profound interior and spiritual simplicity that grounded a whole way of life. This simplicity of prayer, her "way of love," was counter-cultural to much of the prayer proposed for all religious in her age, and is again a witness to the genuine freedom of spirit nourished by her prayer and her life.

A member of the "active" religious community founded by a contemporary of Dame Gertrude More, Mary Ward's Institute of the Blessed Virgin Mary, concluded her study with a judgment that fittingly concludes this one: "In my opinion, Gertrude More, like her saintly ancestor, is a woman for all seasons, and not of one order or nation or century."[32]

NOTES

1. Augustine Baker, O.S.B., *The Inner Life of Dame Gertrude More,* ed. Benedict Weld-Blundell, O.S.B. (London: R. T. Washbourne Ltd., 1910) 18.

2. Ibid.

3. See Thomas Merton, "Self-Knowledge in Gertrude More and Augustine Baker" in *Mystics and Zen Masters* (New York: Farrar, Strauss and Giroux, 1967) 154–170.

4. David Knowles, O.S.B., critical of Baker's work in some respects, judged his teaching on divine inspirations, when properly understood, to be "perhaps the most original and valuable part of his work." "Father Augustine Baker" in *The English Mystical Tradition* (New York: Harper Torchbooks, 1961) 179.

5. Baker, *Inner Life,* 72–73.

6. Ibid., 76–79.

7. Ibid., 235. See also Baker's *The Substance of the Rule of St. Bennet,* ed. Benedictines of Stanbrook Abbey (Worcester: Stanbrook Abbey, 1981).

8. Augustine Baker, O.S.B., *The Writings of Dame Gertrude More*, ed. Benedict Weld–Blundell, O.S.B. (London: R. T. Washbourne Ltd., 1910).

9. Evelyn Underhill, *Mysticism* (New York: E. P. Dutton and Co., 1961) 87–89.

10. "Confessions," #34. In the following paragraphs, sources in her writing will be indicated in the text: A for "Apology," C for "Confessions," each with appropriate page or excerpt number.

11. Quoted in the Benedictines of Stanbrook, *In a Great Tradition* (New York: Harper and Brothers, 1956) 15.

12. Frideswide Sandeman, O.S.B., "Dame Gertrude More," in *Benedict's Disciples,* ed. David H. Farmer (Leominster: Fuller Wright Books, 1980) 278.

13. Baker, *Inner Life,* 293. The final chapter of the book is Father Baker's account of her illness and death; the Appendix of some twenty pages, from which the above is quoted, is a reflection on Dame Gertrude that he requested from a community member, perhaps the infirmarian, Sister Hilda.

14. Placid Spearitt, O.S.B., "The Survival of Medieval Spirituality Among the Exiled Black Monks," *American Bemedictine Review,* 25 (1974) 305.

15. See the most recent edition, *Holy Wisdom: Directions for the Prayer of Contemplation,* Intr. Gerard Sitwell, O.S.B. (Wheathampstead: Anthony Clarke Books, 1972). The book remains the subject of some controversy; this introduction provides a helpful summary. See also David Lunn, *The English Benedictines 1540–1688: From Reformation to Revolution* (New York: Barnes and Noble, 1980) 211–213, 216–217.

16. *In a Great Tradition,* 29.

17. Ibid., ch. 1.

18. *RB 1980: The Rule of St. Benedict,* ed. Timothy Fry, O.S.B. (Collegeville: Liturgical Press, 1981) 295–297.

19. Merton, *Mystics and Zen Masters,* 152.

20. Marion Norman, I.B.V.M., "Dame Gertrude and the English Mystical Tradition," *Recusant History* 13 (1976) 198.

21. Philip Jebb and David M. Rogers, "Rebirth," in *The Benedictines in Britain,* ed. D. H. Turner et al (New York: George Brazillar, 1980) 94.

22. Ibid., 197. See also Helen C. White, *English Devotional Literature: 1600–1640* [University of Wisconsin Studies in Language and Literature #29, 1930] Reprinted (New York: Haskell House, 1966) 127–133.

23. Knowles, *The English Mystical Tradition,* 152.

24. For details regarding this and the following fourteenth century texts, see Spearitt, "The Survival of Medieval Spirituality," especially 287–288, 303–307, 310–314.

25. Merton, *Mystics and Zen Masters,* 136.

26. *Julian of Norwich: Showings,* trans. Edmund Colledge, O.S.A. and James Walsh, S.J. "The Classics of Western Spirituality" (New York: Paulist Press, 1978) 22.

27. *In a Great Tradition,* 152–153.

28. Baker, *The Inner Life,* 96.

29. Baker, *The Writings,* 215.

30. Lunn, *The English Benedictines,* 217.

31. Baker, *The Inner Life,* vii–viii.

32. Norman, "Dame Gertrude and the English Mystical Tradition," 210.

Notes on Contributors

NANCY BAUER, O.S.B., a member of the Sisters of St. Benedict, St. Joseph, Minnesota, has a bachelor's degree in photojournalism from the University of Minnesota and a master's degree in theology with a monastic studies specialization from the School of Theology, St. John's University, Collegeville, Minnesota. From 1978 to 1989 she was both a reporter and photographer for the *St. Cloud Visitor,* the newspaper of the St. Cloud Diocese; since 1989 she has been its editor.

ANNE BEARD, O.S.B., a member of the Benedictine Sisters of St. Walburg Monastery, Covington, Kentucky, received her B.A. in English from the University of Kentucky and an M.A. in English from Miami University, Oxford, Ohio. She did further graduate work both in folklore at Indiana University and in communications at Michigan State University. For twenty years she was a textbook editor for several free-lance design and production firms in Chicago. Within recent years she served as her community's editor for internal and external newsletters, publications, and communications. Anne died of cancer on February 24, 1996, the hour for celebrating First Vespers of St. Walburga, the patronal feast of the monastery to which she belonged since 1987.

MARY RICHARD BOO, O.S.B., a Benedictine of St. Scholastica Priory, Duluth, since 1953, earned a master's degree in English from Saint Louis University and a doctorate in the same field from the University of Illinois, Champagne-Urbana. From 1960 until her retirement (1994), she was involved in teaching and administration at the College of St. Scholastica, Duluth. She is the author of *House of Stone,* the history of her religious community.

JOAN BRAUN, O.S.B., a Benedictine of St. Scholastica Priory, Duluth, since 1942, has a master's degree in art history and a master's and doctorate in library science from the University of Michigan. Her ministries have included teaching and administration at the College of St. Scholastica, and teaching at the University of Michigan Library School. She is currently director of her community's Spiritual Resource Center.

ALBERTA DIEKER, O.S.B., a member of the Benedictine Sisters of Queen of Angels Monastery in Mt. Angel, Oregon, earned an M.A. in European history from St. Louis University and a Ph.D. in the same field from the University of Oregon. She teaches Church history at Mt. Angel Seminary and is the executive secretary of the American Benedictine Academy.

JEREMY HALL, O.S.B., a member of St. Benedict's Monastery, St. Joseph, Minnesota, holds a Ph.D. in religious studies from Marquette University. She has taught at the College of St. Benedict, St. John's University, Collegeville, and Creighton University. For the past decade, while living as a hermit at St. Benedict's, she has done extensive work in monastic retreats.

DEBORAH HARMELING, O.S.B., a member of the Benedictine Sisters of St. Walburg Monastery of Covington, Kentucky, is the Director of Library at the Athenaeum of Ohio, a graduate school of theology in Cincinnati, Ohio, where she is also a faculty member and part of the seminary formation team.

MARY MICHAEL KALIHER, O.S.B., a member of the Benedictine Sisters of Annunciation Priory in Bismarck, North Dakota, received her artistic training from Kann Institute of Art in West Hollywood, California; her B.A. from the College of St. Catherine, St. Paul, Minnesota; and an M.A. from the University of Notre Dame. She has illustrated two books: *Father de Smet* by Louis Pfaller, O.S.B., and *The First Sioux Nun* by Ione Hilger, O.S.B. Her illustrations and photography have appeared in various magazines. She does free-lance art work and tutors students at the University of Mary in Bismarck.

JANE KLIMISCH, O.S.B., a member of the Benedictine Sisters of Sacred Heart Monastery, Yankton, South Dakota, is a professor emerita at Mount Mary College. She received her undergraduate and doctoral degrees in music and the humanities from St. Mary-of-the-Woods College, the American Conservatory, and Washington University in St. Louis. A teacher, composer of liturgical music, author, and monastic liturgist for many years, she has recently written a history of the Benedictine Federation of St. Gertrude (Toronto: Peregrina Press).

LINDA KULZER, O.S.B., a Benedictine from St. Benedict's Monastery in St. Joseph, Minnesota, earned her B.A. in English from the College of St. Benedict, her M.A. in educational psychology from The Catholic University of America, and her Ph.D. in higher education with a minor in religion and culture from Syracuse University. She spent most of her professional life in college teaching and administration and has had a long-term interest in monastic history with a special focus on medieval monastic women.

EMMANUEL LUCKMAN, O.S.B., is a member of the Benedictine Abbey of St. Walburga in Boulder, Colorado, founded in 1935 from the Abbey of St. Walburg in Eichstätt, Germany, where the relics of St. Walburga have been venerated since 1035. She holds a master's degree in systematic theology from St. Thomas Theological Seminary in Denver and has served her community as director of guests and director of vocations. She is currently doing doctoral studies in historical theology at Marquette University.

GLADYS NOREEN, O.S.B., is a Benedictine Sister of Perpetual Adoration in St. Louis. She is studying for an M.A. in religious studies at Washington University, St. Louis. She is a registered nurse, at present the administrator of her congregation's health care, the superior of the Health Care Community, and an instructor of an internovitiate course.

JOHNETTE PUTNAM, O.S.B., a member of the Benedictine monastery of St. Scholastica, Atchison, Kansas, received her B.A. in English from Mount St. Scholastica College and her M.A. in monastic studies from St. John's University School of Theology, Collegeville. She did further graduate studies in English at St. Louis University and at the University of Notre Dame. She served in the ministries of education and has been active in the spiritual renewal of the monasteries of the Federation of St. Scholastica, acting as president from 1978 to 1990. She is the director of the Sophia Center at Mount St. Scholastica and serves as an instructor in the community's formation program.

ROSEMARY RADER, O.S.B., a member of the Benedictine sisters of St. Paul's Priory, St. Paul, Minnesota, earned a B.A. in history and Latin from the College of St. Catherine, an M.A. in Latin literature from the University of Minnesota, a Ph.D. both in the history of religions and the humanities from Stanford University, and has studied in Italy and Oxford, England. In her ministry as an educator, she has taught at Arizona State University, Stanford University, the University of San Diego, and St. John's University, Collegeville. From 1984 to 1992 she served her community as prioress and from 1990 to 1993 as President of the Conference of American Benedictine Prioresses. She authored *Breaking Boundaries: Male/Female Friendship in Early Christian Communities* (Paulist Press, 1982). Presently she is visiting associate professor in the history of Christianity at St. Olaf College, Northfield, Minnesota.

HILDEGARD RYAN, O.S.B., a member of the Benedictine community at Jamberoo Abbey, Australia, holds a B.A. from the University of

Queensland, a degree in Scripture studies from the Institut Catholique de Toulouse, a certificate in religious studies and in pastoral liturgy from the Institute of Faith in Queensland, and in 1995 completed a bachelor of divinity degree at the Melbourne College of Divinity. Within her community she serves as sub-prioress, choir director, director of studies, and as a member of the formation team. As the director of oblates and in ministry to guests, she gives conferences and workshops on Scripture, the Rule of Benedict, monastic history, liturgy, and *lectio divina*.

MIRIAM SCHMITT, O.S.B., a Benedictine of Annunciation Priory in Bismarck, received her B.S. in finance from St. Louis University, an M.S. in institutional administration from the University of Notre Dame, and an M.A. in liturgical studies from the School of Theology, St. John's University, Collegeville. She did additional graduate work in monastic spirituality at St. John's at the School of Theology, spent a semester in their Jerusalem Program and another semester as resident scholar at the Institute of Ecumenical and Cultural Research. She has served as educator, financial administrator, and prioress of her community (1980-1984). Currently she is both a lecturer and writer on medieval women monastics and mystics, spiritual mentor, retreat director, and adjunct faculty member for the United Methodist Spiritual Formation Academies sponsored by the Upper Room and conducted throughout the United States.

M. ZITA WENKER, O.S.B., is a member of the Sisters of Jesus Crucified at Regina Mundi Priory in Devon, Pennsylvania. She received her M.A. in theology with a monastic studies concentration from the School of Theology, St. John's University, Collegeville. She is the editor of her community's spirituality bulletin, teaches in the initial and on-going formation programs, and serves as the director of music and liturgy.

TERESA WOLKING, O.S.B., a member of the Benedictine Sisters of St. Walburg Monastery in Covington, Kentucky, earned her B.A. at Villa Madonna College (now Thomas More College) and her M.A. in English at the Catholic University of America. She serves as the monastery's archivist and as substitute teacher at her alma mater, the Villa Madonna Academy.

CATHERINE WYBOURNE, O.S.B., a Benedictine of Stanbrook Abbey in Worcester, England, read history at Girton College, Cambridge, and did three years of research and three years in banking before entering Stanbrook Abbey in 1981. Her community works have ranged from looking after poultry to printing. Her most recent publication, with Columba Cary-Elwes, is *Work and Prayer* (Burns & Oates, 1992).